D0948623

WITHDRAWN

Out of the Wilderness

Out of the Wilderness

he Emergence of
an American Identity in
Colonial New England

John Canup

Wesleyan University Press
Middletown, Connecticut

Copyright © 1990 by John Canup

All rights reserved

Chapter 2 appeared in somewhat different form in the *Proceedings of the American Antiquarian Society*, volume 98 (1988), copyright © 1988 by the American Antiquarian Society, and is reprinted with permission. Chapter 6 appeared in somewhat different form in *Early American Literature*, Volume 24 (1989).

All inquiries and permissions requests should be addressed to the Publisher, Wesleyan University Press, 110 Mt. Vernon Street, Middletown, Connecticut 06457.

Library of Congress Cataloging-in-Publication Data
Canup, John, 1952–
    Out of the wilderness : the emergence of an American identity in colonial New England / by Canup John.—1st ed.
        p.   cm.
    Includes bibliographical references.
    ISBN 0-8195-5226-7
    1. New England—Civilization—17th century.   2. New England—Civilization—18th century.   I. title.
    F7.C28   1990   89-16541
    974′.02—dc20

Manufactured in the United States of America

First Edition

To my mother and
the memory of my father

Preface

irst, to acknowledge debts and claim kin. Nathaniel Hawthorne, who was (as Michael Colacurcio has reminded us) "our first significant intellectual historian," may be responsible for my initial interest in colonial New England, but my primary scholarly inspiration came from that prime inspirer of American Puritan studies, Perry Miller—and specifically from *The New England Mind: From Colony to Province* (1953).[1] At the beginning of my research, when I had (quite properly) more ambition than ideas, I planned to build a grand new structure on Miller's foundation. After elaborating a general theory of provincialism, I would go on to anatomize the culture of late seventeenth- and early eighteenth-century New England—with particular emphasis on changing attitudes toward the homeland and the emergence of an "American" identity among erstwhile Englishmen.

I have not abandoned all of my early ambitions for this project, even at this late stage, but I have certainly revised my ideas about the true subject of the work. As I explored the dark forest of material that seemed to obscure my original topic, I realized that the fundamental problem remained the intellectual genealogy of New England's provincialism, not the nature of the mature phenomenon. Miller had begun to excavate the roots of the subject in his ample biography of the Puritan "errand," and I could easily have followed his lead in that direction—with a myriad others for company. Yet the colonial promotional literature, which I had at first regarded as mere "background material," made it clear that my central focus would have to be on the colonists' intellectual and emotional reactions to the physical circumstances of America itself: the climate, the terrain, flora and fauna—and the native inhabitants, the Indians.

Here again, I discovered Miller leading the way—however circuitously. In *From Colony to Province*, Miller was obviously aware of the challenges that settlement in America had posed for Puritan social and religious ideals, but more important for my purposes were his essays on nineteenth-century American thought in *Errand into the Wilderness* (1956) and *Nature's Nation* (1967). Especially striking, from the perspective of evolving American attitudes toward the natural world, was the contrast between the Romantic veneration of Nature as a component of the "National Ego" and the Puritan aversion toward the merely "natural" in anything. Instead of "Nature's Nation," the founders of New England aspired to the Culture's (as well as God's) Country. Thus Miller confirmed my growing interest in what he regarded as "*the* American theme": "Nature versus civilization."[2]

Although that theme does lie at the heart of this book, my pursuit of it has taken me in rather un-Millerian directions. Along the way I encountered two scholars' work that—despite considerable differences in style, methodology, and interpretation—encouraged me in the course I was following. The marks of John Seelye and Richard Slotkin's influence, far more than Perry Miller's, are surely evident throughout these pages. Seelye, above all among contemporary laborers in this field, also has at least one quality of Miller's that few of his true disciples (including those whose discipleship takes the form of opposition) possess: the wit and stylistic panache to demonstrate that early American writing, far from being just dead words relating to dead controversies, may have some life left in it as literature. I have tried not to betray this tradition—with what success I leave the reader to judge.

Many teachers, colleagues, and friends have fostered the

completion and publication of this book. Lest they be required unfairly to share blame as well as credit, I will name only a few who are most directly implicated in the results: John K. Nelson, Joel Williamson, Robert Bain, Dale T. Knobel, and Michael Hill. The secretarial staff—and especially Jude K. Swank—of the history department at Texas A&M University contributed greatly to making the manuscript presentable for the press. Portions of the book, in somewhat different form, first appeared in *Early American Literature* and the *Proceedings of the American Antiquarian Society*. I am grateful for permission to put this material to other uses—and for the editorial suggestions of Everett Emerson, of *EAL,* and Sheila McAvey, of the AAS. I am also indebted to Peter J. Potter, of Wesleyan University Press, for his early (and continuing) interest in the work, while Jeannette Hopkins brought her formidable editorial experience to bear on my stylistic quirks and interpretive obliquities. The book is entirely the better for her guidance and advice. I have tried to make a small payment on my greatest, indeed unpayable, debt in the dedication.

Contents

Illustrations

Out of the Wilderness

Prologue

MONG the many works devoted to the intellectual and cultural history of colonial New England, this book, I believe, is something of an oddity—in part because of its reluctance to allow the Puritan leadership to determine the course of its inquiry. Rather than retracing the religious and political controversies that occupied the intellectual foreground in the seventeenth century, I have focused on a genre of thought so fundamental and pervasive that the Puritan intellectuals would not have acknowledged it as a distinct body of discourse: a subtle but troubled debate on the threat that the physical and human environments of America seemed to pose for the transplanted English culture. We owe much of our understanding of colonial New England to the rich "internalist" tradition of scholarship (so "internal" in some cases as to be neo-Puritan in sympathy), and I have frequently drawn upon it in the following pages.[1] But our sense of how New England's intellectuals became American is distorted unless we also consider their awkward, often self-defeating responses to specifically American challenges from outside their own culture.

Accordingly, in my first two chapters I address the colonists' reaction to the physical circumstances of America, and I base my discussion on the promotional and descriptive literature of the earliest years of colonization—with an excursion into somewhat darker regions of the Puritan mentality in Chapter 2. By attending to the rhetoric of this literature, I have found that the writers, despite their obvious intention to inspire confidence in the colonial venture's ultimate success, inadvertently conveyed rather contradictory impressions: that American nature was deeply alien and antagonistic to English culture, that there was a disparity so great between the natural environment of the New World and the familiar landscape of England that a fully successful transplantation of culture would be unlikely—and perhaps impossible. In developing this argument, I have not introduced the botanical term *transplantation* arbitrarily; it is present in the rhetoric itself, indicating the writers' tendency to think of colonization through organic analogies and correspondences. This tendency both reflected and reinforced an underlying concern that transplantation into an alien environment would transform English people into "Americans"—new creatures more compatible with the wilderness of America than with the relatively tame England that had formed their native temperament.

Of course, the process of cultural transplantation went on anyway, but even as the colonists conquered the wilderness, the custodians of English culture continued to worry about what the victory meant for the victors. The magistrates and ministers who assumed the responsibility of maintaining the spiritual and civil health of New England suffered from a vaguely defined but nonetheless powerful suspicion that exposure to American nature had strengthened the wilderness of human nature within the men and women upon whom the future of a godly, civil New England depended. The Puritan colonies seemed threatened by a gradual moral and cultural degeneration that only the guardians of the public welfare could prevent.

The influence of the physical environment was abetted by what the colonists were inclined to regard as the even worse example of the native peoples of America—the central concern of Chapters 3–5. Seventeenth-century environmental thought encouraged a view of the Indians as an organic growth shaped by natural influences—and thus perhaps an indication of what English people might become in the same

surroundings. Colonial writers used many rhetorical strategies to counter the threat of "savage" contamination, but
the fear of assimilation to the native human environment
persisted. An occasional English renegade helped to keep the
fear alive by becoming an "Indian" outright, while efforts
to eliminate the Indians' bad example had complex, ironic
repercussions. Peaceful conversion of the native peoples to
Christianity and English civility was only a modest success.
Nor did military victory in the Indian wars preclude cultural
defeat.

From the perspective of the emerging Puritan orthodoxy,
certain black sheep within the New England flock confirmed
America's ability to elicit disorder from the transplanted English. And, as with the Indians, the orthodox response was
finally inadequate. The case of Roger Williams—while providing new grounds for the traditional association of wilderness, madness, barbarism, and heresy—made it clear that
black sheep did not always make good scapegoats.

When the third generation of New Englanders reached
maturity, a tradition of thought had developed that insistently
questioned the success of cultural transplantation and the
colonists' ability to maintain their inherited Englishness. I
believe this tradition helps to account for the provincial embarrassment third-generation intellectuals felt before the culture of metropolitan England. The growing sense of provincial inferiority also explains some aspects of the provincial
generation's ambivalence toward a distinct "American" identity and the compensatory appeal of an idealized England.
But the celebration of English identity merely confirmed the
assumptions that provoked it. The emergence of American
Anglophilia was sure evidence that New Englanders were no
longer English in the relatively effortless, unquestioning way
their ancestors had been.

In the final chapter I discuss three central figures in the
intellectual history of colonial New England who represent
three stages in the emergence of a provincial mentality: John

Winthrop, Jr., Increase Mather, and Cotton Mather. More than anyone else, Cotton Mather illustrates the painful condition of being torn between two fundamentally incompatible identities. He was unable to think of himself exclusively as either an American or an Englishman, nor could he completely renounce one identity in favor of the other. Although Mather was still devoted to the inherited Puritan traditions that had helped to set New England apart from Old, he suffered from provincial embarrassment in the face of metropolitan culture, while craving recognition and acceptance as an intellectual by metropolitan standards. Apparently convinced of American inferiority, Mather looked for an explanation in the notion that life in the alien environment had induced a "Criolian degeneracy" among the English colonists—and especially among the "tame Indian" English born in America.

With the appearance of the Boston-born Benjamin Franklin, toward whom I can only gesture in closing, there is evidence of a more mature stage of New England provincialism. Franklin was an emblematic figure who was able to reject the compromised American-English identity of Cotton Mather for the relatively simple identity of an English provincial. He accepted his country's inferior provincial status and made his own accommodation with its limitations, looking for intellectual and literary models not in the New England past, but in the English present. For Franklin, the giants of the Puritan tradition receded into the shadows, overwhelmed by the rising glory of Augustan English culture, and Franklin turned to bask in the warmth of the imperial sun. Yet Franklin's "English" identity was a delusion—evidence of an "Americanization" Franklin and his contemporaries would be unable to acknowledge until changing relations between England and its American colonies made a radical redefinition of national identity inescapable.

As a Southerner, I trust that I will not be found guilty of confusing New England with the continent as a whole. I am aware that my account of the emergence of a provincial mentality would be greatly complicated by the inclusion of material from regions other than New England, but I believe that my regional focus is warranted by the peculiar intensity of New England's cultural anxieties. I am also aware that much recent scholarship emphasizes the success of transplantation and the progressive "Anglicization" of colonial culture—especially in New England; insofar as this scholarship deals with material culture, agricultural practices, and political or social institutions, I have no great quarrel with it.[2] But the relative success of such transplantation should not blind us to the darker emotional side of the tortuous process of trying to re-create England in America. For the language that New England's intellectuals used to express their ambivalent impressions of their own Americanization reveals considerable malaise beneath the surface of material success. By offering this book as a key into that language, I hope to illuminate the anxiety these English colonists experienced as they became, despite themselves, American.

Chapter 1

The Transplanted English Vine

LTHOUGH the founders of New England began with considerable faith in the superiority of English culture to American nature, the utter strangeness of the place shook their confidence. New England, despite its deceptively familiar name, meant a new air to breathe, new foods to eat, and a new climate that often disappointed English expectations. The Creation in America had also been oddly profligate and whimsical: this was a land where vast flocks of pigeons blotted out the sun while frogs sang in the treetops.[1] And if Old England in its settled maturity babbled of green fields, New England howled of wilderness. Consequently, transplantation to America posed a challenge to the colonists' sense of themselves as English people: it gave them a new land, which they desired, but it also threatened to give them a new identity, something much less desirable in a century acutely conscious of national distinctions.

Thus Sir Thomas Browne, in his *Religio Medici,* ran strongly against the national grain by picturing himself as a man without "nationall repugnances." Having traveled and studied on the Continent, he was well aware of the habitable lands beyond the demiparadise of England. In an age of rampant chauvinism, his temperament molded him to the cosmopolitan ideal: "I am of a constitution so generall, that it consorts, and sympathizeth with all things; I have no antipathy, or rather Idio-syncrasie, in dyet, humour, ayre, any thing." He could even contemplate complacently the thought of the French sitting down to "their dishes of frogges, snailes, and toadstooles." In short, "I am no Plant that will not prosper out of a Garden. All places, all ayres make unto me one Country; I am in *England,* every where, and under any meridian."[2]

William Bradford expressed a much less cosmopolitan frame of mind when he recalled the "neither unreasonable, nor unprobable" objections the Pilgrim Fathers had considered before transplanting themselves to America. They carefully consulted their cherished antipathies and idiosyncrasies, worrying that "The chang of aire, diate, and drinking of water, would infecte their bodies with sore sickneses, and greevous diseases." It had been difficult enough to uproot themselves from "their native soyle" and put down new roots in the well-cultivated Low Countries; now they faced a wilderness transplantation that would challenge more severely their ability to survive and prosper, as English people, out of England's garden.[3] Even Browne, despite his desire to escape the hobbles of cultural parochialism, could not avoid the idea that to be at home everywhere was to be "in *England,* every where."

The metaphor of "Plant" and "Garden" acquired more than merely rhetorical significance, despite Browne's rejection of the analogy in his own case. The contemporary literature concerned with English "plantations" tended to accept the botanical metaphor's implication that Englishmen and plants were similarly dependent on the natural environment for their native "temperament." In 1630, when the Reverend John Cotton preached the farewell sermon to John Winthrop's New England–bound fleet, he chose for his text 2 Samuel 7:10 ("Moreover I will appoint a place for my people Israell, and I will plant them . . ."), and in explicitly addressing the question "What is it for God to plant a people?" he explained: "It is a Metaphor taken from young Impes [shoots or saplings]; I will plant them, that is, I will make them to take roote there; and that is, where they and their soyle agree well together, when they are well and sufficiently provided for, as a plant suckes nourishment from the soyle that fitteth it."[4] Cotton, who within a few years would follow in Winthrop's wake to become teacher to the Boston congregation, clearly hoped for a successful planting—at least in spiritual terms. He accordingly couched his warning against degeneration in a biblical reference: "have a tender care that you looke well to the plants that spring from you, that is, to your children, that they doe not degenerate as the Israelites did. . . . *Jer*. 2. 21. *I planted them a noble Vine, holy, a right seede, how then art thou degenerate into a strange Vine before mee?*"[5] Given this analogy, ominous conclusions followed: if the English "Impes" found no soil to fit them in America, if American nature itself proved to be fundamentally hostile to English culture, "the transplanted *English* Vine" (as a later New Englander, Samuel Sewall, would describe his country) risked degeneration into a strange new American growth.[6]

From Nova Britannia to New England

The rhetoric of degeneration that lurked between the lines of the colonial promotional tracts expressed more than popular "antipathies" and ignorant prejudices: it also reflected a formidable intellectual tradition that ascribed much of individual and cultural temperament to environmental influences. Classical humoral physiology assumed that human beings were in many ways creatures of the climate in which they lived. This notion—with its corollary of an organic correspondence between men, plants, and animals—led to the obvious conclusion that a people could not leave their native environment, as in the process of colonization, and retain indefinitely their native identity.[7] In the sixteenth century the French jurist (and environmental theorist) Jean Bodin, building on inherited ideas about the relationship of culture and environment, argued that while people "transplanted into another countrey, . . . shall not be chaunged so soone, as plants which draw their nourishment from the earth: yet in the end they shall be altered."[8] Nathanael Carpenter, fellow of Exeter College, Oxford, and one of Bodin's foremost English disciples, agreed that men, as well as plants and animals, "being transported into other regions, though a long time retaining their native perfection, will notwithstanding in time by litle and litle degenerate." And Carpenter, still following Bodin, applied this principle specifically to colonization: "Colonies transplanted from one region into another, farre remote, retaine a long time their first disposition, though by litle and litle they decline and suffer alteration."[9]

Virginia offered the first real test of this theory for English settlers: Would they, by little and little, lose their "native perfection" on the shores of the Chesapeake? Carpenter did not venture an explicit answer, though he had heard that English corn and cattle "translated" to Virginia had already undergone a "great alteration."[10] But lest such rumors encourage pessimistic appraisals of the probable fate of English people there, promoters assured readers that their countrymen did not degenerate completely after exposure to Virginia's environment. Pocahontas's teacher, Alexander Whitaker, included in his *Good Newes from Virginia* (1613) the glad tidings that "The aire of the Countrey . . . is very temperate and agreeth well with our bodies."[11] And in 1620 the preacher-poet-promoter William Crashaw wrote that life in the colony posed no threat to the English temperament: "*our brethren in Virginea*, who some of them have been there many yeeres, . . . doe not complaine of any alteration caused by distemper of the Climate."[12]

But bad news leaked out with the good. Word reached England that Virginia, increasingly obsessed with growing the "herbe of hell," was something less than the "earthly Paradice" it had been called.[13] Aside from such problems as starvation, inadequate shelter, and hard work in hot weather, the promoters had to acknowledge that a physical "seasoning" was necessary before English bodies could feel truly at home. This process often proved fatal, and it also provided grounds for concluding that the successfully seasoned colonists were in danger of cultural translation.[14]

It was possible to answer objections to Virginia's embarrassments by arguing that the colony, though obviously different from England in many respects, was potentially its equal or even its superior. As early as the 1580s, Thomas Hariot, resident polymath of Sir Walter Raleigh's first Roanoke Island colony, described the land around "Pommeioocke" as being "soe fruit full and good, that England is not to bee compared to yt."[15] And in the seventeenth century, William Strachey, sometime secretary of the Jamestown colony, said of English fruits and vegetables transplanted to Virginia that they not only grew as well there as in England, but with better taste.[16] On the other hand, Strachey understood that it would not help his case to pretend that Virginia was heaven on earth. He admitted that Jamestown was not an ideal site for a settlement, but rather than have his readers thank God they were still at home, he hastened to add that England had Jamestowns of its own. Plumstead in Kent, he reminded them, was notorious for its agues and fevers. Since no one condemned all of Kent because of this one unhealthy spot, so Virginia should not be damned because of Jamestown.[17]

Strachey, perhaps unawares, had stumbled upon a clever means of preserving the appearance of objectivity while undermining doubts about the virtues of transplantation. He conceded Virginia's limitations but argued that Virginia was flawed only as England itself was flawed. The promotional force of this comparison lay in its subtle equation of homeland and colony—an equation made more explicit in such titles as Strachey's own *Virginia Britania* (1612) and Robert Johnson's *Nova Britannia: Offering Most Excellent fruites by Planting in Virginia* (1609).[18] These titles attested to their authors' belief that Englishmen would surely be more willing to venture themselves in the New World if they were convinced that it was a new England—a mirror of its parent even in its imperfections. The problem for Virginia was that the comparison might seem to apply more accurately to other regions further north.

Richard Eburne, vicar of the parish church at Henstridge, Somerset, clearing *A Plain Pathway to Plantations* (1624), implied in passing that environmental objections to cultural transplantation were fundamentally irrelevant. Having in effect declared culture independent of nature, he could offer his readers the miracle of a colonization that allowed the colonists to remain at home. To unbelievers and skeptics, he preached that the kingdom of England was within them: "if you will needs live in England, imagine all that to be England where Englishmen, where English people, you with them, and they with you, do dwell. (And it be the people that makes the land English, not the land the people.)" Colonization, then, was not properly a foreign transplantation at all, but the imaginative imprinting of an English identity upon a land that, as a cultural tabula rasa, had no identity of its own. Simply by their presence, the colonists would bring English order to an American chaos. "So you may find England . . . ," wrote Eburne, "where now is, as I may say, no land."[19]

With such rhetorical weapons, Eburne attacked the stay-at-home mentality of Englishmen who were "wedded to their native soil like a snail to his shell or, as the fable is, a mouse to his chest."[20] Yet for those who remained, despite Eburne's sober arguments, so "besotted" with "the immoderate love of our own country" that it was "almost impossible upon any advantage to get them out of it,"[21] other strategies were clearly necessary. It was not enough to be told that the kingdom of England lay within if the fond conviction persisted that the land of England was the only proper habitation for the people of England. Thus, when Captain John Smith named a stretch of the North American coast "New England," he put into motion a powerful rhetorical engine for the promotion of colonization—the name being both testimony to the region's "English" environmental temper and prophecy of its English colonial future.[22] Following Smith's lead, later promoters

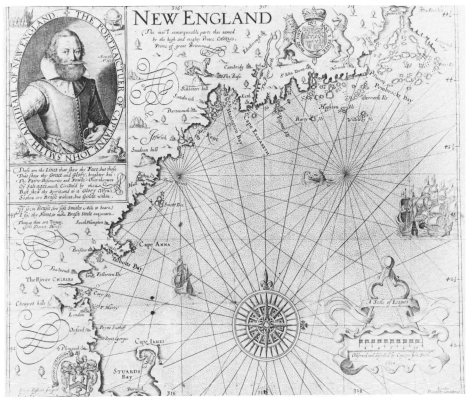

Captain John Smith's map of New England from *The Generall Histo-rie of Virginia, New England, and the Summer Isles*, made after his 1614 exploration of a stretch of the North American coast that he named "New England." *Courtesy, American Antiquarian Society*

carefully fostered the general impression that, in the words of the Pilgrim Father (and promotional writer) Edward Winslow, "one can scarce distinguish New England from Old."[23]

In preaching this colonial gospel, the promotional tracts began with the premise that the quality of any land depended (next to God) on "the temperature and disposition of the foure Elements, Earth, Water, Aire and Fire."[24] Consequently, the promoters repeatedly assured their readers that New England's environment did not contradict its name—or that, if there was a discrepancy, it could easily be resolved in New England's favor. William Wood, author of one of the century's most appealing promotional works, observed that "To wipe away all groundlesse calumniations, and to answer to every too curious objections, and frivolous question (some so simple as not ashamed to aske whether the Sunne shines there or no) were to run in infinitum."[25] But Wood and his fellow promoters took seriously their audience's apparent need to be convinced that the air of America was compatible with English lungs, that the soil was hospitable to English crops, that English cows could graze safely on American grass, and that English people could drink American water (in moderation) and remain "as healthfull, fresh, and lustie, as they that drinke beere."[26] If "all our severall Graines" found in New England "a fitting Soyle for their nature," and if even the colonists' livestock seemed to "like well of this Countrey,"[27] English people should suffer no ill effects through transplantation.

It proved difficult, however, to "like well of" the weather, which was both hotter and colder than it should have been, given the contemporary assumption that climate was largely a function of latitude: though New England corresponded in latitude to the south of France, the winters were hardly comparable. Wood replied that while the colony was not an exact reflection of its namesake, its present was, climatically, Old England's past. The homeland had lost the dubious felicities that the colony still enjoyed: "who is there," Wood asked, "that could not wish, that *Englands* Climate were as it hath

NEVV
ENGLANDS
PROSPECT.

A true, lively, and experimen-
call defcription of that part of *America*,
commonly called N ꜱ vv E ɴ ɢ ʟ ᴀ ɴ ᴅ:
difcovering the ftate of that Countrie, both as it ftands to our new-come
Englifh Planters; and to the old
Native Inhabitants.

Layingdowne that which may both enrich the
knowledge of the mind-travelling Reader,
or benefit the future Voyager.

By W ɪ ʟ ʟ ɪ ᴀ ᴍ W ᴏ ᴏ ᴅ.

Printed at *London* by *Tho. Cotes*, for *Iohn Bellamie*, and are to be fold
at his fhop, at the three Golden Lyons in *Corne-hill*, neere the
Royall Exchange. 1 6 3 5.

New Englands Prospect, a promotional work by William Wood written
in 1634 to assure readers that New England's environment was
suited to the English people. *Courtesy, American Antiquarian Society*

beene in quondam times, colder in Winter, and hotter in Summer? or who will condemne that which is as *England* hath beene?" Wood had transformed the voyage to America into a sort of time-travel in which the English, rather than losing their ancestral climate, would find it restored to them.[28]

It was a seductive idea—perhaps too obviously seductive in a genre that constantly risked arousing suspicion through excessive enthusiasm or cleverness. Eburne clearly assumed that many of his readers regarded the promotional tracts as "idle books, fables, . . . not worth the looking on."[29] And in fact, hyperbolic reports made some spokesmen for the Massachusetts Bay colony uncomfortable after they had experienced the reality for themselves. The greatest disillusionment may have come to the Reverend Francis Higginson of the Puritan settlement at Salem: he died of a fever contracted in the air he had praised as positively therapeutic.[30] But great expectations easily bred great disappointments for others.

Deputy Governor Thomas Dudley's letter of March 1631 to the Countess of Lincoln was largely a recitation of woes— the work of a man who had not found in America what he had been led to expect. He repeated some of the standard promotional clichés, noting for example that there was "a pure air to breathe in" and "good water to drink, till wine or beer can be made." Yet he made clear his resentment, sharpened by the bitterly cold weather in which he wrote, of the "too large commendations of the country and the commodities thereof" that had helped lure him to New England. He went to the heart of the matter with characteristic bluntness: "I do the more willingly use this open and plain dealing, lest other men should fall short of their expectations when they come hither, as we to our great prejudice did, by means of letters sent us from hence into England, wherein honest men, out of a desire to draw over others to them, wrote somewhat hyperbolically of many things here." Dudley still believed the colony was God's work, but he did not think that he and his neighbors were laboring in a paradise.[31]

NEW-ENGLANDS
PLANTATION.

OR,
A SHORT AND TRVE
DESCRIPTION OF THE
COMMODITIES AND
DISCOMMODITIES
of that Countrey.

in the year 1629.

Written by M*r*. *Higgeson*, a reuerend Diuine
now there resident.

Whereunto is added a Letter, sent by M*r*.*Graues*
an Enginere, out of *New-England*,

The third Edition. enlarged.

LONDON,
Printed by *T.* and *R. Cotes.* for *Michael Sparke*, dwelling
at the Signe of the *Blue Bible* in *Greene-
Arbor.* 1 6 3 o.

New-Englands Plantation, a 1630 promotional tract by Francis Higginson, who claimed "to report nothing but the naked truth" about New England, including descriptions of both "commodities" and "discommodities." *Courtesy, Massachusetts Historical Society*

Higginson, one of Dudley's "honest" but hyperbolic writers, anticipated such criticism when he prepared his account of *New-Englands Plantation* (1630) for the press. He noted the "idle Proverbe" which said that *"Travellers may lye by authoritie,"* but as a "Preacher of Truth" he sought "to report nothing but the naked truth, and that both to tell you of the discommodities as well as of the commodities."[32] Higginson faithfully, if halfheartedly, included his brief list of "discommodities,"[33] but otherwise the genre in which he wrote helped to frustrate his devotion to the truth. The promotional task seemed to demand, if not outright lies, at least some cosmetic retouching of unattractive facts. The promoters became the victims of their own rhetoric: since they needed to convince themselves, as much as anyone else, that transplantation would not lead inevitably to cultural or physical degeneration, they sacrificed skepticism to the colonial vision.

Balancing precariously between naked truth and barefaced lies, the promotional literature continued the process of verbally inventing New England. In time, the name would come to seem less a whim of John Smith's than a natural expression of the region's inherently English identity. Robert Cushman, in a 1621 sermon delivered in Plymouth colony, demonstrated how completely he accepted the idea that New England must be, in almost every respect, a new England. According to Cushman, the area was "so called not only (to avoid novelties) because Captain Smith hath so entitled it in his Description, but because of the resemblance that is in it of England, the native soil of Englishmen." Its climate, he thought, was much the same as England's, and in topography and soil it recalled Kent and Essex. In Cushman's eyes he was surrounded by a remarkably familiar countryside, "full of dales and meadow ground, full of rivers and sweet springs, as England is." But Cushman pushed comparison toward geographical equation: he believed that New England, like Old, was an island, "and near about the quantity of England, being cut out from the main land in America, as England is from the main of Europe, by a great arm of the sea."[34] New England indeed. It was as if the reflecting surface of the Atlantic had reproduced the exact image of the homeland in the New World.

Though Cushman's geography was wrong, his eagerness to assume that New England, like Britain, must be an island grew from impulses impervious to mere fact. Cushman, as the Pilgrims' representative to their English investors, did not long remain in America, but he had found a strangely alluring (and long-lived) means of making himself at home there. In the 1670s a variation on the mirror-image notion emerged in the Reverend William Hubbard's description of New England as environmentally "most resembling the Countrey from whence it borrowed its appellation."[35] And Cotton Mather, in his *Magnalia Christi Americana* (1702), wrote that his native region was, more than any other colony, truly English: it was the mother country's "most *resembling daughter*."[36]

Yet words alone could not invent a New England from the raw material of American nature. Not content simply to rely on rhetorical alchemy to effect the necessary transmutation, the colonists wanted to see their desires realized materially in the surrounding landscape. Unfortunately, much of what they saw around them remained stubbornly alien. Despite the geocultural gospel preached by the promotional evangelists, deeply ingrained habits of thought conspired with the physical environment to suggest that New England was not a domestic pastoral landscape, but a howling wilderness. A fully successful transplantation seemed to require that the colonists subdue the wild nature of America before it could devour them.

A Howling Wilderness—or a Second England?

It was tempting to disguise New England's wilderness qualities beneath a veil of pastoral imagery, and Thomas Morton (of "Merry Mount") yielded to the temptation wholeheartedly. In his *New English Canaan* (1637) he wanted to display the charms of New England "as in a Landskipp," and he apparently intended his verbal portrait to convey the same general euphoria that his contemporaries expected to experience when looking at "Landskipp" painting.[37] As Morton looked at his subject, his vision blurred, and a soft mist of pastoral cliché settled upon New England's terrain, cloaking its less alluring features from the harsh light of plain prose. Here were

> so many goodly groves of trees, dainty fine round rising hillucks, delicate faire large plaines, sweete cristall fountaines, and cleare running streames that twine in fine meanders through the meads, making so sweete a murmering noise to heare as would even lull the sences with delight a sleepe, so pleasantly doe they glide upon the pebble stones, jetting most jocundly where they doe meete and hand in hand runne downe to Neptunes Court, to pay the yearely tribute which they owe to him as soveraigne Lord of all the springs. Contained within the volume of the Land, [are] Fowles in abundance, Fish in multitude; and [I] discovered, besides, Millions of Turtledoves one the greene boughes, which sate pecking of the full ripe pleasant grapes that were supported by the lusty trees, whose fruitfull loade did cause the armes to bend: [among] which here and there dispersed, you might see Lillies and of the Daphnean-tree: which made the Land to mee seeme paradice: for in mine eie t'was Natures Masterpeece; Her cheifest Magazine of all where lives her store: if this Land be not rich, then is the whole world poore.[38]

Morton presented what he regarded as the perfect answer to those "who cannot imagine that there is any Country in the universall world which may be compared unto our native soyle."[39] But even Morton at his most imaginative could not paint over all evidence that New England was in many respects far from being the "New English Canaan" he envisioned. Before he published his flattering portrait of Massachusetts, the Pilgrim historian William Bradford had sketched its refutation in a stark tableau of the Pilgrims' stunned reaction to Cape Cod. According to Bradford, as he and his friends looked into the "wetherbeaten face" of New England they did not see Nature's Masterpiece, but "a hidious and desolate wilderness, full of wild beasts and willd men."[40]

Of course, when Puritans considered the New England forest, they often could not see the literal trees for the typological wilderness; an exclusively literal interpretation of Bradford's description is thus impossible.[41] Nevertheless, America resembled a wilderness as the seventeenth-century English understood the word: a living, green labyrinth harboring wild beasts and wild men, the antithesis of contemporary England's relatively tame, deforested landscape. And New England, which paradoxically seemed closer to an older England of the early Middle Ages than to a "new" version of the domestic environment the colonists had left behind, evoked attitudes toward wild nature that had no place for the mother country's emergent nostalgia for the wildwood.[42]

In contrast to the "artificial wildernesses" and "False Labyrinthes" of England's formal gardens—where gentlemen and their ladies could flirt with ancient confusion without encountering ferocious beasts, bandits, wild men, or supernatural terrors[43]—New England's forests offered the unaccustomed prospect of literal bewilderment in what William Wood called "the strange labyrinth of unbeaten bushy wayes in the woody wildernesse."[44] And while in 1596 an English writer could remark that "Wee [in England] are not troubled with poysoning Serpents, nor with fierce Lyons, or with devouring Tigers, Beares, Wolfes, Panthers or any such hurtfull beastes as other nations are,"[45] his countrymen who later went to live in New England could not make the same boast. Perhaps they were in no danger of meeting "Tigers" in America's woods, but those woods were full of other creatures that either had never roamed the English countryside or, to say the least, had long since become rarities there.[46]

In the promoters' attempts to "tame" such beasts, they may have confirmed their readers' worst suspicions about the exotic nature of America. Francis Higginson's list of discommodities included one that appeared especially discommodious: "This Countrey being verie full of Woods and Wildernesses, doth also much abound with Snakes and Serpents of strange colours and huge greatnesse: yea there are some Serpents called Rattle Snakes, that have Rattles in their Tayles[,] that will not flye from a Man as others will, but will flye upon him and sting him so mortally, that he will dye within a quarter of an houre after. . . ." Higginson rushed to defang this monster, adding that the snakes seldom harmed anyone (though "About three yeeres since an *Indian* was stung to death by one of them") and that the country produced an antidote in "an Hearbe called Snake weed."[47] But literal-minded readers apparently concluded from Higginson's account that the rattlesnake could in fact "flye," while one rumor held that it could kill a man with its breath. William Wood tried to repair the damage with a rather ambiguous disclaimer: "This is a most poysonous and dangerous creature, yet nothing so bad as the report goes of him in *England*"—which was not saying much, considering the report.[48] And Thomas Morton had declared with greater confidence that "it is simplicity in any one that shall tell a bugbeare tale of horrible, or terrible Serpents, that are in that land."[49] Yet as late as 1672 readers could find in the English traveler and naturalist John Josselyn's *New-Englands Rarities Discovered* the disturbingly vague revelation that the rattlesnake "poysons with a Vapour that comes thorough two crooked Fangs in their Mouth."[50]

Bears, wolves, and lions (or the rumor thereof) called for similar cosmetic treatment. Morton attacked the first of this forbidding trio by acknowledging frankly, "If I should not speake something of the beare, I might happily [haply] leave a scruple in the mindes of some effeminate persone[s] who conceaved of more dainger in them then there is cause." He argued that while this beast was "a tyrant at a Lobster," it posed no threat to people: "Hee will runne away from a man as fast as a litle dogge."[51] And Wood implied that the English were more likely to eat the bear than the other way around, "Beares being accounted very good meate, esteemed of all men above Venison."[52] As for lions, Morton was certain that "there are none in New England: it is contrary to the Nature of the beast to frequent places accustomed to snow."[53] But Wood was more cautious—and more reluctant to set his readers' minds completely at ease: "I will not say that I ever saw any my selfe, but some affirme that they have seene a Lyon at *Cape Anne* which is not above six leagues from *Boston*: some likewise being lost in woods, have heard such terrible roarings, as have made them much agast; which must eyther be Devills or Lyons."[54] Prospective colonists could draw their own conclusions and take their own chances—of falling prey to the devil (who "walketh about, seeking whom he may devour") or merely to his bestial emblem.[55]

It was not roaring, however, but howling that conclusively marked New England with the stigma of wilderness. Though wolves had been considered extinct in England for generations,[56] the colonists were audibly reminded of their continued presence in America. Morton, using much the same terms he had applied to the bear, quickly dismissed the wolf threat: "They are fearefull Curres, and will runne away from a man, (that meeteth them by chaunce at a banke end,) as fast as any fearefull dogge."[57] Still, the thought of testing the wolf's courage, by chance or otherwise, surely appealed to few of Morton's readers. Wood denied that the wolves were a great danger to people, and the larger livestock seemed safe. But goats, swine, and calves were vulnerable—especially red calves, which the wolves evidently mistook for deer, a more familiar prey. The problem was especially bad in the fall and early spring, when the wolves followed the deer as they moved closer to the settlements. At such times the wilderness seemed to speak to the colonists in its own native tongue: "Late at night, and early in the morning, they set up their howlings, and call their companies together at night to hunt, at morning to sleepe." Despite the wolves' supposed harmlessness to human beings, Wood concluded that the authors of these "howlings," so alien to English ears, were "the greatest inconveniency the Countrey hath, both for matter of dammage to

private men in particular, and the whole Countrey in generall." Worst of all, though wolves were regularly killed by the
English as well as Indians, "Yet is there little hope of their
utter destruction."[58] If so, to that extent New England would
never fully realize the promise of its name.

To be sure, the environmental contrast between England
and America was not entirely to the latter's disadvantage. The
Indians had not been far wrong in concluding, as they told
Roger Williams, that the colonists had come to America because they lacked fuel at home.[59] Viewed from the perspective
of Old England's timber shortages, New England's forests
could appear as so much firewood in the rough. And whatever
might be said for or against wolves, bears, lions, and rattle-
snakes, other animals of the wilderness promised large profits
in the fur trade. But to regard trees and fur-bearing animals
as valuable commodities was not necessarily to contradict the
traditional aversion to wild nature; concern for "commodity"
simply added a powerful commercial motive for deforestation
and extermination of predators.[60] By clearing the forests,
the colonists could strike a blow for civilization and warm
themselves (twice, their descendants would say) at the same
time.[61]

Unfortunately for such expectations, as colonization proceeded there were signs that the transplanted English vine
was in danger of being choked in the rank, resurgent growth
of the wilderness. For a brief but crucial period New England
may well have seemed increasingly remote environmentally
from the English model. The Indians had kept the forest
undergrowth under control by periodic burnings, but the
wilderness quickly began to reclaim lost territory as the English replaced the original inhabitants.[62] The number of
wolves also apparently increased after the colonists' arrival,
thanks in part to the new source of food provided by imported
livestock.[63] The anonymous author of the "Essay on the Ordering of Towns" (ca. 1635) was clearly mindful of the contradiction to civilization implied by the wolf menace. Could the

colonists sink so low as to tolerate an animal whose presence in England would be unthinkable? As the "Essay" argued, "it hath in some other Cuntries ben accounted a shamefull misery to induer the tyrany of such spoyleing beasts without laboring for Resistance and Revenge." By enduring the wolf's tyranny, the colonists seemed in danger of proving themselves less competent than the Indians in defending civility: "I have often hearde (by seemeing credible men) that Wolves are much more increased since our Nation came then when the Indians possessed the same, and a Reason rendred, that they were dilligent in destroying the Yonge. And is not this a dishonor unto our Christian newe Common wealth: to the very name of our nation yf not to the nature of our proffession."[64] If the wolves and their wilderness environment, far from retreating before the advancing frontier of English culture, continued to thrive amidst the settlements, the colonists would have to acknowledge that they were less the pioneers of civilization than the harbingers of its degeneration.

To avoid dishonoring their nation and religious profession by failing to subdue America, the colonists embraced their commission of Christian stewardship and set about bringing nature under control—with considerable success.[65] By 1653 Edward Johnson, the town clerk and militia captain of Woburn, Massachusetts, was able to present his *Wonder-Working Providence of Sions Saviour in New England* as the literary complement of deforestation and wolf extermination, the book being a rather rough-hewn testimony to the material progress of transplantation at midcentury: "[T]his remote, rocky, barren, bushy, wild-woody wilderness, a receptacle for Lions, Wolves, Bears, Foxes, Rockoones, Bags, Bevers, Otters, and all kind of wild creatures, a place that never afforded the Natives better then the flesh of a few wild creatures and parch't Indian corn incht out with Chestnuts and bitter Acorns, now through the mercy of Christ [is] becom a second England for fertilness in so short a space, that it is indeed the wonder of the world."[66] In Johnson's wonder-filled pages, readers could discover the colonists "t[r]anslating the close, clouded woods into goodly corn-fields"[67] while familiar names from England are imposed upon older Indian identities. Just as Shawmut becomes Boston, so other "savage" or uninhabited sites assume the dignity of Cambridge, Ipswich, Hingham, Dorchester, Roxbury, Salisbury, Sudbury, and so on—the Adamic prerogative of the assigning of names linking the American New Jerusalem emotionally as well as verbally to Old England.[68]

If the colonists hoped to find in America a refuge where they could enjoy Christ and his ordinances "in their primitive purity,"[69] primitivism was not an ideal for them in any other sense. In many ways, New England had even surpassed its parent in material comforts:

there are not many Towns in the Country, but the poorest person in them hath a house and land of his own, and bread of his own growing, if not some cattel: beside, flesh is now no rare food, beef, pork, and mutton being frequent in many houses, so that this poor Wilderness hath not onely equalized England in food, but goes beyond it in some places for the great plenty of wine and sugar, which is ordinarily spent, apples, pears, and quince tarts instead of their former Pumpkin Pies. Poultry they have plenty, and great rarity, and in their feasts have not forgotten the English fashion of stirring up their appetites with variety of cooking their food.[70]

Johnson was not so carried away as to forget that the stirring up of appetites was hardly the approved Puritan fashion. These new Israelites had not left the fleshpots of Egypt behind, and as they fed on the land's bounty, they apparently began to mistake the New Jerusalem for Vanity Fair: "there [are] here (as in other places) some that use these good creatures of God to excess."[71] Yet, while the threat of a spiritual apostasy looms over Johnson's vision of worldly prosperity, the physical realization of New England's English destiny remains central to the book's meaning.[72] Johnson spread before his readers a banquet of nature reformed by culture, praising the "very laborious people, whose labours the Lord hath so blest, that in the roome of dismall Swampes and tearing Bushes, they have very goodly Fruit-trees, fruitfull Fields and Gardens."[73] The promotional prophecy of a fully domestic New England stood forth in the *Wonder-Working Providence* as an accomplished fact: wolf and wilderness had retreated before the relentless advance of poultry and peas.

But the very insistence of the claim perversely implied the doubts that made such a claim necessary. As Johnson perhaps suspected, the complete transplantation of English culture would ultimately prove impossible. Because of the undeniable environmental disparities between the two Englands, the process of imprinting an English form on the American landscape necessarily involved accommodation on both sides.[74] In America, where English culture was from the beginning a thing of artifice, the colonists could never regard their way of life as the natural product of England's garden, an inalienable environmental birthright. And however successful the more material aspects of transplantation, the victory was much less conclusive in other ways.[75] Increasingly, the colonial custodians of culture would wonder if the wilderness, vanquished on the objective level, had not simply retreated to the subjective—to take root in the supposed victors' minds, where it could continue the fight in the inner wilderness of human nature.

Chapter 2 *The Disafforestation of the Mind*

NE of the most unsettling (and most unforeseen) consequences of colonization was New England's strange ability to breathe new life into Old World metaphors—especially metaphors that suggested a correspondence between the subjugation of the physical environment and the mastery of human nature. For example, John Donne, in his poem "To Sr *Edward Herbert*," made some observations concerning this correspondence that would have had much stronger meaning for the guardians of civility in early New England:

> Man is a lumpe, where all beasts kneaded bee,
>   Wisdome makes him an Arke where all agree;
>
> . . . .
>
> How happy is hee, which hath due place assign'd
>   To his beasts, and disaforested his minde!¹

Even before that preeminent Puritan Ark, the *Arbella*, unloaded its passengers onto the American Ararat in 1630, the ship's captain pointed out the colonists' more-than-metaphorical beastliness by complaining to John Winthrop that they "were very nasty and slovenly, and that the gundeck, where they lodged, was so beastly and noisome with their victuals and beastliness, as would much endanger the health of the ship."² Winthrop saw that the mess was cleaned up, but after the human cargo had been released into the pure air of New England, he found no release from the task of ensuring that these frequently unruly "beasts" kept their due place in the social order.

While the colonists went on with the domestication—and the attendant disafforestation—of the land, it was imperative that they not neglect the ongoing disafforestation of their inner wildernesses. Winthrop understood this because he had wrestled often enough with his own inner beast, in that warfare of the spirit against what he called "this wanton bruitishe fleshe."[3] And it followed logically that what was true of human nature individually must also be true of human nature collectively. In 1645, again in his role of Puritan Noah, Winthrop warned against the sort of brutish, headstrong "liberty" that made men "grow more evil, and in time to be worse than brute beasts." Indeed, the liberty of undisciplined nature was itself, in Winthrop's rhetoric, "that wild beast, which all the ordinances of God are bent against, to restrain and subdue it."[4]

In the context of New England—which Winthrop once described as a place "where are nothing but wild beasts and beastlike men"[5]—the "wild beast" of human nature threatened to draw encouragement from an environment much wilder than the landscape of England. In America, the fearful symmetry of external and internal wilderness strained the tenuous continuity of civility upon which the successful transplantation of culture seemed to depend. So long as the wilderness remained potent, either as objective reality or as myth, like would call to like, and the wild terrain would find a sympathetic response in the wild nature of the colonists. If Winthrop and his colleagues were to fail in their custodial duties, the English themselves might emerge as the true "beastlike men" of New England.[6]

"Beasts in the Shape of Men"

The environmental circumstances of America intensified a danger that Europeans of the seventeenth century assumed was present universally in the human soul. Humanity's rather precarious place in the hierarchy of creation implied not only the hopeful prospect of eventually climbing (or being lifted) into the realm of pure spirit, but also the possibility of being dragged downward by the lusts of the "bruitishe fleshe" into a bestial condition. The complementary notion of the composite soul—which ascribed bestial as well as rational faculties to human beings—held equally disturbing implications for the stability of human reason. "In briefe," Sir Thomas Browne concluded, "we all are monsters, that is, a composition of man and beast," a condition that made it necessary "to have the Region of Man above that of Beast, and sense to sit but at the feete of reason."[7] But if sense refused to sit meekly at reason's feet like a faithful hound, the beast would become master of the man—who would then have only the mockery of his divine image to testify to his human identity. In an essential moral sense, he would have become, in fact, a bestial monster.[8]

Although the Puritans shared these ideas with other Europeans of their century, an unusually strong sense of fallen humanity as creatures utterly depraved and deranged in all their faculties made Puritan ears especially sensitive to the growlings of the beast within. "Let us consider our selves," the Reverend Thomas Hooker of Hartford, Connecticut, invited his readers, "a company of poor, miserable, sinful, and damned Creatures, sinful dust and ashes, dead dogs."[9] In offering this invitation—and in including himself in his audience—Hooker was probably quite conscious of his own (very lively) bestial nature. According to Cotton Mather, Hooker was "a man of a cholerick disposition, . . . yet he had ordinarily as much government of his choler as a man has of a mastiff dog in a chain; he 'could let out his dog, and pull in his dog, as he pleased.' "[10] Mather seems to have been especially fascinated with this imagery, and he greatly admired his predecessors in the New England ministry who were able to keep their canine appetites under control. Citing a "philosopher of old [who] called our passions by the just name of *unnurtured dogs*," Mather lauded Samuel Whiting for keeping "these dogs with a strong chain upon them."[11] Similarly, John Eliot, famous in Mather's pages for his efforts at self-mortification and his zeal in recommending it to others, provoked in Mather the reflection that "We are all of us compounded of those two things, *the man* and *the beast*; but so powerful was the *man* in this holy person, that it kept the *beast* ever tyed with a short tedder, and suppressed the irregular *calcitrations* of it."[12]

It is easy to imagine Mather's envy of such exemplary self-control, since he struggled so painfully with "the irregular *calcitrations*" of his own inner beast. Mather obsessively abased himself in his diary with "the Sense of my own Sinfulness, and Filthiness." Convinced that he was "the most filthy Sinner out of Hell," Mather confessed, "Lord, I *am viler than a Beast before Thee!*"[13] But the most striking instance of Mather's willingness, even eagerness, to confront this side of his nature occurred one day when he was engaged in an elemental act that clearly demonstrated his equivalence to an animal: "I was once emptying the *Cistern of Nature*, and making *Water* at the Wall. At the same Time, there came a *Dog*, who did so too, before me. Thought I; 'What mean, and vile Things are the Children of Men, in this mortal State! How much do our *natural Necessities* abase us, and place us in some regard, on the same Level with the very *Dogs!*'" In response, Mather resolved to provoke his spirit to "rise and soar, and fly up, towards the Employment of the *Angel.*" On future occasions of this sort he would focus on "some holy, noble, divine *Thought*; usually, by way of *occasional Reflection* on some sensible Object which I either then have before me, or have lately had so." He hoped that this would leave some "*Tincture of Piety*" to compensate for the degrading behavior to which his mortal state compelled him.[14]

But Puritans seldom confined their revulsion to their own acts. Corporal punishments were considered especially apt for offenses that most clearly revealed the human "beast" in others: New Haven's law code specified "brutish folly" and "bestly cruelty" as among the cases in which "*Stripes*, or whipping" was "a correction fit."[15] Sermon rhetoric also tended to dehumanize the ungodly—as when Thomas Shepard told his flock in Cambridge, Massachusetts, that those who would not pray to God were worthy to live only "among bears, and wolves, and beasts in the wilderness."[16] Significantly, in light of this view, animals played a prominent role in witchcraft cases—either as familiars, as forms assumed by the supposed witch, as victims of the witch's spells, or (perhaps most revealing) as models for the behavior of human victims, who often seemed to descend to a bestial state during their affliction.[17] Even in John Cotton's categorization of hypocrites as either "Goats" or "washed Swine" there was an intimation of a full moral correspondence quite at odds with references to Christ's sheep or lambs.[18] Heresy also suggested a lapse into a more bestial frame of mind: the heresiarch Samuel Gorton and his followers were compared to "beasts in the shape of men."[19] And Roger Williams, who had himself been driven out of Massachusetts as an unclean beast, was not above exploiting the implications of George Fox's surname. For Williams that name was no mere pun; the "finger of God" had pointed out this verbal emblem as a clue to the Quaker's true nature.[20]

Such rhetoric may have tempted the Puritans to try to purge themselves by projecting their fears onto heretical or unregenerate scapegoats. And in some respects New England was ideally suited for such a strategy—since the orthodox magistrates could expel the "goats" into the surrounding wilderness where they presumably belonged. But certain especially seductive, or especially elemental, lusts persisted in reminding the godly that the wilderness within harbored strange creatures who were only partly human.

"The Cry of Sodom Enquired Into"

A particularly insidious stimulus to the brute within was that powerful solvent of human reason which, as one writer put it, left "The man confounded with the Beast": "O Potent Rum!"[21] As Cotton Mather declared bluntly, "The man who does make *himself Drunk,* does make himself a *Beast.*"[22] Similarly, fornication, "wherein men show their brutishness," could unseat reason and enthrone the bestial soul in its place.[23] But if alcohol or fornication degraded humanity to the level of the animals, another form of lust confirmed the fragility of human identity in even more appalling ways: sexual bestiality. Given the seventeenth-century concern with preserving the uneasy distinction between humans and beasts, it is not surprising that the question of human relations with domestic animals was especially troubling.[24] In a predominantly agricultural society, contacts between animals and their owners were bound to be frequent and close, but it was important that they not be too close. Any sexual interaction across species boundaries was greatly abhorred, not least because of the suggestion that humans could, if provoked by bestial lust, join with the animal kingdom in a horrifyingly literal sense. Sexual bestiality was also disturbing in that, like drunkenness or fornication, it could not be safely isolated and identified with an objective ideological or doctrinal error. How was society to account for this impulse except by reference to the corrupt nature that all shared? The temptation to bestiality was thus a germ that society carried within it, a chronic infection that required vigilant monitoring and persistent efforts of suppression.

In the period 1640–1642 Winthrop was sufficiently disturbed by three outbreaks to make special note of them in his journal. The first case involved a "wicked fellow, given up to bestiality"—so given up to it that by his own confession "he never saw any beast go before him but he lusted after it."[25] Then, in 1641, as if to confirm the infection's spread, a young servant in Salem "was found in buggery with a cow, upon the Lord's day." William Hackett (or Hatchet), about eighteen or twenty years old, tried to deny that he had actually gone through with the act, but the court decided otherwise. He received the death penalty—as prescribed by Leviticus—and the guilty cow was killed as a prelude to his own execution.[26]

Winthrop sought to deflect responsibility for this wickedness from the society that had harbored Hackett by observing that "he was noted always to have been a very stupid, idle, and ill-disposed boy, and would never regard the means of instruction, either in the church or family." Still, as he faced the prospect of the noose, "his hard heart melted." Hackett made a full confession and began to display the usual signs of regeneration—and not a moment too soon, with his execution scheduled for the next day. In light of this sudden, hopeful change of heart, the authorities delayed the inevitable for another week. Winthrop believed that the Lord had admitted Hackett's soul "to his mercy." But mercy in this case belonged to the Lord alone, not to the Massachusetts Bay magistrates, who were more concerned with justice. Hackett's timely conversion could not save him from the gallows.[27]

In 1642 word of the case of George Spencer reached Winthrop from New Haven. It seems that a sow there had given birth to a pig with certain "human resemblances." Specifically, as Winthrop reported the details, it was bald and (most revealing) "it had also one eye blemished, just like one eye of a loose fellow in the town." Sure enough, when the loose fellow—Spencer—was urged to confess, he admitted his paternity, though perhaps merely on the mistaken assumption that he would thereby get off with lighter punishment. Despite subsequent efforts to retract his confession, he too was hanged.[28]

New Haven seems to have been especially afflicted by this form of lust. In 1647 the same sort of paternal resemblances that had helped to convict Spencer got Thomas Hogg into trouble. It is likely that the unfortunate man's name in itself suggested the same accusing finger of God that would put Roger Williams onto George Fox's trail. When another suspicious-looking litter of pigs appeared, Hogg became the prime suspect. In a strange instance of using bestiality to obtain evidence of bestiality, the authorities confronted Hogg with his supposed partner in crime: "they bid him scratt the sow that had the monsters, & immedyatly there appeared a working of lust in the sow, insomuch that she powred out seede before them, & then, being asked what he thought of it, he said he saw a hand of God in it." The magistrates were inclined to agree: the hand of God was clearly pointing out the filthy handiwork of Thomas Hogg. Still, the evidence was not enough to convict him of a capital offense; though Hogg was whipped for other misconduct, he escaped hanging.[29]

Whatever else these proceedings say about the ignorance and credulity of the New England justices (who were, after all, at the mercy of their century's conventional wisdom in such matters), there can be no more vivid testimony to the contemporary belief in the possibility of dissolving the boundaries between humans and animals through sexual communication. Bestiality demonstrated that the man who engaged in the act was as much of a monster as his unnatural issue. Cotton Mather, recording with fastidious horror yet another New Haven case, referred to the guilty man himself as a "monster" who had been seen "confounding himself with a *bitch*" and "hideously conversing with a *sow*." In calling this miscreant a "hell hound" and a "*bewitch'd beast*," Mather added rhetorical force to the implicit assumption that these hideous, confounding conversations permitted the melding of what should have remained two distinct realms of creation.[30]

The definitive New England statement on the confounding effects of bestiality came from Samuel Danforth, pastor of Roxbury, Massachusetts, in *The Cry of Sodom Enquired Into; Upon Occasion of The Arraignment and Condemnation of Benjamin Goad, For his Prodigious Villany* (1674). Benjamin was a Roxbury lad of seventeen or eighteen years, and the prodigious villainy consisted of his having committed "Bestiality with a Mare . . . at noon day in an open yard." As punishment for this particularly flagrant violation of human identity and God's law, Goad was sentenced to be executed on April 2, 1674, when (according to precedent) the mare "was first

THE
Cry of Sodom

ENQVIRED INTO;

Upon Occasion of

The *Arraignment* and *Condemnation*

OF

BENJAMIN GOAD,

For his Prodigious Villany.

Together with

A Solemn Exhortation to Tremble at Gods Judgements,
and to Abandon Youthful Lusts.

By S. Danforth

Isa. 26.9. ——When thy Judgements are in the earth, the inhabitants of the world will learn righteousness.

Psal. 119.118. Thou hast troden down all them that err from thy statutes: for their deceit is falshood.

ver. 119. Thou puttest away all the wicked of the earth like dross: therefore I love thy Testimonies.

ver. 120. My flesh trembleth for fear of thee; and I am afraid of thy Judgements.

1 Pet. 2. 11. Dearly beloved, I beseech you as strangers and pilgrims, abstain from fleshly lusts, which war against the soul.

Cambridge: Printed by Marmaduke Johnson 1674.

The Cry of Sodom Enquired Into, a jeremiad against bestiality, written by Samuel Danforth, pastor of Roxbury, Massachusetts. Incidents of bestiality in New England fueled Puritan fears that the boundaries between humans and animals could be dissolved. *Courtesy, American Antiquarian Society* knocked in the head under the Gallows in his sight."[31] Goad's crime, among other current vexations, prompted the General Court to set aside a day of humiliation a week before the execution,[32] and Danforth seized the opportunity to clarify without equivocation the threat that bestiality posed to those who gave in to it. In his sermon to the people of Roxbury, Danforth acknowledged that bestiality was only one type of uncleanness among many others—including self-pollution, whoredom, adultery, incest, and sodomy. Those who wallowed in any of these lusts were "*Dogs* and *Swine*." But if this were true of "the lusts of Uncleanness" in general, it was more blatantly true of bestiality. "This is monstrous and horrible *Confusion*," said Danforth; "it turneth a man into a bruit Beast. He that joyneth himself to a Beast, is one flesh with a Beast."[33]

This was the golden age of the jeremiad, and as one of its virtuosi, Danforth could not resist exploiting Benjamin as a goad to incite the rising generation to greater efforts of self-discipline. His audience also surely expected to learn from Danforth not only society's justification for visiting such an extreme penalty on the boy, but the extent to which society shared the shame and guilt of his horrible deed—itself both sin and affliction. Danforth did not disappoint them. He reminded his younger listeners (and their parents or guardians) that Benjamin had been "extremely addicted to Sloth and Idleness; which is a great breeder and cherisher of Uncleanness." With such evidence before them, could anyone doubt that "Lust is usually warm and stirring in idle bosomes"? Warm lust had obviously stirred in Goad until God had abandoned him to his bestial desires. In reviewing his rather spotted career, Danforth posited a natural progression from "Disobedience to his Parents," through "Lying, Stealing, Sabbath-breaking," and neglect of catechism, to "Self-pollution, and other Sodomitical wickedness." The chain of causation seemed clear: it was only a short step from sloth to sodomy.[34]

Without accusing the entire congregation of complicity in bestiality, Danforth still managed to suggest that they were not wholly untainted by the evil to which Goad, in his "licentious liberty," had yielded. What Goad had done "in the sight of the Sun, and in the open field, even at Noon-day; proclaiming his sin like *Sodom*," was to give open release to a basic corruption that all men harbored, like a familiar serpent, in their breasts. By implication, all New England—indeed, all humanity—stood convicted along with Goad, and if the people looked into their own hearts they would find similar (if not quite so horrible) sins that were equally deserving of God's judgment. Danforth assured his audience that "The gross and flagitious practises of the worst of men, are but Comments upon our Nature. Who can say, I have made my heart clean? The holiest man hath as vile and filthy a Nature, as the *Sodomites*, or the men of *Gibeah*."[35]

Perhaps the congregation was sufficiently scandalized by Goad, despite his youth, to take this message as more than a variation on a rather threadbare theme. Surely their awareness of the beast within was especially strong as they left the meetinghouse that day. But Danforth, by stressing the universal qualities of Goad's bestiality, left his flock a way out of their filthy mire. If Goad's sin compromised his humanity and set him apart from society, he was nevertheless useful as a scapegoat for his neighbors, having simultaneously polluted his community and furnished the means for a ritual purge. As Danforth put the case, "Though he be a Youth in respect of years, yet he is grown old in wickedness, and ripe for Vengeance. The Church cannot be cleansed, untill this wicked person be put away from among us. . . . The Land cannot be cleansed, untill it hath spued out this Unclean Beast."[36]

But could the land really cleanse itself by spewing out such unclean beasts? In order for the scapegoat to fulfill his purifying function, there would have to be a sharp distinction between the realm of civilization and the wilderness into which the goat was to carry his burden. In a material sense, the expansion of settlement in New England was gradually making the distinction clear enough. But bestiality complicated matters: just as it blurred the inner boundary between man and beast, so it also weakened the comfortable external dichotomy of civilization and wilderness. The occurrence of bestiality within the area of English culture suggested that while the colonists might conquer the wilderness as a physical presence, its moral influences were less easy to combat. And if the curse of wilderness had taken root in the colonists and their culture, no scapegoat could possibly draw off all the corruption they would generate.[37]

In the early 1640s, when bestiality was threatening to assume epidemic proportions, William Bradford shared John Winthrop's need to deal with this phenomenon in the history he was writing. Bradford reacted to bestiality with an abhorrence equal to Winthrop's, but he was more willing to confront the environmental implications. He was obviously mindful that the Pilgrims' pretensions to social as well as doctrinal purity focused critical attention on their ability to practice what they preached. They had in fact "so narrowly looked unto, and severly punished" wickedness that they had been "somewhat censured, even by moderate and good men, for their severitie in punishments." Now, events suggested that their efforts had really been futile. Something in America resisted Puritan discipline and was breaking out in foul eruptions—and not just in the old familiar forms of drunkenness and fornication, for "even sodomie and bugerie, (things fearfull to name,)" had cropped up "oftener then once."[38]

One case in particular was enough to raise doubts in Bradford's mind about the inward health of his colony. In 1642 all the uncleanness of an unclean year came to a head in the bizarre career of Thomas Granger of Duxbury. Only sixteen or seventeen years old, Granger had left his parents' home in Scituate to serve in the family of Love Brewster, Elder William's son. But despite the good example of this "honest man," Granger fell into practices that both repelled and strangely fascinated Bradford. "Horrible it is to mention," he admitted, "but the truth of the historie requires it."[39] He seemed drawn to expose

Granger to the light of history so that he could rid himself of the fear that Granger's sins were somehow a natural consequence of transplantation into a wilderness environment.

The horrible truth was that Granger had committed "buggery . . . with a mare, a cowe, tow goats, five sheep, .2. calves, and a turkey." He had apparently been gratifying his bestial lusts for some time before he was caught in the act with the mare ("I forbear perticulers," Bradford tersely commented). Upon examination, Granger confessed in full, and the authorities—with some difficulty—went about rounding up the suspected accomplices. In a perverse, monstrous (though surely inadvertent) parody of the last judgment, Granger had to separate the guilty sheep from the innocent. As Bradford explained, "wheras some of the sheep could not so well be knowne by his description of them, others with them were brought before him, and he declared which were they, and which were not." This done, the animals and Granger (in that order) were dispatched on the authority of Leviticus—and "A very sade spectakle it was," Bradford assures us.[40]

Naturally enough, the Plymouth magistrates were interested in finding out how Granger had acquired such eccentric tastes, and they were doubtless relieved to learn that, in this case at least, bestiality was imported, not homemade, sin. According to the boy's testimony, "he was taught it by an other that had heard of shuch things from some in England when he was ther, and they kept catle togeather." This reassuring revelation allowed Bradford to blame part of the recent carnival of crime on the mixed multitude that had followed the Pilgrims into the wilderness "for the loaves sake."[41] As he might have added, it also followed (from Numbers 11:4) that "the mixt multitude that was among them fell a lusting."

So it did, but the Granger incident was clearly more than a matter of one boy's unfortunate choice of sexual expression. At bottom, as always, there lay "our corrupte natures, which are so hardly bridled, subdued, and mortified." This root of evil ran so deep that it could account for any act of wickedness, without distinction of mere geography. Still, it was the sort of explanation that explained too little by explaining too much. Bradford ultimately had to confront the possibility that Plymouth's corruption—as represented by Granger—was related specifically to American circumstances. Something about the place seemed to attract the attention and energies of the devil. Indeed, the Pilgrims could consider themselves flattered if Satan harbored a special grudge against them for their devotion to "holynes and puritie." Bradford admitted he "would rather thinke thus, then that Satane hath more power in these heathen lands, as som have thought, then in more Christian nations, espetially over Gods servants in them."[42] If America proved to be Satan's, not God's, country, then the Pilgrims had settled in an environment that, through its diabolic nature, would frustrate any transplantation of civility and Christianity.[43]

Rather than confront openly such an ominous conclusion, Bradford hurried on to other explanations that reassured him of the basic soundness of the colonial venture: perhaps repressed wickedness was simply breaking forth like a dammed stream; perhaps Plymouth was more rigorous in exposing and punishing evil—thus creating the false impression that the colony actually suffered more from human depravity than other lands that complacently allowed the filth to remain hidden. "Besides," he observed, "here the people are but few in comparison of other places, which are full and populous, and lye hid, as it were, in a wood or thickett, and many horrible evills by that means are never seen nor knowne; wheras hear, they are, as it were, brought into the light, and set in the plaine feeld, or rather on a hill, made conspicuous to the veiw of all."[44] Thus, Bradford contrived to tell his horror story of bestiality while simultaneously absolving America and himself (as Christian magistrate) from any direct complicity in the matter. But the strained, and apparently unconvincing, nature of this rhetorical gambit is revealed in the strange reversal of imagery that he applied to the contrast between America and Europe. Under Bradford's hands, civil, populous, cultivated Europe takes shape improbably as "a wood or thickett" that conceals evil, while America oddly emerges as a "plaine feeld" or (even more resonant) "a hill, conspicuous to the veiw of all."

This comforting rhetoric was undermined not only by the inconvenient persistence of America's own relatively abundant (by comparison to England) woods and thickets, but also by the wilderness connotations of bestiality. Bradford clearly wrote from within the tradition that viewed the wilderness as the antithesis of civilization and a place where men were in danger of degenerating to the level of wild beasts.[45] From this perspective, Thomas Granger, in the literal wilderness condition of Plymouth colony, was merely pursuing with perverse abandon the brutal fate that also subtly threatened his neighbors.

Since Bradford saw fit to withhold the essential details, it is impossible to reconstruct the exact circumstances of Granger's crime. Like Benjamin Goad, he may actually have committed the act in a "plaine feeld" or "open yard." But in October 1681, long after William Bradford had ceased to worry about such matters, a case of bestiality arose in Plymouth that moved much further toward confirming the connection of bestiality, wilderness, and the devil. Thomas Saddeler was haled before the court and charged with "buggery" with a mare. The formal statement of the charge warrants quotation at some length:

thou, haveing not the feare of God before, nor carrying with thee the dignity of humaine nature, but being seduced by the instigation of the divill, on the third of September in this present yeer, 1681, by force and armes, att Mount Hope, in the jurisdiction of New Plymouth, a certaine mare of a blackish couller then and there being in a certaine obscure and woodey place, on Mount Hope aforsaid, neare the ferrey, then and there thou didest tye her head unto a bush, and then and there, wickedly and most abominably, against thy humaine nature, with the same mare then and there being felloniously and carnally didest attempt, and the detestable sin of buggery then and there felloniously thou didest committ and doe, to the great dishonor and contempt of Almighty God and of all mankind, and against the peace of our sovereign lord the Kinge, his crowne, and dignity, and against the lawes of God, his majestie, and this jurisdiction.[46]

In effect, the court had summed up for Saddeler the fundamental grounds of the culture's revulsion against his "detestable sin." Whatever challenge bestiality posed for the king's dignity, it was obvious enough that this crime represented a monstrous assault on "the dignity of humaine nature." The court also seemed determined to drive home the point that Saddeler had not merely endangered his own humanity; his sin was also an affront to "all mankind"—and specifically to that part of mankind that had ventured its destiny in New England.

As if to revive Bradford's old fear, the court also allowed the image of America as Satan's hunting park to emerge in its accusation that Saddeler had been "seduced by the instigation of the divill." But where his act occurred was as loathsome as how or why it was committed. Saddeler had succumbed to the devil's promptings not in a plain field or upon a hill, but "in a certaine obscure and woodey place"— and Mount Hope at that, a site that only a few years earlier had been the haunt of King Philip and the Indians whom, in the hysteria of a bloody war, the people had been encouraged to regard as bestial and demonic.[47] Against this background, Saddeler seemed no mere frontier rakehell, to be lumped in with ordinary fornicators and drunkards. He dramatically symbolized the precarious condition of English civility (let alone essential humanity) in an alien environment. Even so, by 1681 the court was less willing to seek a full catharsis. Although Saddeler was not hanged, he was whipped publicly and forced to stand on the gallows with a noose about his neck. His forehead was branded with a "P" for pollution, and he was ordered to leave the colony.[48]

By this time it may have seemed that New England, compared to Old, was peculiarly plagued by this evil.[49] The crime of bestiality had been a capital offense in England since the sixteenth century, but English court records indicate that prosecution was relatively rare.[50] Roger Thompson has suggested that bestiality was "statistically insignificant" in the New England court records as well.[51] Still, with New England's smaller population and less dense settlement (aside from its superior pretensions to moral discipline), a handful of cases within a few years—as in the 1640s—was enough to raise the suspicion that the colonists were for some reason strangely susceptible to this form of degeneracy. In the year after the Saddeler case, an English writer who was no friend of the reigning orthodoxy in New England suggested as much when he charged that "there be some of the Brethren that do love to embrace their likeness, (to wit a Beast;) choosing rather to have familiarity with a Beast or a handsom Boy, than use their own Wives."[52]

William Bradford was probably right in ascribing the greater evidence of bestiality in Plymouth to the magistrates' diligence in bringing the guilty to trial. And it is possible that the Puritans' intense biblical-mindedness—especially in their reading of Leviticus—encouraged them to detect and prosecute crimes that justices in England were more inclined to ignore. Two years after Samuel Danforth inquired into the cry of Sodom, a writer in England remarked that "Such crimes as these are rarely heard of among us."[53] Rarely heard of does not mean rarely committed. Bestiality may indeed have been a common practice in England's rural areas—as Granger hinted when he confessed that he had acquired the habit from a man who, in turn, had picked it up among keepers of cattle in England.[54]

Yet Bradford was in no position to make a transatlantic comparison of court records—nor was he much concerned with questions of statistical significance. He simply suspected that bestiality had loomed less ominously over the community in England. The question of whether America belonged to God or the devil would remain to torment the guardians of English culture in New England until a mental "disafforestation" had assigned due place to New England's bestial passions. Throughout the seventeenth century, thanks to men like Granger, Hogg, Goad, and Saddeler, the complete success of cultural transplantation remained far from certain.

Humanity, Civility, and Christianity

For Puritan New England, the essential antithesis to human bestiality lay in a trinity of values enshrined in the 1648 Massachusetts law code: "humanitie, civilitie & christianity."[55] And in service of these values, the magistrates worked to establish and enforce the "good laws" without which, according to William Hubbard, men and women were "but like cattle without a fence, . . . apt to run wild and grow unruly."[56] The ministers, for their part, cultivated the church, "Gods Garden, or Orchard, his Paradise"—in distinction to the world outside, which was "as a wildernesse, or at best as a wide field, where all manner of unclean, and wilde beasts live and feed."[57] God's gardeners faithfully cautioned against letting the tender English shoots "grow up in sinfull ignorance and profanenes of life, letting them grow like wilde plants, or rather like the wilde asse-colt which snuffs up the winde at her pleasure."[58]

The urgency of preserving humanity, civility, and Christianity as defenses against bestial nature also helps to explain the Puritan leaders' intense commitment to communalism as a social ideal. If the people were allowed to yearn freely toward the greener, wilder prospects that beckoned from beyond the pasture fence, they might in time find themselves among those "that account it their happiness to live in the wast howling wilderness, without any ministry, or schooles, and means of education for their posterity."[59] Such people, in the words of Edward Johnson, had "run out so far in this Wilderness" that they had not only forsaken "the assembly of the Lords people" but were apparently in danger of forsaking the assembly of humanity itself—"horse, kine, sheep, goats, and swine being their most indeared companions."[60] This would not do. Though the Puritans had sought a place of refuge far from the roots of their ancestral culture, they had not intended thereby to sever all ties to the human community. Beasts might live alone in a wilderness, but not human creatures: they were social beings, not isolatoes.

The idea of people as social animals was yet another ancient commonplace that threatened to acquire new life in the novel conditions of the New World. In his essay "Of Frendship" Francis Bacon had repeated a statement of Aristotle's that had enormous potential for illuminating the dangers of a solitary wilderness life: "It had beene hard for him that spake it, to have put more Truth and untruth together, in few Words, then in that Speech; *Whosoever is delighted in solitude, is either a wilde Beast, or a God.* For it is most true, that a Naturall and Secret Hatred, and Aversation towards *Society*, in any Man, hath somewhat of the Savage Beast; But it is most Untrue, that it should have any Character, at all, of the Divine Nature."[61] The bestializing effects of solitude were related to the supposed tendency of the solitary condition to breed mental disorders—especially melancholy, which in circular fashion increased the isolatoes' estrangement from their fellow creatures. As Thomas Walkington observed in *The Optick Glasse of Humors* (1631), melancholy "causeth men to bee alienated from the nature of man, and wholly to discarde themselves from all societie."[62] And Robert Burton, with his own massive authority on this subject, identified "Voluntary solitariness" as an important cause of melancholy. "These wretches," wrote Burton of those who chose idle solitude over society, "do frequently degenerate from men, and of sociable creatures become beasts, monsters, inhuman, ugly to behold, *misanthropi.*"[63]

The Puritan shepherds knew that America provided ample opportunity to withdraw from society and degenerate, perhaps, into wild beasts or monsters. At best, a lone colonist in the backwoods might become a cranky misanthrope—at worst, the monstrous beast represented by Granger, Hogg,

Goad, and Saddeler. To forestall such an outcome, the voice of cultural orthodoxy in New England reiterated the doctrine that human society was essential to human identity. John Cotton wrote that "Society in all sorts of humane affaires is better then Solitariness." Nor was it simply a matter of preferring neighborliness to a sullen hermit's life. Society and consultation with others were necessary to stave off the ravenings of the beast within: "Thus pride of heart [in keeping one's own counsel too closely] maketh a man of a savage nature; wild beasts love to goe alone, but tame by flocks and herds."[64]

Paradoxically, part of the problem was that in a spiritually charged world it was impossible to be truly alone. Sir Thomas Browne liked to pursue his thoughts on the spiritual mysteries to an "*oh altitudo,*" but not to an *oh solitudo,* because he believed that "there is no such thing as solitude." Of course, nothing could "subsist without the concourse of God, and the society of that hand which doth uphold their natures." But even "in a Wildernesse" "a man is never alone, not onely because hee is with himselfe, and his owne thoughts, but because he is with the devill, who ever consorts with our solitude, and is that unruly rebell that musters up those disordered motions, which accompany our sequestred imaginations."[65] New Englanders did not need Browne's reminder to be alert to the inescapable companionship of the devil. The colonist Thomas Tillam, speaking for the Lamb of God in his poem "Uppon the first sight of New-England June 29 1638," had already warned them to

> . . . beware of Sathans wylye baites
> hee lurkes amongs yow, Cunningly hee waites
> to Catch yow from mee; live not then secure
> but fight 'gainst sinne, and let your lives be pure. . . .[66]

But if the Puritans were aware of the need to avoid the sort of solitude that allowed lurking Satan to catch hold of their "sequestred imaginations," they eagerly sought the solitude that they could share with God. The intense piety that drove a man like Governor Edward Hopkins of Connecticut to pray so hard he bled from the nose also drove pious Puritans to withdraw from the world into private meditation—either in quiet "closets" or in the open countryside, apart from the crush of society.[67] Thomas Shepard discovered this satisfaction when he was a student at Cambridge in England. On one occasion—still in his wild-colt phase—he woke up in embarrassing circumstances in another student's room after a Saturday-night drinking bout. Sickened by what he called his "beastly carriage," he fled the strange chamber "in shame and confusion, and went out into the fields and there spent that Sabbath lying hid in the cornfields." There, in the fields, he sought relief from the contaminations of society and pondered his sins.[68]

Even in America, where simple unfamiliarity with the forest made abstracted meanderings less advisable, the practice of outdoor meditation persisted. According to Cotton Mather, Jonathan Mitchell as a young man at Harvard (where he became Shepard's ministerial heir apparent) "would sometimes, on the Saturday, retire into the woods, near the town, and there spend a great part of the day in examining of his own heart and life."[69] Though Mather, an urban creature by nature, usually confined his personal exercises in self-mortification to the privacy of his study, on a visit to Lynn in 1683 he refreshed himself by taking contemplative walks away from the town. As he recorded in his diary, "I enjoy'd many happy Hours, in the countrey-Retirements of the Fields."[70] It is important to note that Mather spoke of "countrey-Retirements" in "Fields," not wilderness-entanglements in the forests. In recording Mitchell's pious walks in the woods, he also carefully observed that Mitchell, while venturing into the forest, stayed "near the town." Still, Puritans were willing within bounds to use the natural sanctuary of the forest for their devotions. Roger Clap did not distinguish between fields and forests when he advised his children, "You may Pray alone in the Woods, as Christ did in the Mountain: You may Pray as you walk in the Fields, as Isaac did."[71] And

Jonathan Edwards, benefiting from the more domesticated character of eighteenth-century Connecticut, made forest meditations a habitual part of his religious exercises. In his "personal narrative" he related how, as a child prodigy of piety, he "had particular secret places of my own in the woods, where I used to retire by myself; and used to be from time to time much affected." He obviously felt he had been affected for the good, not seduced by the devil, in such retreats, since he continued the practice in his later years. At a more mature age, he still "used to spend abundance of my time, in walking alone in the woods, and solitary places, for meditation, soliloquy and prayer, and converse with God."[72]

The fact that it was acceptable to pray alone (even in the woods) did not mean that it was all right to live alone (and certainly not in the woods). A faithful Christian like Jonathan Mitchell or Jonathan Edwards might venture into the forest for meditation, but in the end the wilderness colloquy with God would have to be broken off in order to return to the enclosed garden, as God had ordained. It proved difficult, however, to confine the transplanted culture as a whole to a formal garden when so much wild growing room lay beyond the garden walls. It was by no means certain that New England could simultaneously subdue the earth and preserve its valued social cohesiveness, when the English plants seemed so determined to become running vines in the wilderness.[73]

Nevertheless, the Puritan governments took up the challenge—most notably in the 1635 Massachusetts law requiring that all houses be built within half a mile of the meetinghouse. As the ultimate futility of this law made clear, such measures were simply unworkable under the conditions of an expanding colony.[74] But the defense of humanity, civility, and Christianity demanded at least a show of resistance to the inevitable. In the summer of 1650 some earnest residents of Hartford respectfully asked the Connecticut General Court for permission to plant a new town at Norwalk, and the court, in a revealing statement, replied that they "could not but, in the generall, approve of the indeavours of men for the further improvement of the wildernes, by the beginning and carrying on of new plantacions in an orderly way."[75] The court could thus sanction wilderness "improvement," but only if it went forward "in an orderly way." The expansion of culture could be carried on safely only by coherent communities, not by isolatoes or single families who were likely to lose their solitary souls in the wilderness before they could subdue it.

Plymouth colony agreed with Connecticut in condemning the disorderly method of wilderness settlement. In May 1652 Joseph Ramsden got into trouble by living "with his family remotely in the woods from naighbours." The authorities warned this backwoods Ishmael "to bring his wife and family, with all convenient speed, near unto some naighborhood." But apparently the warning did no good, since in June 1656 the General Court took notice that "Joseph Ramsden hath lived long in the woods, in an uncivell way, in the woods, with his wife alone." The man had been given four years to save himself from barbarism, and it seemed he would not do it. The court therefore ordered "that hee repaier downe to sume naighborhood betwixt this and October next, or that then his house bee pulled downe."[76]

It was doubtless a simple matter to pull down Ramsden's house, but the authorities could not so easily eliminate the wilderness attractions that would continue to draw other Ramsdens into the forest and away from civility. Almost twenty years later, in June 1675, the Plymouth General Court summoned three men to give some explanation "for theire residing in the goverment without order, and not attending the publicke worship of God, liveing lonely and in a heathenish way from good societie." The court ordered these disorderly, heathenish characters to attend religious services "and live otherwise orderly" or they would have to leave the colony.[77]

The New England Crusoe

In many ways, the transplanted culture of New England found itself in a situation similar to that of Robinson Crusoe—

himself an early eighteenth-century product of the Puritan imagination, by way of Daniel Defoe. Like the New England colonists, Crusoe on his island was in a wilderness condition, cut off from the roots of his culture and forced to supply the comforts of society from limited resources. Yet, like the lone penitent confessing his sins to God and examining his soul in a wilderness retreat, Crusoe appreciated that a solitary condition had certain benefits as well as liabilities. After two years on the island he became, as he thought, reconciled to his isolato's fate: "I gave humble and hearty Thanks that God had been pleas'd to discover to me, even that it was possible I might be more happy in this Solitary Condition, than I should have been in a Liberty of Society, and in all the Pleasures of the World. That he could fully make up to me, the Deficiencies of my Solitary State, and the want of Humane Society by his Presence, and the Communications of his Grace to my Soul. . . ." Crusoe was also conscious that his material condition, though somewhat straitened by his shipwreck and the wildness of the island, was not hopeless—especially when he applied his natural ingenuity to the raw materials he found lying about him. "I am divided from Mankind, a Solitaire, one banish'd from humane Society," he thinks near the beginning of his exile, "But I am not starv'd and perishing on a barren Place, affording no Sustenance."[78]

In time, however, events revealed that Crusoe was not as secure as he had thought. Practical applications of his reason saved him from death by starvation or exposure, but Crusoe remained in other respects a man in peril, a man in danger of succumbing to influences that he scarcely understood. If he did not degenerate into a melancholy misanthrope or a human "beast," he drew remarkably close to a bestial condition. Crusoe's factual prototype, Alexander Selkirk, reportedly "tam'd some Kids, and to divert himself would now and then sing and dance with them and his Cats."[79] True to his model, Crusoe accepted beasts as his daily familiars: his parrot, his goats, his cats, and his dog. And after over twenty years on the island, he confessed that he was "naturaliz'd to the Place." Even as he had imposed much of his own vision of civilization on the environment, it had also imprinted something of its character on him. He realized he had taken on a savage appearance, wearing goatskin clothes "of a most barbarous Shape."[80]

Above all, Crusoe's peace remained incomplete so long as there was a chance that "Savages" would find his hideaway and devour him. Moreover, he was troubled by the fear that, while he could at times feel himself alone with God, there was also a less benevolent spiritual presence on the island, a presence that seemed somehow linked to the threat of savage attack. When, after many years of solitary life, Crusoe came upon a human footprint on the beach, he wondered at first if the print might be the mark of the devil. He quickly rejected this explanation, but having looked upon that portentous sign, he could live in security no longer—at least until he had confronted the human devils that terrorized him merely by this mute rumor of their existence.[81]

Crusoe ultimately triumphed over the cannibals, and even adopted one of them as his companion. This relieved his solitary condition, but it complicated his situation by raising the prospect of cultural contamination through familiarity with a savage. Crusoe accordingly resolved to remake Friday in his own image, rather than meet the Indian halfway. Friday must learn to speak Crusoe's language ("I began now to have some Use for my Tongue again"), and one of the first words he learns is "*Master.*" Friday must also embrace his master's religion, he must wear clothes patterned after Crusoe's (however "barbarous"), and he must learn to eat in the English manner. When Crusoe discovered that Friday still hankered after human flesh, he let his servant know that he would kill him if he indulged this forbidden taste.[82]

The colonists of New England—a collective Crusoe, despite continued communications with England—also struggled with their environment and applied their reason toward adjusting the land to fit their material needs. And, like Crusoe, they tried to enjoy a wilderness communion with God while remaining aware that the devil lurked in their midst. Though some of them verged on bestial degeneration, society as a whole drew back from that oblivion. And when they encountered the native peoples of America, they accepted the challenge of converting them into docile Fridays who could understand the meaning of English civility, the English God, and the word "Master." Yet in the case of these Puritan castaways there was no real prospect of escape from their voluntary exile. A few individuals might abandon the experiment in favor of a return to England, but no ship would arrive to rescue them as a culture from a deepening acquaintance with America. The New England Crusoes were left indefinitely in their transatlantic retreat, alone with themselves, their God, the devil, and their native Fridays. And though Defoe's Crusoe succeeded in taming his wild companion, it was by no means certain that the New England colonists would be able so easily to convert the Indians to English manners. On the contrary, the Indians enjoyed some limited (but still impressive) success at converting the English to their own wild ways. The Indians of New England were not the cannibals of Defoe's imagination, but by confronting the English with an example of what naturalization to the untamed American environment might mean, they greatly complicated the colonists' efforts to disafforest their own minds as well as their adopted land.

Chapter 3 *Indian Origins and Colonial Destinies*

EW ENGLAND, in addition to reinvigorating the colonists' sense of bestial nature, challenged their complacency toward the process of cultural change that they believed had formed the distinct national identities of the world's peoples. Along with other Europeans of their century, the English owed much of their historical perspective to the Bible, a source that seemed to describe the fragmentation and dispersal of culture from an original Edenic unity. The expulsion from the Garden, the divergent paths of Noah's sons after the Flood, the loss of linguistic coherence after the fall of Babel's tower: all had been stages in this ultimately degenerative course. Now, for Europeans of the age of colonization, the migration to America loomed as the next step in degeneracy—if transplantation into the New World's alien environment strained the bonds of Old World tradition to the breaking point.[1]

The English could seek consolation for the loss of their antediluvian place among undifferentiated humanity in the glorification of their own demiparadise island, but chauvinism was no guarantee that English culture was not mutable through dispersal along distant shores. Should the colonists find themselves condemned in their pride of conquest to a confusion of tongues and national identities (with the consequent loss of civility and Christianity as well), the trans-lation of England to America would result in the translation of

Englishmen into Americans—a metamorphosis no Englishman would willingly invite.[2]

The Lesson of O'Hanlan's Breech

And yet, the fate of English colonists who had been translated to Ireland suggested that such a metamorphosis was
indeed possible. Just as England was making its first feeble
attempts to establish permanent settlements on the other side
of the Atlantic, it had become apparent that the attempt to
"plant" English people on the other side of the Irish Sea was
not working out to complete satisfaction. Despite the creation
of an English Pale of settlement—in effect a seedbed for the
transplantation of English culture—and despite legal barriers
designed to fend off any contamination from the native Irish,
the English seemed in danger of losing their long battle to
convert Ireland into a smaller facsimile of their homeland.
Though many colonists continued to display a fastidious contempt for the Irish and their "wild shamrock manners," others
had proved all too willing to embrace Irish customs—as well as
the Irish people. The resulting emergence of a "degenerate"
Anglo-Irish population became a topic of considerable concern to English theorists of colonization and empire.[3]

One such theorist, the poet Edmund Spenser, addressed
the Anglo-Irish scandal in his *View of the Present State of Ireland*,
a work in dialogue form written in 1596, though not printed until 1633.[4] Spenser's view of England's Irish problem
emerges from the conversation between Irenius (the author's
principal mouthpiece) and Eudoxus, who reacts with proper
horror and indignation to the suggestion that the English
could prove so traitorous to their national identity as to throw
it over for the inexpressible barbarism of the Irish. Irenius,
referring to the long history of his country's involvement in
Ireland, an undistinguished record stretching back to the
reign of Henry II, concedes that the descendants of the original colonists "abide still a mighty people"—that is, "of so many

as remain English of them." Eudoxus can hardly believe his English ears: "What is this that ye say of so many as remain English of them? Why are not they that were once English abiding English still?" Sadly, no: "the most part of them," Irenius admits, "are degenerated and grown almost mere Irish, yea and more malicious to the English than the very Irish themselves." Within the Pale (primarily Leinster), civility was holding its own with more success, but elsewhere—especially in Connaught and Munster—the English were "as very patchocks as the wild Irish, yea and some of them have quite shaken off their English names and put on Irish, that they might be altogether Irish." Even some of the "old English" gentry had become, according to Irenius, "as Irish as O'Hanlan's breech, (as the proverb there is)."[5]

But would the lesson of O'Hanlan's breech translate to America? The compass rose of empire pointed directly through Ireland, and English colonial promoters sighted westward along that line with natural ease. Ireland itself began to take on an American cast, one writer describing it as an island "in the Virginian Sea."[6] And as the distinction between Ireland and America became blurred in the imperial prospect, the distinction between Indians and Irishmen also became less clear. The rhetoric English writers had devised to describe the Irish seems to have served as a rough draft for descriptions of the American Indians—themselves, apparently, as "Irish" as O'Hanlan's breech, and perhaps as subversive of English culture.[7]

One group who decided to risk the possibility of an "Indian" destiny did so, in part, because they wanted to escape a more immediate threat of the same kind in Holland. Before the founders of Plymouth colony set out across the Atlantic, they had already become aware of the dangers such dislocations posed for the continuity of culture. In William Bradford's account of the considerations that had led the Pilgrims to abandon Holland for the New World, the problem of their children's increasing acculturation to Dutch life was largely a matter of maintaining moral discipline in the highly competitive, highly seductive urban environment: "many of their children, by these occasions [of poverty and hard work], and the great licentiousnes of youth in that countrie, and the manifold temptations of the place, were drawne away by evill examples into extravagante and dangerous courses, getting the raines off their neks, and departing from their parents. . . . So that they saw their posteritie would be in danger to degenerate and be corrupted."[8] Yet Bradford's words suggest that in "departing from their parents" the English children were also departing from their English identity. Presumably, then, by coming to America the Pilgrims sought a place where they might have a better chance of making certain that their children would remain English. In America, there would be no other well-established European culture nearby—no "evill" but attractive Dutch examples—to tempt them into abandoning the language and customs of their ancestors.[9]

This explanation of the founding of Plymouth colony was stated much more explicitly by Bradford's fellow Pilgrim Edward Winslow. In *Hypocrisie Unmasked* (1646) Winslow, recalling the motives that had prompted him and his friends to settle in America, noted "how grievous [it was, in Holland] to live from under the protection of the State of *England*; how like wee were to lose our language, and our name of English."[10] And Nathaniel Morton, Bradford's nephew, put the matter even more bluntly in his 1669 history of the New England colonies. According to Morton, one reason the founding generation had left Holland was the possibility that "their Posterity would in a few generations become *Dutch,* and so lose their interest in the *English* Nation."[11] The colonists' commitment to the transatlantic continuity of English culture was thus woven into the fabric of their official history.

Bradford seems to have addressed his work largely to Plymouth itself. Winslow and Morton were more aware of the need to reaffirm New England's filial loyalty to the mother country and refute charges that the colonists were seeking de facto

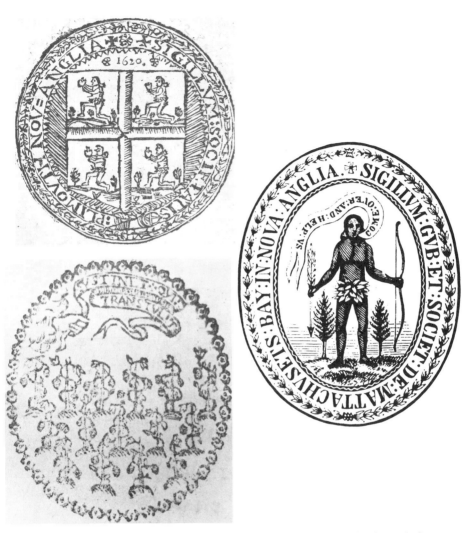

The seals of the first Puritan colonies in New England: above left, the Plymouth seal; above right, the Massachusetts Bay Colony seal; below left, the Connecticut Seal, depicting fifteen vines below the inscription, "Sustinet Qui Transtulit" ("He who has transplanted us sustains us"). *Courtesy, Massachusetts Historical Society*

independence. The Pilgrim Fathers would, however, have seen more than merely political meaning in one critic's contemptuous charge that, even in the 1660s, the Plymouth colonists remained, in fact, "Mungrell Dutch."[12] Although the intense Dutch-English rivalry of these years made any reminder of the colonists' questionable loyalty especially embarrassing to them, the reference to their "Mungrell" nature also took advantage of their continuing sensitivity to charges that they were not as English as they should be.

For in America, the threat of cultural contamination remained. In 1622, two years after the founding of Plymouth, an English writer had noted the colonial danger of "falling away from God to Sathan" and becoming "utterly savage" like the Indians.[13] And in 1624 Richard Eburne championed Newfoundland as an English colony because, among other attractions, "the country for the most part is utterly void of all inhabitants, savages or other, so that there is no fear of enemies in it nor of corruption of language or blood from it."[14] But the lands sheltered within the arm of Cape Cod were not "utterly void of all inhabitants"—despite the Pilgrims' intentions of settling in "some of those vast, and unpeopled countries of America, which are frutfull, and fitt for habitation; being devoyd of all civill inhabitants."[15] In the face of America's "salvage, and brutish men, which range up and downe, litle otherwise then the wild beasts of the same,"[16] the example of the Dutch would fade into comparative insignificance.

An Indian Wilderness

The colonial debate over the origins and historical role (secular and spiritual) of the American Indians acquired a peculiar importance, especially among those who were trying to create a "New England" in the New World. It was possible, of course, to agree with the sixteenth-century writer who dismissed the origins question as a subject of purely academic interest:

... howe the people furst began
In that contrey or whens they cam
For clerkes it is a questyon[.][17]

Or perhaps, as the English writer Philip Vincent declared, "It
were needlesse curiosity to dispute their originall, or how they
came hither. . . . Their correspondency of disposition with us,
argueth all to be of the same constitution, & the sons of *Adam*,
and that we had the same Maker, the same matter, the same
mould." As if to put the best face on what might otherwise
seem an unflattering "correspondency," Vincent suggested
that the Indians were "seldome seene violent, or extreme in
any passion."[18]

Still, the primary occasion for Vincent's *True Relation of the
Late Battell fought in New England, between the English, and the
Salvages* (1637) was itself sufficient evidence that these exemplary stoics could appear violent and passionate enough under the proper stimulus. Vincent noted that "as soyle, aire,
diet; & custome make ofttimes a memorable difference in
mens natures, so is it among these Nations." The Indians
living near the English "have shewed themselves very loving
and friendly" and, therefore, "much hath beene written of
their civilitie and peacefull conversation"—at least "untill this
yeare." The blatant fact of the Pequot War forced Vincent to
consider the dangerous implications of his environmental
interpretation. Just as Nature could teach wisdom, so also she
could instill more violent traits. If the body's humors became
"exagitated," the fiery element within would become dominant. Under such influences, the "stately warlike" Pequots
had yielded to their most barbarous inclinations.[19] The war
could be diagnosed as the natural consequence of a humoral
imbalance.

So it was possible to explain away the contradiction that
while the promotional tracts had praised the "civilitie and
peacefull conversation" of some of these people, others had
lately proved rather uncivil and violent. But Vincent apparently did not consider that he had another contradiction on

his hands: his argument on environmental determinism badly undermined his assurance that the origins of the Indians were of little importance. Their very "correspondency of disposition" with the English argued that the colonists, as people of "the same constitution," were equally subject to the same environmental influences. It was more than "needlesse curiosity," then, to understand just how these Indian offspring of the original parent had come to be what they were and where they were—especially if the "where" was largely responsible for the "what."[20]

The Indians themselves offered one explanation of their origins. They told Roger Williams that they had "*sprung* and *growne* up in that very place, like the very *trees* of the *Wildernesse*."[21] Williams shared with his European contemporaries a somewhat different idea of the original creation of humanity, and though he was willing to report the Indians' theory to his readers, he did not intend them to take it at face value. But the notion of the Indians as an organic product of the American environment was consonant with the colonists' own inclinations to regard the native peoples as the human face of the American wilderness. Moreover, this interpretation reinforced the application of botanical analogies to the process of colonization. Having transplanted themselves from England's Garden into "an Indian Wilderness,"[22] the colonists were testing their ability to maintain their Englishness despite both Indians and wilderness.

In a verse catalogue of New England's trees, William Wood referred to the forest as an "*Indian* Orchard."[23] And while his conscious emphasis was on "Orchard," not "*Indian*," he could not prevent the roots of meaning from reaching out in both directions. An "orchard" was precisely what the colonists wanted to make of their Indian wilderness—just as promoters of the Indian missionary work proposed "to Plant the *Indians as a spirituall Garden,* into which Christ might come and eat his pleasant fruits."[24] Yet until such transformations could be accomplished, the colonists would have to accommodate their

English palates to the bitter taste of wilderness and savagery. Wood revealed that in literal terms there was little danger of the colonists' developing a fondness for the wild fruits of New England. The Indian orchard's cherries, unless "very ripe," were "nothing neare so good" as the English variety: "they so furre the mouth that the tongue will cleave to the roofe, and the throate wax horse with swallowing those red Bullies (as I may call them,) being little better in taste."[25] This opinion carries the conviction of a man who had put the fruit in question amply to the test. But Wood might just as easily have been characterizing, through metaphor, English attitudes toward the uncultivated Indians—those "red Bullies" of the forest whose barbarous nature was such a bitter pill for the English to swallow. Whatever chance there might be for converting the Indians into plants suitable for a spiritual garden, there was apparently some hope that these native trees might be "converted." According to Wood, *"English* ordering may bring them to be an *English* Cherrie, but yet they are as wilde as the *Indians.*"[26] By explicitly raising the analogy of wild cherry and wild Indian, Wood carelessly opened the gates to a flood of ominous implications. As always, there was the danger that before the necessary English ordering could take place, the colonists themselves would take on the pungent savor of the wilderness.

But if the Indians had not simply grown up like the very trees of the wilderness, then the original Americans loomed even larger in significance as a clue into the possible effects of colonization. For if the theory of indigenous, organic origins were dismissed, the Indians would have to be regarded as the first colonists of the New World—and therefore the best available illustration of America's influence on transplanted cultures. Unhappily for Englishmen who were contemplating the meaning of their colonial venture, the Indian "precedent" seemed to point not toward the perfection of humanity, civility, and Christianity, but toward cultural degeneration and spiritual corruption—a troubling prophecy if it indeed proved applicable to the English themselves. To some extent, the early writers of New England appreciated the danger-ous implications of the Indian-origins question, and as they sought to solve the mystery they favored answers that permit-ted the greatest optimism for their own future in America. But close attention to their arguments and rhetoric reveals that their overt strategies harbored contradictory, self-subver-sive meanings. Despite the writers' conscious intentions, these rhetorical contradictions led inexorably to the conclusion that if the key to the colonists' destiny lay encoded in the origins and nature of the American Indians, then England would find in America its grave—not a new field for spiritual growth and national expansion.

Jews in America

By the 1630s and 1640s the essential humanity of the Indi-ans was no longer in serious doubt. As Roger Williams remarked (in agreement with Philip Vincent and many oth-ers), "From *Adam* and *Noah* that they spring, it is granted on all hands."[27] From Adam, obviously, given the intellectual hegemony of biblical history; but Noah complicated the pic-ture. Though Noah's place on the universal family tree did not disrupt the unity of humankind, his descendants had wandered away from the paternal hearth into cultural diver-sity. From an Old World perspective, the Indians were the most far-flung branch of Noah's tribe—and thus the culmina-tion of the age-old process of colonization-as-degeneration. That they were indeed "degenerate" was clear to most English observers. Thomas Shepard, who consciously meant them no harm, still called them "the dregs of mankinde" and asked, "what Nation or people [were] ever so deeply degenerated since *Adams* fall as these Indians . . . ?"[28] Earlier, the English geographer Nathanael Carpenter had traced "the present *Ignorance* and *Barbarisme* of the *Americans*" directly to their decline from the original Noachian culture: "Their descent being from *Noah* and his posterity, they could not at first but have some forme of *discipline,* which afterwards being by long processe of time or incertainty of *tradition* neglected & obliterated, they fell back into such waies as their owne depraved nature dictated or the devill malitiously suggested."[29]

The danger of building upon this deceptively solid basis of inquiry was the historical symmetry that appeared between the Indians' ancestors' "degenerate" eastward migration from the Ark and the English colonists' westward movement toward the same destination—where they might in time perfect the symmetry by becoming indistinguishable from the other ignorant and barbarous Americans. Without confronting these implications, William Hubbard, of Ipswich, Massachusetts, nevertheless affirmed that the first colonists of Massachusetts Bay "were not much unlike the family of Noah at their first issuing out of the ark, and had, as it were, a new world to people; being uncertain where to make their beginning."[30] Whether or not Hubbard realized it, his reference to Noah made the question of ends as important as the problem of beginnings. The comparison was implicitly a warning to any genealogist who might venture to trace the stages of the Indians' descent: the resulting genealogy could easily shadow forth the colonists' own descent into barbarism and apostasy.

The inadvertent prophecy of degeneration was a problem especially in the efforts to determine from which branch of the family tree the wild fruit of the Indians had grown. Among Noah's three sons—Ham (or Cham), Sem (or Shem), and Japheth (or Japhet)—the last seemed the least likely candidate for Founding Father of the Indian line, since Europeans generally regarded Japheth as their own remote ancestor. Ham, however, was available, and in *The Historie of Travell into Virginia Britania* William Strachey had established an English precedent for pressing him into service as the most convenient solution to the puzzle. Ham, by making the double mistake of looking upon his father's nakedness and then telling his brothers about it, had incurred for his own son Canaan the curse of being "a servant of servants . . . unto his brethren."[31] This fate apparently provided sufficient grounds for assuming that Ham and Canaan, as rebellious outcasts from the Ur-family, must be the source of all cultural degeneracy in the postdiluvian world. As Strachey argued, "we may conclude, that from Cham, and his tooke byrth and begynning the first universall Confusion and diversity, which ensued afterwardes throughout the whole world, especially in divine and sacred matters, whilst yt is said agayne of the Children of Sem, and Japhet, how they being taught by their elders, and content with their owne lymitts and confynes, not travelling beyond them into new Countryes as the other, retayned still (untill the comming of the Messias,) the only knowledge of the eternall, and never chaungeable triuth."[32]

Strachey could explain both the Indians' genealogy and their current barbarous condition by pointing to their accursed ancestors' reckless wanderings after the Flood. The problem with Strachey's theory was that the Hamitic fate seemed to bear far too close a correspondence to the English colonists' own wayfaring habits. The Indians were not only part of "the scattering of Noah his children and Nephewes, with their fameliees (as little Colonies)" over the earth, but, as members of "the vagabond Race of Cham," they had been among "the only far Travellors, and Straglers into divers and unknowne countries, searching, exploring and sitting downe in the same."[33]

Strachey's thesis was, in effect, a projection of the rhetoric of colonization into a distant historical mirror, and the image that was reflected back to the "little Colonies" of English people in the seventeenth century was less than flattering. The English themselves were becoming a "vagabond Race" and "Travellors . . . into divers and unknowne countries." Like Ham's posterity, they had ceased to be "content with their owne lymitts and confynes" and were expanding far beyond them into a New World. In the 1620s and 1630s some of them would also become vulnerable to the charge of being rebellious outcasts. Were they not equally in danger of furthering the "universall Confusion and diversity" that Ham had unleashed? Strachey clearly had intended no such prophecy (unless, conceivably, as a subtle warning to the latter-day sons of Japheth not to ape their Indian cousins' degeneration), but his rhetoric betrayed him into meanings that subverted his conscious strategies.

The New England writers who later approached the Indians' genealogy from a similar biblical perspective found an alternative answer that neatly solved the problem of origins while seeming to permit a more optimistic appraisal of the colonists' future in America: What if the Indians were of the tribe of Sem? John White, of the Massachusetts Bay Company, moved uncertainly toward that conclusion in *The Planters Plea* (1630). He knew that "Some conceive the Inhabitants of *New-England* to be *Chams* posterity, and consequently shut out from grace by *Noahs* curse, till the conversion of the Jewes be past at least." But White, eager to get on with the Indians' conversion (and equally eager to urge that duty as a reason for settling New England), was reluctant to concede the point. Even if the Indians were the children of Ham, White refused to allow that dubious fact to rule out their redemption: "*Noahs* curse reacheth but to one branch, to *Canaan*, and as Interpreters conceive, with especiall relation to the extirpation of that part of his issue which inhabited *Judea,* by the children of *Israel.* It is too much boldnesse then to curse where God hath not cursed, and shut out those from the meanes of grace, whom God hath not excluded."[34] White was willing to recognize the Indians as Hamitic only if he could at the same time secure their right to the Gospel. His millennial notions, based on Romans 11:25, led him to believe that "the fulnesse of the *Gentiles* must come in" before the Jews could be reclaimed— a necessary prelude to the climax of Christian history. Since White hoped the Jews' conversion was near, it seemed imperative to Christianize the Gentile Indians as soon as possible:

"this is the houre for the worke, . . . the opening of the eyes of those poore ignorant soules, and discovering unto them the glorious mystery of Jesus Christ."[35]

But just how ignorant were these poor souls? And how difficult would it be to reveal to them this "glorious mystery"? White believed that there were no "Reliques of any of those principles which belong to that Mysterie, although in some place may be discovered some foot-steps of the knowledge of GOD, of the Creation, and of some Legall Observations." The Indians' knowledge of Christianity may have been, understandably, slight, but their ideas of the Creation bore a close resemblance to the account given in Genesis. Further, their "Legall Observations" seemed strangely consonant with other matters recorded in the Old Testament. White had heard "that they separate their women in the times appointed by the Law of *Moses,* counting them and all they touch uncleane during that time appointed by the Law." Now whose footsteps were these? White was not sure: "whether upon any other ground, or by a tradition received from the *Jewes,* it is uncertaine. Some conceive, their Predecessors might have had some commerce with the *Jewes* in times past, by what meanes I know not." White seems not to have considered the already well-worn idea that the Indians themselves might be Jews (at least in origin), but he passed along some remarkable evidence that pointed, however vaguely, in that direction: "Howsoever it bee, it fals out that the name of the place, which our late Colony hath chosen for their seat, prooves to bee perfect Hebrew, being called *Nahum Keike,* by interpretation, *The bosome of consolation.*" This suggestive coincidence was itself so "perfect" that White regretted the colonists had redundantly substituted another Hebrew name (Salem) for the supposed Indian-Hebrew original.[36]

Yet the specter of cultural degeneration remained potent— since if the Indians were Semites, they had certainly lost all but the faintest traces of their heritage in the migration that had brought them to America. Nevertheless, in the 1640s and

1650s, when writers in both Englands became obsessed with the conversion of the Jews as a crucial stage in the millennial timetable, there was a tendency to seize upon every resemblance between Indian and Jewish customs as evidence that by converting Indians the colonists were aiding the fulfillment of prophecy.[37] Especially influential in this respect were Thomas Thorowgood's books purporting to discover "Jews in America"—namely, the Indians, who, as the new-found Lost Tribes of Israel, were now to be gathered in with the Christian flock.[38]

The Reverend John Eliot of Roxbury, excited by millennial prospects and mindful of his public role as a champion of Indian conversion, was eager to reap the benefits of the Indians' "Jewish" heritage. He was too cautious to assert unequivocally that the Indians were in fact what was left of the Lost Tribes, but the idea was too useful to resist. Eliot's historical imagination (inspired by Scripture) pictured to him a "great Easterne expedition" of Semites away from the unity of the Ark. If the Ten Lost Tribes, in their own "dispersion . . . to the utmost ends of the Earth eastward," had followed in the tracks of Semitic pioneers, they might well have ended up in the New World. And there, presumably, the Jews of America awaited the realization of prophecy in their reclamation and conversion—perhaps through the humble means of the Apostle Eliot.[39]

Though Eliot's "learned Conjectures" encouraged hopeful anticipations of the Indians' imminent conversion, his Jewish-Indian genealogy concealed meanings just as disturbing as those Strachey had stumbled upon while tracking Ham's posterity. In both cases it seemed that someone had colonized the New World long before the English, and those "first planters of *America*," as Eliot called them,[40] had lost all but a few vestiges of their language, religion, and ancestral customs during their "great Easterne expedition." Like Strachey, Eliot could not afford to confront these implications directly, but his oddly subversive strategy as a scriptural genealogist had involved him in an inadvertent prophecy of what might happen to the most recent planters of America. While Eliot looked forward to glorious conversions and the fulfillment of millennial hopes, his rhetoric hinted that the English, in their own great western expedition, would join the Indians in a new Babel rather than reintroduce them to the language of Canaan.[41]

To be sure, the prospect of degeneration could prove useful as a means of frightening Japhetic New Englanders into supporting their colony's fundamental cultural institutions. In the early 1660s Jonathan Mitchell—championing the interests of Harvard College—reminded his audience that "wee in this Country being farre removed from the more cultivated parts of the world, had need to use utmost care & diligence to keep up Learning & all Helps of Education among us, lest degeneracy, Barbarism, Ignorance and irreligion doe by degrees breake in upon us." And to introduce this warning, Mitchell intentionally confronted the postdiluvian parallel: "It is an observation not to be despised concerning the sons of Japhet that they Transplanting themselves into places remote from the seat & Center of Religion & Learning (in those first ages of the new world after the Flood) did in a little time lose both, tho the first planters were pious & Religious."[42] But the very boldness with which Mitchell made this "observation not to be despised" suggested that it was also not to be taken too seriously. It was merely an exhortation in the familiar form of a threat, and as such it assumed its own success. The sons of Japhet in New England—descendants of those pious and religious "first planters" who had braved the Atlantic flood while transplanting themselves to the New World—would not abandon Harvard. And so long as Harvard stood, Babel would not break out among them.

Perhaps; but such rhetoric remained volatile, despite Mitchell's efforts to keep it well under control. And as for the Lost-Tribes idea, with its much more ambiguous implications, it never really caught on outside the relatively small circle directly interested in the missionary projects. By the late 1650s Eliot himself was having second thoughts about the Jews-in-America argument. Among other inconveniences, conversions (Jewish or Indian) were simply not as plentiful as had been hoped.[43] The way was thus cleared for darker views of the Indians' origins and probable role in Christian history. In 1674, when Daniel Gookin, magistrate and militia officer, completed his *Historical Collections of the Indians in New England,* he admitted that the picture had clouded: "Concerning the original of the Savages, or Indians, in New-England, there is nothing of certainty to be concluded."[44] And yet, the need for a certain conclusion remained.

As might be expected from the magistrate in charge of Indian converts, Gookin still seemed to favor the notion "that this people are of the race of the ten tribes of Israel"—though they had been "reduced . . . into such woful blindness and barbarism, as all those Americans are in."[45] Even so, he realized that few would agree with him. With reduced expectations for the Indians' conversion had come reduced estimations of their ancestry. Significantly, the prevalent theory of the 1670s—that they were descended from "Tartars, or Scythians, that live in the northeast parts of Asia"[46]—provided little room for arguing that in their "colonization" of America they had demonstrated the power of geographic dispersal to induce cultural degeneration and spiritual apostasy. If the Indians had descended from Scythians (who, despite presumably Japhetic origins, had declined into the classic pattern of barbarism), they had been barbarians all along, and no real comparison with the English as colonists was possible.

Gookin knew that the Scythian theory, despite its flaws, had geography in its favor. Granted that the first inhabitants of America had probably entered by way of northeast Asia, then who had been better situated to undertake the migration than Scythians? Gookin was willing to concede this point of entry, but he refused to close it to errant Israelites: "suppose it should be so, that the origination of the Americans came from

Asia, by the northwest of America, where the continents are conceived to meet very near, which indeed is an opinion very probable; yet this doth not hinder the truth of the first conjecture, that this people may be of the race of the ten tribes of Israel."[47] The consequent view of the Indians as a people who, from Jewish origins, had been "reduced" to "barbarism" in their progress toward an American destiny supported the colonization-as-degeneration theme (and its potential application to the English colonists) that had lurked in Eliot's "Conjectures."

Gookin stated that it was a "custom and manner" of the Ten Tribes "to keep themselves distinct from the other nations they lived amongst; and did commonly intermarry only with their own people"—characteristics that were quite consonant with the separatist and "tribal" tendencies of English Puritanism. "[A]lso," he continued, "their religion being so different from the heathen, unto whom they were generally an abomination, as they were to the Egyptians; and also partly from God's judgment following them for their sins: I say, it is not impossible but a considerable number of them might withdraw themselves; and so pass gradually into the extreme parts of the continent of Asia; and where-ever they came, being disrelished by the heathen, might for their own security, pass further and further, till they found America; which being unpeopled, there they found some rest."[48] Rest; and, apparently, cultural oblivion. With some changes in wording and tone, this passage could serve as a rough draft of William Bradford's account of the Pilgrim Fathers' own search for security and rest—including the underlying fear of degeneration and corruption that had encouraged them to renounce exile in Holland for a new life in "unpeopled" America.[49]

It is unlikely that Gookin intended any such parallel to the English colonists. His musings were meant as mere speculation on a problem that would elude solution "until the day, wherein all secret and hidden things shall be manifested to the glory of God." But, as in Eliot's case, the language in which he phrased his conjectures led subversively toward other conclusions than their author intended. Whoever the Indians were (or had been), it remained the colonists' duty "to reduce them from barbarism to civility" and "to rescue them out of the bondage of Satan." This, said Gookin, was the aim of his "tractate."[50] Unhappily, his inadvertent subtext argued that the English themselves might be "reduced" from civility to barbarism under the seductive bondage of Satan.

It is hardly surprising, then, that it became increasingly attractive to assume that the Indians, instead of degenerating in America, had been degenerate barbarians from the beginning. It is especially revealing that in the last years of the century, when Cotton Mather came to consider Indian origins, he could not take the Indian-Israelite theory very seriously—despite his obvious respect for John Eliot.[51] Mather might look forward to the millennium as hopefully as any of the men of Eliot's generation, but he had apparently concluded that if he had to wait till the "Jewish" Indians were converted, he would be waiting a long time. Instead, Mather strongly favored the barbaric Scythians as the most likely progenitors of America's own barbarians, a people to whom their Christian neighbors owed a certain evangelical duty, but who were probably beyond redemption.[52] More than most, Mather acknowledged this duty, but he also harbored a deep-rooted suspicion that the proposed beneficiaries were hardly worthy of it.[53] He certainly was reluctant to honor them by assuming that they were the long-lost Tribes of Israel, the ancient people of God who would have to be gathered in before the climax of Christian history. When Cotton Mather thought of Indians, he thought more often of Satan than of Christ.

Satan's Colony

Rejection of the Jews-in-America idea did not mean an end to the problem of colonization-as-degeneration. William Hubbard had easily dismissed the suggestion of Indian Israelites in his *General History of New England* (written in 1680), but what he was tempted to put in its place was in some respects much worse. Hubbard had read the correspondence between the English theologians William Twisse and Joseph Mede on America's role in the millennial scenario, and Mede's speculations made sense as a solution to the Indian-origins problem: "His conceit is, that when the devil was put out of his throne in the other parts of the world, and that the mouth of all his oracles was stopped in Europe, Asia, and Africa, he seduced a company of silly wretches to follow his conduct into this unknown part of the world, where he might lie hid and not be disturbed in the idolatrous and abominable, or rather diabolical service he expected from those his followers; for here are no footsteps of any religion before the English came, but merely diabolical."[54] Gone, obliterated, are the "footsteps" of the Lost Tribes, and in their place have appeared the cloven-hoof prints of Satan and his Indian colonists. Because of the common assumption that the Indians' religion was "merely diabolical," many English readers would have found it easy to imagine such a close paternal relationship between Satan and his "silly wretches"—especially in the last quarter of the century, when patience for the Indians' conversion had long since begun to wear thin. Moreover, it obviously flattered the English and confirmed their sense of superiority to regard the Indians as the children of the devil. But the image of America as Satan's colony also had a serious catch in it, insofar as it suggested that America was peculiarly under the devil's influence.[55]

This notion would have been especially disturbing to colonists who harbored some hope of building the New Jerusalem in New England. Twisse confessed to Mede that this had been his own hope for the English colonies, though Mede's reply had promptly disabused him of "such odd conceits." He had already heard that the dream of Indian conversion was fading and that the colonists themselves were threatened with spiritual decline. "But what? I pray, shall our *English* there degenerate and joyn themselves with *Gog* and *Magog*?"[56] That was precisely Mede's suspicion.

Mede supposed that America had been "first inhabited since our Saviour and his Apostles times, and not before." The Indians had been lured there by the devil, who, challenged by the rise of Christianity in the Old World, sought to reserve a realm for himself in the New: "accordingly he drew a Colony out of some of those barbarous Nations dwelling upon the Northern Ocean, (whither the sound of Christ had not yet come)" and planted them where his rule would be secure. Mede further assumed that America, as the devil's private domain, was to serve ultimately as the opposition's staging ground, though he wished the colonists there no ill and hoped that they could at least give Satan a little competition on his own turf before they utterly degenerated. "I will hope," he wrote, "they shall not so far degenerate (not all of them) as to come in that Army of *Gog* and *Magog* against the Kingdom of Christ; but be translated thither before the Devil be loosed, if not presently after his tying up. And whence should those Nations get notice of the glorious happiness of our world, if not by some Christians that had lived among them?"[57]

Mede presented his "fancy" as "built upon mere conjectures," but Twisse was impressed nonetheless: "Call that which you write *Fancies,* as your modesty suggests; I cannot but entertain them as sage conceits."[58] Of course, Mede and Twisse could easily enough take this rather dim view of America's future from their remote perspective in England. The prospect from New England was somewhat different. The colonists had not crossed the Atlantic in order to enlist in the army of Gog and Magog. They much preferred to see themselves as the army of the Lord, preparing for the final assault against Antichrist.[59] Mede's "sage conceits" thus threw in their faces the prophecy of a monstrous (if partial) apostasy, and there was surely little comfort in his concession that some of them might be "translated" away before the rest took their place alongside their Indian comrades in the devil's legions.

Still, the logic of their jeremiad rhetoric drew them toward Mede's suspicion that America would prove to be the devil's country, not God's. In 1677, while addressing "the Danger of Apostacy," Increase Mather alluded to "Dr. *Twiss* his Opinion that when New Jerusalem should come down from Heaven *America* would be the seat of it," but he also conceded that "*The present Generation in New-England is lamentably degenerate.*"[60] Almost twenty years later he noted that "it is the Judgment of very Learned men; that in the Glorious Times promised to the Church on Earth; *America* will be Hell."[61] And in his *Dissertation Concerning the Future Conversion of the Jewish Nation* (1709) Mather again looked to Mede for guidance. The "Jewish Nation" whose conversion he contemplated was not to be found among lost Indian Israelites. It seemed more likely that, as Mede had suggested, the Indians were Gentiles who were destined to serve Gog and Magog.[62]

Others remained unconvinced. In 1697 Samuel Sewall took the field against what he called "this Antick Fancy of *America's* being Hell." Instead, he offered a "Vindication of *America*" that was also an effort toward vindicating the Indians' claim to a nobler destiny than either Mather or Mede would allow them: "if *America* be laid out as a Rendezvous for *Gog* and *Magog,* this must needs tend to supersede all Desire and Endeavour for their Recovery." Rather than abandon the Indians to the devil, Sewall revived the Jews-in-America argument, proposing that "the *English* Nation, in shewing Kindness to the Aboriginal Natives of *America,* may possibly, shew Kindness to *Israelites* unawares."[63]

But to speak of such possibilities (and such kindness) in the 1690s was, for a New Englander, to embrace intellectual nostalgia. For all his eccentricities, Cotton Mather (the balanced weights of whose name suggest New England's own alternative to Gog and Magog) was more in tune than was Sewall with their era's dominant attitude toward the Indians' origins and probable destiny. Mather kept well away from the notion that the Indians had degenerated into savages only after they arrived in America: he thought they "had been forlorn and wretched heathen ever since their first herding here."[64] This was perfectly consonant with his assumption that they were, in fact, the descendants of nomadic Scythians. But Mather's language could imply an active herdsman as well as a passive herd: How had this herding of wretched heathen been accomplished? On the surface, Mede's answer must have seemed as good as any.

Mather took an interest in Mede's theory as early as the 1680s, and in *Magnalia Christi Americana* (1702) it heavily influenced his view of America's original settlement: "though we know not *when* or *how* those Indians first became inhabitants of this mighty continent, yet we may guess that probably the devil decoyed those miserable salvages hither, in hopes that the gospel of the Lord Jesus Christ would never come here to destroy or disturb his *absolute empire* over them."[65] Mede thus provided a tentative answer to the Indian-origins problem, but in such a way that it became necessary to disentangle the legions of Gog and Magog from the more recently arrived legions of God—lest it seem that the English had indeed gone to America to defect to the opposition. Though others might look upon America as the devil's empire, for Mather the rocks of New England were potentially the foundation stones for the New Jerusalem. Mede's theory was, after all, "but conjecture. . . . However, I am going to give unto the *Christian reader* an *history* of *some feeble attempts* made in the American hemisphere to anticipate the state of New-Jerusalem, as far as the unavoidable *vanity of human affairs* and *influence* of Satan upon them would allow of it."[66]

But there was the rub: the vanity of human affairs and the influence of Satan (which, if Mede was right, was especially potent in America). Mather simply could not escape his rhetoric's logic of degeneration. And it was by no means clear that he could follow Mede's lead in respect to the Indians without falling into the Slough of Despond over New England's ultimate role in Christian history. In the *Magnalia* Mather could only sound again the old warning that perversely affirmed the danger of apostasy that he might otherwise have denied. As he told the descendants of the Founders, "if they make a *squadron* in the *fleets* of *Gog* and *Magog*, [they] will be *apostates* deserving a room, and a doom with the *legions* of the *grand apostate*, that will deceive the nations to that *mysterious enterprize*."[67]

Eventually, Mather's increasing attraction to a specifically "American" identity led him to reject Mede's theory: "I that am an American must needs be Lothe to allow all *America* still unto the Devils possession, when our Lord shall possess all the rest of the world."[68] But he clearly remained uneasy about the question of how much influence Satan exercised in New England. The events of the early 1690s had certainly not been reassuring. Mather inaugurated that decade of Indian warfare with a troubled assessment of *The Present State of New-England* (1690). In this sermon, preached "Upon the News of an *Invasion* by bloody *INDIANS* and *FRENCH-MEN*, began upon Us," the prospect of war seemed to raise the specter of Mede's conjectures. Mather cautioned his countrymen that if

the Blessed God intend that the Divel shall keep *America* during the Happy *Chiliad* which His Church is now very *quickly* Entring into, . . . then our Lord Jesus will within a few Months break up House among us, and we go for our Lodging either to *Heaven* or to *Europe* in a very little while. But if our God will wrest *America* out of the Hands of its old Land-Lord, *Satan,* and give these *utmost ends of the Earth* to our Lord Jesus, then our present conflicts will shortly be blown over, and something better than, *A Golden Age,* will arrive to this place, and this perhaps before all our *First Planters* are fallen a sleep.[69]

Though Mather longed for the advent of such a Golden Age, the outcome (as always) seemed in doubt. "Now," he admitted, "Tis a dismal *Uncertainty* and *Ambiguity* that we see ourselves placed in."[70] And Mather's odd pairing of alternatives—an exit to Heaven or Europe—suggested that an escape from this frustrating ambiguity might mean an escape from America itself. Indeed, the possibility of an escape to a heavenly, idealized Europe would appear increasingly attractive to Mather's father, who came to regard England as heaven's doorstep, the most suitable location from which to take his leave of earth.[71] But while waiting in uncertainty for this crisis to arrive, it was no encouragement to find America's old landlord trying to evict his unwanted Christian tenants. It seemed to Cotton that "The *Devils* are stark mad, that the *House of the Lord our God,* is come into these Remote corners of the World; and they fume, they fret prodigiously, That some of their old Vassals and Bondslaves here, begin to *pray* unto the Almighty God."[72] When, within two years, the devils began to fret even more prodigiously in the neighborhood of Salem, it appeared that New England was coming under an unusually direct assault from the invisible world—though not without the assistance of very visible allies. In *Decennium Luctuosum* (1699) Mather suggested that the Salem episode had "some of its Original among the *Indians,* whose chief *Sagamores* are well known unto some of our Captives, to have been horrid *Sorcerers,* and hellish *Conjurers,* and such as Conversed with *Daemons.*"[73]

As Gog and Magog thus began to stir in the womb of America—with the Indians' hellish conjurers acting as midwives—Mather's contradictory impulses as a Puritan historian became especially painful. For all his millennial optimism, Mather was often whistling in the dark. *Magnalia Christi Americana,* as (in Perry Miller's words) "a colossal jeremiad,"[74] was also at war with itself, being a self-subversive effort to sing in Virgilian tones the wonders of New England's history while rather discordantly lamenting the ever-imminent apostasy. And the deep note of warning on which the book ends simply reinforces the sense of a deeper underlying dissonance of motive: "God knows what will be the END."[75] Cotton Mather did not. But wherever his rhetoric led him, he seemed unable to evade the suspicion that America's destiny was monstrous degeneration and apostasy.

Canaanites in America

Though the attempt to establish the Indians' historical meaning by accounting for their origins proved worse than futile, another strategy initially promised to be much less subversive. In typology the Puritan scholars discovered a way to escape millenarian pessimism—while also avoiding the Jews-in-America conundrum. Rather than proclaiming the Indians as the Lost Tribes, the colonists themselves could assume the dignity of "the *New-England-Israel*," and the wilderness around them would then become "the place which God decreed to make a *Canaan* to you."[76] This done, it simply remained for the English to make Canaanites of the Indians— thereby defining them as the accursed races from whom God's people were to wrest their Promised Land.[77]

Typology thus made it possible to distinguish clearly between the destinies of English Israel and Indian Canaan, and there was no need to mention Gog and Magog. Unfortunately, the typological rhetoric summoned forth its own monsters. In their close reading of biblical history, the Puritans could hardly have ignored the fact that the Israelites' strong sense of "election" involved an equally strong fear of contamination from alien cultures. Settlement of the original Canaan had been effected through conquest, not through assimilation with the powerful idolatrous tribes already on the land.[78] The application of this precedent to the colonization of New England had grave consequences, rhetorical and otherwise, for both Indians and English.

Genesis recorded that God had given to the seed of Abraham the lands of "The Kenites, and the Kenizzites, and the Kadmonites, And the Hittites, and the Perizzites, and the Rephaims, And the Amorites, and the Canaanites, and the Girgashites, and the Jebusites"[79]—a list that could easily be made to correspond to the Algonquian tribes occupying New England's coastal lands. Moreover, God had arranged, in the fullness of time, to clear the land of these tribes in order to make way for his followers: "mine Angel shall go before thee, . . . and I will cut them off."[80] In the meantime, there was to be no accommodation with the condemned peoples: "ye shall not walk in the manners of the nation, which I cast out before you."[81] Be forewarned: "if ye do in any wise go back, and cleave unto the remnant of these nations, even these that remain among you, and shall make marriages with them, and go in unto them, and they to you: Know for a certainty that the Lord your God will no more drive out any of these nations from before you; but they shall be snares and traps unto you, and scourges in your sides, and thorns in your eyes, until ye perish from off this good land which the Lord your God hath given you."[82]

Judging by their actions, the colonists of the New England Israel took this warning to heart as they confronted the "Uncircumcised Heathens" surrounding them.[83] They had not come three thousand miles to perish from the good land they believed the Lord had given them, and from the earliest stages of settlement they erected legal barriers to reinforce the cultural defenses they hoped to maintain between themselves and the Indians. For example, in 1647 the Connecticut General Court, by limiting the Indians' opportunities to own or lease lands near the English settlements, tried to prevent the two peoples from becoming too neighborly, "Forasmuch as divers inconveniences fall out by letting land to the Indeans, whereby they mix themselves in their labours with the Inglishe, and therby the manners of many young men are lyable to be corrupted."[84] In the spirit of biblical injunctions against intermarriage with Canaanites, the English colonists were officially discouraged from mixing themselves with the Indians in other ways. According to John Josselyn, "An *English* woman suffering an *Indian* to have carnal knowledge of her, had an *Indian* cut out exactly in red cloth sewed upon her right Arm, and injoyned to wear it twelve moneths."[85] But if this Scarlet Indian was a vivid emblem of the New England Israel's determination to preserve itself inviolate from the Canaanite pollution, it was also clear evidence that the Puritans' efforts to remain culturally pure were not a complete success.

The Puritans were apparently well aware, however, that

the most direct way to avoid the Indian scourge was simply to complete the scripturally sanctioned conquest. There were signs that the Lord, true to his word, had already begun to destroy the heathen in the plague or epidemic that preceded settlement. John Winthrop drew the inevitable conclusion: "if God were not pleased with our inheriting these parts, why did he drive out the natives before us?"[86] And according to William Hubbard, the Pilgrims' ability to survive in the midst of potentially hostile Indians had reminded them "of God's promise to the people of Israel in their passage toward the possession of the land of Canaan, where he engaged to them concerning the Canaanite and the Hittite, that he would by little and little drive them out from before his people, till they were increased, and did inherit the land."[87]

Little wonder, then, that these people occasionally confused themselves with the biblical conquerors of Canaan (though the Puritans' attacks on the Indians were hardly a strict historical parallel to the original Israelites' wars of conquest). Little wonder also that they did not idly stand by and watch the destroying angel do its work unassisted. An ominous note sounds in the literature of Indian-English relations when specific references to the Indians as the accursed races of Canaan appear. Both the Pequots and King Philip were branded as "Amalekites" or "Amalek"—a role that Hubbard defined in the title-page epigraph for his narrative of King Philip's War: "And the Lord said unto Moses, Write this for a Memorial in a Book, and rehearse it in the ears of Joshua; for I will utterly put out the Remembrance of Amalek from under heaven, *Exod. 17. 14.*"[88] In light of such rhetoric, it seems that Samuel Gorton had not been merely indulging in overwrought polemics when, in 1646, he charged that "some of the Ministers have rendred [the Indians] unto the people as *Hittites, Cananites,* and *Peresites,* urging it as a duty unto the *English* to put them to death."[89]

Some among the English—Roger Williams most notably—opposed this reasoning. Williams's rejection of the typological approach to Indian-English relations was consistent with his general assault on New England's tendency to see itself too literally as the latter-day antitype of the biblical Israel. In *The Bloudy Tenent, of Persecution, for cause of Conscience* (1644) he argued that Israel's conquests had no real parallel in any contemporary situation. Regarding Europe's religious wars, he asked, "Where have *Emperours, Kings,* or *Generals* an immediate call from God to destroy whole Cities, City after City, Men, women, Children, Old and Young, as *Joshua* practised?" And the answer followed inevitably from Williams's convictions: "This did Israel to these seven Nations, that they themselves might succeed them in their Cities, Habitations, and Possessions. This onely is true in a spirituall *Antitype,* when Gods people by the Sword (the two-edged Sword of *Gods Spirit*) slay the ungodly and become *Heires,* yea fellow *Heires* with *Christ Jesus, Romanes* 8."[90] Further, in *Christenings make not Christians* (1645) Williams brought this observation home to a specifically American context: "How oft have I heard both the English and Dutch (not onely the civill, but the most debauched and profane) say, These *Heathen* Dogges, better kill a thousand of them then that we *Christians* should be indangered or troubled with them; Better they were all cut off, & then we shall be no more troubled with them: They have spilt our *Christian* bloud, the best way to make riddance of them, cut them all off, and so make way for Christians."[91]

Williams abhorred this facile assumption that "Christians" might righteously cut off the Indian "Heathen"—especially when these terms were, in his view, so badly misapplied. For Williams, only true, spiritual Christians could regard themselves as God's own people; no state could claim to be as a whole truly "Christian." Consequently, it was dangerous arrogance to restrict the term "Heathen" to unconverted people like the Indians and then use it as an argument for extermination. Who were the true heathen? Not the naked savages of America alone: "I answer, All People, *civilized* as well as *uncivilized,* even the most famous States, Cities, and the Kingdomes of the World: For all must come within that distinction." In the face of the evolving New England rhetoric of national election, Williams was insisting upon a strict distinction between spiritual and national identity.[92]

Unlike those who were apparently so eager to claim the status of a uniquely chosen, covenanted people, Williams could afford to approach the Indians relatively free of the fear of cultural contamination. As a separatist, he certainly resisted the corrupting mixture of sacred and profane as much as, or more than, any of his fellow Puritans. And, with regard to the prospects of converting the Indians themselves to Christianity, he was concerned that this conversion not be "a mixture of the manner of worship of the true God, the God of Israel, with false gods & their worships."[93] But Williams's intense desire for spiritual purity, along with his insistence on the need to distinguish the proper spiritual applications of typology from inappropriate worldly uses, may have freed him from an obsession with mere cultural purity. The conflation of cultural and spiritual identity seemed more understandable in the case of biblical Israel. As Williams assumed, "the people of Israel were all the Seed or Offspring of one man *Abraham* . . . and so downward the Seed of *Isaac* and *Jacob*, hence called the *Israel* of *God*." But this ethnic continuity was lacking elsewhere: "now, few *Nations* of the World but are a mixed Seed, the People of *England* especially[:] the *Britaines*, *Picts*, *Romanes*, *Saxons*, *Danes* and *Normans*, by a wonderfull providence of God being become one *English* people."[94] Why worry about cultural purity when the English had already been thoroughly "mixed" beyond any hope of purification?

But the deadly equation of Indians and Canaanites was simply too valuable for the Puritan colonies to abandon—since, among other services, it supported the idea that the colonies' destiny lay not in degeneration but in the realization of the New Jerusalem, an edifice the Indian Canaanites must not be permitted to undermine. In 1631 Edward Howes wrote from England to his friend John Winthrop, Jr., in Massachusetts: "I pray god account you and preserve you all as worthy stones in buyldinge his newe Jerusalem, and that ye may be conformable to the head stone Christ Jesus, whoe make ye wise to the salvation of your owne soules, your generations after you and the poore heathen with you; that ye become not a prey to the spoyler, and your children turne heathen."[95] In principle, the colonists would have been glad to serve as the means of the poor heathen's conversion, but if these heathen proved to be agents of the spoiler and threatened to lure their children to destruction, Indian conversion would have to wait until the English had made sure of their own supremacy on the land. The rhetoric of extermination was rooted in a conviction that the English might well perish unless they were faithful in carrying out the Lord's vengeance on the Indians—especially when more peaceful means of conversion had failed. The colonists pursued their conquest not merely out of land greed or blood lust, but out of the belief that they could not tolerate indefinitely a source of cultural contamination in their midst.

In any case, despite plague and warfare and missionaries, the Indians stubbornly resisted extermination, long remaining as potential snares or scourges to the New England Israel. And though the Indian-Canaanite conflation provided a convenient justification for violently supplanting the native peoples, it also confirmed the threat they posed for the invaders. Had not the Lord (speaking through Moses) told his followers that if they did not "drive out the inhabitants of the land" as ordered "it shall come to pass, that I shall do unto you, as I thought to do unto them"?[96]

The jeremiad mentality itself fed on the fear that New England's spiritual degeneration would follow the pattern of the Israelites' unholy alliances with Canaanites. John Cotton, in his 1630 sermon to Winthrop's fleet, planted the seeds of this fear by warning that the colonists' children must not be allowed to "degenerate as the Israelites did."[97] And what

Cotton sowed, later writers reaped in abundance. Michael Wigglesworth—the pastor, poet, and physician of Malden, Massachusetts—described in "God's Controversy with New-England" (1662) the Lord's astonishment upon finding that the Founders' children had indeed proved "A Generation even ripe for vengeance stroke"—though he had "ruin'd fearfully" the "curst Amalekites, that first / Lift up their hand on high / To fight against Gods Israel."

> Such were that Carnall Brood of Israelites
> That Josua and the Elders did ensue,
> Who growing like the cursed Cananites
> Upon themselves my heavy judgements drew.

Of course, salvation with repentance was still available, but until his carnal brood repented, God had a variety of scourges to get his point across.[98]

Wigglesworth's poem illustrates the jeremiad's tendency to deal in foregone conclusions: after Joshua and his generation, decline is inevitable.[99] But the Canaanite provocation to declension is unusually prominent in this American context. Wigglesworth's formula forced upon him the assumption that the New England Israelites had in fact grown "like the cursed Cananites" of the New World. And in a jeremiad of 1696 Cotton Mather confirmed this assumption by directly linking "Indianization" with the sins of Canaan:

The Land was fearfully Defiled, by the Impieties of the *Indians*, which were the first Inhabitants. Now, is it not *A Wonderful & an Horrible Thing*, for so many *English* have Succeeded them, to *Indianize*, and by the *Indian* Vices of *Lying*, and *Idleness*, and *Sorcery*, and a notorious want of all *Family Discipline*, to become obnoxious unto the old Score, and Store of wrath due unto the Land? . . . Is it not a *Wonderful & an Horrible Thing*, that in such a Land as this, there should be the Sins that made the *Old Land of Canaan, Vomit out her Inhabitants*? For so did those Infandous, & Confounded, Mixtures [in religion], that have openly shown their Heads among our selves.[100]

Consequently, Wigglesworth and Mather could not call for spiritual reformation without also implying that the transplantation of English culture to America had been a failure, that Englishmen were already taking on the evil character of the heathen barbarians in their defiled transatlantic Canaan.

But Wigglesworth and Mather were not alone in this rhetorical maze. All efforts to fit the Indians into a frame of meaning that would appease both the colonists' sense of destiny and their ideal of cultural purity ultimately proved self-subversive. As long as Indians remained in New England or around its borders—whether as Lost Tribes, Scythians, the devil's colonists, or latter-day Canaanites—they remained a thorny snare, especially for New England's intellectuals, confronted at every turn with the prophecy that they were destined to suffer the "heavy judgements" of spiritual declension and the growth of a "degenerate" American identity.

Chapter 4   *"Wild Men of Mine Own Nation"*

N August 12, 1585, Ralph Lane, governor of the English colony on Roanoke Island, complained in a letter to Sir Philip Sidney of "having, amongst savages, the charge of wild men of mine own nation, whose unruliness is such as not to give leisure to the governor to be almost at any time from them."[1] Lane, a prosaic man of military background, thus hinted to the author of the great Elizabethan prose romance that America was not realizing in all respects the Arcadian promise that some of its promoters (including Lane himself) had predicted for it.[2] In this supposed Arcadia, the unwelcome presence that marred the paradisiacal prospect was not so much the traditional memento mori, nor were the Indians necessarily the most serious flaw in the landscape. The real difficulty lay in the innate savagery of the men under Lane's command—an embarrassing trait that, like a grinning death's-head, mocked the colonists' pretenses to discipline and good order. The ideal antithesis of Indian barbarism and English civility was breaking down, leaving Lane with the sense of being caught between two tribes of savages—between one he had found in America and another he had brought with him from England. And at the moment it was the latter tribe, the home-bred savages, that seemed to worry him most.

Perhaps Lane was exaggerating in order to excuse his own apparent failure to maintain proper discipline in a dangerous situation. But his words take on deeper resonance when read from the perspective of England's later efforts to colonize America. In the seventeenth century the problem of controlling English "wild men" amongst the native "savages" of America continued to try the patience of colonial authorities. Something in America seemed to hold out to unruly men the opportunity to give free rein to their repressed wildness, to throw off traditional restraints and live masterless. Since wildness and ungoverned freedom were characteristics Europeans often associated with the Indians—as well as with their own corrupt natures—the appeal to embrace a wilderness liberty became in effect an invitation to a growing "Indianization" of colonial manners and morals.[3]

Prophetic Encounters

The example of native "savages" was not a prerequisite for English wildness in the New World—witness the 1609 wreck of the *Sea Venture*, with its subsequent mutinies, on Bermuda. The *Sea Venture*, flagship of a Virginia-bound fleet of nine vessels, carried about one hundred and fifty men, women, and children—as well as the colony's acting governor, Sir Thomas Gates. Several days away from the Chesapeake, the ships sailed into a July hurricane, and though most of them eventually reached Virginia, the *Sea Venture*, after four days in the storm, ran aground. Since the rocks where it lodged kept it from sinking, the ship's crew and passengers saved not only themselves but their tools and some supplies. Even so, they were still in peril, for these "Devil's Islands," by reputation "a most prodigious and enchanted place," foreshadowed the New World's ability to provoke disorder among the colonists.[4]

Silvester Jourdain—who, with William Strachey, was one of the two eyewitness chroniclers of these events—tried to take the curse off Bermuda by describing it as an earthly paradise like those already common in New World promotional literature: "my opinion sincerely of this island is that whereas it hath been and is still accounted the most danger-ous, infortunate, and most forlorn place of the world, it is in truth the richest, healthfullest, and pleasing land (the quantity and bigness thereof considered) and merely natural, as ever man set foot upon."[5] But the island's enchantments resembled Circe's as much as those of paradise. The English found the place well stocked with wild swine,[6] and once ashore some of the company seemed determined to imitate their unruly behavior. The wildest castaways, who were far less afraid of the pleasant island's devils than of ending up as servants in a hellish Virginia, decided that the established authority had been broken up along with the *Sea Venture*, and as one ring-leader, Stephen Hopkins, argued, "they were all then freed from the government of any man." Strachey, far more skepti-cal than Jourdain of Bermuda's virtues, lamented: "Lo, what are our affections and passions if not rightly squared? How irreligious and irregular they express us!" And "what," he asked, "hath a more adamantine power to draw unto it the consent and attraction of the idle, untoward, and wretched number of the many than liberty and fullness of sensuality?"[7]

Gates finally regained control—but only with considerable difficulty. The cedar groves of Bermuda, foreshadowing the forests of the mainland, had offered the English a convenient setting in which to play Wild Man—or Robin Hood: one group of mutineers "by a mutual consent forsook their labor . . . and like outlaws betook them to the wild woods."[8] And though most of these rebels soon grew tired of roughing it and returned to beg the governor's pardon, two men remained when the rest, after eleven months on the island, left for Virginia in two well-named boats, *Deliverance* and *Patience*, cobbled together from the remains of the *Sea Venture* and timber from the island. With Patience came Deliverance for all but the two left behind, whose conspicuous absence on the last stage of the crossing doubtless served as a reminder that the victory of order over anarchy had been incomplete.[9]

The wreck of the *Sea Venture* in certain respects prefigured the voyage of the *Mayflower* eleven years later and the planting of Plymouth colony. From Strachey's account, it is clear that the religious motive that would eventually launch the Pilgrims on their passage to America had had something to do with the disorder on Bermuda. Strachey pointed out that one of the leading mutineers was "suspected . . . for a Brownist" (or separatist)—the same charge that orthodox Anglicans used to condemn the Pilgrim Fathers. To Strachey it seemed self-evident that heresy and civil disorder went hand in hand. At least the suspected Brownist, John Want, was certainly "both seditious and a sectary in points of religion."[10]

When the *Mayflower* arrived on the coast of Cape Cod in November 1620, the Pilgrims were threatened with a civil disaster remarkably similar to the events on Bermuda. Since the Cape lay too far north for their Virginia Company patent, some of the passengers concluded that they were no longer under any obligations of civil obedience. As William Bradford recalled in his history, there were "discontented and mutinous speeches that some of the strangers amongst them had let fall from them in the ship; That when they came a shore they would use their owne libertie; for none had power to command them." To counter such threats, the Pilgrim leaders adopted the expedient of the "Mayflower Compact," creating by their own authority "a civill body politick" to antidote the heady fumes of "libertie."[11]

On uninhabited Bermuda, the colonists had found no competition for the role of "wild men." In New England, native-born "wild men" were already there. For the English, the Indians represented the same seductive "libertie" that had threatened order on Bermuda and on the *Mayflower*. Bradford, on the Pilgrims' initial reconnaissance of the Cape, blundered into a noose ("a very pretie devise") the native hunters had set to catch deer (the "snares and traps" of the heathen indeed!), an entanglement that suggests the cultural inversion the English would suffer by becoming too intimately entangled with the people they found there.[12]

The Pilgrims first sighted the Cape's native inhabitants on November 15, 1620, when a party investigating the bay shore for a suitable site for a colony saw a group of people with a dog. The people promptly disappeared into the nearby woods "and whisled the Dogge after them." The English took them for another party of the *Mayflower*'s crew who had gone ashore earlier. When they recognized their mistake, the Pilgrims chased after them; or, as Bradford explained, "after they knew them to be *Indians* they marched after them into the Woods, least other of the *Indians* should lie in Ambush." The English, in their heavy armor, could not catch up with the "Savages."[13] But the Pilgrims' intrusion on Cape Cod did begin a complex intermingling of English and American destinies, a transforming process whose early intimations confronted them at almost every stage of their search for an acceptable place to plant their colony.

During their exploration of the Cape, the Pilgrims came upon several intriguing mounds, or "heapes of sand," that were obviously artificial. In some of these mounds they were delighted to discover caches of corn—a lucky find, given their need for a locally tried and proven crop. Bradford ascribed this boon to the highest source: "sure it was Gods good providence that we found this Corne, for els wee know not how we should have done, for we knew not how we should find, or meete with any of the *Indians*, except it be to doe us a mischiefe." The provident Indians had inadvertently done them a service by providing seed for the Pilgrims' first native harvest. With some pangs of conscience, which they soothed by assuring themselves that they would repay the Indians, the English appropriated the corn.[14]

The English found in their rummagings certain evidence that a process of acculturation or intermingling between the Old World and the New had already begun on the Cape. At the site of an abandoned Indian dwelling, the Pilgrims "found a great Ketle, which had beene some Ships ketle and brought out of *Europe*," and which they commandeered, "at length after much consultation," to help carry away the corn—hushing their consciences with the promise to return it "if we could find any of the people, and come to parley with them." Nearby, they discovered even more substantial signs that they were not the first Europeans to venture upon this sandy ground. Rotting into the soil of the Cape was "the remainder of an old Fort, or Palizado, which as we conceived had beene made by some Christians"—but exactly by whom they did not speculate.[15]

But it was in one of the mounds that the Pilgrims discovered the most powerful, if enigmatic, sign of a mingled Indian-European destiny. The Pilgrims had resisted digging very far into the first mounds they happened upon, suspecting them (correctly) to be graves, "because we thought it would be odious unto them to ransacke their Sepulchers." But after uncovering the seed caches, they discovered another mound that was "much bigger and longer then any we had yet seene." Beneath the soil they found "the bones and skull of a man." In itself this was not surprising, but "The skull had fine yellow haire still on it." The man was apparently a European. He was surrounded in death by material clues of his past life: "a knife, a pack-needle, and two or three old iron things. It was bound up in a Saylers canvas Casacke, and a payre of cloth breeches." Even more interesting, he was buried with a second, smaller body. In a small bundle alongside the sailor were "the bones and head of a little childe . . . ; there was also by it a little Bow, about three quarters long, and some other odd knackes."[16]

The English "brought sundry of the pretiest things away with us, and covered the Corps up againe" before going off to look for more corn. But the mound, with its double burial, did puzzle them: "There was a varietie of opinions amongst us about the embalmed person; some thought it was an *Indian* Lord and King: others sayd, the *Indians* have all blacke hayre, and never any was seene with browne or yellow hayre; some thought, it was a Christian of some speciall note, which had dyed amongst them, and they thus buried him to honour him; others thought, they had killed him, and did it in triumph over him."[17] As John Seelye has suggested, "this incredible couple" was indeed "a figure of prophecy": "For whatever brought the castaway sailor to America; whatever bound him to the red man, planted him with an Indian child in the earth of the New World, left him like a Corn God to flower as a nation; whatever brought the Pilgrims to his grave—whatever caused all those patterned accidents is a mystery intimate with the destiny of the Old World in the New."[18] The white man buried with what might well have been his own half-Indian child was proof and prophecy that the identity of Europeans could become confused with the native peoples of America.

On Friday, March 16, 1621, as the Pilgrims were holding a meeting to settle certain matters relating to defenses against the "Savages," one of the savages walked up boldly and interrupted their discussion. "[H]e was the first *Savage* we could meete withall," but not, after all, entirely alien: "hee saluted us in English, and bad us well come."[19] The startled Pilgrims soon learned that this Indian, named Samoset, "had learned some broken English amongst the English men that came to fish at *Monchiggon*." Samoset in turn introduced them to Squanto, "the onely [surviving] native of *Patuxat*, where we now inhabite." Some years earlier he had been kidnapped by a Captain Thomas Hunt to be sold as a slave in Spain, but he managed eventually to get to England, where he "dwelt in *Cornehill* with master *John Slanie* a Marchant." Consequently, he "could speake a little English."[20] Now, having recently returned by an English ship to his native land, Squanto possessed skills as an interpreter that made him of great value to the colonists: Bradford called him "a spetiall instrument sent of God for their good beyond their expectation."[21] But his bilingualism was also a tacit reminder of the mutual acculturation the English feared. His abilities to bridge the language gap apparently left him stranded between cultures—unable to return to the lost world of "*Patuxat*" and equally unable to assimilate fully into the new Plymouth. When he died suddenly of "an Indean feavor" in 1622, Squanto asked Bradford "to pray for him, that he might goe to the Englishmens God in heaven, and bequeathed sundrie of his things to sundry of his English freinds, as remembrances of his love; of whom they had a great loss."[22] Squanto had been so dispossessed of his own cultural inheritance (as well as of his native lands) that he was resigned to continuing in the company of Englishmen (and "the Englishmens God") even after death.

The question was, would any of the English suffer the same dispossession, perhaps ending up at last not in an English heaven, but an Indian hell? Improbable as it seemed, here was an Indian from Cornhill, London, who had crossed the Atlantic to speak to and for "his English freinds" in his old homeland. No small part of the prophetic meaning of the grave on the Cape stems from the fact that the Pilgrims named the area where they found the buried granaries *"Corne-hill."*[23] In blundering about through the Cape's tangled underbrush, in digging into the cold sandy soil in search of clues of the Indians' lives, in taking the measure of the land and in trying to discover a place for themselves in it, the colonists were in effect defining the terms of their fate. Would their translation be not simply a carrying-across of culture from one side of the Atlantic to the other, but a translation of English people into "Americans"? Were Squanto and the emblematic grave on the Cape prefigurations of their own colonial destiny? An answer was implied by the fact that the English colonial experience, reaching from England through Ireland toward Roanoke and Jamestown (with the interesting stopover on Bermuda), had been marked at almost every stage by cases of colonists who found accommodation to the local variety of savagery easier than resistance.

"Lives and Manners Amongst the Indians"

The "degenerate" Anglo-Irish "patchocks" and the renegade English soldiers who deserted to the wild-Irish enemy were surely lurking darkly in the thoughts of Ralph Lane, a veteran of the English campaigns in Ireland, when he complained of the English "wild men" at Roanoke. At Jamestown, John Smith sought to maintain discipline among wild Englishmen in similarly frustrating circumstances: "Much they blamed us for not converting the Salvages," he recalled bitterly, "when those they sent us were little better, if not worse."[24] Some desperate men ran away to join the "Salvages" in the forest, preferring to embrace barbarism rather than remain civilized (and hungry) in the settlement.[25]

But even when Smith, after his departure from Jamestown in 1609, had diverted some of his interest from Virginia to New England, he continued to worry that a desire for "dissolute liberty" was endangering the success of colonization.[26] He had hoped to solve the problem by supervising the settlement of New England personally, to make certain that the colonists there would avoid Virginia's mistakes. He seems to have harbored some hope of accompanying the Pilgrims on their voyage, but the impoverished separatists rejected his services because he placed far too great a value on them. Smith vented his spite on "your Brownists of England, Amsterdam, and Leyden," who had established Plymouth colony without his assistance and "whose humorous ignorances, caused them for more than a yeare, to endure a wonderfull deale of misery, with an infinite patience; saying my books and maps were much better cheape to teach them, than my selfe."[27] In Smith's eyes the Pilgrims were the victims of a hypocritical, canting self-will and of the same lust for "dissolute liberty" that had plagued the colonists in Virginia and on Bermuda (did Smith recall that a "Brownist" had tried to sabotage the castaways' escape from the island?): "they would not be knowne to have any knowledge of any but themselves, pretending onely Religion their governour, and frugality their counsell, when indeed it was onely their pride, and singularity, and contempt of authority; because they could not be equals, they would have no superiours."[28]

If any of the Pilgrim Fathers ever read this indictment, it

surely burned as bitter wormwood and gall. Who else but themselves had been so piously devoted to divinely ordained authority and social order? They had been so earnest in resisting the infection of savagery among themselves that they even ventured out to eradicate incipient savagery in other nearby English settlements that might, through an example of degeneration, encourage the same tendency in Plymouth. In 1622 Thomas Weston, an English merchant who was also an investor in the Pilgrims' Indian trade, financed an independent trading settlement on the coast north of Plymouth, at Wessagusset. The "Westonians" were a commercial competitor for the "Plymotheans" and, as Bradford described them in his history, "an unruly company" with "no good govermente over them" who would surely come to grief.[29] Weston's colony began with adequate supplies and great expectations, but it was soon in trouble. Just as John Smith had taken some satisfaction in the Pilgrims' early period of suffering, so Bradford took a certain pleasure in recalling the fate of these "unruly" competitors. He was also evidently relieved that their collapse had removed an embarrassing exception to the rule that English civility must reign unchallenged. Their failure, in Bradford's account, was a clear result of "their great disorder," a disorder leading them toward cultural degeneration. For one thing, the leader of the colony "was taxed by some amongst them for keeping Indean women, how truly I know not." The mere suggestion of such an abomination was enough to provoke the wrath of men who took the biblical prohibition against intermarriage with the heathen as a binding law. Meanwhile, as supplies of food ran low, the biblical fate of becoming hewers of wood and drawers of water to the heathen descended upon some members of Weston's colony: "others (so base were they) became servants to the Indeans, and would cutt them woode and fetch them water, for a cap full of corne." Others became thieves: they "fell to plaine stealing, both night and day, from the Indeans, of which they greevosly complained." But the wages of theft, even theft from Indians, were in some respects more humiliating than servitude, since "in the end they were faine to hange one of their men, whom they could not reclaime from stealing, to give the Indeans contente."[30] This incident, illustrating English subservience to heathen justice, was a blow to the pretense of English superiority; it would also return to haunt them in a suitably "improved" version in Samuel Butler's anti-Puritan *Hudibras.*[31]

The Westonians, as Bradford saw it, had betrayed their culture and national identity. Having begun badly, they ended up in social dissolution, completely at the Indians' mercy, scrounging for food like swine. "At last most of them left their dwellings and scatered up and downe in the woods," Bradford wrote, "and by the water sides, wher they could find ground nuts and clames, hear .6. and ther ten. By which their cariages they became contemned and scorned of the Indeans, and they begane greatly to insulte over them in a most insolente maner."[32] It was simply a confirmation of suspicions to learn that one of the Westonians "was turned salvage" outright.[33]

Before this contagion of "salvage" behavior (and the likely effects of the Indians' "insolente maner") could reach Plymouth itself, the Pilgrim leaders decided to act, sending Miles Standish—"a man of very little stature, yet of a very hot and angry temper"[34]—to cut off the leaders of a supposed Indian conspiracy against the English before they could put their plans into effect. He addressed himself to his task with ruthless efficiency. In a surprise attack on the Indians, he quickly killed the men he took to be the principal leaders of the conspiracy—one of whom had told Standish to his face that "though he were a great captain, yet he was but a little man." Standish's actions, by inviting further trouble with the Indians, also efficiently put an end to the Westonian colony. The colonists wisely abandoned the settlement. Standish returned to Plymouth with the head of the chief "conspirator."[35] And Bradford saluted the Westonians with a rather vengeful valediction: "This was the end of these that some time bosted of their strength, (being all able lustie men,) and what they would doe and bring to pass, in comparison of the people hear, who had many women and children and weak ones amongst them; and said at their first arivall, when they saw the wants hear, that they would take an other course, and not fall into shuch a condition, as this simple people were come too."[36]

"[A] mans way is not in his owne power," Bradford concluded piously; "God can make the weake to stand; let him also that standeth take heed least he fall."[37] But when John Robinson, the Pilgrims' old pastor in Leyden, heard about these events, he expressed his misgivings in a letter that Bradford later copied into his history: "Concerning the killing of those poor Indeans, . . . oh! how happy a thing had it been, if you had converted some, before you had killed any; . . . You will say they deserved it. I grant it; but upon what provocations and invitments by those heathenish Christians?" Robinson's words must have touched Bradford's conscience, since he took the trouble to indicate in a note that the "heathenish Christians" in question were the Westonians, not the Plymotheans.[38] But Robinson, after all, had written these words in Europe. In America, where the "provocations and invitments by those heathenish Christians" galled the Pilgrims at least as much as the Indians, it was more difficult to perceive any injustice in Standish's actions. The heathenish Christians were gone, and the "insolente" Indians had been taught a lesson.

Bradford, writing to England in September 1623, professed a rather surprising sympathy for the Westonians as he sought to excuse Standish's actions: "We went to reskew the lives of our countrie-men, whom we thought (both by nature, and conscience) we were bound to deliver, as also to take veng[e]ance of them [the Indians] for their villanie entended and determined against us, which never did them harme. . . ." But in his history, as he said, "I have but touched on these things breefly, because they have allready been published in printe more at large."[39]

The "at large" to which Bradford referred was Edward Winslow's *Good Newes from New England* (1624), a work that doubled as promotional tract and apologia. Winslow sought to put the best face possible on what might well have seemed an unprovoked massacre of innocent Indians. The Pilgrims had not killed the suspected conspirators merely out of blood lust; they had simply been performing a painful and unpleasant duty: "this business was no less troublesome than grievous, . . . especially for that we knew no means to deliver our countrymen and preserve ourselves, than by returning their malicious and cruel purposes upon their own heads, and causing them to fall into the same pit they had digged for others; though it much grieved us to shed the blood of those whose good we ever intended and aimed at, as a principal in all our proceedings."[40] Winslow's professions of regret over the need to kill a few of the heathen before converting them might ordinarily have gone down smoothly enough in England, thus giving an early promise of his future reputation as "a Smooth toungued Cunning fellow."[41] But his words ring hollow when read alongside his avowed reason for publishing his account of the Pilgrims' actions. The Westonians, the supposed beneficiaries of the Pilgrims' concern, had proved themselves ungrateful wretches and were slandering their deliverers in England. So Winslow reluctantly appeared in print before the public, "the rather, because of a disorderly colony that are dispersed, and most of them returned, to the great prejudice and damage of him [Weston] that set them forth; who, as they were a stain to Old England that bred them, in respect of their lives and manners amongst the Indians, so, it is to be feared, will be no less to New England, in their vile and clamorous reports, because she would not foster them in their desired idle courses."[42] Almost despite himself, Winslow suggested that a laudable concern for the Westonians' safety and a humane reluctance to kill Indians did not quite cover the situation. The real problem was that the "disorderly colony" of competitors, so timely dispersed, had threatened through "their lives and manners amongst the Indians" to dissolve the distinction between Englishmen and savages. The Westonians and Indians were both stains on New England, stains that Captain Standish had tried to wash away with blood.

Aside from its promotional and propagandistic intentions, Winslow's tract, like Bradford's history, does speak from genuine concern about the conflict between civility and savagery. Looking back upon the shocking degeneration of Weston's colony, Bradford and Winslow could easily reflect that there, but for the grace of God, had gone the Pilgrims themselves. They had begun life in New England as a weak, impoverished band of outcasts, stumbling through the thickets on Cape Cod, battling disease and hunger, watching their friends and families die. And were the "unruly" Westonians really so different from the Pilgrims when, in danger of starvation, they "brake the earth, and robbed the Indians' store"?[43]

It is likely, then, that the Pilgrims did recognize a certain unflattering resemblance between themselves and their sister colony to the north. The Westonians, as scapegoats for Plymouth's own fears of degeneration, gave the Plymotheans a chance to demonstrate both their practical superiority and their abhorrence of the "disorder" the other colony represented to them. Whatever might be true of other unruly companies of Englishmen, John Smith had been wrong about this group of "Brownists." However inexperienced in the ways of colonization, they most definitely were not bent upon "dissolute liberty" or the contemptuous rejection of authority. In their own lives among the Indians, they were determined to preserve their English manners and identity.

The infection of savagery was not eliminated by the dissolution of Weston's colony. In March 1630 James Sherley, one of the "adventurers" in the colony's Indian trade, informed the Pilgrims in a letter that he and his associates had decided to diversify their investments by sending over "one *Edward Ashley* (a man I thinke that some of you know)" to establish a new trading post at Penobscot. Indeed, the Pilgrims knew the man well enough to have conceived an ill opinion of him. Ashley was of course another unwelcome source of competition and a further complication of their already tortuous relations with the English investors. To be sure, the Adventurers offered to include the Pilgrims as partners in this new project, asking them at least "to offer him all the help you can, either by men, commodities, or boats; yet not but that we will pay you for any thing he hath." And Sherley assured the Pilgrims that they still had their backers' primary loyalty and concern: "Ther is none of us that would venture as we had done, were it not to strengthen and setle you more then our owne perticuler profite."[44]

The well-seasoned founders of Plymouth were not so sure, having long since become aware of the frequent discrepancy between the Adventurers' fair promises and their niggardly efforts in the colonists' behalf. But this cannot fully account for the intense dislike the Pilgrims conceived for Ashley. Bradford came closer to the fundamental reasons when he remarked that "though he [Ashley] had wite and abillitie enough to menage the bussines, yet some of them knew him to be a very profane yonge man; and he had for some time lived amonge the Indeans as a savage, and wente naked amongst them, and used their manners (in which time he got their language), so they feared he might still rune into evill courses (though he promised better), and God would not prosper his ways."[45] The Pilgrims who knew Ashley were thus afraid that the business he would "menage" at Penobscot would inevitably degenerate into a ménage of savagery and English depravity. According to Bradford, Ashley had already given abundant evidence of his willingness to throw off his own identity and, chameleonlike, accommodate himself to his surroundings. Bradford's parenthetical reference to Ashley's Indian-English bilingualism also hints at a deeper fear. The nightmare image of an English wild man cavorting naked among the savages was a perfect emblem of what the

Pilgrims most feared for themselves and the other Englishmen around them. Still, like it or not, the Adventurers were committed to this man, and the Pilgrims had to accept him.

After arriving in New England, Ashley wasted no time in asking Plymouth for supplies of corn, wampum, "and other things." The Pilgrims' hospitality was sorely tried, but they apparently concluded that it would be best to play along with him in order to blunt the edge of his competition and to avoid offending the Adventurers. After all, they reasoned, Ashley "might gett supplies of these things els wher" if they refused to help him: "So they, to prevent a worse mischeefe, resolved to joyne in the bussines, and gave him supplies in what they could, and overlooked his proceedings as well as they could." To better "overlook" Ashley, that "very profane yonge man," the Pilgrims made use of the services of "an honest yonge man" of their own. Into Ashley's camp they insinuated as their representative and spy Thomas Willett, "Which yonge man being discreete, and one whom they could trust, they so instructed as keept Ashley in some good mesure within bounds."[46]

To the Pilgrims' chagrin, Ashley's success as a trader soon greatly exceeded their own accomplishments, not least because Plymouth "fell very short of trading-goods" in the shipments from England, while Ashley was "farr better suppleyed then them selves."[47] Ashley seemed to be proving that an inclination to "rune into evill courses" could be more profitable than Plymouth's efforts to trudge the path of righteousness. But for the time being the Pilgrims could do little more than nurse their grudge and complain, as Ashley's fortunes rose. It was painfully obvious that the Adventurers were more impressed with their profane young man's profits than they were worried about his weakness for savagery. They not only favored him in their shipments of supplies, but they also held up his success as a reproach to the Pilgrims.[48] The founders of Plymouth, measuring success by a rather different standard, had resisted as well as they could becoming ensnared in the traps of the heathen. Ashley apparently had no qualms about entangling himself in their snares, and yet he prospered while the Pilgrims suffered. Again: let him that standeth take heed lest he fall.

Ashley did not manage as well when he became fouled in the toils of the law. Bradford, with obvious satisfaction, noted that Ashley's downfall came when he *"was taken in a trape, . . . for trading powder and shote with the Indeans."* Such "disorderly Trading" had been explicitly forbidden in a royal proclamation. What the Pilgrims' wrath could not accomplish, the king's wrath could: "some in authoritie" seized Ashley and his goods—"above a thousand weight of beaver" (it was a day of reckoning in more ways than one). And as much as the Pilgrims were glad to see Ashley go, they were inclined to extend their hospitality to the fruits of his labor, lest the furs also be carried away to England: "the goods were freed, for the Gov[erno]r here made it appere, by a bond under Ashleys hand, wherin he was bound to them in 500 *li.* not to trade any munition with the Indeans, or other wise to abuse him selfe." But abuse himself he had, and not just by selling weapons to savages: "it was allso manifest against him that he had commited uncleannes with Indean women, (things that they feared at his first implyment, which made them take this strict course with him in the begining)." As with the Westonians, it was all simply a confirmation of their worst suspicions. Under the circumstances, it is also difficult to tell whether Bradford was more pleased or disturbed by this vindication of his forebodings about Ashley. In any case, it all turned out in Plymouth's favor: "they gott their [*sic*] goods freed, but he was sent home prisoner."[49]

Back in England, after a stay "in the Fleet," Ashley managed to regain his freedom "by the means of friends." And though he hoped to return to New England, he eventually went in the opposite direction, to Russia, where he could apply his "good skill in the beaver trade" (Bradford could now safely grant him that much) without offense to Puritans. But just as Bradford assumed that God had intervened to prevent Ashley from reinflicting himself on New England, so it seems that Providence, by prompting "some marchants" to hire him as their agent in Russia, had something to do with his unhappy demise: on his way home he was lost at sea; "this was his end."[50] And a fitting end it was, Bradford must have decided. The Pilgrim historian did not bother to point the moral explicitly, but it was clear enough.

Morton's Revenge

As the Pilgrims watched the relatively brief drama of Edward Ashley conclude, they were in the midst of a somewhat longer (yet somewhat livelier) entertainment centering upon the American career of Thomas Morton. From the time he first set foot in New England, probably in 1624, until his death in 1647 in Maine, Morton was intermittently a focal point for many of the Puritans' most persistent anxieties about life in a wilderness. The ship that deposited him on the shore of Massachusetts Bay—Morton's Ark, his *Mayflower*—was called the *Unity*, a name fraught with irony, as it turned out.[51]

Like the Westonians and Ashley, Morton also served the Puritans as a scapegoat, a role to which he seems to have been born—even his personal seal featured the head of a goat.[52] To the Puritan colonists of New England, Morton was a creature of the cloven hoof, an unclean beast, an Old World satyr self-transplanted to thrive and revel in the forests of America. Not surprisingly, the Puritans moved quickly to drive him out before he could breed others of his kind. But unlike the Westonians and Ashley, Morton proved an especially clever and articulate goat, whose reply to his Puritan opponents achieved a relatively permanent form in print. Though the Puritans did effectively spoil his hopes for a stake in New England's future, Morton had his revenge.[53]

William Bradford made the clearest statement of the case against Morton in his history of Plymouth. There, Morton figures as a source of the same infection that had plagued the colonists at Bermuda, Jamestown, and Wessagusset. Arriving as part of a plantation under the leadership of "one Captaine Wolastone, (a man of pretie parts,)" Morton seized control when the captain decided to abandon his "Mount Wollaston" settlement for Virginia, a labor-hungry colony where he could easily and profitably dispose of his servants. As in Bermuda, the prospect of life as a servant in the Chesapeake was more than enough to provoke rebellion. While Wollaston was away, surveying the situation in Virginia and selling the first batch of servants "at good rates," Morton arranged a coup d'état against the man Wollaston had left in charge. Morton, "haveing more craft then honestie, (who had been a kind of petiefogger, of Furneffells Inne,)" launched his scheme by plying his comrades with "strong drinck and other junkats." The metamorphosis of Mount Wollaston into Merry Mount had begun: "after they were merie, he begane to tell them, he would give them good counsell"—specifically, that by putting him in charge they could avoid the fate of being "carried away and sould for slaves with the rest." As Bradford summarized Morton's "good counsell," it was the old appeal to servants to become masterless: "so you may be free from service, and we will converse, trade, plante, and live togeather as equalls, and supporte and protecte one another, or to like effecte."[54]

Whether or not this was an accurate account of Morton's call to rebellion ("to like effecte" inevitably raises doubts), the general consequence was clear to Bradford: it was nothing less than an invitation to disorder, the same sort of appeal that had almost made an anarchic debacle of the *Mayflower*. But in this case there were no defenders of order to intervene, and the worst consequences followed without opposition. "After this they fell to great licenciousnes, and led a dissolute life, powering out them selves into all profanenes. And Morton became lord of misrule, and maintained (as it were) a schoole of Athisme." They also consumed a great deal of alcohol—drinking "as some reported, 10*lis.* worth in a morning." With their wits thus properly befuddled, "They also set up a May-pole, drinking and dancing aboute it many days togeather, inviting the Indean women, for their consorts, dancing and frisking togither, (like so many fairies, or furies rather,) and worse practises. As if they had anew revived and celebrated the feasts of the Roman Goddes Flora, or the beasly practieses of the madd Bacchinalians."[55]

By assuming the dubious dignity of the Lord of Misrule and by erecting his "idle or idoll May-polle,"[56] Morton was apparently seeking to introduce into New England some of the worst habits of Old. In Puritan eyes, his frolics were simply the remains of the ancient idolatry and devil-worship of their benighted ancestors. For many years they had been preaching against this sort of thing in England, only to find that now they had to deal with it again in America—though in the absence of fair English maids, willing and eager to be led into the May woods, Merry Mount's Lord of Misrule was recruiting Indian women, an especially shocking New World variation on the Old World theme.[57]

Further, while Bradford did not explicitly make the connection, mention of May Games and May Poles might well have conjured up thoughts of Robin Hood and his merry men, who as characters of romance had long figured in the May festivities and masques.[58] Morton thus appeared on the wilderness stage of New England as a more perverse and more dangerous version of the rusticated Duke in *As You Like It*, who took up residence "in the forest of Arden, and a many merry men with him," where they lived "like the old Robin Hood of England." Of course, Shakespeare's treatment of this theme involved an escape from the corruptions of civilization into the literary landscape of pastoral convention: "They say many young gentlemen flock to him every day, and fleet the time carelessly, as they did in the golden world."[59] But Merry Mount was not the Forest of Arden, and Bradford thought he had good reason to fear that Morton would attract not young gentlemen seeking a lost Arcadia, but disgruntled servants of Plymouth: "they saw," Bradford wrote, "they should keep no servants, for Morton would entertaine any, how vile soever, and all the scume of the countrie, or any discontents, would flock to him from all places, if this nest was not broken; and they should stand in more fear of their lives and goods (in short time) from this wicked and deboste crue, then from the salvages them selves."[60]

The image of Morton as a potential New England Robin Hood also points, by way of Bradford's reference to fairies, toward Robin Goodfellow, another figure widely associated with midsummer nights' forest revels. To a Puritan, however, this Robin would be more likely to savor of nightmare than of woodland pleasures. By the early seventeenth century the fairies had exchanged much of their malevolent reputation for a role as diminutive, "puckish" creatures whose mischievous pranks were hardly the stuff bad dreams were made on. But some of the scent of brimstone still clung to them. In one 1578 work they had been compared to "Furies madde, and Satyres wild," and for many common people the nicknames "Goodfellow" and "good neighbors" were means of propitiating potentially harmful spirits.[61]

But Morton, dancing (as fairies, or furies, danced) around his idol in the New World greenwood,[62] was no "Goodfellow" to Bradford, nor was he likely to find acceptance as a "good neighbor" in Plymouth. Far from wanting to propitiate him, the Puritans were more interested in exorcising him altogether. Like Milton's Comus, Morton had his own "wicked and deboste crue," a dangerous source of "Riot and ill-manag'd Merriment":

> . . . night by night
> He and his monstrous rout are heard to howl
> Like stabl'd wolves, or tigers at their prey,
> Doing abhorred rites to *Hecate*
> In their obscured haunts of inmost bow'rs.[63]

Morton's "abhorred rites," echoing the "barbarous dissonance" of Comus's revels,[64] grated on Puritan ears. New England had its own native wolves to fill the nights with howling; Morton's wild call, demonstrating that Englishmen could figuratively join in, was simply too much to bear in silence.

The founders of Plymouth and Massachusetts Bay were committed to the preservation of their English identities and English culture. But Morton had brought with him a bit of Merrie England that the Puritans had hoped to leave behind. He had compounded his offense by including Indian women in the traditional May festivities, thereby demonstrating the easy compatibility of England's pagan heritage with the barbarians of America. For the Puritans, this grew from a weakness, a rottenness in the root of English culture that they would have to prune away if they were to realize their own dream of a Puritan New England.[65]

Unfortunately for Morton, the same qualities that made him a source of anxiety for Puritans also made him an ideal scapegoat. But before his hostile neighbors could drive him out, they needed a case against him that would stick in Old England as well as New. Bradford, in relating the story of the fall of Merry Mount, tried to make it clear that the Lord of Misrule had brought his troubles on himself. All the "riotous prodigallitie and profuse excess" proved costly, and Morton, "thinking him selfe lawless," had sought to supplement his income by taking up the forbidden trade of firearms with the Indians.[66] Or so Bradford charged. It is far from certain that Morton was actually guilty of the crime that so conveniently excused the destruction of his settlement, though there is no doubt that Bradford's fear of the consequences of selling guns to Indians was genuine.[67] The Plymouth governor probably came closer to stating his fundamental grievance when he complained to England that Morton and company were "living without all fear of God or common honesty; some of them abusing the Indian women most filthily, as it is notorious."[68] Whether or not Morton had ever put a musket in an Indian's hands, this filthy "abuse" was more than sufficient warrant for the swift exercise of Puritan justice.

As the agent of their vengeance, the Pilgrim Fathers chose Miles Standish. Thanks to the captain's skills (or thanks to the intoxication of Merry Mount's defenders), the Lord of Misrule was deposed and packed off to England.[69] Yet, like a recurrent nightmare, Morton soon returned and had to be exorcised again, this time through the agency of Massachusetts Bay. According to Bradford, Morton was now under suspicion of having added murder to his other misdeeds. This charge seems even more dubious than the accusation of firearms trading, especially since Morton never stood trial for murder when he again reached England.[70] Still, Bradford asserted confidently that the Massachusetts authorities had a warrant from England for Morton's arrest and, consequently, felt justified in sending him home to answer for his crimes. "[A]nd for other his misdemenors amongst them, they demolisht his house, that it might be no longer a roost for shuch unclaine birds to nestle in."[71]

To their disappointment, however, this was not the end of Thomas Morton. Unclean bird or scapegoat, he also apparently had the nine lives of a cat, for "he got free againe, and write an infamouse and scurillous booke against many godly and cheefe men of the cuntrie; full of lyes and slanders, and fraight with profane callumnies against their names and persons, and the ways of God."[72] If he could not return to his old nest at Merry Mount, Morton was determined to see that his enemies' foul deeds came home to roost.

The "infamouse and scurillous booke" with which Morton sought to wreak his vengeance on the Puritans was *New English Canaan* (1637). However infamous and scurrilous, it was also a study in impudent mockery, a witty anti-Puritan tract that achieved its most subversive effects by pillorying its antagonists with their own rhetoric. In his version of the rise and fall of Merry Mount, Morton turned the tables on his enemies, holding them guilty of the very evils with which they had charged him. The Puritans of Plymouth and Massachusetts Bay, not "mine Hoste of Ma-re Mount," were the real traitors

NEW ENGLISH CANAAN
OR
NEW CANAAN.

Containing an Abſtract of New England,

Compoſed in three Bookes.

The firſt Booke ſetting forth the originall of the Natives, their
Manners and Cuſtomes, together with their tractable Nature and
Love towards the Engliſh.

The ſecond Booke ſetting forth the naturall Indowments of the
Country, and what ſtaple Commodities it
yealdeth.

The third Booke ſetting forth, what people are planted there,
their proſperity, what remarkable accidents have happened ſince the firſt
planting of it, together with their Tenents and practiſe
of their Church.

Written by Thomas Morton of Cliffords Inne gent, *upon tenne
yeares knowledge and experiment of the
Country.*

Printed at AMSTERDAM,
By JACOB FREDERICK STAM.
In the Yeare 1637.

New English Canaan, a promotional work and anti-Puritan tract by
Thomas Morton, whose conduct as "Lord of Misrule" was described
by William Bradford in his history of Plymouth Plantation. *Courtesy,
Massachusetts Historical Society*

to English culture; they, not the Lord of Misrule, were most in danger of degenerating into wild people or savages. Morton, by contrast, emerged in his book as the champion of tradition and cultural continuity, the custodian of the good old ways, "with Revels and merriment after the old English custome."[73]

Morton made it clear that, whatever the Puritans thought was going on at Merry Mount, he had in fact rejected the possibility of a genuine amalgamation with the Indians.[74] True, in "The Songe" he composed to grace his revels around the May Pole, Morton had extended a suggestive invitation to the Indian women: "Lasses in beaver coats come away, / Yee shall be welcome to us night and day."[75] And in his extremity, temporarily stranded by the Plymouth authorities on the inhospitable Isle of Shoals awaiting his banishment, he was happy to be "releeved by Salvages that tooke notice that mine Host was a Sachem of Passonagessit [the Indian name for Merry Mount], and would bringe bottles of strong liquor to him, and unite themselves into a league of brother hood with mine Host."[76] In the absence of English girls, Morton was willing to make do with Indian "Lasses," just as he was perfectly content, in a pinch, to welcome Indian men into the brotherhood of the bottle. But if "mine Host" met the "Salvages" on a level of equality as revelers and pot companions, he kept his distance in other respects. He had not, after all, translated himself into the Sachem of Passonagessit; instead, he and his men had "translated the name of their habitation from that ancient Salvage name to Ma-re Mount."[77]

At times, in order to shame the Puritans by comparison, Morton made gestures in the direction of the Noble Savage: "I have found the Massachusets Indian more full of humanity then the Christians; and have had much better quarter with them." But he quickly added an important qualification: "I observed not their humors, but they mine . . . : for I know that this falls out infallibly where two Nations meete, one must rule and the other be ruled, before a peace can be hoped for: and for a Christian to submit to the rule of a Salvage, you will say, is both shame and dishonor: at least it is my opinion, and my practise was accordingly, and I have the better quarter by the meanes thereof. The more Salvages the better quarter, the more Christians the worser quarter, I found; as all the indifferent minded Planters can testifie."[78] In the first part of this statement Morton is in complete agreement with the Puritans. From this perspective the spectacle of the Westonians' submission to Indian justice should have scandalized him as much as it had the Pilgrims. In the last sentence, Morton and the Puritans part company. Clearly, Morton was not embracing savagery in making invidious comparisons between his English opponents and the Indians. He tried to remain above the "shame and dishonor" of following Indian customs, as he compromised his Golden-Age vision of the Indians' contented lives by suggesting that their powwows were servants of the devil ("and then you may imagin what good rule is like to be amongst them").[79] Morton's Indians remain "Salvages"—but his real point is that the English Puritans have incurred their own share of shame and dishonor by proving themselves even worse than savages. Presumably, it was the height of hypocrisy for them to sneer at his lasses in beaver coats.

Morton well knew that he was stabbing at a vulnerable spot with such jibes. His tendency to favor his Indian over his English neighbors ran directly against the attitude the Puritans cultivated. Morton noted that it was "an article of the new creede of Canaan, . . . [which] they [would] have received of every new commer there to inhabit, that the Salvages are a dangerous people, subtill, secreat and mischeivous; and that it is dangerous to live seperated, but rather together: and so be under their Lee, that none might trade for Beaver, but at their pleasure, as none doe or shall doe there."[80] In other words, both worldly greed and their arrogant identification with the biblical Israel made it convenient for the Puritans to make more of the Indians' ferocity than Morton's experience warranted. In reply, Morton subtly reversed the usual roles, implying that the true "Canaanites" in this case were the Puritans themselves, while "mine Host" appeared as the spy in their midst, the harbinger of their righteous dispossession. On the other hand, he played along with their typological whims when it was to his advantage to do so. The opportunity to lampoon John Winthrop as "Josua Temperwell" was obviously too good to resist: "And here comes their Josua too among them; and they make it a more miraculous thing for these seaven shipps to set forth together, and arrive at New Canaan together, then it was for the Israelites to goe over Jordan drishod: perhaps it was, because they had a wall on the right hand and a wall on the left hand."[81]

If Morton was willing to humor the Puritans' self-image as the New American Israel, it was primarily as an Israel that had become contaminated through contact with the wilderness and was on the verge of a precipitous decline into a worse-than-Canaanite savagery. Among the prefatory verses "In laudem Authoris," a contribution by one "F.C." asked,

> Why, in an aire so milde,
> Are they so monstrous growne up, and so vilde,
> That Salvages can of themselves espy
> Their errors, brand their names with infamy?[82]

F.C.'s inspiration for these lines surely came from Morton's tale of the Indian sachem whose mother's grave had been spoiled by the English. The offended spirit appeared to her son and urged him "to take revenge of those vild people that hath my monument defaced in despitefull manner."[83] "Vild," as Morton used it here, suggests a conflation of "wild" and "vile," thus linking an impression of general wildness with a deeper, moral vileness—as, in *The Tempest*, Caliban is said to be of a "vild race."[84] Morton obviously found it compatible with his own purposes to give peace to the aggrieved spirit by taking vengeance on "those vild people"—in part by throwing this very charge in their faces. And though the Puritans wanted to believe that Standish's attack on the Indians at

Wessagusset had been a blow for civility and good discipline, Morton forced them to take a disquieting look at the matter from another perspective: After the incident, the Indians began calling the English "Wotawquenange, which in their language signifieth stabbers, or Cutthroates," a suitable name for an essentially "vild" people.[85]

Did the good citizens of Plymouth think of him as "a great Monster"? He would return the compliment by suggesting that, in the pride of their strength, "they, (like overgrowne beares,) seemed monsterous." But Morton's words cut deeper when he aimed at more fundamental targets. By accusing Morton of social "inordinariness," Bradford could set him up as the antithesis of the Puritan ideal. Morton simply retaliated by harping on his enemies' own irregularities. Echoing John Smith, he charged that "they had shaked of their shackles of servitude, and were become Masters, and masterles people."[86]

To back up this point, Morton devoted a chapter to the theme of social instability in New England: "Of the digrading and creating gentry in New Canaan"—a curious tale concerning the willingness of the Puritans to invert the traditional social order to suit their own whims. As evidence, he related how "a zealous Professor" of lowly background benefited greatly from the misfortune of a genuine gentleman who "had incurred the displeasure of great Josua [Temperwell, i.e., John Winthrop] so highly that hee must therefore be digraded." The place of a gentleman having thus become suddenly vacant, the socially undistinguished (but lately prosperous) "Professor" just as suddenly moved up in the world— or, as Morton put it, the upstart "was receaved in like a Cypher to fill up a roome, and was made a Gentleman of the first head."[87]

This episode provided a perfect opportunity for Morton to berate the Puritans for their radical social tendencies while testifying to his own commitment to traditional English values. It also gave him a chance to whet his poetic wit on an especially sensitive side of the Puritans' self-image. While the newly created gentleman had been apprenticed early in life "to a tombe maker," he had eventually been "translated . . . to be the tapster at hell"—that is, a watering hole by that nickname "which is in Westminster, under the Ex-Chequer office." From this subterranean point of departure "hee translated himselfe into New England, where, by the help of Beaver and the commaund of a servant or two, hee was advaunced to the title of a gentleman."[88]

Morton, ostentatiously offended by this series of rude translations, decided to present the ex-tapster with a coat of arms suitable to his new status:

> What ailes Pigmalion? Is it Lunacy;
>   Or Doteage on his owne Imagery?
>   Let him remember how hee came from Hell,
>   That after ages by record may tell
> The compleate story to posterity.
> Blazon his Coate in forme of Heraldry.
>   Hee beareth argent alwaies at commaund,
>   A barre betweene three crusty rolls at hand,
>   And for his crest, with froth, there does appeare
>   Dextra Paw Elevant a Jugg of beare.[89]

Here, then, was a self-infatuated Pygmalion, escaped from hell, eager to mistranslate himself into the counterfeit of a gentleman; and there was Thomas Morton, self-appointed herald, who was just as eager to see him blazoned forth in his true colors. If in doing so "mine Host" inadvertently acknowledged his own pettifogger's close acquaintance with "Hell," he at least managed to point out the stains of alcohol on his antagonist's "Coate." Having ridiculed the Plymouth separatists as "overgrowne beares," he now applied the same imagery, with the irresistible pun, to the Massachusetts Bay Puritans, giving their farcical gentleman "a Jugg of beare" for his frothy crest.

Morton's Puritan Caliban, raising his beery paw to grasp at a dignity that lay above his true station (at the tap), was a complementary image of another aspect of Morton's attack on his opponents. Not only were they socially maladroit; they were also ignorant, heretical louts who lacked respect for traditional learning and, it almost followed inevitably, traditional religion. The colonists at Plymouth were especially vulnerable to both attacks, while Morton found it easy to represent himself as a defender of wit and letters, as well as a faithful observer of the Church of England's order of worship. He emphasized that he angered the Puritans because he "was a man that indeavoured to advaunce the dignity of the Church of England; which they, (on the contrary part,) would laboure to vilifie with uncivile termes: enveying against the sacred booke of common prayer, and mine host that used it in a laudable manner amongst his family, as a practise of piety."[90] Moreover, it was but a short step from heresy to treason: Morton further suggested that the separatists' rejection of the king's church was inextricably bound up with a rejection of the king himself. There were "none of the Seperation that regarded the duety they owe their Soveraigne, whose naturall borne Subjects they were, though translated out of Holland, from whence they had learned to worke all to their owne ends. . . ."[91] Again, Morton was reviving old fears and concerns that the founders of Plymouth would gladly have laid to rest. Against suggestions, such as Edward Winslow's, that the Pilgrims had left Holland for America to retain their place in the English world, Morton was arguing that Holland had, in fact, weaned them from their motherland and had encouraged their headstrong, self-willed rebelliousness.

But Morton clearly found his strongest case against the Pilgrims in their religious practices. He could smugly note that while the separatists condemned his May Pole as "an Idoll" and "the Calfe of Horeb," they used the same language against the Church of England, maintaining that "the booke of Common prayer is an idoll: and all that use it, Idolaters."[92] Morton, with Archbishop Laud surely in mind as one of his most important readers, was obviously content to be branded an "Idolater" in these terms. And what did the separatists value instead? "[T]he meanes, they crie, alas, poore Soules where is the meanes?" And what were these precious "meanes"? Concisely glossing his point with the marginal note, "*Booke learning despised,*" Morton allowed his heretics to condemn themselves out of their own mouths: "the booke of common prayer, sayd they, what poore thinge is that, for a man to reade in a booke? No, no, good sirs, I would you were neere us, you might receave comfort by instruction: give me a man hath the guiftes of the spirit, not a booke in hand." Guided by this "spirit" (of ignorance), "like the Serpent, they did creepe and winde into the good opinion of the illiterate multitude."[93]

By portraying the Pilgrims' message as an appeal to the "illiterate multitude," Morton established the disruptive, if not anarchic, overtones of the separatists' cause. Doubtless with Archbishop Laud again in mind, Morton pointed out that "The Church of the Seperatists is governed by Pastors, Elders and Deacons, and there is not any of these, though hee be but a Cow keeper, but is allowed to exercise his guifts in the publik assembly on the Lords day, so as hee doe not make use of any notes for the helpe of his memory: for such things, they say, smell of Lampe oyle, and there must be no such unsavery perfume admitted to come into the congregation." The results were much what might be expected from cow keepers who found the perfume of the scholar's lamp offensive. As Morton observed, demonstrating that he had burned a little oil himself at one time or another, "Socrates sayes, *loquere ut te videam*. If a man observe these people in the exercise of their gifts, hee may thereby discerne the tincture of their proper calling, the asses eares will peepe through the lyons hide."[94]

Giving his readers a peep into a separatist meeting, Morton in effect raises the curtain on a farce, as "these illiterate people" display their gifts. Here is "*A Tapster,*" ill-met once again: he "begins a text that is drawne out of a fountaine that has in it no dreggs of popery," being instead "the Cup of repentance" which is, of course, "filled up to the brim with comfortable joyce," offering "a comfortable cordiall to a sick soule." After the tapster, with his message learned (presumably) in "Hell," comes "*A Cobler*" ("a very learned man indeed"), who plays his own variation in the tones of his trade. He "exhorts them to walke upright, in the way of their calling, and not, (like carnall men,) tread awry." And so on, with the efforts of other gifted "asses." Morton's contempt is vicious: "Well, if you marke it, these are speciall gifts indeede: which the vulgar people are so taken with, that there is no perswading them that it is so ridiculous." Morton had no doubt whatsoever as to the ridiculous nature of "the meanes, (O the meanes,) that they pursue."[95]

Especially ridiculous to Morton was the effect of their ignorance and contempt of learning in professional matters outside the pulpit. Once more, ignorance appears as the natural catalyst of social disorder, as Morton takes up the story "Of a Doctor made at a Commencement in New Canaan," a companion piece to his tale of the rise of the Tapster from Hell, though here the unlucky target is more clearly identifiable as Samuel Fuller, the Pilgrims' physician. Morton spares him the indignity of being singled out explicitly ("What luck is it I cannot hit on his name[?]"), but nameless as "Doctor" Fuller remains, his identity is obvious through the thin veil Morton allows him. For one thing, this Doctor is a man of "speciall gifts"—that is, "hee could wright and reade." His preparation for his profession lay primarily in the fact that "hee was bred a Butcher," and in Morton's account his practice seems to answer to his training. For those who complained of being "ill at ease" after the ocean crossing, he diagnosed "winde"—an illness contracted "by gapeing feasting over board at Sea." Whatever his faults in diagnosis, his treatment worked to perfection: "hee handled the patient so handsomely, that hee eased him of all the winde hee had in an instant." Among this good physician's other remarkable cures was one he arranged for "Captaine Littleworth" (John Endecott): "hee cured him

of a disease called a wife." If anything, Morton's parting words
for Dr. Fuller were more scathing than his poetic salute to his
Tapster: "in mine opinion, hee deserves to be set upon a
palfrey and lead up and downe in triumph throw new Canaan, . . . that men might know where to finde a Quack-
salver."[96]

Morton, who claimed to have cured his dog of snakebite
"with one Saucer of Salet oyle powred downe his throate,"[97]
may have been unqualified to pass authoritative judgment on
Fuller as a physician, but in matters of wit he surely regarded
himself as perfectly qualified to judge the Puritans. In fact,
they seem never so confused and out of their intellectual
element as when confronted by his poetry. Their inability to
interpret (or decipher) Morton's May-Pole verses gave him
another good opportunity to celebrate his talents while laugh-
ing at his critics. Although he wrote his poems "according to
the occurrents of the time, it, being Enigmattically composed,
pusselled the Seperatists most pittifully to expound it."[98] Morton dismissed his opponents as "those Moles" and noted as
an added insult that his merry crew perfectly understood "the
true sence and exposition of the riddle that was fixed to the
Maypole, which the Seperatists were at defiance with." Above
all, Morton replied with supreme contempt to the notion that
the pole "was in memory of a whore." The Puritan Moles
were simply too benighted to realize "that it was a Tro-
phe erected at first in honor of Maia, the Lady of learning
which they despise, vilifying the two universities with uncivile
termes, accounting what is there obtained by studdy is but
unnecessary learning." The Puritans' mistake was in not considering "that learninge does inable mens mindes to converse
with eliments of a higher nature then is to be found within
the habitation of the Mole."[99]

In this manner, Morton stood forth proudly as the defender
of everything good in the English tradition: the old games and
revels, sharp wit, orthodox religion, social order, sound learning. By contrast, the Puritans were left with a role that was

hardly to their liking: the epitome of radical innovation and cultural degeneration. Having consigned them to the bestial heap as "Moles" and "overgrowne beares," Morton completed the caricature by linking the Puritans more directly to the Indians. He managed this trick by means of the Indian-origins question. As much as anyone, Morton realized how volatile this topic was, how likely it was to backfire with unforeseen consequences for those who toyed with it. As Morton opens his own careful discussion of the question, it is difficult to resist the impression that he is parodying the sort of search for cultural "footsteps" that he could have found in the words of John White or William Wood (his archrival as a promotional writer). "After my arrivall in those partes," he begins, "I endeavoured by all the wayes and meanes that I could to find out from what people, or nation, the Natives of New England might be conjectured origin[a]lly to proceede."[100]

Morton's primary "wayes and meanes" were linguistic. It seemed to him that the Indians spoke "*a mixed language*" with affinities to both Latin and Greek. For example, native place-names were highly suggestive of classical Mediterranean influences: "Many places doe retaine the name of *Pan*, as Pantneket and *Matta pan*, so that it may be thought that these people heretofore have had the name of *Pan* in great reverence and estimation, and it may bee have worshipped *Pan* the great God of the Heathens."[101] And though it might have puzzled dull-witted Puritans to trace these curious Mediterranean "footsteps" to America, Morton thought he had a possible answer: "I am bold to conclude that the originall of the Natives of New England may be well conjectured to be from the scattered Trojans, after such time as Brutus departed from Latium."[102] For those able to appreciate a cleverness that lay beyond the comprehension of moles, this surprising conclusion was a revealing glimpse into Morton's satirical motives and strategy.[103]

Through his reference to Trojans and Brutus and Latium, Morton was conjuring up the notion that an exodus of people and culture had followed the destruction of Troy. Aeneas

had first led his Trojans to Latium, but, in time, as a consequence of wars with the Latin peoples, the Trojans under
Brutus ("the forth from Aneas") had once again been "dispersed" over the world—perhaps as far as America. This
explained the supposed echoes of Greek and Latin in the
Indian language, since "there is no question but the people
that lived with him [Brutus], by reason of their conversation
with the Graecians and Latines, had a mixed language that
participated of both . . . ; for this is commonly seene where 2.
nations traffique together, the one indevouring to understand
the others meaning makes them both many times speak a
mixed language, as is approved by the Natives of New England, through the coveteous desire they have to commerce
with our nation and wee with them."[104]

The question of such a mixture of languages arising naturally from the meeting of peoples would have done little to
ease the Puritans' own fears of linguistic and cultural contamination—especially since Morton had specifically argued that
"both" parties would eventually "speak a mixed language."
But Morton's strategy aimed much further than linguistic
insecurity. His theory that the Indians were transplanted Trojans would have struck many seventeenth-century English
readers as a thinly veiled reference to the old belief that
the British people themselves were the descendants of the
eponymous Brutus: from Brutus, Britons. Morton had introduced his chapter on Indian origins with the apparently re-
dundant observation that he had found in New England "two
sortes of people, the one Christians, the other Infidels."[105]
But now he was subtly implying that, genealogically speaking,
there was actually only one sort. The Indian natives and the
English newcomers were kinsmen, however estranged and
altered by time and chance.[106] To portray the meeting of
Indians and Englishmen as a long-delayed family reunion
was meant to be quite a joke on a people who were (as Morton had noted) so desperately intent upon distancing themselves from the supposedly vicious, treacherous, alien barbarians.

But the Brutus legend proved useful to Morton in another way. Despite the skepticism of scholars, the story long retained its hold on the English historical imagination—perhaps because the assumption of Trojan origins provided a suitably ancient and heroic ancestry. The Stuarts used it to bolster the prestige and legitimacy of the British monarchy. It is not surprising, then, that royalists caught up in the growing tension between the king and parliament tended to accept the Brutus story, while the opposition favored Germanic origins.[107] Though Morton may seem to verge on parody in his variation on the Trojan-origins theme, it is far more likely that he regarded an acceptance of the Brutus legend as sound testimony of his loyalty. All questions of genuine belief aside, by paying lip service to official Stuart historiography Morton could use his own political orthodoxy as a means of emphasizing the Puritans' rebellious image. For the coveted royalist audience in England, Morton's Trojan genealogy was a profession of solidarity, but for the despised Puritan audience in New England, it was a gesture of defiance.

Another defender of Stuart legitimacy, the poet Michael Drayton, linked the British empire's expansion to America with the "Trojan" heritage of the British people in his ode "To the Virginian Voyage": "in regions far," he urged the descendants of Brutus,

> Such heroes bring ye forth
>   As those from whom we came,
>   And plant our name
> Under that star
> Not known unto our north.[108]

But if Morton was right, such "heroes" had long since sprung forth in America and were there waiting to embrace their English cousins. The Puritan colonists were surely not amused. Morton was forcing a kinship upon them they could not afford to acknowledge—just as they could not afford to tolerate Morton himself and his sly, winking suggestions that Old Briton, Merrie England, and Savage America were somehow intimately related and perfectly compatible.

Morton's wits failed him, however, when he made the serious mistake of giving the Puritans another chance at him after he had published his scurrilous book. In 1643 "mine Host" returned to the scene of his revels, and Puritan New England seized the opportunity to make him dance to a somewhat different tune. Morton arrived in Plymouth in the fall.[109] On January 4, 1644, Edward Winslow wrote John Winthrop to declare, "for my part . . . [I] would not have this serpent stay amongst us," and he backed up his judgment with an appeal to general sentiment: "indeed Morton is the odium of our peop[le] at present, and if he be suffered (for we are diversly minded) it will be just with God who hath putt him in our hands . . . that afterward we shall suffer for it."[110] Official opinion in Winthrop's colony was much the same. If anyone was to suffer, it must be Morton. John Endecott was driven to the edge of paranoia by his vision of Morton as the epitome of anti-Puritan interests: "It is most likelie that the Jesuites or some that way disposed have sent him over to doe us mischiefe to raise up our enemies round about us both English and Indean."[111] Three days after the embattled Endecott poured out his fears, another concerned Puritan penned similar thoughts to Winthrop, praying "that you would not permit that vyle person Morton to pas without some due punishment for he hath in my Judgment Abused the Cuntry very much and that In print."[112]

For the last time, Morton felt the effects of Puritan justice. The people he had abused ("and that In print") arrested him, threw him in jail, and kept him there over the winter of 1644–45. Though they released him in 1645 to take up exile in Maine, he did not long survive. He died at Agamenticus (later known as York) in 1647.[113] Even dead, however, Morton remained a creature of nightmare, figuring as a bugbear in Puritan histories, while for the opponents of the New England Way, he became something of a hero. After the Restoration, with the Stuarts back in power, the anti-Puritan Samuel Maverick was moved to declare the *New English Ca-*

naan "the truest discription of New England as then it was that ever I saw." True to his name, Maverick could easily identify with Morton, and his outsider's perspective allowed him to appreciate the fundamental nature of Morton's "odium" for the Puritans: he had simply "touched them too neare."[114]

The Holy Wild Man in New England

Though at first glance it would not seem that Thomas Morton and Roger Williams had much in common, they played remarkably similar roles in the early history of New England. The Puritans attacked both as dangerous opponents of their order, and both retaliated with essentially the same strategy—an ironic inversion of Puritan rhetoric. Yet no one would be tempted to regard them as true allies against an emergent Puritan orthodoxy. Morton, as a fellow Englishman, shared a basic national identity with the people he ridiculed, but in other respects he was a maverick in their midst, a Dionysian among Calvinists and a Cavalier among Roundheads. Roger Williams, on the other hand, was a scapegoat (or black sheep) from within the Puritan flock itself—and thus a much more intimate and subversive challenge to the Puritan impulse toward orthodoxy and consensus.

As in Morton's case, Williams's threat to the Puritan order carried a suggestion of wilderness contamination and accommodation with Indian savagery. Yet in a 1638 letter he assured John Winthrop that he was "not yet turned Indian."[115] And when he encountered men who did seem inclined to "turn Indian," he reacted with unambiguous disapproval. For several months before his letter to Winthrop, Williams had been writing about William Baker, a renegade colonist who had abandoned his own nation in favor of its Pequot enemies. Baker, wrote Williams, had "turned Indian in nakedness and cutting of haire" and had learned to "speake much Indian." It almost went without saying that he had completed the offense by committing "uncleanenes with an Indian Squaw." Greatly concerned about what "this fire brand" might accomplish in league with his Pequot friends, Williams offered suggestions about how to bring him to justice. After Baker had paid for his crimes under the lash at Hartford, Williams wrote to Winthrop that "This fellow notorious in villany" was still "worthy to be watcht even by the whole Countrey and to be dispersed from the Pequts."[116]

But if this literal sort of Indianization scandalized Williams, he was not at all averse to using the English fear of Indian-wilderness contamination for his own rhetorical purposes. He was quite willing to play the wild man on the wilderness stage to which his rivals had banished him, but only as the "Holy Wild Man"—a New World Elijah or John the Baptist who accepted the wilderness as merely the necessary backdrop for his call to repentance.[117] Even the Indians had their use as supporting characters: "In *wildernesse*, in great *distresse*, / These *Ravens* have fed me."[118]

Williams was well aware that Elijah-fed-by-ravens was not the only biblical model for the part he was offering to play. There was also Nebuchadnezzar-grazing-with-the-oxen, a precedent that inconveniently seemed to partake more of genuine wildness, bestiality, and madness.[119] Williams, resisting any identification with the Bible's more deranged and "unholy" wild men, liked to think that he could still recognize "Indian madness" when he saw it (for instance, in their sharp trading practices), and he could heartily pray "The Father of Lights cause us to bless him for and with our reason, remembering Nebuchadnezzar."[120] By all available evidence, he valued his own God-given "Lights" highly, and he used them to write closely (often tediously) reasoned discourses on points of controversy. But his antagonists in these paper debates usually professed to find more darkness than light in his pages.

William Bradford, while granting that Williams was "a man godly and zealous, having many precious parts," found him "very unsettled in judgmente."[121] Later Puritan historians generally agreed. William Hubbard characterized Williams as a victim of "over-heated zeal," a man who even before coming to America had been regarded as "divinely mad; as if his too much zeal, as Festus said of Paul's too much learning, had made him beside himself."[122] Cotton Mather, who could well have considered himself an authority on over-heated zeal, dealt with Williams in a section of his *Magnalia* called "Little Foxes; Or, The Spirit of Rigid Separation in One Remarkable Zealot." Mather diagnosed Williams's ailment as *"quixotism"* and described his infectious threat in appropriately "quixotic" imagery: "there was a whole country in America like to be set on *fire* by the *rapid motion* of a windmill, in the head of one particular man."[123]

Rhode Island and Providence Plantations, thanks to the presence of Williams and other black sheep (Anne Hutchinson, Samuel Gorton), soon replaced Merry Mount and the Westonian colony as the principal realm of disorder in New England. But if the image of Rhode Island as a harbor and breeding ground for heresy is essential to an understanding of Williams's own image in the minds of his orthodox neighbors, it is important to recognize that his view of himself and his colony was quite different. As improbable as it may have seemed to his most zealous detractors, Williams's transition from outsider-in-the-Bay to patriarch-in-Providence led him to speak more often as the champion of civility and order.[124]

Upon occasion, Williams could convey as well as anyone the sense of being an island of English culture in a sea of Indian barbarism. Near the beginning of the Pequot War, he told Winthrop that "our dangers (in the midst of these dens of lions) now especially, call upon us to be compact in a civil way and power." In a resolution he drew up to establish more effective civil order in Providence, he spoke of the town's situation as being "remote from others of our countrymen amongst the barbarians."[125] In November 1637 he wrote to Winthrop that he had heard some colonists from Charlestown were thinking about moving into his neighborhood. And though Williams already felt himself uncomfortably wedged between the Indians on one side and Plymouth's claims on the other, he was still unwilling to turn away newcomers: "I know not the persons, yet in generall could wish . . . that these wayes might be more trod into these inland parts, and that amongst the multitudes of the Barbarous, the neighbourhood of some English Plantation (especially of men desiring to feare God) might helpe and strengthen."[126]

These were not the words of an Elijah, content to be fed by Indian ravens in the midst of a howling wilderness. Here, Williams was posing as a pioneer—willing to offer his colony, not as a source of contamination, but as a frontier post against the threat of barbarism. In 1656, hoping to be allowed to buy arms and powder from Massachusetts Bay merchants, he reminded the Bay authorities of his strategic importance to them: "We have been esteemed by some of you, as your thorny hedge on this side of you; If so, yet a hedge to be maintained; if as out sentinels, yet not to be discouraged."[127] Perhaps thinking of the wilderness surrounding Providence, he wrote in *The Bloody Tenent Yet More Bloody* (1652) that "if the *sword* and *balances* of *justice* . . . be not drawn and held forth, against *scandalous* offenders against *civil state*, that *civil state* must dissolve by little and little from *civility* to *barbarisme*, which is a *wilderness* of *life* and *manners*."[128]

Williams appeared to equally strong effect as a champion of traditional intellectual culture, despite his sympathy with radical Puritans in both Englands who valued the gifts of the spirit above the rewards of formal study. Although he regarded England's universities as corrupt, parasitic, latter-day monasteries and praised lay preachers like Samuel How, a cobbler, who performed the Lord's work "without humane *Learning*," he carefully noted that How had become an accomplished "*Textuary* or Scripture learned man." Like How, he himself was a formidable "*Textuary*," and, as he remarked, "I have not been altogether a *stranger* to the *Learning* of the

Aegyptians." Indeed, "I heartily acknowledge that among all the *outward Gifts* of God, humane learning and the *knowledge* of *Languages*, and good *Arts*, are excellent and excell other outward *gifts*, as far as *light* excels *darknesse*, and therefore that *Schools* of *humane Learning*, ought to be maintained . . . and cherished."[129]

In matters of education and scholarship—"humane" or spiritual—Williams regarded himself as allied with the forces of light. He vigorously opposed any attempt to depend excessively on the teachings of the spirit. When, in the 1650s, the Quakers introduced themselves to New England and orthodox Puritans reacted with horror (for the Reverend John Norton, the official voice of that orthodoxy, the Quakers' teachings were a "contagious influence" that needed "to be antidoted"),[130] there was no more resolute opponent of Quakerism in New England than Williams. He stopped far short of advocating civil punishments to effect a cure; preferring instead to speak and write against the doctrinal disease, he spent four days in 1672 debating three Quaker spokesmen (disciples of George Fox) in Providence. The compatibility of his argument with orthodox opinion in Massachusetts Bay is apparent since his account of the debates was then printed and sold in Boston. *George Fox Digg'd out of his Burrowes* (1676) seems to have rehabilitated Williams in the eyes of the Bay ministers. At least William Hubbard, in writing of Williams's "great and lamentable apostasy," granted that "he did a little recover himself" through his anti-Quaker polemics.[131]

For Williams, as for Norton, the Quakers were the antithesis of civil and spiritual order. He even went so far as to charge that Quakerism tended "To reduce Persons from *Civility* to *Barbarisme.*"[132] He was especially offended, in this regard, by the Quakers' apparent contempt for common courtesy. Williams argued "that in our *Native Countrey*, and in all *civilized Countreys*, the civility, Courteous Speech Courteous Salutation, and respective Behaviour was generally practised, opposite to the cariage of *Barbarous & Unciviliz'd People*." In an

American context, these words carried a far greater weight
of meaning than they would have supported in England,
where civility and courteous speech were no longer starkly
opposed to the rude taciturnity of any *"Barbarous & Unciviliz'd"* neighbors: "We *English* were our selves at first wild and
savage *Britains*: Gods mercy had civilized us, and we were
now come into a wild and savage Countrey, without *Manners*,
without *Courtesie*, so that generally except you begin with a
What Chear or some other *Salutation*, you had as good meet
an *Horse* or a *Cow*, &c. And hath not the *Quaker spirit* been
such a *Spirit* amongst us?"[133]

Williams was not about to let George Fox (or his followers)
get away with the old trick of shaming his English opponents
by comparing them unfavorably with the natives. He noted
that "*G. Fox* in his book affirms that the *Conversation* of these
very *Barbarians*, in many things were better then his *Opposites*
&c." It was easy for Williams to question Fox's authority, since
Fox had not yet been to New England when he had offered
this opinion—"but since I have heard that the *Quakers* have
commended the spirit of the *Indians*, for they have seen them
come into *English Houses* and sit down by the fire, not speaking
a word to any body." It remained merely to point the obvious
conclusion in a marginal gloss: "*The Indians and Quakers of one
Spirit.*"[134]

Not content to unite Quakers and Indians in the bonds of
bad manners, Williams sought also to establish his opponents'
kinship with lower orders of creation. For Williams the Quakers' "*bruitish Irreverence* to all their Superiours" was no mere
lack of traditional courtesy and deference, nor simply evidence
of an affinity with Indian barbarism, but rather "a most *proud*
and *monstrous Bestiality.*"[135] Further evidence that the Quakers'
"*bruitish spirit*" fell short of "a sober and well grounded *Humanity*" (in more than one sense) came from "that *whorish* and
monstrous act of your *Women* and Maidens, stripping themselves *stark naked*, by your Spirit, and with a face of *brass*
coming into the open *streets*, and publick *Congregations* of Men

and Youths. This *Spirit* . . . is such a piece of unnaturall and bruitish *Impudence*, that I cannot hear of the like amongst *Jews* or *Gentiles*, yea not amongst the most Savage, Base and Barbarous of them all (all Circumstances considered)."[136]

Williams believed that this nakedness confirmed the blatantly bestial nature of Quakerism, since such behavior was "only practised by the *Bruites*, and sometimes by *Indians*, and *Whores* in their drink, when all *Modesty* and *Reason* is overwhelmed with more then common *Drunkenness*."[137] But Williams in making this charge carelessly exposed himself to a Quaker counterattack. One of his opponents rose to confess that "he had been a *Quaker* 19 years and yet had never seen a woman *Naked*, and some of the *Quakers* said to me aloud, *when didst thou see any of our women Naked?* and another of them said, *We did not think that thou wouldest have been such a wicked man*." Though Williams had foolishly allowed himself to be taken in his own snare, he at least knew how to get out: "I said unto my *Antagonists*, seeing some *Heat* is risen about these matters, I will if you please go on"—to another point.[138]

Williams had many other complaints about the Quakers—including "Their *New Way* of *feeling* and *grabling* the *hand* in an *uncouth, strange* and *Immodest* way" in place of the traditional "*holy Kiss*" of Christian greeting.[139] Williams also took advantage of the fact that the name of the Quakers' leader was George Fox. Williams did not really need this excuse to think of Fox as an animal, since he also called him "this *poor wild Asses Colt*." But how could he resist the opportunity (God-given, at that) to play on all the implications of the name of "this *wild Fox*"?[140] His opponents evidently suspected that his frequent references to Fox and Burroughs (i.e., to their book, *The Great Mystery*) were not rhetorically innocent—that he was, in other words, "speaking of *G. Fox* and *E. Burrowes* in scorn and derision." Williams denied that he had meant to pun, "yet this Passage was the occasion of the *Title* of the *Book*: For the finger of *Gods* most wise and holy Providence is often wonderfully seen in small, unexpected & inconsiderable

Turns and Occasions." Thus, the Quaker antagonist who had brought this Providence to his attention was himself acting as *"Digitus Dei* the finger of God directing and pointing me to so proper and pertinent an use and Application."[141] This was no mere pun; it was a veritable call from God to portray his enemies in their true, bestial light. So Williams was off in a flash, "to follow this *Fox* into his holes and *Burrowes*, and to hale him out before God, Angels and Men as a most greedy audacious *Fox* and *Wolfe*, not sparing the Son and Lamb of God, nor his precious Lambs and Sheep."[142] The Quaker's answers to his critics became recognizable as "meer simple *barkings* of dogs or foxes compar'd with the rational and prudential Answers of a man."[143]

Fox's crude barkings prompted Williams to make one of his most unequivocal defenses of formal education.[144] To an accomplished textuary like Williams, the Quakers' relative neglect of Scripture in favor of what they took to be direct spiritual revelation was a sure sign of their true (unholy) inspiration: "It is no wonder this Spirit of Lying cries out so fiercely against the Schools of Learning in *Old and New England*, it knows that the right and regular propagation of natural, of civil, and especially of *Divine Knowledge* scatters the thick Fogs of the *Quakers* affected hellish ignorance."[145] Little wonder then that Fox reasoned and disputed so awkwardly. His "loose and wild Spirit" in debate goaded him into "Leaps and Skips like a wild *Satyre* or *Indian*, catching and snapping at here and there a Sentence, like Children skipping ore hard places and Chapters, picking and culling out what is common and easie with them to be paid of and answered."[146] Williams's own exhaustive point-by-point argumentation hardly seems preferable, but he was clearly satisfied that Fox's Indianized (or infantilized) method was in perfect accord with his other faults. He denied that Fox could even write sensibly in his native language; Fox's book was full of "Boyes English," and not just because of "his *Northern Dialect*" or printer's errors. The Quaker's grammatical solecisms (like his name) were nothing less than "the finger of the most High, and most Holy," that remarkable *Digitus Dei*, pointing out through Fox's illiteracy the hollowness of his doctrine.[147]

An appreciation of Williams's more conservative tendencies is necessary in order to put his truly radical side in better perspective. In his debates with the Quakers he was speaking near the end of a long lifetime of bitter (and embittering) doctrinal battles. A crabbed, vindictive spirit is often apparent beneath his puns and witty invective.[148] But if he now had emerged as an ally of established orthodox opinion, he had in earlier days often been something of a wily beast himself. He was a crafty, clever manipulator of language, an elusive opponent in a debate. Though in his old age Williams found the strength to hunt with the orthodox hounds, in his even more vigorous youth he was far more inclined to run with the foxes.

A Key into the Language of Roger Williams

Williams's banishment from Massachusetts Bay in 1635 and his subsequent flight into the wilderness provided the necessary background for his most subversive attack on the dominant ideology of Puritan New England. In fact, Williams began his assault on the expectations of the Bay authorities by choosing a wilderness exile in place of the return trip to England that the magistrates had planned for him.[149] He rejected any notion of serving as a scapegoat for his antagonists, becoming instead a wilderness prophet to witness against his judges. Williams's wilderness exile gave him the appropriate context for such a prophetic role while providing a rich source of wilderness imagery with which to frame his argument.

In appraising Williams's strategy of turning his sufferings to his own rhetorical advantage, it is useful to remember that the Massachusetts Bay authorities had not pounced on him without warning like a wolf. The General Court's proceedings against Williams were leisurely enough to give him plenty of

time to prepare for his banishment. And Williams, by reject-
ing a return to England in favor of the Narragansett country,
doubtless brought many of his hardships upon himself.
Nevertheless, those hardships were apparently real enough:
events had forced him to begin his flight during the severe
winter of early 1636. In considering such circumstances, it is
also important to remember that Williams, unlike many other
colonists of his generation, was an urban creature—a son of
London, not the English countryside. If the wilderness of
New England daunted those who, like William Bradford,
were largely accustomed to the absence of urban comforts, it
must have been even more of an ordeal to Williams. In effect,
Williams experienced a double exile, living not only relatively
remote from the principal areas of settlement in the Bay, but
also "so many thousand miles distant in *America*" from the
land of his birth.[150]

Whether or not Perry Miller was right in concluding that
Williams "enjoyed feeling sorry for himself," he was certainly
justified in observing that "No other New England writer
makes quite so much of an incantation out of the very word
'wilderness,' and none of the others who also endured great
hardships so loves to expatiate on them."[151] Indeed, Williams
became an unrivaled virtuoso at playing upon the themes of
the wilderness condition. His sufferings (real or imagined)
gave him a powerful rhetorical edge against his opponents
who had remained in relative comfort in Boston or Salem
while he, "being destitute of food, of cloths," had been "exposed to the mercy of an howling Wildernesse in Frost and
Snow, &c."[152]

This characteristic reference to the wilderness's cold
"mercy" drew attention to the apparent absence of that virtue
in his judges—the men who had condemned him, a sick man
at that, "without mercy and humane compassion . . . to winter
miseries in a howling Wildernes."[153] Above all, Williams directed these words toward John Cotton, holding him especially responsible for his fate. Williams said he had written

letters to Cotton "in which I proved and exprest, that if I had perished in that sorrowfull Winters flight; only the blood of Jesus Christ could have washed him from the guilt of mine."[154] How would Cotton feel, he asked, "to be pluckt up by the roots, him and his, and to endure the losses, distractions, miseries that doe attend such a condition[?]" Williams believed that "had his soule been in my soules case, exposed to the miseries, poverties, necessities, wants debts, hardships of Sea and Land, in a banished condition; he would I presume, reach forth a more mercifull cordiall to the afflicted." He would grant that Cotton at least still had the capacity for mercy. "But he that is despised and afflicted is like a lamp despised in the eyes of him that is at ease: *Job*."[155]

Cotton had no intention of allowing Williams to play Job at his expense. Cotton preferred to compare Williams to the Apostle John and his confinement on Patmos, "a desolate Wildernesse, destitute (for the most part) of Inhabitants: yet he maketh no expresse mention of his Banishment, nor of the howling Wildernesse, nor of frost, and snow, and such winter miseries." How did Williams measure up to this example? "Mr. *Williams* . . . aggravateth the banishment of such an one as himselfe, by all the sad exaggerations, which wit and words could well paint it out withall."[156] Making as light of Williams's "sad exaggerations" as possible, Cotton suggested that his antagonist, far from being deathly ill when he had to light out for the territory, was himself the sickness. Williams's growing influence "provoked the Magistrates rather then to breed a winters spirituall plague in the Countrey, to put upon him a winters journey out of the Countrey."[157] Though Cotton denied that the banishment was his doing, he obviously approved of it.[158]

But granted that Williams had been banished, what did banishment mean in America? Cotton wondered "if it be in proper speech a punishment at all in such a Countrey as this is, where the Jurisdiction (whence a man is banished) is but small, and the Countrey round about it, large, and fruitfull:

where a man may make his choice of variety of more pleasant, and profitable seats, then he leaveth behinde him. In which respect, Banishment in this Countrey, is not counted so much a confinement, as an enlargement, where a man doth not so much loose civill comforts, as change them."[159] It was an interesting point, yet in portraying wilderness exile as a mere change of "comforts," Cotton was contradicting the antithesis of wilderness and civility that was an essential element of the Puritan self-image in New England. Cotton even went so far as to deny (albeit with irony) that his own situation in Boston was as comfortable as Williams supposed. As Cotton saw it, Williams had obtained his own "ease" only by renouncing the weighty social responsibilities his gifts ordinarily would have imposed upon him. Further, "As for my being at ease, (as he calleth it) had he been a little longer acquainted with the faithfull discharge of a Ministers office, he would not judge it such a state of ease. If I durst allow my selfe to seeke, and take mine ease, I should sooner choose a private solitary condition in his Wildernesse, then all the throng of employment in this numerous society."[160]

This surprising remark runs so contrary to Cotton's defense of society elsewhere that, even assuming an ironic intention, his view of Williams's "solitary condition" seems brazenly disingenuous.[161] And a poem Cotton wrote on his migration from Boston in Old England to a new Boston in a new England suggests that his real attitude toward wilderness exile did not jibe with his view of Williams's forest comforts. He speaks of the memory of old Boston as a tonic for his faltering spirits in his new home:

> When I think of the sweet and gracious company
> That at *Boston* once I had,
> And of the long peace of a fruitful Ministry
> For twenty years enjoy'd:
>
> The joy that I found in all that happiness
> Doth still so much refresh me,
> That the grief to be cast out into a wilderness
> Doth not so much distress me.[162]

The key word here is "grief," not "ease." Cotton's deeper sense of exile in Boston also emerged during the course of his pamphlet war with Williams. Cotton was in America when his opponent, temporarily back in England where he had better access to books and the press, began to publish his side of the argument. In his reply, Cotton apologized for not having read a book to which Williams had referred, noting "I have not had the Liberty to get [it], in these remote ends of the world."[163]

If Cotton was not sure that he could really be at ease "in these remote ends of the world," he was relatively certain that a wilderness was precisely where Williams belonged. Williams was an unruly wilderness branch that could bring forth only "bitter, and wild fruit."[164] In "orthodox" minds, then, the effect of Williams's flight into the wilderness was ultimately to reaffirm, not negate, the distinction between wilderness and Christianity—though his choice of the wilderness as a place of exile and refuge also tended to reinforce the Puritans' worst fears about America itself. Williams's case seemed to prove that in America heresy could find unlimited room for "enlargement" in a compatible, nourishing environment. But Williams would use wilderness imagery to suggest that the most serious problem of savage contamination lay within the orthodox "gardens" of the surrounding Puritan colonies.

Williams launched this strategy in his first published work, *A Key into the Language of America*, a book he wrote on a 1643 return voyage to England and ushered into print on his arrival. The language in question was the Algonquian dialect of the Narragansetts, and in practical terms Williams was offering his researches into that language as a "key" for admitting others to its mysteries. But the book also opened to Williams and his readers the peculiar rhetoric of America, enabling him to introduce an Indian accent into the debate over wilderness contamination and cultural degeneration. The *Key* itself was a work forged in his wilderness ordeal amongst the Indians. As he explained, "I drew the *Materialls* in a rude lumpe at Sea, as a private *helpe* to my owne memory, that I might not by my present absence *lightly lose* what I had so *dearely bought* in some few yeares *hardship*, and *charges* among the *Barbarians*." He realized "It is expected, that having had so much converse with these *Natives*, I should write some litle of them."[165]

Out of this "converse" with the Indians that his banishment had made possible, Williams fashioned far more than a simple account of their lives and language. His Indian conversation became the pretext for an assault on the Puritan colonies' pretensions to true civility and Christianity. Specifically, Williams's experience had revealed to him that the wilderness, as an emblem of man's inner nature, was a natural setting for the sort of persecution that had driven him beyond the pale of settlement in New England. "The Wildernesse is a cleere resemblance of the world," he wrote, "where greedie and furious men persecute and devoure the harmlesse and innocent as the wilde beasts pursue and devoure the Hinds and Roes."[166] Williams found this observation remarkably useful in his polemic against his own pursuers.

The image of the world as a wilderness was already a commonplace in Christian thought when Williams took it up, and in his other works he often used it in rather commonplace ways.[167] But in his *Key* Williams discovered a peculiarly American context for this imagery, one that would allow him to identify his orthodox opponents with the beast-haunted wilderness they were attempting to subdue. In a chapter devoted to the Indians' hunting practices, Williams drew a clever analogy to his own experience of persecution. Identifying himself with the most vulnerable game animal of the wilderness, the deer, he managed to identify his tormentors with the predators: "all wild creatures, and many tame, prey upon the poore Deere (which are there in a right Embleme of Gods persecuted, that is, hunted people . . .)." And by way of further illustration, he related an incident that suggested an allegory of his own banishment. "I remember," he wrote, "how a poore

Deere was long hunted and chased by a Wolfe, at last (as their manner is) after the chase of ten, it may be more miles running, the stout Wolfe tired out the nimble Deere, and seasing upon it, kill'd: In the act of devouring his prey, two *English* Swine, big with Pig, past by, assaulted the Wolfe, drove him from his prey, and devoured so much of that poore Deere, as they both surfeted and dyed that night."[168]

It is possible to decipher this passage in fairly simple terms: Williams, of course, is the deer; Boston seems the most likely candidate for the wolf; Plymouth and Salem are left in the roles of the greedy swine.[169] Williams's identification with the deer is also strengthened by his observation that the Indians believed the deer possessed "a Divine power in them."[170] But Williams himself offered a more general interpretation of the parable: "The Wolfe is an Embleme of a fierce bloodsucking persecutor," while with "The Swine of a covetous rooting worldling, both make a prey of the Lord Jesus in his poore servants."[171] Williams, that poor servant of Jesus, had been thus "devoured" by his persecutors, but he was determined not to prove a quiet, digestible morsel. As he remarked in one of his poetic efforts, "Gods children are sweet prey to all, / But yet the end proves sowre."[172]

Williams apparently found this role as Circe (changing Puritans into swine—and wolves) so congenial that he returned to it in his argument against John Cotton on the subject of persecution for differences of conscience. In *The Bloudy Tenent* (1644) he wanted "to give *alarme* to my selfe, and all men to prepare to be *persecuted* or hunted for cause of *conscience*."[173] This was, he declared, "the greatest violence and hunting in the *wildernesse* of the whole *World*."[174] And recurring to the image of the deer, he found that the people of God "(as *Gods Venison*)" were "most sweet when most hunted."[175] In *The Bloody Tenent Yet More Bloody*, he further lectured Cotton that "The *Church* of *Christ* is a *congregation* of *Saints*, a *flock* of *sheep*, humble, meek, patient, contented, with whom it is *monstrous* and impossible, to couple cruel and persecuting *lyons*, subtle and hypocritical *Foxes*, contentious biting *dogs* or greedy and rooting *swine*, so visibly declared and apparant."[176] But obviously the would-be sheep of the orthodox Puritan flock had proved to be wolves (or bears, or lions, etc.) in sheep's clothing. It seemed that in New England a horrible metamorphosis had occurred. Williams professed his amazement "that such as are the *sheep* and *lambs* of *Christ*, should be so monstrously changed and transformed into *lyons, beares*, &c."; they had even fallen to citing Scripture "for this their *unnatural* and monstrous change and *transformation*."[177]

By raising the question of such a "monstrous change," Williams was following essentially the same strategy Thomas Morton had used in calling the Puritans "vild" and "overgrowne beares." Though Williams's motives were hardly the same as Morton's, he was seconding mine Host's suggestion that his opponents had undergone a "*transformation*" that had brought them into a moral conformity with the American wilderness. It is true that Williams was as dependent on scriptural precedents as on his own wilderness experience for this imagery (for example: "Behold, I send you forth as sheep in the midst of wolves: be ye therefore wise as serpents, and harmless as doves"—Matthew 10:16). And the rather tame, wolfless condition of England was clearly of slight importance in Williams's description of Archbishop Laud as "that late bloody *Woolfe*" who had been "an *instrument* of the bloody hunting and *worrying*" of God's "poor *Lambs*."[178] Still, such clichés took on added meaning when applied to men who had experienced a change of environment from a civil, ordered landscape to a literal wilderness. It seemed to Williams that John Cotton, for instance, had found his own key into the most brutal language of America as a result of his transplantation across the Atlantic. In *The Bloudy Tenent* Williams pointed out "how fully this worthy *Answerer* [Cotton] hath learned to speake the roaring *language* of *Lyon-like Persecution*, far from the *purity* and *peaceablenesse* of the *Lambe*, which he was wont to expresse in *England*."[179]

As Williams realized, however, Scripture could also support a view of heretics and false prophets as wolves ("For I know this, that after my departing shall grievous wolves enter in among you, not sparing the flock"—Acts 20:29). And Cotton took advantage of this precedent to give Williams a dose of his own rhetoric. In *The Bloudy Tenent, Washed, And Made White in the Bloud of the Lambe* (1647) Cotton answered Williams's talk about wolves and hunting with a more "orthodox" variation on that theme: "Now it is a part of a Shepheards protection of his sheepe, to drive away wolves from sheepe-folds. And it is the like part of good Magistrates to drive away false Prophets from the Churches, whom our Saviour calleth ravening wolves, *Matth.* 7.15." Especially "when the Wolfe runneth ravenously upon the sheep, . . . is it then against the Nature of the true Shepheard to send forth his Dogs to worry such a Wolfe, without incurring the reproach of a persecutor?"[180] Cotton could trust Williams to know exactly what he meant.

Williams was not one to suffer defeat gladly at his own game. Rather than meekly accepting his role as a threat to the orthodox flock, he continued to force the wolfish mantle onto Cotton's back. In his rebuttal of Cotton's attempt to wash the blood from the disputed tenet, he insisted upon a crucial distinction between the spiritual and civil realms. While the magistrates (Cotton's "Dogs") might consider themselves justified in "worrying" anyone who attacked the people in a civil way, it was wrong to use civil force or punishments to deal with spiritual offenders whom the orthodox clergy regarded (perhaps mistakenly) as heretical "wolves." For such spiritual wolves, there could be only spiritual remedies.[181] Needless to say, Williams would have denied that he was a wolf, in either the civil or spiritual senses, and by keeping the focus on Cotton's own role as a persecutor, he kept his antagonist on the defensive.

Again like Thomas Morton, Williams was aware that comparisons of his opponents to the American Indians were a convenient means of linking his persecutors to the American wilderness. It was thus hardly consistent of him to deny this strategy to George Fox when he had used it to such good effect in his own earlier polemics. As he had declared in the *Key*, he wanted his book "to bring some short *Observations* and *Applications* home to *Europe* from *America*."[182] He was also, however indirectly, bringing home several pointed observations to a specific community of Europeans living in America. The general tendency of these applications was to question the English colonists' easy assumption of superiority over Indian barbarism. From Williams's perspective (as from Morton's), it proved possible to find more true virtue in the supposed "barbarians" than in the English who prided themselves on their "civility."[183]

But Williams was no more a devotee of the Noble Savage than Thomas Morton had been. If anything, he was far more willing than Morton to take a darker view of Indian culture. Williams, like the Puritan ministers of Massachusetts Bay, was firmly convinced of the fundamental bestiality and depravity of unregenerate human nature, whether that nature clothed itself in fine silks or buckskins. He exempted neither himself nor any other specimen of humanity when he declared that "we are not only like to, but Infinitely (as I may say) worse then the wildest Beasts that perish."[184] Far from thinking of the Indians as noble innocents, he was capable of referring to them (selectively) as "mad dogs," "wild barbarous wretches," the "dregs of mankind," and "a barbarous scum and offscouring of mankind."[185] Nor were Indian enemies safe from the club he used to beat the English "wolves." On July 10, 1637, he wrote to John Winthrop that he would "deale with them wisely as with wolves endewed with mens braines."[186] And during King Philip's War he used the same language to convince John Winthrop, Jr., that he was on the right side: "I presume you are satisfied in the necessitie of these present hostilities, & that it is not possible at present to keepe peace with these barbarous men of bloud, who are as justly to be repelld & subdued as wolves that assault the sheepe."[187]

Williams was also in agreement with his orthodox neighbors in an abhorrence of any contamination from the Indians' customs of worship. In describing for his readers the Indians' religious practices, he had to forgo firsthand experience, so fearful was he of risking direct exposure to their unholy rites: "for after once being in their Houses and beholding what their Worship was, I durst never bee an eye witnesse, Spectatour, or looker on, least I should have been partaker of Sathans Inventions and Worships, contrary to *Ephes.* 5.11."[188]

But if the Indians were more blatantly devoted to Satan than most men, Williams persisted in asserting the essential racial and spiritual unity of mankind—an assertion that, however idealistic, was also useful in his paper war with Massachusetts Bay. An especially imaginative means of making this point emerged from his attempt to describe the Indians' language. He did not want to make his book into a dictionary or grammar, and he also rejected the idea of working his Indian vocabulary into a polished, formal dialogue. Still, his linguistic *Key* was no random list of words and phrases; as he pointed out, "(with no small paines) I have so framed every Chapter and the matter of it, as I may call it an Implicite Dialogue."[189] In other words, he presented the Indian vocabulary and grammar through brief, direct statements that seem to constitute the skeleton of a conversation—with the English translation set over against the original. In adopting this device, Williams risked making the Indian language (and the culture to which it gave expression) even more alien than his readers already regarded it. Perhaps they felt many of their worst suspicions confirmed as they compared the rather commonplace English phrases with the tongue-twisting Indian equivalents. The spaces between the two columns of words could thus perform the distancing function of the cultural barrier the English sought to maintain between themselves and the native peoples of America. This seems especially evident when the "Implicite Dialogue" touches upon the very absence of mutual understanding:

Nippenowántawem.	*I am of another language.*
Penowantowawhettûock.	*They are of a divers language.*
Mat nowawtau hettémina.	*We understand not each other.*[190]

Thus Williams's dialogue becomes inadvertently an emblem of cultural antagonism and incompatibility. And yet the counterbalancing effect of the English translation also suggests that the ground between is potentially a place of meeting, a linguistic neutral zone in which meanings can converge and blend. The "Implicite Dialogue" is an exercise in linguistic and cultural counterpoint that invites both sides to lose their discrete identities in a harmony of understanding—the key to which Williams had placed in his readers' hands.

Cowâutam?	*Understand You?*
Nowaûtam.	*I understand.*
. . . .	
Awanagusàntowosh.	*Speake English.*
Eenàntowash.	*Speake Indian.*[191]

If the mutual acculturation that Williams sketched out in his *Key* seems rather limited and hypothetical, he was nevertheless providing support for a much more fundamental point: human nature, as well as language, was universal, despite the forms in which it could express itself. And just as it was possible to "translate" (carry across) words into another language to reveal a basic universal meaning, so it was possible to bridge the intervening distance between different cultural identities. As Williams put it:

> Boast not proud *English*, of thy birth & blood,
> Thy brother *Indian* is by birth as Good.
> Of one blood God made Him, and Thee & All,
> As wise, as faire, as strong, as personall.

And in case his proud readers could not draw the obvious conclusion from this, he gave them a prod in the right direction with the next stanza:

> By nature wrath's his portion, thine no more
> Till Grace *his* soule and *thine* in Christ restore,

> Make sure thy second birth, else thou shalt see,
> Heaven ope to *Indians* wild, but shut to thee.[192]

Here Williams was not simply asserting that the Indians and English would have to measure themselves against a common spiritual standard; he was also suggesting that regenerate Indians (however "wild") would easily outrank unregenerate Englishmen in the judgment of God—especially considering that the English would have less excuse for their failings. He assured his readers,

> I could never discerne that excesse of scandalous sins amongst them, which *Europe* aboundeth with. Drunkennesse and gluttony, generally they know not what sinnes they be; and although they have not so much to restraine them (both in respect of knowledge of God and Lawes of men) as the *English* have, yet a man shall never heare of such crimes amongst them of robberies, murthers, adulteries, &c. as amongst the *English*: I conceive that the glorious Sunne of so much truth as shines in *England*, hardens our *English* hearts; for what the Sunne softeneth not, it hardens.[193]

In a book published in England, Williams was addressing himself primarily to the sins of England, but he had New England in mind as well, especially as he noted that the Indians "have a modest Religious perswasion not to disturb any man, either themselves *English*, *Dutch*, or any in their Conscience, and worship."[194] Certainly he seems to speak for Thomas Morton as well as himself when he observes, "It is a strange *truth*, that a man shall generally finde more free entertainment and refreshing amongst these *Barbarians*, then amongst thousands that call themselves *Christians*."[195] And the Indian ravens that fed this Elijah had often performed similar services for other lost Englishmen in the American wilderness—thereby further shaming the exclusiveness and jealousy of the colonists in New England: "I have heard of many *English* lost, and have oft been lost my selfe, and my selfe and others have often been found, and succoured by the *Indians*."[196]

In the light of such virtues, it seemed of little consequence that, as barbarians, the Indians lacked some of the superficial polish of English manners. Though many wore their hair long, there were roundheads among them: "some cut their haire round, and some as low and as short as the sober *English*; yet I never saw any so to forget nature it selfe in such excessive length and monstrous fashion, as to the shame of the *English* Nation, I now (with griefe) see my Countrey-men in *England* are degenerated unto."[197] What if they painted themselves in barbarous patterns? Were the English completely without sin in this respect? "It hath been the foolish Custome of all barbarous Nations to paint and figure their Faces and Bodies (as it hath been to our shame and griefe, wee may remember it of some of our Fore-Fathers in this Nation.)"[198] If the Indians wore much less clothing than the English would think proper, at least they had not abused what little clothing they had by enslaving themselves, as many Englishmen had, to the whims of fashion. "The best clad *English-man*," Williams said, "Not cloth'd with Christ, more naked is: / Then naked *Indian*."[199] At the final judgment, what would clothes matter when all stood naked before God?

> Two Worlds of men shall rise and stand
> 'Fore Christs most dreadfull barre:
> *Indians*, and *English* naked too,
> That now most gallant are.[200]

The general effect of such comparisons was to portray the English as (relatively speaking) moral barbarians, while the Indians emerged as a people of great natural civility whose barbarous practices were largely explained, if not fully excused, by their ignorance. "There is a savour of *civility* and *courtesie* even amongst these wild *Americans*, both amongst *themselves* and towards *strangers*," Williams said, and he followed this observation with a poetic application:

> The Courteous *Pagan* shall condemne
> *Uncourteous Englishmen*,
> Who live like Foxes, Beares and Wolves,
> Or Lyon in his Den.[201]

Englishmen who did behave toward their fellow men as wolves or lions were thus in more accord with the spirit of the wilderness than was the *"Pagan"* who had been made "Courteous" by the light of nature. It would seem, then, that the wolfish, lionlike persecutors in New England were themselves in danger of becoming the true "wild *Americans.*" In view of the barbarous practices of the supposedly civil peoples of the British Isles, the Indians appeared justified in making the condemnation Williams put into their mouths:

> We weare no Cloaths, have many Gods,
> And yet our sinnes are lesse:
> You are Barbarians, Pagans wild,
> Your Land's the Wildernesse.[202]

If Old England itself had taken on the moral character of a wilderness (even in the eyes of pagan Indians), what hope could there be for a New England that, planted amidst a literal wilderness, seemed determined to cherish the bloody tenet of persecution? As Thomas Morton had appropriated the mantle of Jonah, crying "Repent, you cruell Schismaticks, repent,"[203] Roger Williams assumed a call to witness against his persecutors, calling upon them to repent lest, contrary to their intentions, their identities became submerged in the wild nature of America. Williams left the architects of the New England Way trapped between two blind walls: they were convinced that they could not defend themselves against wilderness contamination and eventual degeneration if they tolerated such "wild men" as himself in their midst; yet he had charged them with demonstrating, through their brutal (and brutish) response to his challenge, that the wilderness had already taken root inside their transplanted garden.

The custodians of New England orthodoxy could easily enough keep Williams and other quixotic scapegoats at a safe physical distance, but before they could feel completely secure they would also have to defuse the deadly irony of his rhetoric by overcoming the cultural and spiritual differences that separated the English from the Indians. They would seek to accomplish this remarkable feat not by succumbing to their own metamorphosis into "wild *Americans,*" but by transforming the Indians, if possible, into the semblance of Englishmen and Christians. By entering a dialogue of conversion with what Williams had called "the People of *America*,"[204] the people of New England would attempt, rather quixotically, to avoid becoming themselves "Americans."

Chapter 5 *The Triumph of Indianism*

o escape Americanization on the Indian pattern, New England waged preventive war, through a variety of tactics, on Indian culture. As a result, less than fifty years after the establishment of the Massachusetts Bay colony, no serious physical Indian menace remained within the area of settlement. And yet, as in the colonists' conflict with the natural environment, the satisfaction of victory was marred by a troubling suspicion that they had paid for their triumph with a more fundamental moral and cultural defeat. Although the English by the end of the 1670s had gone far toward domesticating the land and supplanting its native inhabitants, in their own growing kinship with America they seemed in danger of becoming heirs to the Indians in other, less material, ways.

Patterns to the Heathen

If Roger Williams, under provocation, had contributed to his persecutors' cultural anxieties by charging them with becoming more barbarous than the "barbarians," he had also helped point the way around this humiliating accusation. Just as his own interest in the conversion of the Indians to civility and Christianity was proof that he had not yet "turned Indian," so the same interest among the orthodox colonists would demonstrate that they had not yet "turned American." By uniting themselves with the Indians in a double covenant of Grace and civility, the colonists could refute all suggestions (from within or without) that their English identities were disappearing in the powerful solvent of barbarism.[1] Unfortunately for the colonists' self-image, the goal of Indian conversion proved maddeningly elusive—in part because of the English insistence that the Indians could not hope to embrace Christianity without first embracing the fundamental elements of English culture. As John Eliot said, "I find it absolutely necessary to carry on civility with Religion." Only if the Indians acquired the European habits of "co-habitation, Government, Arts, and trades" would it be possible to wean them from their "Indianisme" to what the English regarded as a better way of life.[2]

In a letter of September 24, 1647, Eliot suggested that the process of weaning had begun. He spoke of his desire to bring God's laws to the Indians, as Moses had brought the Law to the Hebrews, "to convince, bridle, restrain, and civilize them, and also to humble them." He admitted that he had met with initial resistance, but his heart had been lifted when he heard that some Indians, though despairing for their own generation, "thought that in 40. yeers more, some *Indians* would be all one *English,* and in a hundred yeers, all *Indians* here about, would so bee." Little wonder that Eliot was so "moved" when he heard this. He assured these would-be Englishmen that the two peoples were already "one"—except for those great qualifications, civilized labor and true worship, "and would they but doe as wee doe in these things, they would be all one with *English* men." Eliot further told them that he was ready and willing to begin their religious education, in order to bring about this glorious metamorphosis.[3]

But was the Indians' prediction realistic? Eliot, of course, made the most of their prospects for conversion by regarding them as the remains of the Lost Tribes of Israel. It was also possible to take a rather optimistic view of the situation on the basis of historical analogy. England's own past, in addition to demonstrating how some English colonists had shamelessly "degenerated" in Ireland, held out the more reassuring example of how the ancient Britons had been elevated by contact with the Romans. The obvious conclusion was that if the Britons had been able to escape their barbarism, the Indians might be able to do the same—especially if they could perceive how miserable their condition was and the possibility of something better.[4] As Williams observed, "when they heare that about sixteen hundred yeeres agoe, *England* and the *Inhabitants* thereof were like unto *themselves,* and since have received from *God, Clothes, Bookes,* &c. they are greatly affected with a secret hope concerning *themselves.*"[5] Such a "secret hope" encouraged great expectations for the colonists' civilizing mission, but it also imposed a great responsibility. And while history seemed to offer a clear precedent for success, it suggested that failure would not go unpunished. Thomas Shepard called upon "*Gildas* our British Historian" for the interesting thought "that one cause why God let loose the *Saxons* to scourge and root out the *Britaines,* was their deep carelesnesse of communicating unto them [the Saxons] the Christian Religion, when they had their spirits at fit advantage: but I dare not discourse of these matters."[6] Shepard's reticence seems more than scholarly modesty when considered in the light of a possible carelessness in New England of communicating Christianity to the Indians: God might well let loose his New World "*Saxons*" as a scourge to root out these transplanted "*Britaines.*"

As Shepard defined the situation, the English had no safe alternative to fulfilling their missionary obligations—while living up to their professions of civility and piety. For not only were they under the eye of God; they were also closely (and critically) watched by the proposed beneficiaries of their example. Williams wrote that the Indians, "apprehending a vast difference of Knowledge betweene the *English* and themselves, are very observant of the *English* lives."[7] And many years earlier, Robert Cushman had reminded the Plymouth colonists of the need to serve as "a notable precedent to these poor heathens, whose eyes are upon you."[8] In 1630 John Cotton warned John Winthrop's fleet on its departure from England, "offend not the poore Natives."[9] The same year, John White emphasized the need for proper civil and spiritual leaders, "especially in such a Plantation as this in *New-England,* where their lives must be the patternes to the Heathen, and the especiall, effectuall meanes of winning them to the love of the truth." White could not have been very concerned about the eventual success of these means, since he believed that "Withall, commerce and example of our course of living, cannot but in time breed civility among them, and that by Gods blessing may make way for religion consequently, and for the saving of their soules."[10] But this expectation also increased the pressure on the English to ensure that the example of their "course of living" would indeed "breed civility," not new strains of barbarism, among the Indians.

The organizers of the Massachusetts Bay colony tried to discipline their colonists accordingly. The king himself had declared in the colony's charter that they should be so governed that "their good life and orderlie conversation maie wynn and incite the natives of [the] country to the knowledg and obedience of the onlie true God and Savior of mankinde, and the Christian fayth. . . ."[11] And while reminding John Endecott that the Indians' conversion was (as the charter also stated) "the main end of our Plantation," Matthew Cradock of the Massachusetts Bay Company acknowledged that progress toward this end must begin among the colonists: "that it [Indian conversion] may be the speedier and better effected, the earnest desire of our whole Company is, that you have a diligent and watchful eye over our own people, that they live unblamable and without reproof, and demean themselves justly and courteous towards the Indians, thereby to draw them to affect our persons, and consequently our religion."[12]

Given this early resolution, it is surprising to discover suggestions in the late 1640s that the English were not really adequate to the task—and that they might well profit from the Indians' example. In the tracts that New Englanders wrote to recruit interest in their belated missionary efforts, an unflattering comparison was often drawn between the Indians and Old (not New) England, where the tracts were published. The English ministers who contributed prefaces to these progress reports apparently found it easy, from the safe distance of three thousand miles, to offer the Indians to their lukewarm parishioners as models for spiritual emulation.[13] The preface to Thomas Shepard's *Clear Sun-shine of the Gospel Breaking Forth Upon the Indians in New-England* (1648) lamented that "We have as many *sad symptomes* of a *declining*, as these poor outcasts have *glad presages* of a *Rising* Sun among them." It even seemed possible that "if he [God] cannot have an *England* here, he can have an *England* there; & *baptize* & adopt them [the Indians] into those *priviledges*, which wee have *looked* upon as our burthens."[14]

If this scared sinners in England, at least they would not have been as disturbed as their countrymen on the other side of the Atlantic to learn that the new England that God might create in America would be composed, not of transplanted Englishmen, but of transmuted Indians. Similarly, the expanse of water insulating England from direct contact with the "Indian wilderness" surely made it more convenient for the Reverend Henry Whitfield, formerly of New England, to tell the English readers of his *Light appearing more and more towards the perfect Day* (1651), "Brethren, the Lord hath no need of us, but if it please him, can carry his Gospel to the other side of the world, and make it there to shine forth in its glory, brightnesse, power and purity, and leave us in Indian darknesse."[15] It is difficult to imagine that this sort of "Indian sermon"[16] would have conveyed the same meaning in a land where "Indian darknesse" was more than an exotic figure of speech.

But New England could not escape these sermons completely.[17] As Roger Williams noted, they occasionally came from the mouths of the Indians themselves, whence no subtle Noble-Savage irony could be suspected: "I have heard them say to an Englishman (who being hindred, broke a promise to them) You know God, Will you lie Englishman?"[18] And even in a more orthodox source, English readers could reflect with shame upon the Indian who "seeing one of the English . . . prophaning the Lords day, by felling of a tree, said to him, *Doe you not know that this is the Lords day*, in *Massaqusetts? much machet man*, that is *very wicked man, what, breake you Gods Day?*" The edge of this story was blunted by the fact that the "*much machet man*" lived "remote from our jurisdiction." Still, such incidents revealed that Englishmen were capable of becoming less patterns of piety than examples of wickedness to the Indians. "The same man comming into an house in those parts where a man and his wife were chiding, and they bidding him sit downe, he was welcome; he answered, *He would not stay there, God did not dwell there, Hobamook*, (that is *the Devill*) *was there*, and so departed."[19] The reminder that these housemates of the devil were living in "those parts" beyond the Puritan pale could only obscure, not conceal, the dismal fact that an Indian had associated Satan with colonists who should have been living an exemplary life with God.

There was other evidence that contact with the English had degraded, not uplifted, the natives of America. Indian drunkenness, bad enough in itself, became a special embarrassment in light of the notion that there was not much to distinguish an Indian who became "like a *furious mad Beast*" under the effects of a five-day binge and an Englishman who also turned into a beast when in his cups.[20] New England's ministers lamented the degeneracy implicit in the fact that some Englishmen were willing to forgo their missionary duty for the sake of the profits to be reaped by converting the Indians into drunkards. Roger Williams (who also regarded "loose coats" and "breeches" as obstacles to Indian civility)[21] was proud of his abstention from this business. "I might have gained thousands (as much as any) by that trade," he wrote in 1669, "but God hath graciously given me rather to choose a dry morsel, &c."[22] Others, less abstemious, set a different example. Increase Mather, bidding *Wo to Drunkards* in 1673, complained that

Some amongst us (who they are the Lord knoweth) out of Covetousness have sold Liquors and strong drink to these poor *Indians*, whose Land we possess, and have made them drunk therewith. What a fearful sin is that! The First-fathers in this Colony, who are now the most of them in heaven, began this Plantation, in part, out of respect to the Conversion and Salvation of the Natives amongst whom we live; but what woful degeneracy is this, that some should rise up amongst us, that out of love to a little filthy lucre, shall teach them such wickedness as before they were never acquainted with. The *Indians* are of themselves the saddest spectacles of Misery, and the most woful remembrance of the ruines of the righteous and glorious Image of God, that ever mortal eye beheld; but therefore their sin is not a little aggravated, that shall make such poor creatures more the children of Hell then they were before.[23]

Cotton Mather seconded his father by noting that the Indians themselves felt "that by the *Drunkenness* got in among them, they are made yet more *Salvages*: A *Drunken Indian*, what is he but a very *Centaur*? I pray, What are *you* then that make them so?"[24] The trade in alcohol was thus powerful testimony that the English might themselves degenerate before they could elevate the Indians. Thanks to English greed and hypocrisy, the great promise of Indian conversion threatened to end in a drunken stupor, while the colonists' hopes of serving as pious "patternes to the Heathen" proved nothing more than a dream.

"So Dim a Work" among "Such Nasty Salvages"

The Mathers' primary concern for the welfare of the English in their relations with the Indians illustrates a problem that had long plagued colonial efforts to (in Cotton Mather's words) "*Civilize* and *Christianize* the *Salvages*."[25] The colonists were fundamentally more interested in defending English culture against the potential challenge of Indianism. Consequently, the same fear of savage contamination and cultural degeneration that helped motivate the missionary effort also contributed to its failure. In order for conversion to succeed, some colonists would have to meet the Indians halfway in a cultural no-man's-land, and Englishmen were usually too afraid of being unable to make their way back home uncontaminated to risk the venture for very long.

The understanding that Indian conversion would require close and frequent contact with the prospective converts had been present in colonial thought before New England was settled. In 1612 William Strachey asked, "Now, what greater good can we derive unto them then the knowledge of the true and everliving God? and what doth more directly and rarely minister that effect, then Society? and to joyne with them in freindship?"[26] Early promotional writers in New England thus tried to assure readers at home that no real immediate danger lay in cultivating the friendship and neighborhood of Indians. Writing from Plymouth, Edward Winslow declared that "we entertaine them familiarly in our houses, and they as friendly bestowing their Venison on us."[27] Robert Cushman presented a similarly benign view of Indian-English relations: "when any of them are in want, as often they are in the winter, when their corn is done, we supply them to our power, and have them in our houses eating and drinking, and warming themselves; which thing, though it be something a trouble to us, yet because they should see and take knowledge of our labors, orders and diligence, both for this life and a better, we are content to bear it."[28]

Cushman's hint that this was, nevertheless, "something a trouble" to the English, an unpleasant duty that had to be borne in patience, serves as a reminder that the literature of Indian-English relations harbored contradictory messages. In the letters the Massachusetts Bay Company sent to John Endecott, the governor of their early Salem settlement, the company officials tried not merely to impress upon him the importance of winning the Indians' respect; they also advised him to take steps "for the avoiding of the hurt that may follow through our much familiarity with the Indians."[29] It is possible that these men were worried about bringing "hurt" to the Indians—in consonance with a promotional tract of the 1640s in which readers in England learned that "The humanity of the English towards them doth much gaine upon them, we being generally wary, and tender in giving them offensive or harsh language, or carriage, but use them fairly and courteously, with loving termes, good looks and kind salutes." But the colonists were obviously "wary" of the Indians in other ways: "(mistake us not) we are wont to keep them at such a distance, (knowing they serve the Devill and are led by him) as not to imbolden them too much, or trust them too farre; though we do them what good we can."[30] There was a basic contradiction in attitudes here, as well as an incompatibility of motives that would in time greatly limit the ability of the English to "do them . . . good."

This contradiction is apparent in the efforts of the English to learn the Indians' language. Would-be missionaries and their encouragers agreed that conversion depended on conversation. As John White realized, there could be little hope of bringing the gospel to the Indians "untill we may be more perfectly acquainted with their language, and they with ours."[31] In the same spirit, Francis Higginson, freshly arrived in America, wrote to England that "We purpose to learne their Language as soone as we can, which will be a meanes to do them good."[32] Unhappily for this purpose, the Indians' language, upon further acquaintance, impressed the English as "very copious, large, and difficult."[33] William Wood bluntly declared that "Their Language is hard to learne; few of the *English* being able to speake any of it, or capable of the right pronunciation, which is the chiefe grace of their tongue."[34] A decade after Wood wrote, New Englanders were still lamenting "the difficulty of their Language to us, and of ours to them; there being no Rules to learne either by."[35]

Roger Williams had made a tentative first step toward remedying this lack in his *Key into the Language of America*, but elsewhere he confirmed the conventional wisdom that lan-

guage was a labyrinthinc obstacle in the path of salvation. In
Christenings make not Christians (1645) he acknowledged that
his readers, having digested his definition of true conversion
and having been reminded of his work on the Indian language, would reasonably want to know what he had done to
put these ideas and skills to work. Although the opportunity
was certainly there, "it must be a great deale of practise, and
mighty paines and hardship undergone by my selfe, or any
that would proceed to such a further degree of the Language,
as to be able in propriety of speech to open matters of salvation
to them."[36]

Propriety of speech: without it there could be no "conversion" worthy of the name, and while Williams remained committed to overcoming this obstacle, he also knew that the
"mighty paines and hardship" necessary for acquiring such
"propriety" were sufficiently daunting to prevent many Englishmen from putting their hands to the work. In *The Bloody
Tenent Yet More Bloody* (1652), Williams stated his belief "that
none of the *Ministers* of *New England* [including John Eliot],
nor any person in the whole *Countrey* is able to open the
Mysteries of *Christ Jesus* in any *proprietie* of their *speech* or
Language." Because the Indians themselves lacked the "*Art*
and *learning*" that might make this task easier, Williams did
not see how anyone could master their language, even on the
most basic level, "without constant *use* or a *Miracle.*" Since a
miracle was presumably out of the question, there was simply
no alternative to "constant *use*"—and that meant constant,
close association with Indians: "The *Experience* of the Dis-
cusser [Williams himself] and of many others testifie how hard
it is for any man to attaine a little *proprietie* of their *Language*
in common things (so as to escape *Derision* amongst them) in
many yeares, without abundance of *conversing* with them, in
Eating, travelling and *lodging* with them &c. which none of their
Ministers (other affaires not permitting) ever could doe."[37]

By alluding to those "other affaires," Williams recognized
the limits that Massachusetts Bay's congregationalism placed

on the ministers' ability to engage in missionary work. Congregational pastors and teachers were responsible solely to the specific churches that had called them to office; they could not easily neglect their primary duties in order to win heathen souls.[38] But Williams's remarks suggest that more than congregationalism was involved. The necessity of talking, eating, and living with Indians simply ran counter to a deep-rooted revulsion for their way of life. Williams admitted to sharing this revulsion himself. He had done his best "to dig into their Barbarous, Rockie Speech" in order to preach to them,[39] and when the occasion of negotiating with the Indians arose, "God was pleased to give me a painful, patient spirit to lodge with them in their filthy, smokey holes." As a result, he "could debate with them (in a great measure) in their own tongue," but this ability had apparently emerged from an ordeal that only divine assistance could render endurable.[40] It is revealing of Williams's sense of martyrdom in these matters that he chose an analogy based on his impressions of the Indians' "filthy, smokey holes" to illustrate for English readers the need to wean oneself from worldly comforts: Christians should use these "as *English Travellers* that lodge in an *Indian* house, use all the wild *Indians* comforts with a strange *affection,* willing and ready to be gone."[41]

It was already an old story when Williams wrote. In 1613 Alexander Whitaker, contemplating his ambition of preaching to the Indians of Virginia, realized that many people at home would find this desire incomprehensible. Playing on his audience's amazement, he made the most of his self-sacrificing commitment:

I therefore hereby let all men know (and malice it selfe shall never disprove it) that a Scholler, a Graduate, a Preacher, well borne, and friended in England, not in debt nor disgrace, but competently provided for, and liked, and beloved where he lived, not in want, but (for a scholler, and as these dayes be) rich in possession, and more in possibilitie, of himselfe without any perswasion (but Gods, and his owne heart) did voluntarily leave his warme nest, and to the wonder of his kindred, and amazement of them that knew him, undertooke this hard, but in my judgement, heroicall resolution to go to *Virginia,* and helpe *to beare the name of God unto the Gentiles.*[42]

How many others, in the face of similar resistance, could find in themselves the same "heroicall resolution"? By 1651 in New England, John Endecott was able to claim that "there are some Schollers amongst us who addict themselves to the study of the *Indian* Tongue,"[43] but the addiction was presumably never very strong. In 1664 Charles Chauncy, president of Harvard College, argued that more financial encouragement was needed for teachers to the Indians, considering it was a labor "wherin they have to deale w[i]th such nasty salvages."[44] Despite such pleas, John Eliot had to admit in 1671, "I find few English students willing to engage into so dim a work as this is."[45] And even when a rare student, full of altruism and indifferent to the lack of financial reward, felt a call to the work, his family might object. In 1647 John Brock, while at Harvard, was "moved to study for the Indians; but," he added, "my Parents do not like it."[46] Brock's career held to a steadier course, just as English culture in New England kept as clear as possible of the peril of Indian barbarism.

In 1674 Daniel Gookin, concerned with the obvious fact that "the learned English young men" were not much interested in "learning the Indian language," proposed a solution to the problem. Gookin assumed that it was not simply "the difficulty" of the language or the "little encouragement" they received while studying it. There was also "the difficulty in the practice of such a calling among them, by reason of the poverty and barbarity, which cannot be grappled with, unless the person be very much mortified, self denying, and of a publick spirit, seeking greatly God's glory; and these are rare qualifications in young men. It is but one of an hundred that is so endowed." The rarity of such paragons of self-mortification among the English had forced the Indians to supply most of their own teachers.[47] Though this hardly spoke well for the colonists' commitment to the work, it at least suggested that the answer to the missionary crisis lay not in encouraging more English to martyr themselves to "poverty and barbarity," but in using a few promising converts to convey civility and Christianity to their still-benighted countrymen. Indian conversion could thus proceed, while the English kept their own hands clean.

To further such a scheme, Gookin suggested beginning with the youngest, most malleable subjects. He proposed "that the Indians, especially the children and youth, may be taught to speak, read, and write, the English tongue." This could be accomplished either by taking them into English families as apprentices or "by setting up one or two free schools." But there Gookin again ran into the old problem: "a suitable pious person for a schoolmaster will not be willing to leave the English society, and to live constantly among the Indians, as such a work will require." Instead, why not teach the Indian and English children together? This arrangement would "much promote the Indians' learning to speak the English tongue," enabling them "to converse with the English familiarly; and thereby learn civility and religion from them."[48]

Gookin did not pause to consider that the English children might also acquire the rudiments of Indianism from their new schoolmates. But a historical analogy that he raised hinted at a threat of contamination: "it hath been the observation of some prudent historians, that the changing of the language of a barbarous people, into the speech of a more civil and potent nation that have conquered them, hath been an approved experiment, to reduce such a people unto the civility and religion of the prevailing nation." Ireland was the obvious comparison—especially for Gookin, who had lived there. "I incline to believe," he continued, "that if that course had been effectually taken with the Irish, their enmity and rebellion against the English had been long since cured or prevented, and they better instructed in the protestant religion."[49] This argument, by suggesting that if the English wanted to be "the prevailing nation" in New England they would have to change the Indians' language to English, also implied that if this

difficult translation failed, the Indians might remain "in ignorance, and . . . in brutishness and superstition" like the Irish.
Gookin surely recalled that his countrymen had found Irish
culture both a source of "enmity and rebellion" and an incentive to abandon their own ways and adopt the manners of the
natives. It thus seems highly significant that the educational
theorist John Brinsley did not direct his *Consolation for Our
Grammar Schooles* (1622) merely toward the teaching of English "to the rudest *Welch* and *Irish,* yea to the very heathen
& savage, brought up amongst them." He also explicitly offered his plan as a means of preserving "the puritie of our
owne language . . . amongst all our owne people" in those
"ruder countries and places."[50] Gookin avoided any question
of linguistic purity in his own scheme, but Brinsley's anticipa-
tion of this problem suggests that it lurked between the lines
of his optimistic proposals.

Even so, the colonists were willing to put to the test their
faith in the superiority of English culture (and language).
In 1648 John Cotton wrote that some Indians were already
volunteering "to be trained up in English families, and in our
schools."[51] And from the earliest days of colonization there
had been indications that a system of fosterage might enable
Indian children to become apprentices to English culture.
Mine Host of Merry Mount wrote that when he agreed to an
Indian's request to have his son brought up in Morton's house,
"hee was a very joyfull man to thinke that his sonne should
thereby (as hee said) become an Englishman; and then hee
would be a good man."[52] The Puritans of Massachusetts Bay
surely would have doubted that an Indian child could be made
into a good Englishman through cohabitation with Thomas
Morton, but the Indian father's ambitions for his son were,
to English minds, highly laudable and encouraging. When
similar cases arose within the orthodox settlements, Puritan
spokesmen made much of them.[53]

There was apparently no suspicion that by taking young
Indians into service the English were welcoming a Trojan

horse of barbarism within their walls. At least the missionary promotional tract *New Englands First Fruits* (1643) presented a picture of remarkable success: "Divers of the *Indians* Children, Boyes and Girles we have received into our houses, who are long since civilized, and in subjection to us, painfull and handy in their businesse, and can speak our language familiarly; divers of whom can read English, and begin to understand in their measure, the grounds of Christian Religion." Of course, it is hardly surprising that a work designed to prime the pump of missionary contributions dwelt on success stories, and the case history of an Indian who "laboured to transform himselfe into the *English* manners and practises, as if he had been an English man indeed" was typical of the impression the promoters wanted to make. This aspiring Englishman "would be called no more by his *Indian* name, but would be named *William*; he would not goe naked like the *Indians,* but cloathed just as one of our selves; he abhorred to dwell with the *Indians* any longer; but forsaking all his friends and Kindred dwelt wholly with us."[54]

In William the champions of civility and Christianity could picture their plans for conversion working out to perfection. The metamorphosis of identity indicated by William's change of name and adoption of English clothes was qualified, however, by the inability of the English to welcome this convert into the bosom of English society.[55] The same tract that related his case also reminded its readers that the colonists were still careful to avoid too much familiarity with the Indians. And the condescending "as if he had been an English man indeed" suggests that William's progress toward a new identity was far from complete. Few if any colonists would have accepted William as a true compatriot, but they would have been quite comfortable with his desire to conform himself to English culture. Such "converts" would serve as an insulation between the English and the unapologetic, unembarrassed "savages" from whom the English wanted to maintain as much distance as possible.

Daybreak or Sunset of the Gospel

Whether or not William ever achieved complete Angliciza-tion, his example helped the English argue that they were beginning to realize their desire to "skrue by variety of meanes something or other of God into" the Indians, as Thomas Shepard suggestively phrased it.[56] Shepard took a tentatively optimistic view of the prospects for conversion in his *Day-Breaking, If not The Sun-Rising of the Gospell With the Indians in New-England* (1647): "me thinkes now that it is with the Indi-ans as it was with our New-English ground when we first came over, there was scarce any man that could beleeve that English graine would grow, or that the Plow could doe any good in this woody and rocky soile. . . . so wee have thought of our Indian people, and therefore have been discouraged to put plow to such dry and rocky ground, but God having begun thus with some few it may bee they are better soile for the Gospel then wee can thinke."[57] Perhaps the seeds of the gospel would take root and grow, however slowly, in this rocky soil—and perhaps they would flourish as good "English graine." But Shepard's imagery also implied the laboriousness of this task, as well as the cultural violence involved. Moreover, pre-mature optimism about the probable yield risked setting up false expectations.

As the Indians were gathered into towns modeled on the English pattern, as the distinction between "praying Indians" and "Barbarous Indians" began to appear in the conversion literature, and as the Indians began to "manifest a great willingnesse to conform themselves to the civill fashions of the *English*," there seemed genuine cause for optimism.[58] While attending one of Eliot's early "*Indian* Lectures," Shepard "marvailed to see so many *Indian* men, women and children in *English* apparell"—indeed, "you would scarce know them from *English* people."[59] In October 1651 Governor John En-decott, along with Eliot and other English observers, wit-nessed an Indian service in which most of the congregation

wore English clothes, and though they sang the obligatory
psalm in their own language, they sang it to an English tune.
As an eye (and ear) witness, the governor reported that an
Indian who lined out the psalm "read it very distinctly without
missing a word as we could judge, and the rest sang chearfully,
and prettie tuneablie."[60]

This scene (with its background music) might well have
struck the English as emblematic: though the Indians had not
abandoned their own tongue, they were at least using it to sing
in harmony with English practice. Endecott was sufficiently
moved by this display of cultural and spiritual consensus to
introduce the Indians to the jeremiad, "declaring our joy to
see such beginnings, and warning them of the great danger
if they should decline from what they had already come unto,
either in their knowledge, affection, or Christian practice,
incouraging them against what might damp or deter."[61] But
as among the English themselves, such warnings seemed to
anticipate the very declension they were meant to counter.
And if Endecott's rather discouraging encouragement was
not in itself a sufficient deterrent against further Indian interest in Christianity, there were still plenty of other obstacles to
"damp or deter" the natives' conversion.

Indians who ventured upon the road to conversion or assimilation left much of their own culture behind, and while
(like William) they seemed rarely to reach their ultimate destination, they were also barred from returning to the lives
they had abandoned.[62] For the founders of Plymouth colony,
Squanto's life and death in their midst illustrated this difficult
situation. And at the time of the Pequot War, John Underhill
recorded another example of an Indian interpreter whose
service to the English left him in a cultural limbo. Underhill
introduced the anecdote as "A pretty passage worthy observation," but the implications for the principals in the little story
were anything but "pretty." "We had an Indian with us," he
wrote, "that was an interpreter; being in English clothes, and
a gun in his hand, was spied by the [Block] islanders, which

called out to him, What are you, an Indian or an Englishman? Come hither, saith he, and I will tell you. He pulls up his cock and let fly at one of them, and without question was the death of him."[63] The interpreter gave the Indians his answer—and in the language that would increasingly dominate English-Indian relations. Nevertheless, despite its direct, forceful tone, it remains ambiguous. On the one hand, it is possible to regard the interpreter's response as proof that English speech and English clothes could make the man English. This man had at least demonstrated his loyalties by his willingness to kill another Indian. But for Underhill he was still only "an Indian . . . in English clothes." Though "with us," he was not "one of us." A similar cultural isolation emerged in the case of a convert on Martha's Vineyard whom the other Indians reviled for his attachment to the colonists, "for going into an Indian house where there were many Indians, they scoffed at him with great laughter, saying, *Here comes the English man*," a taunt that clearly indicated the *"English man's"* alienation from his own people—without offering conclusive testimony that he was truly English.[64]

In addition to the contempt and ridicule that prospective converts suffered at the hands of their more traditional-minded neighbors, they also had to contend with a deep skepticism among the English toward the Indians' receptivity to Christianity and civility. The missionary tracts' optimism was meant, in part, to answer persistent fears that the Indians, despite all protestations to the contrary, were far too rocky a soil for the gospel. At the same time, there was considerable skepticism toward the missionaries' own sincerity in promoting their project. In 1630, before English audiences had been subjected to full-scale assaults on their consciences and purses in behalf of the missionary effort, John White noted (without agreeing with) the objection that "the pretended end of winning the Heathen to the knowledge of God and embracing of the faith of Christ, is a meere fantasie, and a worke not onely of uncertaine but unlikely successe, as appeares by our fruitlesse endeavours that way, both in *Virginia* and *New-England*, where *New-Plimmouth* men inhabiting now these ten yeares, are not able to give account of any one man converted to Christianity."[65] Even after Massachusetts Bay in the 1640s launched its missionary endeavors, critics remained convinced that the idea was nothing more than "a meere fantasie." As Thomas Shepard admitted in 1648, "I know that some thinke that all this worke among them is done and acted thus by the *Indians* to please the *English,* and for applause from them"—and while Shepard believed that this might be true for many, he still hoped it was not true for all.[66] Whether or not the Indians were frauds, many English readers apparently suspected that the promotional tracts themselves were designed "to please the *English*"—the better to fleece them. In other words, the hopeful reports from God's vineyards in New England were "but a fable, and a device or engine used by some to cheat good people of their money."[67]

The promotional tracts seldom neglected to make an unctuous appeal for more "encouragement" from England. For example, consider the rather fulsome petition for prayers, tears . . . and money in *New Englands First Fruits*. The anonymous writers wanted God

to stirre up the bowels of some godly minded, to pitty those poore Heathen that are bleeding to death to eternall death, and to reach forth an hand of soule-mercy, to save some of them from the fire of hell by affording some means to maintain some fit instruments on purpose to spend their time, and give themselves wholly to preach to these poore wretches, . . . that even their bowels may blesse them in the day of their visitation, and Christs bowels refreshed by their love, may set it on his own score, and pay them all againe in the day of their accompts.[68]

It is difficult to say how many readers were stirred up by this rhetoric, though the tangible results brought in by *First Fruits* were slight.[69] But it is clear that New England was not about to bear the cost of conversion alone. The inadvertent irony of *First Fruits*'s title lies in the ambiguity concerning the source of the golden harvest: the Indians' souls or English purses? Several years after the pamphlet's publication, the former Salem pastor Hugh Peter, one of its original sponsors who had remained in England after the beginning of the Civil War, turned against the missionary appeals. Word reached New England that he "tould Mr Winslow in plaine tearmes hee heard the worke was but a plaine Cheat and that there was noe such thinge as Gosspell conversion amongst the Indians." And while Peter had served on a committee in the army to collect contributions, he had "yett protested against contribut-ing a peny towards it in his p[er]son."[70] Little wonder there was public skepticism when one of the promoters denounced the business as a fraud and refused to contribute his own money.

In New England, doubts about the probable success of Indian conversion grew from persistent fears of the Indians as crafty, subtle enemies who were simply waiting for an opportunity to pounce upon the English. In 1643, the year *First Fruits* appeared in London, the colonists were reaping a crop of reports that the Indians were hatching a plot against them, and ten years later the same mood of encirclement by plotting savages (this time perhaps in league with the Dutch) seized the colonial leadership.[71] Such attitudes affected rela-tions not merely with Indians who were obviously hostile, but also with prospective converts, the distinction between "praying" and "Barbarous" Indians melting under the influ-ence of overheated emotions. John Eliot tried to defend the Praying Indians from suspicions of anti-English conspiracy, but such suspicions were still strong enough to delay the gathering of an Indian church at Natick.[72] And in 1655 the Commissioners of the United Colonies (an organization founded in part to coordinate the Puritan colonies' defenses against the Indians) warned Eliot that since many of his Pray-ing Indians had proved hypocrites, he should not trust them indiscriminately.[73] English communities were also reluctant to allow the Praying-Indian towns to be established too near them, and English congregations were apparently unwilling to regard the Indian churches as their equals.[74] If Thomas Shepard thought he recognized *The Day-Breaking, If not The Sun-Rising of the Gospell With the Indians in New-England*, others could see only a false dawn, if not a sunset.

"All One Indians"

The sense that New England's missionary efforts had not been entirely successful was heightened by evidence that the Indians had enjoyed some success in converting the English to Indianism.[75] When such conversion occurred involuntarily as a result of prolonged captivity, there was at least no suggestion that the victim had actually chosen barbarism in preference to civility. And when the victim was a child, the case might have seemed even less remarkable—especially when the child was the daughter of Anne Hutchinson, whose own death at the hands of the Indians who carried off her daughter was interpreted as divine retribution for her heresy. Even so, the fate of Hutchinson's daughter demonstrated that the English did not possess an impregnable immunity against the infection of savagery. Though the Dutch eventually recovered the girl and returned her to the English, she was hardly the same child who had begun a new life among the Indians four years earlier, as John Winthrop observed: "She was about eight years old, when she was taken, and continued with them about four years, and she had forgot her own language, and all her friends, and was loath to have come from the Indians."[76]

But youthful impressionability was no excuse for the conduct of William Chessbrooke (or Chesebrough), a smith who got into trouble with the Connecticut authorities in 1649 by withdrawing from English society into the neighborhood of potentially hostile Indians. The General Court had already cast an officially disapproving eye on this sort of conduct in 1642, when they observed that "divers persons departe from amongst us, and take up their abode with the Indeans in a prophane course of life."[77] Chessbrooke not only seemed in danger of following the same course; he also posed a threat to the physical safety of other colonists since, as a smith, he could repair guns for his new neighbors. In many respects, Chessbrooke risked betrayal of his culture and national identity. In the words of the Court, "it carried (in the open face of it,) the greater ground of offence, in that by his calling hee was fitted, and by his solitary living advantaged, to carry on a mischeivous trade with the Indians, professly cross [to] the generall orders of the Country, and extreamely prejudiciall to the publique safety . . . ; besides it seemed more than uncomely for a man professing Godliness so to withdraw from all publique ordinances and Xtian society." In his defense, Chessbrooke declared that he had rendered himself harmless by selling his smithing tools, and "hee was fully resolved not to continue in that sollitary condition, but had to himselfe good grounds of hopes (if libberty might bee graunted,) in a shorte time to procure a competent company of desireable men, for the planting of the place." Under these conditions (and with Chessbrooke under a bond of £100 not to engage in any illegal trade with the Indians), the Court was willing to give him a chance to establish a properly ordered English settlement.[78]

The guardians of culture in New England proved especially sensitive to the possibility that a subtle corruption of colonial society was slowly conforming English lives to the "Indian" pattern.[79] William Wood was merely straining for a joke when, in discussing "the churlish and inhumane behaviour of these ruder *Indians* towards their patient wives," he wondered if this would "confirme some in the beliefe of an aspersion, which I have often heard men cast upon the *English* there [in New England], as if they should learne of the *Indians* to use their wives in the like manner, and to bring them to the same subjection, as to sit on the lower hand, and to carrie water, and the like drudgerie." Wood, who certainly had New England's best interests at heart, denied it: "the women finde there as much love, respect, and ease, as here in old *England*."[80] Realizing that a colony without women had limited prospects for survival, he simply wanted his female audience to know that New England would not prove an earthly hell for them.

But in the hands of a malicious adversary, such jests could conceal a sharp barb. In this *Trip to New-England. With a Character of the Country and People, both English and Indians* (1699), the anti-Puritan humorist Edward Ward seemed to suggest that, as to the character of the said English and Indians, there was not much difference: "The [New English] Women (like the Men) are excessive *Smokers*; and have contracted so many ill habits from the *Indians*, that 'tis difficult to find a Woman cleanly enough for a *Cook* to a *Squemish Lady*, or a Man neat enough for a *Vallet* to Sir *Courtly Nice*."[81] From the perspective of Europe, of course, it was a simple matter to look down on the colonials as "Indians," regardless of how this would have rankled in America.[82] There was also a peculiarly Old English attitude in the remark that the pregnant Lucy Downing made in 1637 to her brother, John Winthrop, concerning her prospective emigration to New England: "I confess could a wish transport me to you, I think as big as I am, I should rather wish to bring an Indyan then a coknye into the world."[83] It is not likely that she would have made the same wish so casually in Boston.

But even the authors of the missionary tracts, whose labors would seem to have demanded complete confidence in the English commitment to civility and Christianity, had to admit that at least some Englishmen were apparently determined to be reborn as "Indians" in the New World. The Massachusetts Bay ministers had confessed to the Indians that "there are two sorts of English men, some are bad and naught, and live wickedly and loosely, (describing them) and these kind of English men wee told them were in a manner as ignorant of Jesus Christ as the *Indians* now are."[84] William Leveridge (or Leverich), a minister who had been driven by problems in his English congregation to turn to the Indians for a more receptive audience, wrote that "it pleaseth God to help some of these poor Creatures to look over and beyond the Examples of some of our looser sort of *English,* which I look upon as a great stumbling block to many. . . . yet God gives some of theirs a spirit of discerning between precious and vile, and a spirit of Conviction, to acknowledge (oh that ours would lay it to heart) there is no difference between the worst *Indians,* and such *English,* saying *they are all one Indians.* . . ."[85] Considering that just a few years earlier John Eliot had held out to the Indians the promise of their becoming "all one with *English* men," Leveridge should have been embarrassed to hear Indians claiming that they were already "all one" with some Englishmen—not because of the Indians' progress toward conversion, but because of the vileness of the English.

Perhaps Leveridge's troubles with his English congregation had prejudiced him against the casual assumption of English superiority. After all, he hoped that his readers would "lay . . . to heart" the Indians' awareness of their shortcomings. But such tactics risked provoking a backlash. One Reverend Hanford encountered a storm of reaction when his Connecticut congregation (already inflamed with "the *fire* of *contention*") heard him refer to them in "a certain paper" as "Indian devils." Hanford's contentious people were so incensed that they complained to the Council, who discovered, upon looking into the "certain paper," that Hanford had merely referred to "Every individual among them."[86] Of course, the Reverend Hanford may have been the victim of his own poor enunciation. It is also conceivable that these "individuals" had become so sensitive to charges of Indianization that they could not retain their composure in the face of what must have seemed the most extreme expression of this charge they had yet "heard."

The Sword of the Wilderness

There was a nagging anxiety that conversion had not really eliminated New England's Indian problem—and perhaps had even helped to emphasize the colonists' own spiritual failings. There was also a much more direct and violent response to the Indian challenge, on the assumption that if the heathen could not be converted, it might be necessary to destroy their ability to compete for cultural dominance in New England.[87] This conclusion had long existed as an alternative to the more superficial optimism of a peaceful conversion. In 1609 Robert Gray argued that "surely so desirous is man of civill societie by nature, that he easily yields to discipline and government, if he see any reasonable motive to induce him to the same." But if the savage variety of "man" resisted all reasonable motives and persuasions, force was justified in imposing "civill societie" upon him.[88]

During the Pequot War, Roger Williams noted that the colonists' "great pretences" about converting the Indians rather easily gave way to the opinion that "all must be rooted out etc."[89] Under the pressure of outright hostilities, the Indians loomed in the colonists' thoughts not as souls to be won for Christ, but as the accursed heathen destined to be driven out before the advancing armies of God's New American Israel. And far from dying out with the war, such opinions continued to surface in periods of tension between colonists and Indians. In 1660 problems with the Narragansetts produced the reflection that "all candidnes and clemency towards these beastly minded and mannered Creatures seemes rather to embolden them in (not only uncivil and inhumane) but in tendency to bloody practices." In the wake of a purported attempt by some Narragansetts to kill Connecticut's deputy governor, Captain John Mason, the captain's countrymen concluded that "it is high time to renew upon the memory of these Pagans the obliterate memorials of the English."[90] Surely no one knew so well what this meant as Mason himself, who had participated in the butchery of the Pequots years earlier at their Mystic fort—an attack that in its brutality had disgusted the Narragansett spectators, then the embarrassed, uneasy allies of the English.[91]

Although as late as July 1675 the Connecticut Council was still referring to "the propagation of the Gospell amongst the Natives of this country" as a fundamental goal of their settlement,[92] such noble "pretences" (to borrow Roger Williams's word) would have a difficult time surviving the next two years fully intact. It is especially surprising that on the eve of New England's bloodiest Indian war, Daniel Gookin could seriously refer to hopes that "Philip," or Metacomet, might be converted to Christianity. Gookin himself was wary of being too optimistic about this, but he was also clearly hopeful that Philip would in time begin the pilgrimage toward conversion, leading his people after him.[93] In this quixotic hope Gookin was to be utterly disappointed. This Philip was no Macedonian asking for help, and there was in New England no Paul adequate to the task of forcing "help" upon him.[94] In a very short time the English would conclude of Philip, as Prospero had concluded of Caliban when he found that his rude servant was involved in a plot to kill him, that they had on their hands

> A devil, a born devil, on whose nature
> Nurture can never stick; on whom my pains,
> Humanely taken, all, all lost, quite lost.[95]

The war with Philip began, symbolically, with the murder of John Sassamon, "a very cunning and plausible *Indian*," according to William Hubbard, "well skilled in the English Language, and bred up in the profession of Christian Religion." Sassamon had been "a Schoolmaster at *Natick*, the *Indian* Town," but for a time had deserted the fold in order to join Philip, whom he served as secretary and adviser, only to return to Natick in repentance. There, he "did apply himself to preach to the *Indians*, wherein he was better gifted than any other of the Indian Nation; so as he was observed to conform more to the English manners than any other Indian." Presumably "out of faithfulness to the *English*," this model convert (or reconvert) also betrayed his former Indian master to his English friends, alleging that Philip was plotting against them. In return, Sassamon was "murdered" by Philip's assassins.[96] At least this was Hubbard's version of Sassamon's fate, and it has the virtue of providing (however inadvertently) a symbol of the English failure fully to bridge the chasm of culture that separated them from the Indians. The death of John Sassamon—the man "well skilled in the English Language," the man of such exemplary conformity "to the English manners," the man who sacrificed his loyalty to Philip out of his greater "faithfulness to the *English*"—symbolized the destruction of whatever shaky structure the English might have begun to erect toward Philip and his people. It was also as if the death of this paragon of the Anglicized Indian left the English free to relax their efforts to be optimistic about the Indians' prospects for conversion and to give in, instead, to their darkest suspicions about the true source and nature of the Indians' "cunning."

This is not to say that New England's ministers allowed their congregations to escape all responsibility for King Philip's War. In July 1675 John Eliot, informing John Winthrop, Jr., that Indian backsliders had used English examples as a justification for their own transgressions (they claimed "We doe but as thei doe"), expressed his hope "that one effect of these warrs may be to reform these great sin[ner]s among the English."[97] Other preachers had the same idea. Certainly Increase Mather did his best to "improve" the war as a variation on the jeremiad—a form that took on a sharper edge under the friction of Indian attacks. In *An Earnest Exhortation To the Inhabitants of New-England* (1676) Mather earnestly exhorted his audience to take notice of the signs indicating "that we have in great part forgotten our *Errand* into this Wilderness." Consequently, God was once again warning New England (as he had warned Jerusalem), "be thou instructed, lest I depart from thee, and thou become desolate without an *English* Inhabitant." Wielding "the Sword of the Wilderness" against a wayward people, God had set "*vile Indians* upon the backs of his Children to scourge them."[98]

Mather was also aware (with Thomas Shepard) of the lesson of Gildas, the British historian who had suggested that when the Britons neglected their missionary duties toward the Saxons, God had used these invaders to punish them. Drawing a disturbing analogy to New England's relationship with the Indians, Mather lamented that the colonists had made so little progress toward converting the natives. As a result, they were courting disaster: "The Histories of our own Nation Declare, that whereas there were famous Christian Churches amongst the ancient *Brittains,* yet when in process of time, they scandalized the *Heathen Saxons,* who lived amongst them, *and neglected to use means for their Conversion unto Christ.* God was displeased with those Churches, so as to dissipate and drive them out of their Land by those very Heathen Nations, whose conversion they should have but did not endeavour, let us consider of it in the fear of God." He went on to assure his latter-day Britons of ultimate victory—"If we mind and seek the things of Christ as we ought to do."[99] But his *Exhortation* had expended most of its effort toward putting the "fear of God" into people who had apparently been far more successful in scandalizing than in converting the heathen. Were "those very Heathen Nations" now engaged in dissipating and driving the English out of their land?

In *A Brief History of the Warr with the Indians in New-England* (1676), the work Mather published in tandem with the *Earnest Exhortation,* he related the story of one English soldier who was so disturbed by the colonists' initial lack of military success that he became "possessed with a strong conceit that God was against the english, whereupon he immediately ran distracted, and so was returned home a lamentable Spectacle."[100] Mather did not run distracted or make a lamentable spectacle of himself, but he used the news of English defeats to milk the jeremiad formula for all it was worth—short of suggesting that God was doubtless going to destroy New England completely.[101] The Puritans' convenant with God promised them an eventual salvation from "so dreadfull a judgment" as the war represented,[102] but in the meantime—before the mechanism of public humiliation, covenant renewal, reformation of sins, and judicious thanksgiving had time to work—New England could expect to suffer justly for its failure to measure up to God's (and Mather's) expectations.[103]

An interesting variation on the Sword-of-the-Wilderness theme came from William Hubbard, Mather's principal rival in New England as a historian of the war.[104] Despite considerable differences in interpretation, Mather and Hubbard shared certain fundamental assumptions about the war and its meaning for New England. In *The Present State of New-England* (1677) Hubbard was largely in agreement with Mather in his view that "God in his Wisdom [hath] suffered so much of the rage of the Heathen to be let loose against his people here, as to become a scourge unto them, that by the wrath of men, praise might be yielded to his holy Name, yet hath he in his abundant goodness restrained the remainder that it should not consume." The Lord punished, but he did not destroy utterly: "God grant that by the *Fire* of all these Judgments [Boston had also recently suffered one of its periodic fires], we may be purged from our Dross, and become a more refined people, as vessels fitted for our Masters use."[105]

Still, if this sounds rather Matherian, in other respects Hubbard demonstrated a reluctance to adopt the jeremiadic approach to the war.[106] Despite his talk of the Indians as "a *sharp scourge*" and despite his overheated rhetoric of fiery "*Judgments*," Hubbard explicitly rejected any suggestion that his country was peculiarly ripe for vengeance. The universality of human depravity was sufficient proof that New England was not exceptional in its susceptibility to divine chastisement. And "if Enquiry be made into the *moral* and *procuring Causes*, whereby God hath been provoked to let loose *the Rage of the Heathen* thus against us; It is not hard to give an Answer. The *Sovereign Ruler of the world* need never *pick a Quarrel* with any sort of men (the best of his Servants at all times giving him too just occasion of Controversy with them) or be to seek of

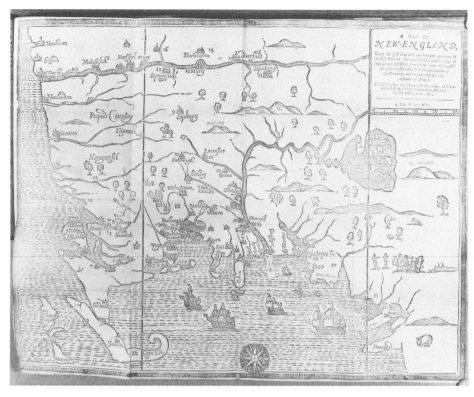

"The White Hills Map" from William Hubbard's 1677 history of King Philip's War, published in Boston as *A Narrative of the Troubles with the Indians in New-England* and in England as *The Present State of New-England.* Courtesy, Massachusetts Historical Society

a ground why to bring *a Scourge* upon them, having also other holy ends why he contends with his People; of which he is not bound to render the world an account."[107]

So much for that potentially embarrassing "Enquiry." But while God might rest undisturbed in his divine silence, Hubbard felt bound to render the world an account on behalf of the scourged party. He dealt with one delicate point by denying that New England's sufferings could be blamed on the colonists' failure to fulfill their missionary obligations to the now-raging heathen. Here, the example of the Virginia massacre of 1622 came in handy. Hubbard believed the Indians had attacked the English there "at that time when they had the greatest hopes of Converting them to Christianity."[108] Knowing that "these late *Uproars* amongst the Indians" might provoke questions about the state of the missionary work and its future prospects—as well as speculations that "the *pious endeavours*" of the missionaries "hath given the first occasion of the Quarrel"—Hubbard pointed to the success these endeavors had achieved in establishing "about *six Societies of Indians* . . . , who have *professedly owned themselves Christians*." He also noted that some of these Indians had "given *notable proof* of their *sincerity*, by fighting against their, and our Enemies."[109] In Hubbard's account, the war grew not from English neglect of the Indians' conversion but from the "natural *barbarousness* and *perfidiousness*" of the Indians themselves—as exemplified most notably by their leader, Philip, "this notorious Traitor."[110]

Hubbard did not deny that the English had done their part in stirring up the heathen—aside from the general sins that had presumably brought God's vengeance down on their heads. He added his voice to the many others deploring the greedy and foolish practice of selling firearms and ammunition to the Indians—a trade that had enabled them to fill their role as "scourges" with murderous efficiency. "It is no small Aggravation of the misery befalling a place or person," Hubbard conceded, "when it is known to be brought about, by means of their own projecting." But Hubbard preferred to confine most of the blame to those outside the Puritan colonies. "*All things considered*," he admitted,

it [the war] may be feared to spring from some *Irregularities and miscarriages* in our *Transactions* and *dealings* with the Indians themselves, according to that known Rule, *In quo quis peccatin eo punitur*, yet must not this be understood, so as to *reflect upon* the People of the *United Colonyes* in the *Gross*: . . . But it hath arisen only from such places & persons as *border* upon us *round about*, both *Southward* and *Eastward*, yet never were, nor would be, subject to the Laws of our *Jurisdiction*, nor had any *Reprover in the Gate*, or *Magistrate* to put the *Offenders* to *shame*.[111]

As further illustration of "that known Rule," Hubbard made it clear that the English who lived too far from their own countrymen and too close to the Indians (in their lives and manners, as well as physical habitation) deserved the obvious consequences: "it hath been observed of many of these *scattering Plantations* in our Borders, that many were contented to live without, yea, desirous to shake off all *yoake of Government*, both *sacred* and *Civil*, and so *Transforming* themselves as much as well they could into the manners of the Indians they lived amongst, and are some of them therefore *most deservedly* (as to *Divine Justice*) left to be put under the *yoke and power* of the Indians themselves. . . ."[112] The expansion of Puritan settlement into the wilderness was also of concern to Hubbard. One reason for the great losses the English had suffered was "the *distance of our Towns* one from the other, so as ofttimes they were destroyed, or in danger thereof, before *any notice* was taken of their danger."[113] In part, this was simply the natural hazard to be expected in frontier regions.[114] But it is likely that Hubbard was afraid that the progressive dispersal of the Puritan towns, no matter how well-ordered in themselves, was bringing the orthodox colonies into closer resemblance to the "*scattering Plantations*" that had seemed bent upon becoming indistinguishable from the Indians who wiped them out.

On this frontier ground, Hubbard again met Increase

Map of the Piscataqua River in New Hampshire and Maine (ca. 1670), showing the expansion of settlement into the wilderness, a source of concern to Puritan leaders. *Courtesy of the British Library, London*

Mather. Like his colleague, Mather was painfully aware of the vulnerability of New England's frontiers to the double threat of heathens and "heathenizing" colonists.[115] Mather also understood Hubbard's "known Rule" on the correspondence of Indianizing sin and Indian-inflicted punishment. More than Hubbard, however, Mather was willing to apply this correspondence to the professed Christians living in the Puritan settlements. The teacher of Boston's Second Church clearly had his hand in the Fast Day proclamation of February 21, 1676, which listed among the sins that cried out for redress "our sinfull heathenizing."[116] In other words, he was concerned that a subtle spiritual and moral declension had given a "heathen" character to people who, however elegant their clothes and the furnishings of their comfortable houses, were revealing a fundamental kinship with the more obviously heathen Indians. *"Consider how this Judgment is circumstanced,* If we mind where it began and by what Instruments, we may well think that God is greatly offended with the *Heathenisme* of the English People. How many that although they are *Christians* in name, are no better then *Heathens* in heart, and in Conversation? How many Families that live like *profane Indians* without *Family prayer?* . . . And in most places Instituted Worship (whereby *Christians* are distinguished from *Heathen*) hath been too much neglected."[117] Following the rule that fitted punishments to sins, it was little wonder that English captives who had been so proud of their outward appearance were "exposed to the burning heat of the sun, and burnt and tauned thereby till they became of an hue like unto these Indians."[118] In effect, the Indians had merely claimed kinship with these hypocritical English, while assisting them in bringing their appearance into a truer conformity with their inner natures.[119]

By hurling these charges at his Boston congregation, Mather was painting as lurid a picture as possible for an audience that had perhaps grown sermon-proof against other jeremiadic strategies. But as he searched for a new way to shame his listeners (and readers) out of their sinful ways, he was drawing upon a fear that ran much deeper than an occasional rhetorical variation on a well-worn theme. Mather was conjuring up the old suspicion that English manners in the American environment were inevitably taking on the taint of heathenism and wilderness. If this was indeed happening in New England in 1676, the conclusion was simple and inescapable: "If we learn the way of the Heathen, and become like them, God will punish us by them." For the future, he could only plead that there be "no more Plantations erected in New England, where people professing Christianity shall live like Indians."[120]

King Philip's War also gave Mather and Hubbard a striking example of an Englishman who had "learned the ways of the Heathen" in a more literal sense. In his *Brief History* Mather noted that at the Great Swamp Fight of December 19, 1675, with the Narragansetts (in which hundreds of Indians were burned alive in their wigwams), one unusual brand had plucked himself from the burning—namely, "a wretched English man that apostatized to the Heathen, and fought with them against his own Country-men, but was at last taken and executed."[121] Joshua Tift found time before his execution to protest that his life among the Indians had not been his idea. The Indians took him captive, he explained, and he then cooperated with his captors in order to survive. But other evidence convinced his scandalized countrymen that this "sad wretch" harbored a weakness for savagery. He had "married an Indian woman," he suffered from gross spiritual ignorance, and he had participated in the fight against the English with an enthusiasm that ill suited a mere captive. Even before the swamp fight, in which he reportedly fired on the English many times, killing or wounding several of his countrymen, he had killed and scalped a miller to prove his loyalty to the Indians. It is easy to understand, then, why Tift's capture and execution were reported as "good news."[122] Hubbard recorded his fate with a grim satisfaction that clearly indicates the horror Tift's case held for New England's guardians of civility, Christianity, and simple Englishness:

about *Jan.* 16*th* [1676], the Scouts brought in one *Joshuah Tift,* a Renegado English-man of *Providence,* that upon some discontent amongst his neighbours, had turned *Indian,* married one of the *Indian Squaws,* renounced his Religion, Nation and natural Parents all at once, fighting against them. . . . [When he was caught] he had in his habit conformed himself to them amongst whom he lived. After examination, he was condemned to die the death of a Traytor. As to his Religion he was found as ignorant as an Heathen, which no doubt caused the fewer tears to be shed at his Funeral, standers by being unwilling to lavish pity upon him that had divested himself of Nature it self, as well as Religion, in a time when so much pity was needed elsewhere, and nothing left besides wherewith to relieve the Sufferers.[123]

But it was difficult for Hubbard and his colleagues to sustain a view of the war that emphasized the heathenizing tendencies of the English themselves. Such emphasis, even when projected onto the frontier areas or renegades like Tift, tended to point out the weaknesses in the English defense against barbarism—perhaps foreshadowing the ultimate degeneration of English culture in America. It was far more convenient and reassuring to direct these fears toward the Indians, who were not simply God's scourge but scapegoats upon whom the English could focus their concerns about their own barbarous inclinations. Consequently, King Philip's War provoked exaggerated, virulent expressions of the old habit of viewing the Indians as beasts or devils, creatures at one with the wilderness through which they ranged like wolves.[124]

The logic of the Indian-wilderness rhetoric led to the conclusion that just as the literal wolves and their forest cover would have to be eliminated before the colonists could create a truly new England in the New World, so these human wolves who used the wilderness with such deadly effect against the English would also have to be driven from the land. Further, despite evidence of their service to the English as scouts and soldiers, and despite the brave efforts of some colonists to defend them against suspicions of treachery, the Praying Indians again suffered from a general reluctance among the English to distinguish them from the enemy. As Increase Mather asked, "how many with us have condemned all *Praying Indians*, crying out, they are all nought, there is not one good amongst them?"[125]

Because of this not-one-good-amongst-them attitude, when the English could not get at the Indians they were after, they all too often turned to the ones who were close at hand— usually the Praying Indians. And any Englishman who tried to defend "the poor unarmed Indians our friends"[126] was liable to draw fire as well—as Daniel Gookin, the magistrate in charge of the Praying Indians' civil affairs, discovered. "I cannot join with the multitude," he declared, "that would cast them all into the same lump with the profane and brutish heathen, who are as great enemies to our Christian Indians as they are to the English."[127] Some of the multitude decided to cast Gookin himself into "the same lump" with his Indian friends: "particularly, many harsh reflections and speeches were uttered against Major Daniel Gookin, and Mr. John Elliot, . . . as if they did support and protect those Indians against the English."[128] According to one report, Gookin's "Impertinences and multitudinous Speeches" to the Council in defense of the Indians under his administration provoked "a very worthy Person" to tell him in court "that he ought rather to be Confined among his *Indians,* than to sit on the Bench." And Gookin admitted publicly "that he was afraid to go along the streets."[129]

In response to his critics, Gookin wrote *An Historical Account of the Doings and Sufferings of the Christian Indians in New England, in the Years 1675, 1676, 1677,* addressing it to the New England Company, the London-based agency created to coordinate English support for New England's missionary projects. And though it probably circulated in manuscript in New England, the *Account,* not surprisingly, remained unpublished until 1836.[130] Public opinion would hardly have found Gookin's account of the war palatable, since he combined an apologia for the Christian Indians (and, by implication, himself) with a powerful indictment of English treachery against the people who, properly used, could have served "as a living wall to guard the English frontiers," perhaps thus preventing "the desolations and devastations that afterward ensued."[131] Instead, the English had abused this "living wall," and the sequel was a horror story for both sides.

One of Gookin's best illustrations for the Indians' side of the story came from the Praying Indians of Wamesit, near Chelmsford, Massachusetts. In October 1675, having been unjustly accused of burning a haystack, the Indians' "able men" were brought to Charlestown and imprisoned for questioning. Most of them were soon returned to Wamesit, but on the way they passed through Woburn just as the local militia was going through its exercises. The English lieutenant in charge of the Indians, sensing trouble, "held out his handkerchief as a flag of truce" and presented his commission to conduct the Indians safely home. The Woburn officers accordingly ordered their men not to fire "nor yet to give any opprobrious words." It did no good: "when the Indians were passing by, a young fellow, a soldier named Knight, discharged his musket and killed one of the Indians stone dead, being very near him." An English jury refused to convict Knight of murder, "much contrary to the mind of the bench," on the grounds that "they wanted evidence, and the prisoner plead that his gun went off by accident, indeed witnesses were mealy-mouthed in giving evidence." Despite being sent out repeatedly for further deliberation, "the jury did not see cause to alter their mind, and so the fellow was cleared."[132]

The next month, the same Indians were accused, with no more justification than before, of burning a barn—and this time several men of Chelmsford decided to ignore altogether the judicial inconveniences. On the pretense of going "to scout and look out for the enemy," they meant instead to exterminate the Wamesits: "in pursuance whereof they came to the wigwams, and called to the poor Indians to come out of doors, which most of them readily did, both men, women, and children, not in the least suspecting the English would hurt them. But two of the English being loaded with pistol-shot, being not far off, fired upon them and wounded five women and children, and slew outright a lad of about twelve years old, which child's mother was also one of the wounded; she was a widow, her name Sarah, a woman of good report for religion." The rest of the men held fire, but, as Gookin observed, "that which was done was too much, and was an action very much decried by all wise and prudent men, especially by the magistracy and ministry." This did not prevent the two murderers from being acquitted. Once again, "The jury pretended want of clear evidence; but some feared it was rather a mist of temptation and prejudice against these poor Indians that darkened their way." The Indians, in terror of the English, abandoned their homes for a time, taking "little or nothing with them; but for fear, rather exposed themselves and families to the hardships and sufferings of hunger and cold, than to be under the harsh dealing of cruel men."[133]

In fairness to his countrymen, Gookin acknowledged that the Indians' loyal services in the war helped to abate the general resentment against them, and the Indians' patience under their sufferings softened some hard English hearts.[134] But Gookin pressed his attack further by borrowing the Puritan self-image as Protestant martyrs and awarding it to the Praying Indians, who appear throughout the *Account* as "these poor Christians."[135] The tone of Indian martyrology rises to its highest pitch in Gookin's closing paragraph, where he seems to claim his place in a tradition reaching back through John Foxe to the early church Fathers and the Hebrew Prophets:

There are many other things, that I might have recorded, concerning these poor, despised sheep of Christ. But I fear that which I have already written will be thought (by some) impertinent and tedious. But when I call to mind, that great and worthy men have taken much pains to record, and others to read, the seeming small and little concerns of the children of God; as well in the historical books of Scripture, as other histories of the primitive times of Christianity, and of the doings and sufferings of the poor saints of God; I do encourage my heart in God, that He will accept, in Christ, this mean labor of mine, touching these poor despised men; yet such as are, through the grace of Christ, the first professors, confessors, if I may not say martyrs, of the Christian religion among the poor Indians in America.[136]

In Gookin's version of the war, then, the Indians' "sufferings" at the hands of the English ultimately upstage their "doings" in support of the English. And to a reader sensitive to charges of English heathenizing, Gookin's pious conclusion might well have seemed an attempt to strip the colonists of their own identity as God's saints and bestow it upon these ruder, but perhaps more deserving "professors." Still, most of Gookin's countrymen were surely determined to retain their own all-but-exclusive claim to that identity, reserving a somewhat different role for the Indians: "despised" perhaps, but certainly not the "sheep of Christ." A leader of the Indians on the northeastern frontier, one Squando, apparently claimed "to have *received some Visions* and *Revelations*" from the Europeans' God. William Hubbard found this utterly unacceptable as prophecy, of course, especially considering what this "*Enthusiastical,* or rather *Diabolical Miscreant*" was hearing in his revelations: "*Squando* doth inform them that God doth speak to him, and doth tell him that God hath left *our Nation* to them to *destroy*"—and his followers were willing enough to believe it, since they had still (as of January 1677) "met with *no Affront*."[137] But the English were not obliged or inclined to believe it, though Squando's revelations were strangely consonant with Increase Mather's warning that if the colonists did not learn their lesson, God might leave New England "desolate without an *English* Inhabitant."[138]

Rather than accept their own destruction as divinely ordained, it much better suited the still-lively English inhabitants to reinvigorate the notion, already present in their literature, that the Indians were the latter-day equivalent of the accursed peoples of biblical history who had fallen before the advance of God's Chosen People. This idea conveniently left the Indians, not the English, ripe for righteous destruction. Hubbard believed that "although the Almighty hath made use of them to be a scourge to his People, he hath now turned his hand against them, to their utter destruction and extirpation from off the face of the earth, peradventure to make room for others of his People to come in their room, and in their stead."[139]

The enemy's fate was thus a foregone conclusion. And perhaps the Praying Indians had also read enough of the Bible (or heard enough of it quoted to them) to come to the same conclusion about their own chances for survival. According to Gookin, one of the Christian-Indian leaders confessed that " 'Since the war begun between the English and wicked Indians, we expected to be all cut off, not only by the enemy Indians, whom we know hated us, but also by many English, who were much exasperated and very angry with us.' "[140] And the "wicked Indians" tried to take advantage of this situation to divide the Praying Indians from the colonists by telling them "that the English designed, in the conclusion, to destroy them all, or send them out of the country for bond slaves." There was more than a little truth in the charge. The Indians might well have been sold as slaves, said Gookin, "if the conscientious and pious rulers of the country had not acted contrary to the minds of sundry men."[141]

The newly invigorated view of the Indians as a people ripe for extermination also conveniently helped excuse past failures to make more progress toward their conversion— just as the Indians' failure to convert provided yet another justification for a more violent policy toward them. This perspective on the war lies behind the apparent contradiction in Increase Mather's treatment of its origins. While he was eager to use the Indian attacks as a stick with which to beat English backsliders, telling them that their own sins had brought this judgment upon them, he saw no reason to blame the English for provoking the initial hostilities. He carefully pointed out that the war did not begin in Massachusetts, "nor do the Indians (so far as I am informed) pretend that we have done them wrong. And therefore the cause on our part is most clear, and unquestionable." Plymouth, where the early fighting had in fact begun, could not make quite the same claim, but even there "It is evident that the Indians did most unrighteously begin a Quarrel, and take up the Sword against them."[142]

By holding tight to the colonists' assumed identity as the Chosen People of God, Mather could even argue that the Indians were fighting "to dispossess us, of the Land, which the Lord our God hath given to us." Not only were the Indians violating the will of God; they were also returning evil for the good the English had offered them. As Mather declared in the concluding lines of his *Brief History,* Philip had been given his chance to embrace Christianity, and he had turned it down. The war was consequently a righteous death to Philip and the stubborn heathen ingrates who followed him: "the Gospel was freely offered to him, and to his Subjects, but they despised it: And now behold how they reward us! will not our God judge them? yea he hath and will do so."[143] Thus, in the end, the confident arguments of biblical typology completely overwhelm any historical analogies to Britons who are justly scourged by invading Saxons for their failure to convert the heathen. Even more directly, Mather spoke in his *Earnest Exhortation* of God's "righteous designe utterly to destroy those of the *Heathen Nations* who have refused and horribly contemned the Gospel."[144]

The war also greatly affected English attitudes toward any future chances of converting the Indians. Hubbard revealingly chose martial imagery to suggest how the work might be able to proceed. First, of course, the Indians would have to be civilized, but thanks to the recent conflict, the necessary means had become much clearer. Christian history itself taught that "Divine Providence hath improved the *Roman Sword* to make way for the *Scepter of the Gospel of Peace.*" The methods the English had used before they took up the sword had simply been inadequate to the task: "That Civility that is found amongst the *Natives* of this Country, hath hitherto been *carried on* and obtained, only by the gentle means of *Courtesy, Familiarity,* and such like *civil behaviour,* which in other places was never yet attended with any *eminent success* that way." In Virginia, a bloody massacre had followed attempts to convert the Indians through "*Familiarity* and *kindness.*" New England, it seemed, could hardly hope for any better results, given Hubbard's opinion that "The generality of the Indians in *New-England* are in their *manners and natural disposition,* not much unlike those in *Virginia* living much in the *same Climate.*" Nevertheless (not to give up all hope), out of those who had been "*hardned to their own destruction,* yet *a Remnant* may be *reserved,* and afterward *called forth,* by the power of the Gospel, to give *glory to the God of all the Earth.*" These were glorious words with which to end his book, but in Hubbard's rhetoric "*destruction*" looms menacingly over the prospect of a gracious "*Remnant*"—while the ominous "*FINIS*" seems to refer as much to "The generality of the Indians in *New-England*" as to the book itself.[145]

If the English could view King Philip's War as proof that "*civil behaviour*" had failed as an Indian policy, the war also gave them an opportunity to try uncivil behavior. By this change of strategy, however, they ran the risk of unleashing any savagery that might be lurking under their veneer of civility. When Hubbard argued that the Indians of Virginia and New England were similarly barbarous and perfidious because they lived "much in the *same Climate,*" he clearly did not mean to imply that the colonists had been molded into the same disposition by their lives in that same climate. But the war provided evidence for a contrary conclusion.

In August 1675 the Connecticut Council demonstrated its concern for the maintenance of civility among the colony's troops in the instructions it drew up for Major Robert Treate, the commander of the Connecticut forces. "In all places of your travailes, march or aboade," Treate was ordered, "you are to see well to the carriage and behaviour of all under your command, that it be sober, Christian and comely, both in words and in deeds, according to Gospell profession, before the heathen and in the sight of all men; that so the name of our God be not dishonoured by ourselves while we are endeavouring to vindicate the same against the heathen's wickedness and blasphemies."[145] The phrasing of these orders carried a suggestion that more than the usual need for military discipline was at stake. In order for the English soldiers to represent civility and Christianity against heathen wickedness and blasphemy, the distinction between the two sides must remain as clear as possible. The question was, would the circumstances of warfare with the heathen (and on the heathen's natural terrain) render the antithesis of barbarism and civility meaningless? If so, as Englishman grappled with Indian, they would find themselves locked inextricably in a common destiny.[147]

For example, the English preferred to think that they were above the sort of inhuman torture they ascribed to the Indians. The mutilation of Philip's corpse was seen simply as a backwoods variation on the traditional punishment meted out to traitors: posthumously, he had been quartered, if not drawn.[148] But outright savage torture in warfare was another matter. That was the point Hubbard tried to make when he described the torture of a Narragansett prisoner by the colonists' Mohegan allies. The English, as Hubbard assured his more squeamish readers, were "not delighted in blood," but they had permitted the torture both to oblige the Mohegans and "Partly also that they might have an occular demonstration of the salvage, barbarous cruelty of these Heathen." The English were properly appalled as the Mohegans got down to business by cutting and breaking off their victim's fingers one by one, "the blood sometimes spirting out in streams a yard from his hand, which barbarous and unheard of cruelty, the English were not able to bear, it forcing tears

from their Eyes." In Hubbard's account there is less suggestion
of an atrocity that the Christians should have stopped than of
a spectacle which, however horrible, riveted the attention of
the otherwise theatrically naive Puritans in a catharsis of pity
and terror. The witnesses' pity was lessened by the Narragansett's stoicism, just as Hubbard forestalled his readers' sym-
pathies for the victim by dehumanizing him: when the Mohegans asked the Narragansett what he now thought of the war,
"this unsensible and hard-hearted Monster Answered, He
liked it very well, and found it as sweet, as English men did their
Sugar." He held to this line as the Mohegans gave his toes the
same treatment they had given his fingers, "all the while making him dance round the Circle, and sing, till he had wearied
both himself and them." After the man's legs had been broken,
the entertainment came to an end as the Mohegans bashed his
brains out. Hubbard conscientiously pointed the moral: "Instances of this nature should be Incentive unto us, to bless the
Father of Lights, who hath called us out from the dark places
of the earth, full of the habitations of cruelty."[149]

   John Easton, of Rhode Island, related that when the English took prisoner "a veri decreped and haremless indian"
and the question of what to do with him arose, "sum wold
have had him devouered by doges but the tendernes of sum
of them prevailed to Cut ofe his head." Here, then, was
the strange "tendernes" of men who were supposedly (in
Hubbard's words) "not delighted in blood." Hubbard and
Mather might well have pointed to Easton's rough-hewn style
as a clue to his competence as a witness. And Easton, as a
Quaker, was certainly not an unbiased source. Nevertheless,
his implicit testimony that some English were proving to be
more barbarous than the Indians warrants consideration: "it
is true the indians genaraly ar very barbarus peopell," he
conceded, "but in this war I have not herd of ther tormenting
ani but that the English army Cote an old indian and tor-
mented him."[150] His readers could draw the obvious conclusion for themselves. Despite their pretences to the contrary,

the Puritan colonies accumulated a rather unflattering record of their more "uncivil" responses to the Indian enemy.[151] When they seized the Sword of the Wilderness from the Indians' hands, it proved double-edged: as the colonists cut down the savage scourge, they also cut more of their ties to inherited cultural traditions. In victory, there was still defeat.

A certain measure of this defeat was evident in the material cost of victory. The war took a heavy toll in lives and property, and Indian attacks on the frontier also forced a temporary retreat from the prewar frontiers of settlement. The colonists thus received undeniable proof that after fifty years in America they still had not fully brought their environment under control.[152] The hazards of war forced a new isolation on the scattered towns and villages of New England. In Plymouth colony, at one point the danger from Indians was so great that "all Travelling was stop'd, and no News had passed for a long time together."[153] Twenty years earlier Edward Johnson had celebrated the fact that "The constant penetrating farther into this Wilderness, hath caused the wild and uncouth woods to be fil'd with frequented wayes, and the large rivers to be over-laid with Bridges passeable, both for horse and foot."[154] Now, through the Indians' attacks, the wilderness was re-claiming its losses and reasserting its old chaos over the super-ficial overlay of English order.

In providing for the defense of their towns, the English also understandably displayed a renewed concern for the safety of "out livers and weak places," as many people on the frontier were forced to become "incomers."[155] The colonial governments were careful later to see that the rebuilt settle-ments did not repeat the mistakes of the past. In October 1677 the Connecticut General Court passed an act that was not only a restatement of their social ideal and a definition of the perceived threat; it was also the Court's attempt to effect a timely cure:

Whereas by woefull experiance in the late warr, many of the inhabitants of this country liveing in a single and scattering way, remoate from townships and neighbourhood, have been destroyed and cutt off by the enemie, and theire estates and dwellings made desolate, to the ruine of such famalyes, impoverishment of the countrey and incouragement of the heathen in doeing farther mis-cheife; and that the Providence of God seems to testify against such a way of liveing as contrary to religion, societie in neighbourhood for common safety [*sic*], the posterity of such, most of them, are endangered to degenerate to heathenish ignorance and barbarisme,—this Court, for prevention of such inconvenience and evills and for common safety, doe order that for the future all plantations or townships that shall or may setle in plantation-wise shall setle themselves in such neernesse together that they may be a help, defence and succour each to other against any surpriz, onset or attempt of any comon enemie; and the Generall Court from time to time shall appoynt some committee to regulate such plantation setlement accordingly.[156]

The condemnation of the "single and scattering way" of life testified clearly to the Court's commitment to preserving the proper social and religious environment, but it also sug-gested, in its references to the "mischeife" of the heathen and the danger of heathenish degeneration among the English themselves, a sense of barely averted (but perhaps still im-pending) disaster. Despite the actual victory over the heathen, in the wake of that success New England was long recoiling from the shock. From the perspective of the 1690s, Cotton Mather could point to Massachusetts's ability to regain and even surpass its former strength. Even so, his country's resur-gence had not been complete, just as the danger to it had not ended with the death of Philip and the end of the war: "There are few towns to be now seen in our list [of the colony's towns] but what were existing in this land before the dreadful Indian war, which befel us twenty years ago; and there are few towns broken up within the then Massachuset-line by that war, but what have revived out of their *ashes*. Nevertheless, the many calamities which have ever since been wasting of the country, have so nipt the growth of it, that its later progress hath held no proportion with what was *from the beginning*."[157]

Mather's reference to "the many calamities" that had con-tinued the "wasting" of New England after King Philip's War serves as a useful reminder that the colonists' Indian problem persisted into the next century. Unlike the Amalekites, the Indians had not been completely blotted out, and at the end of the war a hostile frontier still stretched around New England's borders. In his 1678 artillery sermon, *Abraham in Arms*, Samuel Nowell warned the New English Israel that its troubles with the Canaanites were not over, even though the commitment to resist assimilation remained as strong as ever:

The Inhabitants of the land will not joyn or mix with us to make one Body, which is the more likely they are preferred to be thorns in our sides. When *Hamor* and *Sichem* propounded a firm peace with Jacobs Family, they cry *Let us marry together and make one nation* or people: a Policy used by the *French* at this day, not far from us, they may think thereby to escape some scourge that hangs over them; the issue of which we must leave to God. When God intended the Canaanites to be destroyed, he did forbid Israel to marry with them: they were to be thorns to them, and Israel was to root them out in the conclusion: therefore frequent trouble, we may probably and rationally reckon of, to meet with from the heathen. Two Nations are in the womb and will be striving.[158]

Nowell's rather contradictory message was that while ultimate success was certain, in the meantime the wilderness would continue to grow thorns to scourge the English.

By keeping alive the tradition of viewing the Indians as doomed "Canaanites," Nowell neatly disposed of any guilt that might otherwise fall upon the English. But Increase Mather worried that at least some New Englanders, caught up in the overwrought feelings of King Philip's War, had all too eagerly accepted the blood on their hands—without sufficient concern for the guilt this might bring upon them. In his diary entry for March 12, 1676, Mather wrote, "W Clarke's house of Plymo[uth] assaulted by the Indians this sabbath day. 11 persons killd. He s[ai]d to me about a month ago when I told him he should not so condemn all the Indians as he did wishing them hanged &c that then inocent blood would cry. He replied that he would say as the Jews did, their blood be upon me & my Children, which was a dreadful expression & made me fear what would come upon his Children."[159] What had come upon them was a heavy judgment indeed. Would a similar judgment fall upon the children of New England as a whole? Upon Increase's own child, Cotton, there descended with a near-crushing weight the father's concern for the destiny of New England's posterity—especially that part of it that seemed in danger of a heathenish degeneration.

Chapter 6 *"Criolian Degeneracy"*

HILE the ongoing rehabilitation of Cotton Mather's historical reputation has tended to establish him as "the first unmistakably American figure in the nation's history,"[1] Mather himself, as the inheritor of two generations of speculation about the American environment's influence on the transplanted English culture, viewed his "Americanization" with painful ambivalence. The suspicion that the American environment and the Indians were essentially incompatible with Englishness clearly did not originate with Mather. But his compulsion to dramatize New England's problems in the theater of his own career made him peculiarly sensitive to any suggestion that transplantation and assimilation to the New World had resulted in cultural degeneration.[2] Mather defined this danger as "Criolian degeneracy"—a concept through which he sought to diagnose the environmental threat to his native country's, and to his own, "English" identity.[3]

Unfortunately for Mather's image of himself and of New England, a definitive cure proved difficult to discover. Like many Americans since, Mather sought to temper his ambivalent Americanism with an alternative identity derived from his country's English traditions. Just as his environmental ideas were largely inherited, so he did not have to discover the meager consolations of Anglophilia for himself. The history of New England (and the recent history of his own family) provided examples of New Englanders who had tried to escape creolian inferiority and provincial isolation by turning away, figuratively and literally, from America. But such a strategy, as Mather would learn, was costly. It offered a compromised, ambiguous identity: at once English and American—and neither wholly. This provincial compromise, while seeming to point the way out of the creolian labyrinth, merely substituted new frustrations of its own.

John Winthrop, Jr., and the Provincial Compromise

Among the Founders of New England, perhaps John Winthrop, Jr. (son of the first governor of Massachusetts Bay and himself an early governor of Connecticut) had most to offer Cotton Mather as an illustration of the benefits and costs of provincialism as a response to feelings of cultural isolation and inferiority. "Provincialism" in this context encompasses more than a simple state of cultural inferiority.[4] It includes the provincials' awareness of an embarrassing disparity between their culture and the sophistication of the metropolis, and it must take into account their effort to overcome that disparity by remaking themselves according to the metropolitan pattern. New England's provincialism was thus a subjective condition, a state of mind that left the provincials painfully conscious of the threat that distance, time, and an alien environment posed for the transatlantic continuity of English culture. Had the Founders succeeded in transplanting England intact to the New World, such concerns would not have arisen. But when doubts about the prospects for a complete transplantation began to intrude, it became tempting to preserve a sense of Englishness by clinging to a rather attenuated cultural and emotional lifeline across the Atlantic to the homeland. It seemed to offer security against further assimilation, but it also prevented the colonists from accepting their new identity.

In many ways, Cotton Mather came to regard Winthrop as a precursor for his own life and career.[5] Like other notables honored with biographies in the *Magnalia,* he served Mather as a model against which he could measure himself spiritually and intellectually. Winthrop, like Mather, was the son of a famous father, a son who had inherited a certain burden of responsibility as a guardian of New England's most cherished values. And while Mather exaggerated Winthrop's piety (which was hardly of the parental intensity) in order to perfect the parallel,[6] Winthrop's wide-ranging intellectual interests were comparable in many ways to the even greater range of Mather's curiosity. Mather did not share Winthrop's fascination with alchemy and hermetic lore, but he was respectful of this side of Winthrop's career: Mather had his own "spiritual *Alchymie*" to set alongside Winthrop's more material variety.[7] And Mather might well have been speaking of his ideal self when he described Winthrop as a "renowned *virtuoso*" who was "a *Christian,* a *gentleman,* and a *philosopher,* well worthy to be, as he was, a member of the *Royal-Society.*"[8] But most important, implicitly, all of this was accomplished by a man who spent most of his life, not in the intellectual centers of England and the Continent, but in the relatively rustic backwater of New England.

In 1631, when John Winthrop, Jr., first set foot in New England, he was already a seasoned traveler of the Old World. His experiences in Europe, his education, and his intellectual inclinations had begun to breed in him a cosmopolitan mentality similar to that of his contemporary Sir Thomas Browne.[9] As Winthrop prepared to sail in his father's wake to America, he assured the elder Winthrop (in a gesture of pious resignation to God's will) that his travels had taught him an indifference to mere geography—as if his fledgling cosmopolitanism were largely spiritual.[10] In fact, while Winthrop was surely eager to add America to his store of knowledge, he must also have suspected that migration to New England would draw him away from the environment in which he could best follow his intellectual calling.

The transition from Old England to New was cushioned

for Winthrop by correspondence with friends in England—friends who were happy to send him books, news, and assurances that he had not completely lost touch with his old surroundings and interests.[11] Winthrop discovered, in turn, that there was some interest back home in the specimens and observations of American nature that he could provide.[12] But Winthrop's restlessness and irresolution in settling down after he arrived in New England suggest that he found it difficult to find a secure and satisfying role for himself in the new colony. He was ready to sail back to England almost before he had become accustomed to conditions in Massachusetts, and in the fall of 1634 he left on a voyage home. Before he got back to New England in the fall of 1635, he had found himself a new wife (his first spouse having died in America) and had acted as a recruiting agent for his colony in Ireland and Scotland, as well as England.[13] There were obvious personal and official reasons for this voyage, but it is easy to conclude that if these reasons had not existed, Winthrop would have found others. In 1636 his aunt, Lucy Downing, explained her own reluctance to settle in New England in terms her restless nephew doubtless understood: "for ould enlan and London, whoe that knowes them can deny the desireablenes of them, as they are in them selves."[14] Committed to a career in New England, Winthrop continued nevertheless to yearn after his homeland.

In 1641 Winthrop returned to England a second time, seizing the opportunity to forge connections with men who shared his intellectual interests. On a visit to the Continent he may have tried to entice the educational theorist Johannes Amos Comenius to New England to serve as president of Harvard, but Comenius chose to remain in Europe.[15] By September 1643 Winthrop was again "home" in New England with the exciting intellectual climate of Europe fresh in his memory. He faced anew the task of settling down in the remote backwater where fate or Providence had placed him.

In the late 1640s Winthrop, who had long been interested in the development of Connecticut, established a relatively stable home at the mouth of the Pequot River at the center of a settlement generally known in its early days as Nameaug or simply "Pequot." Eventually he would create for himself, on a site overlooking the river, the rather limited New England equivalent of an English gentleman's country seat.[16]

Yet the Indian name perversely remained as a reminder of the disparity between such a place and the image Winthrop had of its future. In 1649, when the growing "Pequot" felt the need for a more suitable English name, Winthrop's tastes almost certainly determined the choice. The town would become "New London" (and the Pequot, in time, would run more sweetly as "the Thames"). In the General Court there was some resistance to this name, on the grounds that it was far too presumptuous for a rustic plantation. Though Hugh Peter, Winthrop's father-in-law, wrote reassuringly from Old London ("Call your plantation London derry or what you please, it will give no offence here"), the Court suggested "Faire Harbour" instead.[17] They could not bring themselves to give final consent to "New London" until March 1658— and then only after citing precedents for their decision. Since the region itself was named after "our deare native Countrey," and since the names of several Old English towns had already reappeared as memorials on the New English landscape, it was fitting to "leave to posterity the memory of that renowned citty of London, from whence we had our transportation."[18] "New England" did seem to demand a "New London," and yet by giving in to that logic the General Court unwittingly furthered their country's entanglement in the frustrations of provincialism. "New London" was finally a reminder of how difficult it would be for the colonial town (and New England as a whole) to measure up to its parent.

In 1648 Winthrop's uncle, Emmanuel Downing, wrote from the Bay urging his nephew "not to burye your talents in those obscure parts."[19] Another correspondent, who wanted

Winthrop to serve as governor of a plantation in Delaware, respectfully informed him, "it is petty that your worship whom heaven hath beautified and earth hath hounnors should live in such a place as pequid whom god hath mad fitt to be guid of a greater poeple."[20] From the perspective of England, "such a place as pequid" was even more of an obscure hole in which to bury such fine talents. In 1655 the polymath Sir Kenelm Digby, who had met Winthrop in England in the 1640s, wrote, "I hope it will not be long before this Iland, your native country, do enjoy your much desired presence. I pray for it hartily." Digby encouraged him to regard himself as being wasted on New England:

Where you are, is too scanty a stage for you to remaine too long upon. It was a well chosen one, when there were inconveniencies for your fixing upon this. But now that all is here as you could wish; all that know you, do expect of you that you should exercise your vertues where they may be of most advantage to the world, and where you may do most good to most men. If I durst be so bold, I would adde my earnest prayres to the other stronger considerations, and beg of you to delay no further time in making your owne country happy by returning to it.[21]

Winthrop was surely pleased with the image of an England made happy by his return, but it was not until 1661 that he granted this favor—as an agent for Connecticut in its effort to obtain a new royal charter. After an interval of almost twenty years in America, Winthrop again found himself at the center of his cultural universe. He returned to New England in 1663 with the charter in hand, but while he was in England he had time to pursue more personal goals, reintroducing himself to the intellectual life of the metropolis. Winthrop renewed his acquaintance with men who were now hatching ambitious schemes for the advancement of knowledge that would soon culminate in the Royal Society, and he proudly accepted election as the first colonial American Fellow of the newly chartered group.[22]

In late 1659, anticipating a voyage to England, Winthrop had written from "these remote westerne parts of the world in New-England" to remind the scientific and social reformer Samuel Hartlib of his existence.[23] Bombarding Hartlib, an acquaintance from the 1640s, with questions about old friends and new discoveries, he apologized: "I am full of more quaeries but I pray excuse me thus farr, for we are heere as men dead to the world in this wildernesse."[24] Hartlib assured Winthrop that he was not forgotten—sending books, answers to Winthrop's questions, and the latest news about his own schemes for promoting the advancement of knowledge.[25] Winthrop, thankful for Hartlib's encouragement, wrote that though he was "contented with a wilderness condition," he was "not without thought of one voyage more into Europe" if he could afford the expense.[26] Having become "a stranger . . . to his native country,"[27] he was reaching out to repossess a heritage he was in danger of losing.

Winthrop's correspondence with Hartlib indicates his provincial longing for closer contact with metropolitan culture; it also provides clues as to why his intellectual affiliations made such contact all the more important to him. Winthrop's scientific interests were largely utilitarian, being focused on Paracelsian medicine and practical applications of alchemy. It was in light of these interests that the New England poet Benjamin Tompson, in his *Funeral Tribute* to Winthrop, described his subject as an *"unimitable Pyrotechnist."*[28] The same general impression emerges from a visitor's reaction to Winthrop's New London establishment in 1656: "Upon my first entrance into your home I believed I was consulting the oracles of the Tripod or the pharmacy of Aesculapius."[29] But, as this description also suggests, Winthrop's alchemical interests linked him to the intellectual community concerned with the hermetic corpus—the works traditionally ascribed to "Hermes Trismegistus." Hermeticism had many adherents in the England of Winthrop's era, including Samuel Hartlib, whose efforts to introduce to Winthrop the notion of an international society of adepti put him in touch, if remotely, with the Rosicrucian schemes circulating in seventeenth-cen-

Monas Hieroglyphica, by John Dee, the Elizabethan alchemist. John Winthrop, Jr.'s identification with Dee extended to the adoption of the "monas hieroglyphica" as a personal emblem. *Courtesy, Massachusetts Historical Society*

tury Europe.[30] Winthrop became, for Cotton Mather, "Hermes Christianus," and Tompson, referring to "His fruits of toyl Hermetically done," clearly regarded him as an accomplished devotee of the occult arts.[31]

Winthrop apparently aspired to be a New World successor to John Dee (1527–1608), the Elizabethan "magus" concerned with practical applications of occult learning.[32] Like Dee, Winthrop was an avid book collector, and his library (the largest alchemical collection in colonial America) included among its most prized volumes works that had belonged to Dee and bore his annotations. (Dee's famous library at Mortlake was in its time the greatest collection of books in England and the center of an informal academy of scholars.)[33] Winthrop's identification with Dee extended even to the adoption of Dee's hermetic device, the *"monas hieroglyphica,"* as a personal emblem. According to Peter J. French, "this astro-chemical hieroglyph was supposed to have a powerful unifying effect on the mind, and when understood and engraved in the psyche, it was to cause marvellous transformations within man."[34] It doubtless reinforced Winthrop's sense of being the heir to a tradition of learning that transcended the cultural limitations of a wilderness.

Yet such learning held certain dangers for a Puritan intellectual. Dee, a genuinely pious man, had regarded his experiments in hermeticism, alchemy, and Kabbalistic angel-conjuring as a benign and divinely sanctioned means for obtaining occult knowledge of great benefit to humanity. But not everyone distinguished these pursuits from black magic, and Dee suffered greatly from a reputation as a sorcerer.[35] Although Puritans in Old England figured prominently in hermetic and Rosicrucian circles, it is unlikely that Dee's philosophy would have been fully palatable to Puritans in Winthrop's New England, had Winthrop felt the inclination to embrace all its ramifications. In 1647 Nathaniel Ward, writing as "the Simple Cobler of Aggawam," declared: "I have ever hated the way of the Rosie-Crucians, who reject things as Gods wisedome hath tempered them, and will have nothing but their Spirits."[36] And Increase Mather, of the next generation, certainly shared the common prejudice against Dee's spiritual investigations. In condemning "the way of Familiarity with *Daemons*," Mather cited not only "a true (as well as a Romantick) Story of *Faustus*"; he also observed that "The Story of the Familiarity which was between Dr. *Dee* and Kellet [Edward Kelley, Dee's medium or skryer], with the Spirits which used to appear to them, is famously known."[37]

Winthrop's calling as a physician made him all the more vulnerable to the same charges that had been made against Dee.[38] New England ministers often studied and practiced medicine as a physical complement to the care they took for their congregations' spiritual health.[39] But a contemporary tradition regarded physicians and other scholars of the material world as peculiarly susceptible to atheism.[40] Sir Thomas Browne began *Religio Medici* ("the religion of a physician") by acknowledging that "the generall scandall of my profession, [and] the naturall course of my studies" might incline people to suppose he had no religion at all.[41] The elder Winthrop was apparently concerned that his son, who lacked a ministerial calling to balance his "naturall" studies, might fall victim to the same professional scandal that troubled Browne. As he cautioned in 1643, "Study well, my son, the saying of the apostle, 'Knowledge puffeth up.' It is a good gift of God, but when it lifts up the mind above the cross of Christ, it is the pride of life, and the high way to apostacy, wherein many men of great learning and hopes have perished.— In all the exercise of your gifts, and improvement of your talents, have an eye to your Master's end, more than your own."[42] In his long career there is little evidence that the younger Winthrop took his father's advice fully to heart.[43]

Winthrop was no necromancer or conjurer of evil spirits, and his interest in alchemy appears to have brought him only greater respect and admiration in New England. Still, his identification with an international community of hermetic scholars surely helped lift his intellectual gaze above the level of New England's cultural horizon. So did his membership in the Royal Society.[44] While in London he exhibited, among other things, the tail of a rattlesnake ("Dr. Merret took it home with him, to make some trial of the powder of it")[45] and brewed "beer" from "Maiz-bread" (it proved "a pale, well-tasted, middle beer. He was desired to keep some of his liquor for a while, to see how it would bear age"). It seems the results were sufficiently satisfactory to warrant publishing Winthrop's report in the *Transactions*.[46] In March 1663, when Winthrop announced his imminent return to New England, the Society urged him to take advantage of this opportunity for maritime experiments.[47] The experiments were a failure, but Winthrop tried to remain an active member in absentia by sending reports and specimens of "American Curiosities" to England.[48]

In certain respects, Winthrop's transatlantic communications with the Royal Society emphasized just how distant and isolated he remained in New England. From Henry Oldenburg, the Society's secretary, Winthrop learned that he and his country seemed from the perspective of London quite exotic. Oldenburg thought it was no more than one hundred miles by land from New England to Virginia and asked "whether young beavers may be disciplin'd; and how farr the Savages doe excell the English, Dutch, and Suedes in diving for them, and fetching them out of their holes?" Winthrop, if so inclined, could have inferred a vague insinuation of degeneracy in Oldenburg's earnest question whether European breeds of dogs "hold the same vertue to a second or third generation in Jamaica, Barbados, Virginia, New England, etc.?" Oldenburg had even heard that "vast numbers of the English are become as wild as the Savages, and that they destroy all accommodations wherever they come, and so remove from place to place as disorderly as the wild Tartars."[49]

Of course, Winthrop could easily correct such misconceptions of life in the colonies—if his letters managed to find their way to England. Winthrop must have been badly discouraged by the difficulty he faced in getting his reports and shipments of specimens across the Atlantic. He frequently complained that his correspondence and packages had been lost on the way, and even when the material got through, the delay could be staggering. From the other side, the problem was just as bad: a letter to Winthrop dated in England December 19, 1665, did not reach him in America until December 1667.[50]

In Winthrop's letters that did arrive, there is a persistent note of melancholy resignation at his relative isolation, especially evident in a 1668 letter thanking Oldenburg for another reminder of his membership in the Society: "It was impossible for me to forgett the happinesse of that station, when for that short time I sojourned in London they were pleased to permitt me to wait upon them at Gresham Colledge (unworthy I acknowledge of that Honour), nor can I possibly (though thus farre distant) forgett my duty to that Society. It is my constant sorrow that (*penitus toto orbe divisus*) my great remotenesse makes [me] so little capable of doing them that service to which my desires & indeavours have beene and are greatly fixed & devoted."[51] Although his remoteness in "this Wilderness" obviously added to the exotic appeal of the "rarities or novelties" he apologetically offered for the Fellows' consideration,[52] he seems largely in earnest when he refers to his "sad & serious thoughts about the unhappinesse of the condition of a Wilderness life so remote from the fountains of learning & noble sciences."[53] In Connecticut he was so "greatly separated . . . from happy Europe"—and thus all the more appreciative for "part of that content with which Christendom is so constantly & abundantly satiated, which yet makes my condition seeme the more unhappy that I am at such a distance from that fountaine whence so many rivelets of excellent things do streame forth for the good of the world."[54]

Winthrop's isolation from the fountain of culture was relieved in a small way by his contacts with men of similar interests in New England—including the Reverend Thomas

Shepard, Jr., of Charlestown, Massachusetts, who greatly appreciated the loan of Winthrop's copies of the *Transactions,* even as they contributed to his own sense of isolation: "it is no small part of our great unhappinesse who dwell in these out-skirts of the earth that we are so little acquainted with those Excellent things that are done, and found out in the world and discoursed of by those learned and worthy personages."[55] Winthrop, as the center of this provincial circle, testified not only to what New Englanders were capable of accomplishing in the larger world, but also to the inability of New England in itself to satisfy fully the aspirations of such a man. He remained a victim of compromised identity, suspended emotionally and intellectually somewhere between Old England and New.

In his old age Winthrop increasingly yearned for a final voyage to England, though his destiny in death as well as in life lay in America. In June 1675, hearing of his plans to leave the colonies, a friend begged him "not to lay your precious bones in England."[56] Winthrop died in Boston on April 5, 1676, and his bones were laid near his father's in Boston's Old Burying Ground.[57] Benjamin Tompson commemorated the occasion with a poem that struck precisely the appropriate (and appropriately inadvertent) provincial tone:

> *England* and *Holland* did great *Winthrop* woe [woo];
> Both had experienc'd Wonders he could doe.
> But poor *New-England* stole his humble Heart. . . .

And for an epitaph, Tompson offered this variation on the same theme:

> Greater Renown than *Boston* could contain,
> Doth underneath this Marble-stone remain:
> Which could it feel but half so well as we,
> 'Twould melt to Tears and let its Prisoner free.[58]

The irony here (as the subject would have appreciated) was that the man who was the dearer to New England because his fame extended so far beyond its shores had also, to some extent, been a prisoner there in life, trapped in the provincialism he could not escape as long as his destiny held him to the stony soil of New England.

Increase Mather and the Consolations of Anglophilia

For Cotton Mather, John Winthrop, Jr.'s illustration of the contradictory attractions and frustrations of a divided identity drew confirmation from a source much closer to home: Increase Mather also encountered the difficulty of reconciling an American destiny with persistent yearnings for a career and recognition in England. Like Winthrop, Increase suspected that New England was not a fully adequate field of action for a man of his abilities, and he consequently suffered from the same sense of provincial isolation.[59]

Though Increase Mather was born in New England and was thus more firmly rooted than Winthrop in America, a specifically American identity meant little to him: Indians were "Americans," Mathers were English.[60] In 1657 he left New England, apparently expecting never to see it again, and returned in 1661 only after the Restoration had spoiled his plans for an English career.[61] Having reluctantly retraced his course to Boston, he agreed to preach at Boston's Second Church only with the understanding that he would be free to leave if he chose. As he admitted in his autobiography, "I had also a great desire to return to England if liberty for Nonconformity should there be granted."[62] And he never fully overcame his aversion to a permanent rustication in Boston. In the early 1660s the city was acknowledged as "the Metrapolis of New England," being "full of good shopps well furnished with all kind of Merchandize and many Artificers, and Trad's men of all sorts,"[63] and in 1672 Mather himself would thank God for settling him in "the most publick place in New England."[64] Still, to Mather, Boston remained a backwater, just as New London and Hartford (and Boston) had been for Winthrop.

The longer Mather lived in Boston, the more he seems

to have longed for an escape to England. Imperial politics eventually gave him his chance. Thirty years after Winthrop's mission to smooth relations between Connecticut and the royal government, Mather undertook much the same errand for Massachusetts Bay. Back in England in the early 1690s, Mather—again like Winthrop—did not confine himself to the pursuit of his official duties but also took the opportunity to bask in the more sophisticated intellectual environment of London. He even found time to have his portrait painted. And like Winthrop, when his work in England was concluded, he had to return to New England—with a renewed (and still unsatisfied) appetite for the pleasures of the metropolis. The spring of 1692 found him back in Boston; by late 1693 he was contemplating another voyage to England—this time on behalf of his alma mater, Harvard College, which was itself in need of a new charter.[65] Mather professed pious, self-denying disinterest in the matter, even claiming that he was reluctant to undertake the voyage. Yet he grasped at the possibility of seeing England again, just as he grasped hopefully at what he regarded as divine assurances "that I should once before I dy, again have an opportunity there to glorify God and the Lord Jesus Christ." When in April 1696 he found himself still in Boston, suffering from an attack of gout in the knee, he considered rather guiltily that his illness might be intended as a divine rebuke for his longing after the voyage. He quickly dismissed the thought with an assertion of selfless resignation that seems less than candid, especially as he contrived at the same time to blame God (or his angelic agents) for encouraging him in his desire:

I am very willing to stay where I have Riches enough, and honor enough. I desire not one grain more of those things to be bestowed on me. I can not think of going from my Relations here, without much Reluctancy. So that if I Return to England it must be purely and only to do greater service for Christ, than in New England I am capable of. The perswasions which have bin in my Heart dè that matter, I can not help. They were wrought in me when Fasting and praying before the Lord. Also, on Lords dayes, when I have bin most in the spirit. And I have left that matter wholly with God.[66]

Increasingly, it looked as if God had decided against him. Mather had already begun to fear "that all my Faith dè an opportunity and Advantage to be put into my hands to glorify God and Christ in England, was only phansy and delusion." At times he could overcome such doubts, but at his low points he was simply at a loss: "As for the strange perswasions I have had concerning my doing service for the Lord again in England I know not what to think of it. Such things are often from Angels. I sometimes think that Angels are ignorant of some future events, but that they cause motions on the spirits of men according to what will in probability come to pass."[67] As time went by it seemed less and less probable that his voyage to England would "come to pass." The spiritual intimations that had encouraged his longing for England now drew his thoughts toward death and regions beyond England's demiparadise.

Mather resigned himself to dying in New England,[68] though the consolation he sought in scriptural parallels suggests that his resignation was incomplete. The Founders had tended to regard England as the Egypt from which they were fleeing to an American Canaan, but Mather reversed this reasoning and consoled himself with the thought that, like Jacob in Egypt, he might see the English Canaan again only through the eyes of his offspring: "However, it shall be as to my selfe, I hope my son Samuel will do service for the Name of Christ in England which is in some sort as if I did so." And of course he would be present there in his writings: "some Bookes of mine printed there will be serviceable to the Interest of Christs Kingdom."[69]

Mather greeted the first day of 1709 as "the first day of that year in which I am to dye and to go into the eternal world! Oh, blessed be God if it be so!"[70] Two years later, still alive and still in Boston, he was making the best of his situation: "I bless the Lord, for his providence in casting my Lot to be in Boston, and among a praying people who have ever had a great Love for me now for the space of near 50 years."[71]

Then, in 1715, his old ambitions were revived.[72] A new king was on the throne, and this required a new agent (or an old agent dusted off for the occasion) in England. Mather declared himself, with blatant understatement, "willing to go." But he would first have to obtain his church's consent. His loving flock unanimously refused to release him from what now must have seemed a deadly embrace: "So that I could not See my call clear notwithstanding the great desire I have had to do some Service for Christ in England once more before I dye. I am now like to dy in New England, whereas 2 months ago I was like to dy in England. My times are in Gods hands; and it is good for me to be where he would have me be. June 17. 1715."[73] On that dying fall, Mather ended his autobiography, and though he lived until 1723 his "great desire" remained unfulfilled. As he had predicted, he died in Boston, in New England.

Cotton Mather and "Criolian Degeneracy"

Increase Mather died not simply in Boston, but in the arms of his Boston-born son, Cotton, whom he had once listed among the chief considerations holding him back from his long-desired voyage to England.[74] When Increase considered that, like Jacob, he might see his Canaan again only through the eyes of his son, the son he had in mind was Samuel, not his firstborn. In 1700 Cotton publicly declared, "Indeed *New England* is not *Heaven*: *That* we are sure of! But for my part, I do not ask to Remove out of *New England,* except for a Removal into *Heaven.*"[75] In fact, Cotton Mather never removed out of New England; it is difficult to think of him outside of Boston.[76]

In the late 1690s, out of filial duty and a tendency to identify with his father's ideas and ambitions, Cotton had joined Increase in praying for the realization of his desire for a mission to England, and Cotton, no less than Increase, was puzzled and shaken by the failure of their *"Particular Faith,"* or Strange

Persuasion, in this mission to pay off.[77] But Cotton was also relieved. When Increase was away in 1690, Cotton had been terrified by the thought that his father might be tempted to remain permanently in England. He wrote an extraordinarily wheedling letter to Increase informing him, " 'Tis not a little trouble unto me to find your so speedy and sudden an inclination in you, to such a dishonorable thing as *Your not returning to New England.*" Cotton pitched his letter as a deathbed request for his father not to desert his family, his church, the college, New England, his dying son. He had "just now been within a few minutes of death by a very dangerous fever, the relics whereof are yet upon me," and he ended his swan song on its deepest note:

> I confess that I write with a most ill-boding jealousy that I shall never see you again in this evil world; and it overwhelms me into tears which cannot be dried up, unless by this consideration, That you will shortly find among the spirits of just men made perfect,
>
> Your son,[78]

Cotton was in raptures when his father overcame temptation and did the honorable thing by returning to New England.[79] And when the possibility of another abandonment arose later in the decade, Cotton had to admit that, however his spirit might yearn for the fulfillment of Increase's Strange Persuasions, "My *Flesh* indeed would be on all Accounts imaginable against my Father's Removal from mee."[80] Cotton's reluctance to part with his father was ambivalent, but, Boston-oriented as he was, he clearly abhorred the thought that Increase might permanently turn his back on his country.

Cotton was perfectly willing, however, to see Increase's prediction of a return to England verified vicariously (and posthumously) in his own biography of his father, *Parentator* (1724). "He never saw *England* any more. Now, what shall we make of This? Will it be enough to say, That he *Misinterpreted* his own *Impression,* when he thought it must needs imply, his own going *in Person* to the other side of the *Atlantic*? But that *this very Book* may sufficiently Accomplish the Praediction?"[81]

Such books were the only means Cotton himself ever found of crossing the Atlantic. Still, he was his father's son, and if he could not share the parental yearning for service in England *"in Person,"* he evidently felt the strong attraction the Old World could exert on an intellectual living in America. Increase bequeathed to Cotton an example—both negative and positive—of the accommodation possible between an English and an American identity. As if in support of the lesson implicit in the life of John Winthrop, Jr., Increase Mather pointed the way toward a provincial compromise that seemed to offer an escape, if not from America, at least from cultural degeneracy. All that was required was the ability to remain both English and American. Thus cultural identity could be harmonized with geographical destiny. But, as Cotton learned, this was not a simple matter to arrange.

Like his father before him, Cotton Mather was sensitive to the suggestion that New England had courted divinely sanctioned destruction by the heathen through its failure to bring them civility and the gospel. And, like his father, Mather cited the prospect of the heathen scourge as a fitting punishment for New England's neglect of its missionary duties— while vigorously denying that those duties had in fact been neglected.[82] This attitude, contradictory enough in itself, was only one aspect of a much deeper ambivalence. Though Mather ostentatiously labored to advance the work of Indian conversion, he could hardly conceal his contempt for the proposed beneficiaries of that work[83]—reserving, however, the full force of his anger for those *"devils in flesh"* who, by actively resisting Christianity or by posing a direct threat to the colonists' safety, merited a "Quick Extirpation."[84]

Yet the unconverted Indians' continuing resistance to extirpation and their persistent hostility toward the English served as undeniable evidence that the transplanted English culture had not rooted itself securely in American soil. This was especially true for the frontier settlements, which were still experiencing the sort of cultural instability that the coastal towns had largely outgrown. Mather was conscious of the frontier as both an extension of civilization into the wilderness and a potential point of invasion for the wilderness into the area of settlement. Accordingly, in his role as cultural and spiritual custodian, he took upon himself the task of lamenting the frontier tendency to neglect the essential Christian responsibilities, and he suggested ways of securing the continuity of culture as it moved inland, away from the established beachheads on the bay.

Mather was willing to consider that the disorderly expansion of settlement itself was part of the problem. In *Observable Things*, a sermon he appended to *Decennium Luctuosum* (1699), he rather circuitously approached this question by elaborately, and contradictorily, declining to inquire "whether those that went before us, might never be too forward in any *Unjustifyable Encroachments*, to possess and command those Lands, which have since proved so Expensive unto us." He was content simply to note that "*Older men* then I, are best able to manage that *Enquiry*, though I also have heard it made." The real difficulty lay in how those lands were settled after the encroachments, and Mather was thus more eager to inquire into the nature of the frontier's principal adversaries, the Indians, as a possible clue into the sins that God had intended those adversaries to punish. In words that would have reminded his father of the 1670s, Mather declared: "It hath been commonly seen, That when the people of God have sinfully come to *Imitate* the *Evil manners* of *other Nations*, God hath made *those* very Nations to be a sore scourge unto them. . . . Now, since the INDIANS have been made by our God, *The Rod of His Anger*, 'tis proper for us to *Enquire*, whether we have not in some Instances too far Imitated the *evil manners* of the *Indians*?" The answer, as obvious and inescapable as it had been for Increase's audience over twenty years before, explained why God was again frustrating the further transplantation of an increasingly heathenized English culture: "If we find these *Indian-Vices* to grow Epidemical among us, Oh!

don't wonder, that our God hath been, with *Indian Hatchets* cutting down the *Tree*, that brings forth *Fruits* thus disagreeable to Him that Planted it."[85]

Mather, so firmly rooted in Boston, recorded in his diary his efforts and resolutions to do something for "the dark Places in our Borders" and "to awaken" in his fellow ministers "a Concern to rescue our Frontiers, from the Vices that Strangely grow upon them."[86] Characteristically, most of Mather's own actions in this cause were literary. In his 1697 life of Sir William Phips, he presented the example of a man who, though frontier-born and a childhood companion of Indians, had overcome these obstacles to win fame, fortune, a knighthood, the royal governorship of Massachusetts Bay, and the respect of Cotton Mather.[87] And in such tracts as *A Letter to Ungospellized Plantations* (1702) and *Frontiers Well-Defended* (1707) Mather attacked the problem of frontier degeneracy much more directly.

Unfortunately, it proved difficult to pretend that the frontier evils grew exclusively on the frontier. In *Observable Things* Mather had observed that the *"Indian-Vices"* plaguing New England were "Epidemical" and not confined to the eastern regions that had felt the full force of the Indian scourge: "I do not go to charge them that were once Inhabitants of the Now Ruined Plantations, with any *Sins,* but what are more or less to be found in all our Colonies."[88] Boston itself, as far from the frontier as any place in the country, was not safe. In a Boston-aimed jeremiad of 1698, Mather pleaded: "let not those that send their sons hither from other parts of the world, for to be improved in virtue, have cause to complain, 'That after they came to Boston, they lost what little virtue was before budding in them; that in Boston they grew more debauched and more malignant than ever they were before!' "[89]

The imagery of budding virtue blighted by malignant growth (like the tree of unsavory fruits cut down by Indian hatchets) grew from the organic analogy underlying much of

Mather's rhetoric on cultural and spiritual degeneracy. With many other New England writers before him, Mather greatly valued the biblical figure of the denegerate vine. As he warned his frontier readers, "Let these *Churches,* Labour to approve themselves well Cultivated *Vineyards.* Beware, O ye *Vineyards* of the Lord, Beware lest *Wild grapes* be Cherished in you."[90] Mather suspected, however, that the growth of wild grapes from the transplanted stock of Christian, English vines was more than a matter of figurative language. In his *Things for a Distress'd People to think upon* (1696) he risked further distressing his people by giving them this to think upon: "It is affirmed, That many sorts of Inferiour Creatures, when Transplanted from *Europe* into *America,* do Degenerate by the Transplantation; But if this Remark must be made upon the *People* too, what can we do, but spend our *Tears* upon such a sad Remark? Our Lord Jesus Christ from Heaven seems to bestow that Rebuke upon us, in Jer. 2. 21. *I planted thee a Noble Vine; How then art thou Turned into the Degenerate Plant of a strange vine unto me!*"[91]

Mather's language tended to confirm the fear that transplantation to America would initiate a degrading cultural metamorphosis, as it encouraged the assumption that Indianization was the logical complement of Americanization. After two generations of English settlement, it had become possible for Mather to appropriate for himself the term "American"— without in the least implying that he was an Indian.[92] Still, the use of this word in reference to New England–born Englishmen augured a subtle, disturbing shift in identity. In 1674 John Josselyn had observed that the phrase "tame *Indian*" was applied to the English natives of New England,[93] and Mather acknowledged this usage by admitting that his son Increase was "a *tame Indian,* for so the Europeans are pleased sometimes to denominate the children that are born in these regions."[94] Harmless enough, perhaps; but the translation of the English into both "Americans" and "tame Indians" suggested that through their adaptation to an alien environment they were meeting the native Indians on a common ground of identity.

Indeed, Mather was willing to consider that the fate of being "born in these regions" had inclined the English toward what he regarded as Indian vices. In 1700 Mather conformed to the celebratory mood of an official occasion in asserting that "The *Comforts* of the *Climate* [of New England], abundantly outweigh the *Hardships* of it."[95] But in a 1724 letter to two English correspondents he raised the subject of "the strange influence that climates appear to have on the humors and manners and actions of the people that inhabit them." For Mather, this was at least one available means of accounting for the fact (as he saw it) that the American-born English were taking on the characteristics he associated with the original Indians: lying, laziness, and lax family discipline. "Now 'tis . . . observable that tho' the first English planters of this country had usually a government and a discipline in their families that had a sufficient severity in it, yet, as if the climate had taught us to Indianize, the relaxation of it is now such that it seems almost wholly laid aside, and a foolish indulgence to children is become an epidemical miscarriage of the country, and like to be attended with many evil consequences."[96]

If the Indians were "intolerably lazy," it seems the English were not much better: "Now I will not complain of my country as if they were not generally a sober, honest, industrious people; yet I must say I wish we did in this matter less answer our climate and Indianize." Perhaps Mather could not suppress a thought of his own tame-Indian son as he referred to the Indians' children as "the most humored, cockered, indulged things in the world."[97] But what were the implications for the father? Though Mather characteristically admitted that his speculations applied equally to himself, he just as characteristically deflected the point by his odd style of contradictory self-mortification:

But for the proof of the article I am now upon, I will rather excuse the rest of my countrymen and exhibit myself unto you as an object for your censures. For if I had not been inexcusably lazy, my letters this year to you would not have come short of the number which in some former years they have arisen to. My friends indeed flatter me as a man of numerous and ponderous employments, and some too wonder at my being able to apply myself unto so many correspondences and other intentions. But you will do me more justice if you censure me as a tame Indian, tainted with the vice of the climate, and rebuke me for my idleness.[98]

Mather signed this letter "Your sincere and well meaning servant."[99] But however well-meaning he was, his rhetorical tricks make his sincerity difficult to appraise. The passage is consequently a fine example of what Kenneth Silverman has called "Matherese": the verbal expression of Mather's ambidextrous personality—one aspect of which was a "self-flattering modesty."[100] When Mather offered himself as proof of the contagion of Indian laziness, he was in effect offering a refutation of the theory he had just put forth. As he and everyone else well knew, what was inexcusable sloth in him would kill other men; his "idleness" was prodigiously productive; and if he was also a "tame Indian," the phrase surely lost much of its derogatory punch. Yet Matherese, despite its awkwardly jocular tone, was dangerously double-edged. The fear of an environmentally induced degeneration had troubled him from the earliest years of his career. It was in 1689, in his first election sermon (an important professional milestone for a young minister of twenty-six), that Mather diagnosed the problem facing New England as "Criolian degeneracy."[101]

It is difficult to say just how or when Mather became aware of the concept of creolism, but as the Spanish-derived term "Creole" pertained to the history of colonial Latin America, it was loaded with significance for Mather's view of the English colonies—especially through the word's connotation of cultural inferiority to metropolitan standards.[102] Perhaps Mather read in Thomas Thorowgood's *Jewes in America* (1650) of "The Criolians, that is, the Spaniards borne in *America*," who were excluded by metropolitan prejudice from civil and ecclesiastical offices.[103] But regardless of where he found the term, he was clearly aware of its ambivalent implications. In the "General

Introduction" to his *Magnalia Christi Americana,* he used it in a relatively neutral (even positive) sense with reference to American-born persons of European ancestry—noting that he would relate "particular instances of Criolians, in our Biography, provoking the whole world with vertuous objects of emulation." Even here, however, Mather echoed the defensive manner and compensatory pride with which Spanish Creoles countered metropolitan condescension and contempt.[104]

Certainly, by yoking "Criolian" with "degeneracy" Mather indicated his awareness that a creolian identity was a mixed blessing at best. But especially significant in this context is the way Mather linked the predictable theme of generational decline to the threat of Indianization and degenerative environmental influences. Above all, the neglect of crucial cultural defenses (the ministry, the college, the local schools) had encouraged the degeneration Mather feared would be the destiny of his country. Without reform, the rising generation seemed doomed to fall: "I know not whether we do or can at this day labor under an iller symptom than the too general want of education in the rising generation, which if not prevented will gradually but speedily dispose us to that sort of Criolian degeneracy observed to deprave the children of the most noble and worthy Europeans when transplanted into America."[105]

Thus degeneration through transplantation had become an immediate danger for New England, unless the "symptom" could be corrected in time. Mather was confident that his country was capable of great things: "our little New England may soon produce them that shall be commanders of the greatest glories that America can pretend unto." But in this rather ambiguous statement the "glories" are strangely qualified by their American setting—as Mather seems to have acknowledged in the warning with which he followed his vision of grandeur: "if our youth be permitted to run wild in our woods, we shall soon be forsaken by that God whom our fathers followed hither when it was a land not sown; and Christianity, which like the sun hath moved still westward unto these 'goings down of the sun,' will return to the Old World again, leaving here not a New

Jerusalem as Doctor Twiss hoped, but a Gog and Magog as Master Mede feared, for the last of the latter days."[106]

In a variety of schemes Mather continued to fight the drift toward degeneracy: ministering to New England's (and especially Boston's) youth; circulating his tracts in Boston and the hinterlands, the better to "Antidote" the "foolish Songs and Ballads, which the Hawkers and Pedlars carry into all parts of the Countrey";[107] resolving to "scatter Books of Piety" among the sailors ("A wicked, stupid, abominable Generation: every Year growing rather worse and worse");[108] advocating *"Regular Singing"* (by note) in place of the idiosyncratic psalmody, or *"howling,"* of New England's congregations;[109] and so on.[110] In the singing controversy of the 1720s, Mather's pointed comparison of "the more polite city of Boston" to the more *"rustic"* countryside (where the English stubbornly cherished their wilderness howling) spoke subtly of a threat that ran far beyond questions of musical taste and performance.[111] The discordant antiphony of "polite" and "rustic" also suggests an inclination to rely upon a relatively un-creolian enclave of English culture (Boston) as an alternative to the more thoroughly creolized manners of colonists who had become far too well attuned to the rude American environment.[112] True, Boston itself could at times be rather discordant and rude—as when "knotts of riotous Young Men" disturbed Mather's rest by congregating under his window at night to "sing prophane and filthy Songs."[113] But beneath his appeal for musical reform was the implicit argument that the answer to creolian degeneracy lay less in loosening such riotous knots than in tightening the colonists' ties to their English identity. The country's salvation as a new England seemed to demand a retreat from America itself in deference to the standards of a distant metropolis.[114]

A Provincial Generation

Massachusetts's political metamorphosis into a province of the empire greatly encouraged the complementary growth of cultural provincialism in late seventeenth-century New England. The loss of the old commonwealth's autonomy and the arrival of a crown-appointed governor (even if he was a native New Englander and a friend and ally of the Mathers) made it difficult to continue regarding New England as a land with a unique destiny. More than ever, the colonies in America appeared as distant extensions of a nation whose center was three thousand miles away. Political "Anglicization," along with the necessary lip service (if nothing else) to English political loyalties, found its cultural and intellectual reflection in a heightened sensitivity and receptivity to English ideas and standards of taste.[115] But closer political and cultural relations between New England and Old also heightened awareness of the disparities that actually divided them.[116]

Certainly there are pragmatic political motives at work in Cotton Mather's declaration (made in 1700 before Massachusetts's governor, the Earl of Bellomont) that "It is no Little Blessing of God, that we are a part of the *English Nation*."[117] And much the same motives (in addition to a transatlantic ecumenical concern) lie behind the *Magnalia*'s vision of New England's founding as less the result of a Puritan rejection and abandonment of England than a reluctant exile or banishment from "the *best Island* of the universe."[118] Yet something more seems present in Mather's proud view of his country as the most English of all England's American colonies. For Mather, America's destiny was English, whatever Columbus might have to say about the matter: "If this New World were not found out first by the English; yet in those regards that are of all the *greatest*, it seems to be found out more *for* them than any other." And in this New English World, New England was obviously the centerpiece—as the name itself suggested: it was "that English Settlement, which may, upon a thousand accounts, pretend unto more of *true* English than all the rest, and which alone therefore has been called New-England."[119] Mather was here not only trying to make the best of the fact that New England would have to accept a new identity for itself, like it or not, as part of the greater English empire; he was also verging on the admission that this new identity might prove useful as a means of escaping the fate of creolian degeneracy. The more New England resembled Old, the more likely its people were to remain *"true* English."

But the strategy of embracing English identity as an antidote to creolism risked accentuating the cultural disparity the strategy was meant to overcome. Provincial New Englanders would have to accept distant England as the unimpeachable standard by which they must measure their own culture, and this requirement inevitably invited a sense of isolation and inferiority. Like John Winthrop, Jr., when Mather addressed his European correspondents and readers he was all too conscious of living "in an infant country entirely destitute of philosophers," an "American Antipodes," and a place (in respect of his readers in Scotland) "a Thousand Leagues beyond your *Ultima Thule.*"[120] And, again like Winthrop, Mather often assumed a self-disparaging, apologetic tone when he presented himself to intellectuals or men of rank on the other side of the Atlantic. Before them he appeared as "a rude American," "an obscure American," frankly aware that "the *addresses* of so mean a person as my self are like to prevail but little abroad with men of learning and figure in the world."[121] As a correspondent (and, eventually, a proud Fellow) of the Royal Society, Mather assumed an especially pronounced pose as an inferior creolian.[122] In a letter of 1713 dealing with "*idiots,*" he anticipated and invited the condescension he certainly feared would be forthcoming by lumping all Americans into this unflattering category—though he subtly tried to distance himself from the general infection: "If you look upon us as generally *idiots,* or but a little superior to such, we ought not to complain of you as having wronged us. And therefore you will not wonder at it that you are entertained from hence with a story of some *idiots,* but rather, that we have anybody in any tolerable manner to relate the story."[123]

Mather was perfectly aware of the exotic appeal his location beyond Ultima Thule gave to his relations of natural curiosities and other matters. As he remarked in *Parentator,* "*Mean Things* brought from a far distant Country, are Usually Well-accepted on the meer account of their being so: and as Well-esteemed as *Great Things* produced nearer Home. . . . And if this Composure be never so Mean, yet you will cast a benign Aspect upon it, for *This* very cause, *It is American.*"[124] Mather hoped the same would be true for himself as author and correspondent, though he could not forget that his "ultramarine" correspondence also "required an exquisite and an expensive Cultivation."[125] Such poses as the obscure American, the near-idiotic scribbler of "*Mean Things,*" masked a powerful craving for recognition as a writer fully comparable to the best the Old World could offer. Abject professions of humility and inferiority must have been especially painful for the man who was capable of acknowledging (even while bewailing) "that particular Lust, my Pride," with its "affectations of Grandeur, and Inclinations to be thought Somebody."[126] He could hardly have contradicted himself more blatantly when he claimed, "I even deprecate a *great Fame* in the World; I cannot with *Pleasure* think of it; it is with *Horror,* if ever I think of it."[127] Only a man who often thought with something less than horror of a great fame in the world could have found the need for such self-mortifying exercises.

Mather's desire (deny it as he would) for recognition both in New England and abroad is of the greatest importance for understanding his ambivalent image of himself as a provincial American and his interest in avoiding any personal taint of creolian degeneracy. Mather was so intensely sensitive to his reputation in his native city and its environs in part because of the importance he placed on Boston's civility and intellectual culture as counterweights to the rusticity of the New England backcountry. He knew that in certain respects Boston was becoming all too sophisticated in all the worst ways: "What! shall there be any bawdy-houses in such a town as this!"[128] And when, in 1721, his advocacy of small pox inoculation exposed him to an especially heavy dose of "vile Abuse," he saw "This miserable Town" transformed into "a dismal Picture and Emblem of *Hell.*"[129] But he remained equally aware (and proud) that Boston was "THE METROPOLIS OF THE WHOLE ENGLISH AMERICA."[130] The city's eminence thus became part of Mather's own credentials as a man of sophistication (of the more respectable sort), and he enjoyed basking in the advantages and distinction of his post in the North Church. In 1682, as a young man on the threshold of his career, he rejected a call to a church in New Haven in preference to remaining in Boston, and it is hard to believe that he would have been satisfied with anything less in New England.[131] Securely established alongside his father, he thanked God "that I should bee as unqualified for the evangelical Ministry, and as unfruitful in it, as any Man; and yett bee settled in the *Metropolis* of *New England,* and enjoy the greatest Auditories in that *Metropolis*; and in my early Youth, bee called forth on the most solemn Occasions, that these Colonies have af- forded."[132]

For Mather, the intellectual nucleus of this great metropolis was his "extraordinary *Library*," an impressive collection "ex- ceeding any man's, in all this Land."[133] And he made extensive (some would say excessive) use of these "several thousands of *Books*"[134] to produce several hundred of his own. In 1699 Mather assumed that he had already written "more Books, . . . than any Man that ever was in this Countrey, or indeed in all *America*," and Kenneth Silverman has conceded that Mather "probably published more than all the New England ministers before his time combined."[135] In 1700, well on his way toward his eventual total of almost four hundred titles, Mather feared that "People were now prejudiced against mee for printing so many Books, and it will be necessary for mee to desist from the Printing of any more."[136] He did not desist, however, and the prodigious flow from his pen continued unabated. In 1712 he boasted to a Scottish correspondent that "Our presses in this town are continually bringing forth new productions for the service of our holy religion; thereof more than two hundred, such as they are, have passed from the mean hand that is now writing to you."[137]

Mather's considerable accomplishments as a writer and scholar were testimony both to his own intellectual vitality and, implicitly, to Boston's value as an intellectual seedbed. But Mather's celebration of Boston as the brightest American jewel in England's crown was marred by a subtle tone of special pleading—as if Mather himself were struggling against the suspicion that Boston was really, by comparison to London, a rather drab and undistinguished place. He praised the productivity of the town's presses (thereby drawing more attention to his own prolific labors), but he was perhaps more concerned with keeping abreast of English and European publications: "Seldome any *new Book* of Consequence finds the way from beyond-Sea, to these Parts of *America,* but I bestow the Perusal upon it."[138] And with respect to his own works, Mather was as interested in where they were published and read as he was in their mere number or volume. In 1693 Mather, who like John Dee longed for intimate conferences with angels, had what he regarded as such a conference, in which a heavenly messenger informed him that he would publish many books in both America and Europe.[139] For Mather, this was no less than divine confirmation of his own ambitions, and he did his best to make the angel's prophecy come true. In 1697 he thanked God for allowing his works "to bee readd, and priz'd, and serviceable, not only all over these *American* Colonies, but in *Europe* also."[140] His "many Writings" did indeed find readers "in both *Englands,*"[141] and even though Mather agonized over the fate of manuscripts (especially his *Magnalia*) that he shipped to England, he still accepted the risks of the crossing and eagerly awaited news of his works' safe arrival and publication.[142]

But the ambition to publish in Old England as well as New subjected Mather to the vagaries of English literary taste, and he was subject to fits of disappointment and authorial rancor when English approval was not forthcoming. After 1710 Mather could point to his honorary doctorate from the University of Glasgow and, after 1713, to his Fellowship in the Royal Society as evidence of his professional standing outside New England.[143] But these honors made little difference to the English printers he tried to interest in tackling what he regarded as his masterpiece, his *Biblia Americana*—a massive biblical commentary that was far too great a challenge for the New England presses. Mather deeply resented this rejection, not least because he had invested much pride as an American in the work. As the title implied, Mather conceived of *Biblia Americana* as "AN AMERICAN OFFER *to serve the Great Interests of Learning and Religion in Europe.*"[144] But Europe was apparently not impressed, and Mather's image of himself as an American author worthy of the Old World's respect was seriously damaged. He doggedly continued to pursue English sponsors for *Biblia,* but with diminishing hopes for success.[145]

As the prospects for getting *Biblia* into print grew worse, Mather's usual self-contradictory professions of humility and unworthiness took on a sharper undertone of bitterness. In a typically "creolian" fashion, he became more pointedly defensive of his American, New England identity. In October 1715, with *Biblia* still in Boston and still in manuscript (the location and condition in which it remains today), Mather complained that English opinion seemed to hold "that a poor American must never be allowed capable of doing anything worth anyone's regarding, or to have ever looked in a book. And the truth is, we are under such disadvantages that if we do anything to purpose, it must carry in it a tacit rebuke to the sloth of people more advantageously circumstanced." Thus Mather was willing to acknowledge his "disadvantages"—but primarily as a means of pointing up English "sloth." By comparison, America's merely circumstantial inferiority seemed more honorable. The English language itself even came under attack as an obstacle to publication: "Had not the work been in the English tongue, my correspondents in the most illustrious Frederician University, who have put singular marks of their favor upon me, would soon bring it into the light."[146]

If *Biblia* brought Mather grief because it never saw the light of publication, other work that did make it into print proved equally a source of pain and bitterness. Mather was pleased to learn that his beloved *Magnalia Christi Americana* had received some favorable notice in England,[147] but he was far more affected by the hostile criticism it also received. Mather offered the *Magnalia,* like the *Biblia,* as a specifically American work, and his specifically American pride was implicated in its fate.[148] He attempted to present the history of New England in a form and style that would command the attention and respect of sophisticated readers. In practice, this meant that while he used a variety of styles in the course of the work, he generally aimed at a mark somewhat above the level of the New England Plain Style. Mather knew how to work within this tradition when it suited his purposes, but more often in the *Magnalia* his purposes tempted him to try for an impressive array of erudition and baroque wit.

In his "General Introduction" Mather offered this revealing apology for his odd blend of the Plain Style and the Baroque: "I cannot say whether the style wherein this Church-History is written, will please the modern cricks: but if I seem to have used . . . a simple, submiss, humble style, 'tis the same that Eusebius affirms to have been used by Hegesippus, . . . Whereas others, it may be, will reckon the *style* embellished with too much of *ornament,* by the multiplicd references to other and former concerns, closely couched, for the observation of the attentive, in almost every paragraph. . . ."[149] Indeed: the *Magnalia* has probably left few readers with the impression that Mather erred on the side of simplicity, submission, or humility. He was clearly justified in supposing that some of "the modern cricks" would not relish his "*ornament.*" Nevertheless, Mather was determined bravely to follow his own inclinations in this matter, confident that cosmopolitan readers of good taste would approve his judgment: "I observe that learned men have been so terrified by the reproaches of pedantry, which little smatterers at reading and learning have, by their quoting humours, brought upon themselves, that, for to avoid all approaches towards that which those feeble creatures have gone to imitate, the best way of writing has been most injuriously deserted. But what shall we say? The best way of writing under heaven shall be the worst, when Erasmus, his monosyllable tyrant, will have it so!"[150] Mather, ostensibly secure in his own erudition and sublimely contemptuous of monosyllable tyrants, indulged his "quoting humours" in the creation of an ornate Burtonian tapestry of "multiplied references."[151]

But in his adoption of a style rich in quotation and ornament, Mather made of the *Magnalia* a massive emblem of his ambivalence toward a purely New England or American identity. A half-century earlier the Reverend Thomas Hooker of Hartford, Connecticut, recognizing a consonance between the plain frontier environment of New England and the Puritan Plain Style, hinted that the colonists' favored form of literary expression, though imported from England, might also become a peculiarly American form of expression. The combination of the Plain Style and America suggested a mutually reinforcing symmetry of language and landscape. As Hooker declared in his *Survey of the Summe of Church-Discipline* (1648),

That the discourse comes forth in such a homely dresse and course habit, the Reader must be desired to consider, It comes *out of the wildernesse,* where curiosity is not studied. Planters if they can provide cloth to go warm, they leave the cutts and lace to those that study to go fine.

As it is beyond my skill, so I professe it is beyond my care to please the nicenesse of mens palates, with any quaintnesse of language. They who covet more sauce then meat, they must provide cooks to their minde.[152]

The *Magnalia,* however, did not come forth in a homely dress or coarse habit. Mather was closely attentive to his verbal "cutts and lace" as he attempted "to go fine." And to please diners with the nicest palates, he ladled on the sauce rather thickly.

In New England—and very close to home—there was apparently some suspicion that Mather had wandered too far from the plain and narrow. Increase Mather, in a preface to one section of the *Magnalia,* praised the contents but curiously reserved judgment on the style: "Whether what is herewith emitted and written by my *son* be, as to the *manner* of it, well performed, I have nothing to say, but shall leave it unto others to judge, as they shall see cause; only as to the *matter* of the history, I am ascertained that things are truly related."[153] Mather's style left him exposed in a vulnerable position, caught midway between the traditions of Puritan taste in New England and the sophisticated audience he hoped to address in England. He had abandoned a creolian plainness in language, just as he had stopped his ears against creolian psalmody, to embrace an ornate prose that he believed would please and impress readers beyond the Atlantic. The style of the *Magnalia* thus appears as both a retreat from an incipient American tradition and the compromise of a distinct American identity with English provincialism. The problem for Mather was that England itself had begun to lose its taste for the style he favored. What he supposed was "The best way of writing under heaven" had come to seem a bit dated under the skies of Augustan England. Mather fell, stylistically, somewhere in mid-Atlantic, in danger of drowning in his own baroque richness.[154]

Mather could at least claim that he had invited the worst. He admitted he could have "Anagrammatized" his name into anonymity. Instead, he trumpeted his authorship: "I freely confess, 'tis COTTON MATHER that has written all these things; *Me, me, adsum qui scripsi; in me convertite ferrum.* ['I wrote it!— I!—vent all your spite on me!']"[155] Some readers were apparently eager to oblige him. The criticism that rankled most came from a fellow historian (and therefore rival), John Oldmixon. In the second edition of *The British Empire in America* (1741) Oldmixon would find flattering things to say about the state of customs and manners in Boston: "The Conversation in this Town is as polite as in most of the Cities and Towns of *England;* many of their Merchants having traded into *Europe,* and those that staid at home having the Advantage of Society with Travellers; so that a Gentleman from *London* would almost think himself at home at *Boston,* when he observes the Number of People, their Houses, their Furniture, their Tables, their Dress and Conversation, which perhaps is as splendid and showy, as that of the most considerable Trades-man in *London.*"[156] But the flattery was marred by condescension—especially insofar as Oldmixon implied that Boston's tradesmanly sophistication was largely imported from England and Europe, not homegrown. And in his first edition (1708, the one read by Mather), Oldmixon certainly had not been inclined to flatter Boston's most eminent homegrown historian, the "very particular and voluminous" Cotton Mather: "there's no considerable Action concerning the Governours or Government, which is in Mr. *Mather's,* but this Historian has included in his History, leaving his *Puns, Anagrams, Acrosticks, Miracles, Prodigies, Witches, Speeches, Epistles,* and other Incumberances, to the Original Author, and his Admirers; among whom, as an Historian, this Writer is not so happy as to be rank'd." Mather's history—"so confus'd in the Form, so trivial in the Matter, and so faulty in the Expression"—reminded Oldmixon more of "School Boys Exercises Forty Years ago, and *Romish* Legends, than the Collections of an Historian bred up in a Protestant Academy."[157]

Mather returned the compliment by referring privately to "the malicious and satanic pen of one *Oldnixson* (some such name) . . . , whose history of New England has far more lies than pages in it."[158] Publicly, Mather continued the attack on Oldmixon and defended his own style against his rival's criticism.[159] But Mather may have been chastened by such censures; at least he was willing to prove that he could write

in more than one style. Regarding one of his later composi-
tions, he wrote, "I could have embellished it with many orna-
ments. But I conscientiously decline the ostentation of erudition lest I disoblige that Holy Spirit, on whom alone I depend
for the success of the essay. Besides, I have in a considerable
number of other books (besides the *Magnalia*) already pretty
well exhausted a good stock of flowers, which ought not to be
presented over again."[160] Even so, Mather could not pass up
the opportunity in his *Manuductio ad Ministerium* (1726) to
defend his "Massy *Way of Writing*"—nor could he resist taking
another shot at Oldmixon.[161] The old grudge was deeply
rooted in Mather's vanity as an author—and in his pride as
an American.

In the summer of 1720, while sending the English hymnist
Isaac Watts "a few more small American treatises," Mather
fell back on pious matter as an apology for manner: "If our
style and manner of writing be, as the historian tells us, inferior
to that of you Europeans, yet the piety inculcated in what we
write is as necessary for them, as for us who are so much
inferior to them."[162] And in a work of the same year, significantly titled *Some American Sentiments on the Great Controversy
of the Time* (namely, Arianism), he stated: "We should not be
insensible, (having been very publicly inform'd of it) *That the
Style and Manner of the* New-England *Writers does not equal that
of the Europeans*: Nor should *he* who now writes, and who
among them is the *least of the Ministers, and the lowest in Merit*,
be without a very humble Sense of his Inability in point of
Sense, as well as of *Style*, to offer any thing worthy of Consideration among the *Europeans*."[163] As always, Mather's confes-
sions of humility are highly ambiguous, and though he ostentatiously parades his inferiority, he is nonetheless pointedly
offering "American" sentiments on "the Great Controversy
of the Time." The double-edged rhetoric of "Matherese"
thus permitted and encouraged the characteristic provincial
compensation for cultural inferiority in an assumption of
moral superiority.

But this aspect of the provincial compromise was ultimately a poor consolation for persistent suspicions of creolian degeneracy. Mather never seems to have felt fully at ease with his divided identity as both a creolian American and an Englishman living in America. If he did not die yearning for a "return" to England, he nevertheless lived out his life in a cultural environment that drew his thoughts toward England while confronting him with uniquely American challenges. Cotton Mather, as "Criolian" and ambivalent Anglophile, is indeed fit to stand as "the first unmistakably American figure"—especially because of the mixed feelings with which he would have resigned himself to the role.[164]

Epilogue

o escape the peculiar frustrations implicit in Cotton Mather's life, it would paradoxically require a more fully provincial generation— one less committed to an inherited American identity and mission, such as Mather represented, and thus freer to attempt an escape from the creolian labyrinth into the less demanding identity of provincial Englishness. New England's intellectuals could then be in a position to reconcile their cultural aspirations with the frank acceptance of their native land as a remote backwater of the empire. They could still look for refreshment to England, where the fountains of culture flowed uncontaminated by American influences—a response that later generations of American intellectuals would continue to find attractive.

Mather, hedging his bets to the last, was finally unable to make his American-English compromise work. But he lived to see a generation that seemed more at ease as English provincials and much less concerned with the need to define themselves, culturally or politically, as Americans. He could have seen the harbinger of mature provincialism in the cosmopolitan style of Benjamin Colman, John Barnard, and other, younger, colleagues in New England's pulpits.[1] He could have read the same signs, although in somewhat different language, in the imitation Augustan wit and satire of Silence Dogood and the "learned *witlings*" of the Boston coffee houses.[2] Mistress Dogood, above all, by lampooning Mather's pose of deep piety and intellectual sophistication, threatened to bring the infection of Oldmixonism within the gates of Boston itself.[3]

Silence Dogood and her gossips were clearly not encumbered with the responsibility of maintaining the Puritan tradition in New England. Consequently, they were more willing to give in to the provincial undertow that was pulling them away from America and toward England—leaving Mather, attached to his American lifeline, struggling in mid-ocean (Silence's own birthplace).[4] Even as the new generation continued to live in America, they accepted it as simply a dim reflection of the English metropolis. When the young Benjamin Franklin looked about him for intellectual and literary models, he looked outward and eastward, toward Addison and *The Spectator,* Newton, Locke, and other leading figures in English thought—not inward toward a more native New England tradition represented by Hooker, Cotton, Shepard . . . or Cotton Mather.[5] Franklin later acknowledged Mather, the erstwhile butt of Silence Dogood's wit, as an influence on his sense of public responsibility, but he pursued his own schemes to "do good" in a spirit for which Mather would have been reluctant to claim responsibility.[6]

Franklin's provincialism suggests that a ready submission to cultural Anglicization was in effect a means of resisting Americanization—or even Germanization. In 1751, after he had transplanted himself from Boston to Philadelphia, he looked forward to the ultimate confirmation of America's Englishness in the day when "the greatest Number of *Englishmen* will be on this Side the Water." But in the meantime, Pennsylvania had to survive the influence of "*Palatine Boors*" who shared Franklin's attraction to the colony. "Why should *Pennsylvania,*" Franklin asked, "founded by the *English,* become a Colony of *Aliens,* who will shortly be so numerous as to Germanize us instead of our Anglifying them. . . ."[7] But Franklin's wholehearted devotion to "Anglifying" himself was ultimately as unsatisfactory as Mather's halfhearted efforts.[8] In fact, Mather would have been largely justified in regarding Franklin as a perverse, unforeseen manifestation of progressive creolization. The irony of Franklin's role is that he illustrates the extent to which Anglicization itself was a symptom of Americanization—insofar as it fostered the growth of provincial "Englishmen" who regarded their English identity as a pose to be imitated from distant metropolitan models, then artificially maintained and coddled in an American environment.

Despite Franklin's continuing efforts to refute charges of American degeneracy,[9] and despite the superficial Anglicization of provincial institutions and material culture, American Anglophilia in the early eighteenth century merely confirmed the actual cultural gap that had grown between Old England and New. Residents of England's own cultural backwaters might be subject to the sorrows of provincialism, but it is unlikely that they suffered also from Anglophilia. The people of Old England did not have to work at being English: they simply accepted their identity as their birthright. When New Englanders began trying to be "English" in painfully self-conscious ways—nurturing their prized identity like the exotic, transplanted sprout it was—they were revealing that they had already become something else. What they had become was not readily apparent to them, of course. It would not be convenient to inquire further into the characteristics that distinguished Americans from the English until relations between England and its American colonies had reached a stage in which reconsiderations of national interest and identity were inescapable.

In 1775, when a group of creolians held the British-occupied city of Boston under siege, a British customs officer named Henry Hulton was certainly not inclined to embrace as fellow Englishmen "such despicable wretches as compose the banditti [i.e., militia] of the country." There was not so much as a single gentleman among them. "They are a most rude, depraved, degenerate race, and it is a mortification to us that they speak English and can trace themselves from that stock."[10] If the ghost of Cotton Mather (that unexcelled authority on mortification), roused from Copp's Hill by all the excitement, happened to look over Hulton's shoulder as he wrote these words, it was surely the ghost that shuddered, not Hulton. Here was unimpeachably English testimony that transplantation to America had indeed transformed Englishmen into "rude, depraved, degenerate" Americans. But this did not mean that the Americans besieging Boston were on the threshold of complete cultural independence. Far from it: Anglophilia remained endemic in America, and the false promise of an alternative English identity continued to hold out false hope for Americans sick of their provincial circumstances. When Americans boldly dissolved the political bands that connected them with the mother country, they did not disentangle themselves from her cultural apron strings.

Intellectually, America long remained a province of England, and no amount of self-consciously nationalistic epics written in a style slavishly imitated from English Augustan models could relieve the dependence. Even as late as 1856, Ralph Waldo Emerson, in *English Traits,* acknowledged England's cultural hegemony: "In all that is done or begun by the Americans towards right thinking or practice, we are met by a civilization already settled and overpowering. The culture of the day, the thoughts and aims of men, are English thoughts and aims. . . . The American is only the continuation of the English genius into new conditions, more or less propitious."[11] It was a statement deeply resonant of the preceding two centuries of New England's history. The founding generation had confronted an alien environment that challenged their English thoughts and aims. The newness of those conditions and the doubtfulness of how propitious they were for the transplanted culture were fundamental considerations for the survival of the English genius in America.

By Emerson's time it had become possible to take a different view of the contrast between the Old World and the New. Struck by England's relatively artificial environment, Emerson turned westward to consider the sublime power of American nature: "There . . . , in America, lies nature sleeping, over-growing, almost conscious, too much by half for man in the picture, . . . and on it man seems not able to make much impression. There, in that great sloven continent, in high Alleghany pastures, in the sea-wide, sky-skirted prairie, still sleeps and murmurs and hides the great mother, long since driven away from the trim hedge-rows and over-cultivated garden of England. And, in England, I am quite too sensible of this."[12] The first generation of New Englanders were also "quite too sensible" of the distinction between garden England and wilderness America. From their response to that contrast grew an ambivalent provincial identity, an identity inextricably linked—as it continues to be, even as American culture has become "too much by half" for nature—to the challenges of acculturation America itself poses for its transplanted peoples.

Notes

Preface

1. In acknowledging Hawthorne as a primary influence, I draw encouragement from Michael J. Colacurcio's *The Province of Piety: Moral History in Hawthorne's Early Tales* (Cambridge, Mass., and London, England: Harvard University Press, 1984). Colacurcio, moreover, confirms my sense of the intellectual kinship between Hawthorne and Miller: see pp. 1–4 (the quotation is from p. 3).
2. Perry Miller, "Nature and the National Ego," in *Errand into the Wilderness* (Cambridge, Mass., and London, England: Belknap Press of Harvard University Press, 1956), p. 205. And see the relevant essays gathered in *Nature's Nation* (Cambridge, Mass.: Belknap Press of Harvard University Press, 1967).

Prologue

1. As an example of what I mean by the "internalist" approach, see Alan Heimert and Andrew Delbanco's *The Puritans in America: A Narrative Anthology* (Cambridge, Mass., and London, England: Harvard University Press, 1985). This collection admirably surveys the literature on the essential religious and political crises as defined by the Puritan intellectuals themselves—from "The Migration" through "The Antinomian Crisis," "The Cotton-Williams Debate," and so on— while slighting the promotional and Indian-war literature that illuminates the Puritans from a different, though no less essential, angle.
2. Examples of estimable work that, through a focus on social history, has convincingly demonstrated many transatlantic continuities in the settlement of New England are David Grayson Allen's *In English Ways: The Movement of Societies and the Transferal of English Local Law and Custom to Massachusetts Bay in the Seventeenth Century* (Chapel Hill: University of North Carolina Press for the Institute of Early American History and Culture, 1981) and (a work much closer to my own concerns) David Cressy's *Coming Over: Migration and Communication Between England and New England in the Seventeenth Century* (Cambridge and New York: Cambridge University Press, 1987). My divergence from their views is the result of my intellectual and literary emphases, not a blanket rejection of their interpretations.

Chapter 1. The Transplanted English Vine

1. For one colonist's astonished description of New England's flocks of passenger pigeons, see Everett Emerson, ed., *Letters from New England: The Massachusetts Bay Colony, 1629–1638* (Amherst: University of Massachusetts Press, 1976), p. 111. William Wood noted the "wonderment" inspired by New England's

"toades which will climbe the topes of high trees where they will sit croaking": *New Englands Prospect* (London, 1634; reprint ed., Boston: Prince Society, 1865), p. 51.

2. Sir Thomas Browne, *Religio Medici*, in *The Major Works*, ed. C. A. Patrides (Harmondsworth, England: Penguin Books, 1977), p. 133.

3. William Bradford, *History of Plymouth Plantation, 1620–1647*, 2 vols., ed. Worthington Chauncey Ford (Boston: Massachusetts Historical Society, 1912; reprint ed., New York: Russell & Russell, 1968), 1:56–57, 28.

4. John Cotton, *Gods Promise to His Plantations* (1630), *Old South Leaflets*, no. 53 (n.d.): 4 (italics reversed), 11.

5. Ibid., p. 14.

6. Samuel Sewall referred to "the transplanted *English* Vine" in his poem saluting the arrival of the eighteenth century—thereby offering his testimony of this image's continuing importance in New England rhetoric. See the revised version printed as a broadside and appended to Sewall's *Proposals Touching the Accomplishment of Prophecies* (1713), reproduced as a plate in *The Diary of Samuel Sewall, 1674–1729*, 2 vols., ed. M. Halsey Thomas (New York: Farrar, Straus & Giroux, 1973), 1:441. John Seelye suggests that "John Cotton's greatest contribution to the subsequent literature of Puritan New England is his figure of the transplanted Vine, the spiritual scion from which an American arbor will grow": see *Prophetic Waters: The River in Early American Life and Literature* (New York: Oxford University Press, 1977), pp. 147–48.

For related uses of vine and grape imagery in the literature, see: Michael Wigglesworth, "God's Controversy with New-England" (1662), Kenneth Silverman, ed., *Colonial American Poetry* (New York and London: Hafner, 1968), p. 69; Nathaniel Morton, *New Englands Memoriall* (Cambridge, Mass., 1669; reprint ed., New York: Scholars' Facsimiles & Reprints, 1937), sig. aᵛ, pp. 197–98; W[illiam] Stoughton, *New-Englands True Interest; Not to Lie* (Cambridge, Mass., 1670), pp. 20, 27; Urian Oakes, *New-England Pleaded with* (Cambridge, Mass., 1673), p. 24; William Hubbard, *The Happiness of a People* (Boston, 1676), p. 49; Samuel Hooker, *Righteousness Rained from Heaven* (Cambridge, Mass., 1677), pp. 15, 17; Edward Taylor, "An Elegy upon the Death of that Holy and Reverend Man of God, Mr. Samuel Hooker," in *The Poems of Edward Taylor*, ed. Donald E. Stanford (New Haven: Yale University Press, 1960), p. 484; and [Joshua Scottow], *A Narrative of the Planting of the Massachusets Colony* (Boston, 1694), pp. 1, 45. A Quaker critic of New England confirmed their worst suspicions: [John Rous], *New-England a Degenerate Plant* (London, 1659).

7. On European environmental thought I have found especially useful: Clarence J. Glacken, *Traces on the Rhodian Shore: Nature and Culture in Western Thought from Ancient Times to the End of the Eighteenth Century* (Berkeley and Los Angeles: University of California Press, 1967); Margaret T. Hodgen, *Early Anthropology in the Sixteenth and Seventeenth Centuries* (Philadelphia: University of Pennsylvania Press, 1964); and the suggestive articles by Karen Ordahl Kupperman on early English reactions to the American climate: "The Puzzle of the American Climate in the Early Colonial Period," *American Historical Review* 87 (1982): 1262–89; "Fear of Hot Climates in the Anglo-American Colonial Experience," *William and Mary Quarterly*, 3d ser., 41 (1984): 213–40; and "Climate and Mastery of the Wilderness in Seventeenth-Century New England," in David D. Hall and David Grayson Allen, eds., *Seventeenth-Century New England: A Conference Held by The Colonial Society of Massachusetts, June 18 and 19, 1982* (Boston: Colonial Society of Massachusetts, 1984), pp. 3–37. On humoral physi-

ology, see the convenient surveys of traditional thought in C. S. Lewis, *The Discarded Image: An Introduction to Medieval and Renaissance Literature* (Cambridge: Cambridge University Press, 1964), pp. 169–74; and E. M. W. Tillyard, *The Elizabethan World Picture* (New York: Vintage Books, n.d.), pp. 66–79.

8. Jean Bodin, *The Six Bookes of a Commonweale: A Facsimile Reprint of the English Translation of 1606 Corrected and Supplemented in the Light of a New Comparison with the French and Latin Texts,* ed. Kenneth Douglas McRae (Cambridge, Mass.: Harvard University Press, 1962), p. 566.

9. Nathanael Carpenter, *Geography Delineated Forth in Two Bookes* (Oxford, 1625; reprint ed., Norwood, N.J., and Amsterdam: Walter J. Johnson and Theatrum Orbis Terrarum, 1976), 2:277, 276 (italics reversed). On the importance of Bodin's work in this era, see Hodgen, *Early Anthropology*, p. 283; and Glacken, *Traces*, pp. 434–36. A copy of Richard Knolles's 1606 English translation of *The Six Bookes* was transplanted to America in the library of William Brewster: see Thomas Goddard Wright, *Literary Culture in Early New England, 1620–1730* (New York: Russell & Russell, 1966), p. 256.

10. Carpenter, *Geography* 2:277.

11. Alexander Whitaker, *Good Newes from Virginia* (London, 1613; reprint ed., New York: Scholars' Facsimiles & Reprints, n.d.), p. 39. On Whitaker, see the biographical note in *The Complete Works of Captain John Smith (1580–1631),* 3 vols., ed. Philip L. Barbour (Chapel Hill and London: University of North Carolina Press for the Institute of Early American History and Culture, 1986), 1:lii–liii.

12. William Crashaw, *A Sermon Preached in London* (London, 1610), quoted in Winthrop D. Jordan, *White Over Black: American Attitudes Toward the Negro, 1550–1812* (New York: W. W. Norton & Company, 1977), p. 240. Jordan's work is especially useful in this context for its discussion of English attitudes toward race, culture, and environment.

13. The phrase "herbe of hell" is Thomas Dekker's: see Robert Ralston Cawley, *Unpathed Waters: Studies in the Influence of the Voyagers on Elizabethan Literature* (Princeton, N.J.: Princeton University Press, 1940), p. 225. Robert Johnson referred to Virginia as an "earthly Paradice" in his *Nova Britannia: Offering Most Excellent fruites by Planting in Virginia* (London, 1609), in Peter Force, ed., *Tracts and Other Papers,* 4 vols. (Gloucester, Mass.: Peter Smith, 1963), 1(no. 6):8.

14. For the promoters' response to Virginia's rumored liabilities, see: William Strachey, *The Historie of Travell into Virginia Britania (1612),* ed. Louis B. Wright and Virginia Freund (London: Hakluyt Society, 1953), pp. 37–38; Whitaker, *Good Newes,* p. 39; and John Smith, *The Generall Historie of Virginia, New-England and the Summer Isles . . .* (1624), in *Complete Works* 2:233. Edmund S. Morgan presents the sound basis for such rumors in his description of living conditions in seventeenth-century Virginia: see *American Slavery, American Freedom: The Ordeal of Colonial Virginia* (New York: W. W. Norton & Company, 1975). On the need for "seasoning," see John Smith, *A Map of Virginia* (1612), in *Complete Works* 1:143, and Strachey, *Virginia Britania,* p. 37. Karen Kupperman has suggested that "Change in the balance of the humors may have been what was meant by use of the word *seasoning* to describe the acclimatization of an English person": see "Fear of Hot Climates," p. 215 (and on the attendant threat of physical or mental changes, see especially pp. 213–17).

15. [Thomas Hariot], "The Drawings of John White," in David Beers Quinn, ed., *The Roanoke Voyages, 1584—1590: Documents to Illustrate the English Voyages to North American Under the Patent Granted to Walter Raleigh in 1584,* 2 vols. (Lon-

don: Hakluyt Society, 1955), 1:419. And see Ralph Lane's letter of September 1585 to Richard Hakluyt the elder: "if Virginia had but Horses and Kine in some reasonable proportion, I dare assure my selfe being inhabited with English, no realme in Christendome were comparable to it": ibid., p. 208.

16. Strachey, *Virginia Britania*, p. 38.

17. William Strachey, *A True Reportory of the Wreck and Redemption of Sir Thomas Gates, Knight, upon and from the Islands of the Bermudas,* in Louis B. Wright, ed., *A Voyage to Virginia in 1609: Two Narratives: Strachey's "True Reportory" and Jourdain's "Discovery of the Bermudas"* (Charlottesville: University Press of Virginia, 1964), p. 83.

18. In their equation of England and America, English writers were following, again perhaps unawares, a precedent established by Columbus and Cortés— who also found it convenient at times to emphasize the similarity, rather than the exotic differences, between the American and European environments. Antonello Gerbi has noted Columbus's eventual decision to describe "the *isla Española,* the 'Spanish Island' " as "a welcoming and familiar dwelling-place, where acclimatization is no problem and where one can live as in the mother country." Cortés, for his part, became convinced that Mexico was "almost like Europe" and could be assimilated into his king's empire "with no discontinuity." Gerbi suggests that "Cortés is thus the first firm advocate of the equation of Europe and America, the first to believe that it was feasible to measure the New World with a European yardstick and assimilate it in every way to the Old World." If so, Cortés was far from being the last. See Gerbi, *Nature in the New World: From Christopher Columbus to Gonzalo Fernández de Oviedo,* trans. Jeremy Moyle (Pittsburgh: Pittsburgh University Press, 1985), pp. 18, 95–96.

19. Richard Eburne, *A Plain Pathway to Plantations (1624),* ed. Louis B. Wright (Ithaca, N.Y.: Cornell University Press for the Folger Shakespeare Library, 1962), p. 12. Eburne was principally concerned with promoting the colonization of Newfoundland, but he also intended his argument to apply to American colonization in more general terms. For biographical background on Eburne, see Wright's "Introduction," pp. xxvi–xxvii.

20. Ibid., p. 90.

21. Ibid., p. 120.

22. For Smith's account of the 1614 voyage that led to the naming of New England, see *A Description of New England . . .* (1616), in *Complete Works* 1:291–370. Everett Emerson has noted that "Calling their dwelling place 'New England' permitted these Englishmen to domesticate their wilderness": *Letters from New England,* p. xviii.

23. Edward Winslow, *Good Newes from New England* (1624), in Alexander Young, ed., *Chronicles of the Pilgrim Fathers of the Colony of Plymouth, from 1602 to 1625* (Boston: Charles C. Little and James Brown, 1841), p. 355. Winslow hinted that he had reservations about the cold weather (see p. 369), yet in the quoted remark he was referring to the climate. See also John Winthrop's letter of July 1630 from New England: "For the Country it selfe I can discerne little difference betweene it and our owne"—an observation surely easier to make in July than in January: *Winthrop Papers,* 5 vols. (Boston: Massachusetts Historical Society, 1929–1947), 2:306–7. On the promotional literature's description of the New England environment, see also David Cressy, *Coming Over: Migration and Communication Between England and New England in the Seventeenth Century* (Cambridge and New York: Cambridge University Press, 1987), pp. 1–20; and Seelye, *Prophetic Waters,* especially pp. 147–58. Emerson's edition of *Letters from*

New England, in addition to providing modern texts of useful documents, also contains valuable commentary on this material.

24. For the clearest expression of this classical approach, see the work quoted here: Francis Higginson, *New-Englands Plantation* (London, 1630; reprint ed., New York and Amsterdam: Da Capo Press and Theatrum Orbis Terrarum, 1970), sig. B^r.

25. Wood, *New Englands Prospect*, p. 61.

26. Ibid., p. 16. For typical promotional reactions to environmental questions, see (in addition to the relevant sections in Wood and Higginson): John White, *The Planters Plea* (London, 1630; reprint ed., New York and Amsterdam: Da Capo Press and Theatrum Orbis Terrarum, 1968), pp. 23–25; Winslow, *Good Newes*, pp. 368–74; Thomas Morton, *New English Canaan*, ed. Charles Francis Adams, Jr. (Boston: Prince Society, 1883; reprint ed., New York: Burt Franklin, 1967), especially pp. 179–82, 228–33; Emerson, *Letters from New England*, especially pp. 96, 110–12; and the material discussed in Cressy, *Coming Over*, pp. 1–20.

27. Higginson, *New-Englands Plantation*, sigs. B2^v–B3^r, B2^r.

28. Wood, *New Englands Prospect*, p. 9. On the promotional difficulties engendered by the New England climate, see Kupperman, "Climate and Mastery of the Wilderness." And on Wood's *Prospect*, see also Cressy, *Coming Over*, pp. 17–18; and Seelye, *Prophetic Waters*, pp. 151–58.

29. Eburne, *Plain Pathway*, p. 22.

30. For Higginson's praise of New England's climate and pure air, see *New-Englands Plantation*, sigs. C^r–C^v. On his death, see his *A True Relation of the last Voyage to New-England* (1629), in Alexander Young, ed., *Chronicles of the First Planters of the Colony of Massachusetts Bay, from 1623 to 1636* (Boston: Charles C. Little and James Brown, 1846), p. 236 n. 2; and Emerson, *Letters from New England*, p. 29. On Higginson's promotional writings, see also Cressy, *Coming Over*, pp. 12–13; and Seelye, *Prophetic Waters*, pp. 148–49. Emerson includes modern texts of *New-Englands Plantation* and related documents, with commentary and notes, in *Letters from New England*, pp. 11–40.

31. Thomas Dudley, "Deputy Governor Dudley's Letter. *To the Right Honorable, my very good Lady, The Lady Bridget, Countess of Lincoln*," in Young, *Chronicles of the First Planters*, pp. 324, 310. And see Cressy, *Coming Over*, pp. 14–15; Seelye, *Prophetic Waters*, p. 148; and Emerson, *Letters from New England*, pp. 66–83 (a reprint of Dudley's letter, with introduction and notes).

32. Higginson, *New-Englands Plantation*, sigs. B^r-B^v.

33. See ibid., sigs. C3^r-C3^v. His fourth and last discommodity suggests the commodious impression he was striving for: "Here wants as yet the good company of honest Christians to bring with them Horses, Kine and Sheepe to make use of this fruitfull Land" (sig. C3^v). See also Emerson, *Letters from New England*, p. 29.

34. Robert Cushman, *Cushman's Discourse [On the Sin and Danger of Self-Love]* (1622), in Young, *Chronicles of the Pilgrim Fathers*, pp. 255–56. Winslow reported in *Good Newes* that the Indians "affirm confidently that it [New England] is an island" (p. 368).

35. William Hubbard, *The Present State of New-England. Being a Narrative of the Troubles with the Indians in New-England* (London, 1677; reprint ed., with introduction by Cecelia Tichi, Bainbridge, N.Y.: York Mail-Print, 1972), pt. 1, p. 1.

36. Cotton Mather, *Magnalia Christi Americana; or, The Ecclesiastical History of New-England*, 2 vols. (Hartford, Conn., 1852; reprint ed., New York: Russell & Russell, 1967), 1:44–45. See also Cotton Mather, *A Pillar of Gratitude* (Boston, 1700), p. 10.

37. Morton, *New English Canaan*, p. 122; and seventeenth century, see Henry V. S. Ogden and Margaret S. Ogden, *English Taste in Landscape in the Seventeenth Century* (Ann Arbor: University of Michigan Press, 1955), pp. 49–53. See also John R. Stilgoe, *Common Landscape of America, 1580 to 1845* (New Haven and London: Yale University Press, 1982), pp. 24–25.

38. Morton, *New English Canaan*, p. 180.

39. Ibid.

40. Bradford, *Plymouth Plantation* 1:155–56. Bradford was not above glossing over the hardships of transplantation when it suited his rhetorical purposes. While his first impressions of New England were still fresh, he contributed to a promotional tract that tended to emphasize the colony's success, despite some obstacles, in establishing itself amidst the natural bounty of the New World: see [William Bradford, Edward Winslow, and Robert Cushman], *A Relation or Journall of the beginning and proceedings of the English Plantation setled at Plimoth in New England* (London, 1622; reprint ed., n.p.: Readex Microprint, 1966)— a work also known as *Mourt's Relation*. The *Relation*'s rather straightforward tone, along with its nearness in time to the events it narrates, has misled some critics into reading it as a rhetorically naive (and relatively factual) document— by comparison to the later *Plymouth Plantation*. See especially Alan Heimert's comments in Alan Heimert and Andrew Delbanco, eds., *The Puritans in America: A Narrative Anthology* (Cambridge, Mass., and London, England: Harvard University Press, 1985), pp. 45, 51–52; and Seelye, *Prophetic Waters*, pp. 105–6. As Seelye observes, however, the *Relation*'s "propaganda motive" denies it an exclusive claim to the truth. Indeed, despite *Plymouth Plantation*'s own propagandistic agenda and more sophisticated rhetoric, its greater distance from the Pilgrims' first glimpse of New England may have allowed it a clearer view of the emotions that glimpse actually produced in the colonists. Moreover, Bradford's memory of the desperate emotional condition of the Pilgrims upon their arrival may have included an especially painful personal element: his wife's death (a possible suicide) by drowning in the harbor at the end of the Cape. See Samuel Eliot Morison, ed., *Of Plymouth Plantation, 1620–1647* (New York: Alfred A. Knopf, 1982), p. xxiv.

41. On the Puritan concept of wilderness, useful works include: Peter N. Carroll, *Puritanism and the Wilderness: The Intellectual Significance of the New England Frontier, 1629–1700* (New York and London: Columbia University Press, 1969); William Cronon, *Changes in the Land: Indians, Colonists, and the Ecology of New England* (New York: Hill and Wang, 1983); Alan Heimert, "Puritanism, the Wilderness, and the Frontier," *New England Quarterly* 26 (1953): 361–82; Roderick Nash, *Wilderness and the American Mind*, 3d ed. (New Haven and London: Yale University Press, 1982); Stilgoe, *Common Landscape of America*; Cecelia Tichi, *New World, New Earth: Environmental Reform in American Literature from the Puritans through Whitman* (New Haven and London: Yale University Press, 1979); George H. Williams, *Wilderness and Paradise in Christian Thought: The Biblical Experience of the Desert in the History of Christianity and the Paradise Theme in the Theological Idea of the University* (New York: Harper & Brothers, 1962); and Michael Zuckerman, "Pilgrims in the Wilderness: Community, Modernity, and the Maypole at Merry Mount," *New England Quarterly* 50 (1977): 255–77. On the meaning of *wilderness* in Puritan rhetoric, see also: Sacvan Bercovitch, "Puritan New England Rhetoric and the Jewish Problem," *Early American Literature* 5 (1970): 63–73; Bercovitch, *The American Jeremiad* (Madison: University of Wisconsin Press, 1978), p. 46 and passim; Tichi, *New World*,

New Earth, especially p. 49; and Tichi, "Spiritual Biography and the 'Lords Remembrancers,' " in Sacvan Bercovitch, ed., *The American Puritan Imagination: Essays in Revaluation* (London and New York: Cambridge University Press, 1974), p. 63.

42. See: Stilgoe, *Common Landscape of America*, pp. 7–12; Nash, *Wilderness and the American Mind*, pp. 1–22; and Keith Thomas, *Man and the Natural World: A History of the Modern Sensibility* (New York: Pantheon Books, 1983), p. 194. On England's changing views of the wildwood, see Thomas, *Man and the Natural World*, pp. 192–223. And on the extent of deforestation there (with the attendant problem of firewood shortages), see: Thomas, *Man and the Natural World*, pp. 192–94; Charles F. Carroll, *The Timber Economy of Puritan New England* (Providence, R.I.: Brown University Press, 1973), pp. 3–21; and Carl Bridenbaugh, *Vexed and Troubled Englishmen, 1590–1642* (London, Oxford, and New York: Oxford University Press, 1976), pp. 98–101, 149. In his 1624 *Plain Pathway to Plantations*, Richard Eburne warned that wood "so fast decays with us that very want of it only within few years is like to prove exceeding hurtful to our land and can be no way repaired but by transplanting the people" (p. 48). But Thomas suggests that "contemporaries exaggerated the depredations on the woods": *Man and the Natural World*, p. 193.

43. Though Robert Burton, in the voice of Democritus Junior, clearly excluded "vast woods" from his Utopia, he accepted "artificial wildernesses" as suitable scenes for pleasant strolls: *The Anatomy of Melancholy*, ed. Holbrook Jackson (New York: Vintage Books, 1977), "Democritus Junior to the Reader," p. 100, and pt. 2, p. 74. And Edmund Spenser linked "False Labyrinthes" with "Delightfull bowres" in *The Faerie Queene*, ed. Thomas P. Roche, with assistance of Patrick O'Donnell, Jr. (New Haven and London: Yale University Press, 1981), bk. 4, canto 10, stanza 24. On "wildernesses" in the gardens of the era, see also Williams, *Wilderness and Paradise*, p. 74 n. 16; and Thomas, *Man and the Natural World*, p. 207.

Natural wilderness, however, continued to carry connotations of danger and moral confusion. In the thirteenth century Bartholomew the Englishman observed that "In woodes is place of deceyte and of huntynge," a place where strangers "ofte erre and go out of the waye": *De proprietatibus rerum* (ca. 1250–60), quoted in John of Trevisa's 1398 translation in G. G. Coulton, ed., *Social Life in Britain from the Conquest to the Reformation* (Cambridge: Cambridge University Press, 1956), pp. 425–26. Bartholomew points the way toward Spenser's labyrinthine Forest of Error (see *The Faerie Queene*, bk. 1, canto 1, stanzas 7, 13) and the "blind mazes" and "leavy Labyrinth" of Comus's forest: John Milton, *Comus*, in *John Milton: Complete Poems and Major Prose*, ed. Merritt Y. Hughes (Indianapolis: Odyssey Press of Bobbs-Merrill Company, 1957), lines 181, 278.

44. Wood, *New Englands Prospect*, p. 80. Wood spoke from experience, having been lost in that labyrinth himself (see pp. 79–80). For other references to the exotic phenomenon of literal bewilderment, see: Bradford, *Plymouth Plantation* 1:164, 222; Dudley, "Letter," p. 334; Wood, *New Englands Prospect*, p. 7; and John Winthrop, *The History of New England from 1630 to 1649*, 2 vols., ed. James Savage (Boston: Little, Brown and Company, 1853), 1:74–75, 118, 120, 171–72, 180; 2:34–35, 101.

45. Thomas Johnson, *Cornucopiae, Or divers secrets* (1596), quoted in Louis B. Wright, *Middle-Class Culture in Elizabethan England* (Chapel Hill: University of North Carolina Press, 1935), p. 36.

46. The presence of wild beasts was an essential component of America's wilderness character: on the etymology of *wilderness* as a place of beasts, see Nash, *Wilderness*, pp. 1–2; and Stilgoe, *Common Landscape*, p. 10. Cole Harris suggests that "There is something of northwestern France before the eleventh- and twelfth-century clearances or of Anglo-Saxon England when beaver, bears, boars, and wolves were still in English forests and commoners hunted freely there, in the experience of seventeenth-century Europeans in North American middle latitudes": "European Beginnings in the Northwest Atlantic: A Comparative View," in Hall and Allen, *Seventeenth-Century New England,* p. 120.

47. Higginson, *New-Englands Plantation,* sig. C3^r.

48. Wood, *New Englands Prospect,* p. 50 (and see pp. 49–51).

49. Morton, *New English Canaan,* p. 213.

50. John Josselyn, *New-Englands Rarities Discovered* (London, 1672; reprint ed., Boston: Massachusetts Historical Society, 1972), p. 38. Morton and Josselyn hardly qualify as Puritan promotional writers, yet in their approach to the New England environment they shared the fundamental assumptions of the Puritan promoters who were trying to "sell" the region to prospective colonists and investors.

51. Morton, *New English Canaan,* p. 209.

52. Wood, *New Englands Prospect,* p. 22. Morton too noted that bear meat was good to eat: "His Flesh is esteemed venison, and of a better taste then beefe" (*New English Canaan,* p. 210).

53. Morton, *New English Canaan,* pp. 214–15.

54. Wood, *New Englands Prospect,* p. 21 (and see p. 22); and see Higginson, *New-Englands Plantation,* sig. B3^v.

55. For the devil as lion, see I Peter 5:8. For an incident in which two colonists were threatened ("as they thought") by "Lyons," see [Bradford et al.], *Relation,* pp. 27–28.

56. In his *Pseudodoxia Epidemica* Sir Thomas Browne stated that "because there are no Wolves in England, nor have been observed for divers generations, common people have proceeded into opinions, and some wise men into affirmations, they will not live therein, although brought from other Countries": *The Works of Sir Thomas Browne,* 4 vols., ed. Geoffrey Keynes (Chicago: University of Chicago Press, 1964), 2:526. And an orator at Cambridge proudly linked his college's doctrinal purity with England's freedom from the taint of heresy's symbol, the wolf: "May the great and good God grant, that this college shall be so tenacious of the truth, that it will be easier to find a wolf in England and a snake in Ireland, than either a Socinian or Arminian in Cambridge!": translation of the Latin original, quoted in Cotton Mather, *Magnalia Christi Americana* 2:33. On the rarity of wolves in England, see: Carroll, *Timber Economy,* p. 5; and Thomas, *Man and the Natural World,* p. 273. On the wolf's significance in European thought and folklore, see: Daniel Bernard and Daniel Dubois, *L'homme et le loup* (Paris: Berger-Levrault, 1981); Barry Holstun Lopez, *Of Wolves and Men* (New York: Charles Scribner's Sons, 1978); and Beryl Rowland, *Animals with Human Faces: A Guide to Animal Symbolism* (Knoxville: University of Tennessee Press, 1973), pp. 161–67.

57. Morton, *New English Canaan,* p. 208.

58. Wood, *New Englands Prospect,* pp. 26–27. For a colonist's encounter with wolves—and with little damage, except perhaps to the colonist's nerves—see [Bradford et al.], *Relation,* p. 29. For other comments on New England's wolf problem, see Emerson, *Letters from New England,* pp. 215, 228, 232.

59. Roger Williams, *A Key into the Language of America*, ed. John J. Teunissen and Evelyn J. Hinz (Detroit: Wayne State University Press, 1973), p. 138.

60. On nature as commodity, see Cronon, *Changes in the Land*.

61. Henry Thoreau remarked as he plowed out of his bean field: "As my driver prophesied when I was ploughing, they warmed me twice, once while I was splitting them, and again when they were on the fire, so that no fuel could give out more heat": *Walden*, in *A Week on the Concord and Merrimack Rivers; Walden; or, Life in the Woods; The Maine Woods; Cape Cod*, ed. Robert F. Sayre (New York: Literary Classics of the United States, 1985), p. 522.

62. See Francis Jennings, *The Invasion of America: Indians, Colonialism, and the Cant of Conquest* (New York: W. W. Norton & Company for the Institute of Early American History and Culture, 1976), p. 29 n. 48. William Wood had noted that because of the Indians' burnings, "in those places where the *Indians* inhabit, there is scarce a bush or bramble, or any combersome underwood to bee seene in the more champion ground. . . . In some places where the *Indians* dyed of the Plague some foureteene yeares agoe, is much underwood, . . . because it hath not beene burned": *New Englands Prospect*, p. 17 (and see p. 8). See also Higginson, *New-Englands Plantation*, sigs. B^v-B2^r; and Morton, *New English Canaan*, pp. 172–73. Charles F. Carroll suggests that the pre-cleared land at the site of Plymouth was "psychologically comforting" to the Pilgrims, since it more nearly resembled England: *Timber Economy*, pp. 48–49.

63. See Carroll, *Timber Economy*, p. 60; and Cronon, *Changes in the Land*, pp. 132, 199–200 n. 9.

64. "Essay on the Ordering of Towns," in *Winthrop Papers* 3:185.

65. On the colonists' success in deforestation and wolf extermination, see Cronon, *Changes in the Land*, pp. 108–26, 132–34, 159–60.

66. Edward Johnson, *Johnson's Wonder-Working Providence, 1628–1651*, ed. J. Franklin Jameson (New York: Charles Scribner's Sons, 1910; reprint ed., New York: Barnes & Noble, 1937), pp. 210, 180. On Johnson I have found especially useful: Edward J. Gallagher, "An Overview of Edward Johnson's *Wonder-Working Providence*," *Early American Literature* 5 (1970–71): 30–49; and Tichi, *New World, New Earth*, pp. 37–66.

67. Johnson, *Wonder-Working Providence*, p. 180.

68. On the significance of place naming, see David Grayson Allen, "*Vacuum Domicilium*: The Social and Cultural Landscape of Seventeenth-Century New England," in Jonathan L. Fairbanks and Robert F. Trent, eds., *New England Begins: The Seventeenth Century*, 3 vols. (Boston: Museum of Fine Arts, Department of American Decorative Arts and Sculpture, 1982), 1:2; and Wayne Franklin, *Discoverers, Explorers, Settlers: The Diligent Writers of Early America* (Chicago and London: University of Chicago Press, 1979), p. 5. On the 1655 naming of Billerica and Groton, William Hubbard observed: "Thus did the inhabitants of New England, that it might not be forgotten whence they had their original, imprint some remembrance of their former habitations in England upon their new dwellings in America": *A General History of New England, From The Discovery to MDCLXXX* (Boston, 1848; reprint ed., New York: Arno Press, 1972), p. 545. With Johnson, however, the transatlantic symmetry in place-names seems to represent, not a mere memento of the homeland, but something closer to an assertion of equivalence.

69. Johnson, *Wonder-Working Providence*, Preface by T. H., p. 22.

70. Ibid., p. 210.

71. Ibid., p. 211.

72. On Johnson's doubts about New England's probable destiny, see Andrew Delbanco, "Looking Homeward, Going Home: The Lure of England for the Founders of New England," *New England Quarterly* 59 (1986): 363–66.

73. Johnson, *Wonder-Working Providence*, p. 72.

74. In agreement with much recent scholarship, David Grayson Allen argues that "Massachusetts was more a new 'England' than a 'new' England." Yet he acknowledges that the reproduction of English culture in American was influenced by American conditions: *In English Ways: The Movement of Societies and the Transferal of English Local Law and Custom to Massachusetts Bay in the Seventeenth Century* (Chapel Hill: University of North Carolina Press for the Institute of Early American History and Culture, 1981), pp. 6, 221. See also T. H. Breen, "Creative Adaptations: Peoples and Cultures," in Jack P. Greene and J. R. Pole, eds., *Colonial British America: Essays in the New History of the Early Modern Era* (Baltimore and London: Johns Hopkins University Press, 1984), pp. 207, 215–16; Stilgoe, *Common Landscape*, pp. 46–47; and Harris, "European Beginnings," p. 121.

75. On the limitations of material culture as evidence of transplantation's success, see John Demos, "Words and Things: A Review and Discussion of 'New England Begins,'" *William and Mary Quarterly*, 3d ser., 40 (1983): 597.

Chapter 2. The Disafforestation of the Mind

1. John Donne, "To Sr *Edward Herbert*. at *Julyers*," in *The Poems of John Donne*, ed. Sir H. J. C. Grierson (London, New York, and Toronto: Oxford University Press, 1933), pp. 170–71.

2. John Winthrop, *The History of New England from 1630 to 1649*, 2 vols., ed. James Savage (Boston: Little, Brown and Company, 1853), 1:12. For Winthrop and the *Arbella*'s captain, the word "beastly" would have had more than merely figurative meaning. E. M. W. Tillyard has noted the "Elizabethan hovering between equivalence and metaphor"—and it is likely that while "beastly" in this case is hovering, it is hovering in the general direction of equivalence. See Tillyard, *The Elizabethan World Picture* (New York: Vintage Books, n.d.), pp. 99–100.

3. *Winthrop Papers*, 5 vols. (Boston: Massachusetts Historical Society, 1929–47), 1:194.

4. Winthrop, *History of New England* 2:280–81. See also *Winthrop Papers* 1:207: "A wilde colte must be well tamed in the ploughe, and then a childe may backe him; so this wanton heart of ours till it be well tamed with afflictions, or suche duties in our callings as are not pleasinge nor easy to the fleshe, there is no rulinge it."

5. Winthrop, *History of New England* 2:104. By "beastlike men," Winthrop meant the Indians, but his view of human nature suggests that he would also have regarded the term as potentially applicable to the English.

6. Richard Slotkin has dealt extensively with the colonists' fear of cultural contamination from Winthrop's "beastlike men" in *Regeneration Through Violence: The Mythology of the American Frontier, 1600–1860* (Middletown, Conn.: Wesleyan University Press, 1973), and in the introduction and commentary in Richard Slotkin and James K. Folsom, eds., *So Dreadfull a Judgment: Puritan Responses to King Philip's War, 1676–1677* (Middletown, Conn.: Wesleyan University Press, 1978). See also the discussion in my chaps. 3 and 4.

7. Sir Thomas Browne, *Religio Medici*, in *The Major Works*, ed. C. A. Patrides

(Harmondsworth, England: Penguin Books, 1977), p. 129. On the hierarchy of creation, the composite soul, and the bestial element in human nature, see: Arthur O. Lovejoy, *The Great Chain of Being: A Study of the History of an Idea* (Cambridge, Mass., and London, England: Harvard University Press, 1936); Tillyard, *Elizabethan World Picture*, pp. 25–36, 66–79; C. S. Lewis, *The Discarded Image: An Introduction to Medieval and Renaissance Literature* (Cambridge: Cambridge University Press, 1964), pp. 152–54; D. W. Robertson, Jr., *A Preface to Chaucer: Studies in Medieval Perspectives* (Princeton, N.J.: Princeton University Press, 1962), pp. 153–54; Perry Miller, *The New England Mind: The Seventeenth Century* (Cambridge, Mass., and London, England: Belknap Press of Harvard University Press, 1982), p. 240; and Keith Thomas, *Man and the Natural World: A History of the Modern Sensibility* (New York: Pantheon Books, 1983), pp. 30–31. For contemporary notions of bestial nature, especially as they were applied to the American Indians, see Bernard W. Sheehan, *Savagism and Civility: Indians and Englishmen in Colonial Virginia* (Cambridge, London, and New York: Cambridge University Press, 1980), chap. 3.

8. See Robertson, *Preface to Chaucer*, pp. 153–54.

9. Thomas Hooker, *The Application of Redemption* (London, 1657; reprint ed., New York: Arno Press, 1972), p. 200.

10. Cotton Mather, *Magnalia Christi Americana; or, The Ecclesiastical History of New-England*, 2 vols. (Hartford, Conn., 1852; reprint ed., New York: Russell & Russell, 1967), 1:345.

11. Ibid., p. 507.

12. Ibid., p. 537. According to Mather, when Eliot sensed that a fellow minister had conceived too high an opinion of himself, Eliot would counsel him: "Study mortification, brother, study mortification!" (1:538).

13. Cotton Mather, *Diary of Cotton Mather*, 2 vols. (New York: Frederick Ungar, n.d.), 1:109, 227, 16–17.

14. Ibid., p. 357. See also ibid., 2:69, 521, 612; Cotton Mather, *The Diary of Cotton Mather, D.D., F.R.S., for the Year 1712*, ed. William R. Manierre II (Charlottesville: University Press of Virginia, 1964), p. 22; and Edmund S. Morgan, ed., *The Diary of Michael Wigglesworth, 1653–1657: The Conscience of a Puritan* (New York: Harper & Row, 1965), pp. 54, 61. Scriptural justification for such attitudes could easily be found in Ecclesiastes 3:18.

15. Charles Jeremy Hoadly, ed., *Records of the Colony or Jurisdiction of New Haven, from May, 1653, to the Union. Together with the New Haven Code of 1656* (Hartford, Conn.: Case, Lockwood & Company, 1858), p. 611. On the peculiarly impersonal nature of Puritan punishment, see Larzer Ziff, *Puritanism in America; New Culture in a New World* (New York: Viking Press, 1973), pp. 143–44; and Kai T. Erikson, *Wayward Puritans: A Study in the Sociology of Deviance* (New York, London, and Sydney: John Wiley & Sons, 1966), pp. 188–90. On the New Haven code, see also Lilian Handlin, "Dissent in a Small Community," *New England Quarterly* 58 (1985): 212. Bradley Chapin includes whipping in his discussion of colonial judicial proceedings: *Criminal Justice in Colonial America, 1606–1660* (Athens: University of Georgia Press, 1983), p. 53; while Jules Zanger argues that Puritan punishments were relatively lenient: see "Crime and Punishment in Early Massachusetts," *William and Mary Quarterly*, 3d ser., 22 (1965): 471–77.

16. Thomas Shepard, *The Parable of the Ten Virgins Unfolded*, in *The Works*, 3 vols., ed. John Adams Albro (Boston: Doctrinal Tract and Book Society, 1853; reprint ed., Hildesheim and New York: Georg Olms Verlag, 1971), 2:584.

17. On the role of animals in witchcraft, see the many instances noted in John Putnam Demos, *Entertaining Satan: Witchcraft and the Culture of Early New England* (Oxford and New York: Oxford University Press, 1982), passim. See also Keith Thomas's discussion of witchcraft in *Religion and the Decline of Magic* (New York: Charles Scribner's Sons, 1971), pp. 433–583 (especially pp. 445–46, 524–25).

18. John Cotton, *The New Covenant* (1654), in Perry Miller and Thomas H. Johnson, eds., *The Puritans*, rev. ed., 2 vols. (New York: Harper & Row, 1963), 1:314.

19. Edward Winslow, *Hypocrisie Unmasked* (London, 1646; reprint ed., New York: Burt Franklin, 1968), p. 61.

20. Roger Williams, *George Fox Digg'd out of his Burrowes*, in *The Complete Writings of Roger Williams*, 7 vols., ed. Reuben Aldridge Guild et al. (New York: Russell & Russell, 1963), 5:53.

21. Sarah Kemble Knight, "The Journal of Madam Knight," in Miller and Johnson, *The Puritans* 2:431.

22. [Cotton Mather], *A Monitory, and Hortatory Letter, To those English, who debauch the Indians, By Selling Strong Drink unto them* (Boston, 1700), p. 6. On the use of "beastly" to describe cases of drunkenness, see, for example, Nathaniel B. Shurtleff and David Pulsifer, eds., *Records of the Colony of New Plymouth in New England*, 12 vols. (Boston, 1855–61), 1:75; 3:212.

23. A New Haven magistrate, quoted in Roger Thompson, *Sex in Middlesex: Popular Mores in a Massachusetts County, 1649–1699* (Amherst: University of Massachusetts Press, 1968), pp. 36–37. On the bestial connotations of sex, see Winthrop D. Jordan, *White Over Black: American Attitudes Toward the Negro, 1550–1812* (New York: W. W. Norton & Company for the Institute of Early American History and Culture, 1977), pp. 32–33. On Puritan attitudes toward sexual practices, see also: Edmund S. Morgan, "The Puritans and Sex," *New England Quarterly* 15 (1942): 591–607; Lawrence Stone, *The Family, Sex and Marriage in England, 1500–1800* (New York: Harper & Row, 1977), passim; Henry Bamford Parkes, "Morals and Law Enforcement in Colonial New England," *New England Quarterly* 5 (1932): 441–47; David H. Flaherty, "Law and the Enforcement of Morals in Early America," *Perspectives in American History* 5 (1971); 201–53; and Kathleen Verduin, " 'Our Cursed Natures': Sexuality and the Puritan Conscience," *New England Quarterly* 56 (1983): 220–37.

24. See Thomas, *Man and the Natural World*, pp. 36–41; and Robert F. Oaks, " 'Things Fearful to Name': Sodomy and Buggery in Seventeenth-Century New England," *Journal of Social History* 12 (1978): 277. Oaks's article is the fullest consideration to date of bestiality as a social phenomenon in colonial New England, though, as his subtitle suggests, he is largely concerned with a broader spectrum of "deviant" activities—including homosexuality. See also Chapin, *Criminal Justice in Colonial America*, pp. 38–39, 127–29.

25. Winthrop, *History of New England* 2:26.

26. Ibid., pp. 58–60; Nathaniel B. Shurtleff, ed., *Records of the Governor and Company of the Massachusetts Bay in New England*, 5 vols. (Boston, 1853–54), 1:339, 344. For the colonial laws on bestiality (derived from Leviticus 20:15–16), see: Max Farrand, ed., *The Laws and Liberties of Massachusetts, Reprinted from the Copy of the 1648 Edition in the Henry E. Huntington Library* (Cambridge, Mass.: Harvard University Press, 1929), p. 5; John D. Cushing, ed., *The Laws of the Pilgrims: A Facsimile Edition of "The Book of the General Laws of the Inhabitants of the Jurisdiction of New-Plimouth. 1672 & 1685"* (Wilmington, Del.: Michael Glazier, 1977), p. 4 (original pagination of 1672 laws); J. Hammond Trumbull and Charles

Jeremy Hoadly, eds., *The Public Records of the Colony of Connecticut*, 15 vols. (Hartford, Conn., 1850–90), 1:77; and Hoadly, *Records of . . . New Haven, from May, 1653, to the Union*, pp. 576–77. Oaks presents a convenient summary of the details of the Hackett case in " 'Things Fearful to Name,' " pp. 274–75.

27. Winthrop, *History of New England* 2:58–60.

28. Ibid., p. 73. And see: Charles Jeremy Hoadly, ed., *Records of the Colony and Plantation of New Haven, from 1638 to 1649* (Hartford, Conn.: Case, Tiffany & Company, 1857), pp. 62–73 (where a more detailed inventory of the "human resemblances" is available); John M. Murrin, "Magistrates, Sinners, and a Precarious Liberty: Trial by Jury in Seventeenth-Century New England," in David D. Hall, John M. Murrin, and Thad W. Tate, eds., *Saints & Revolutionaries: Essays on Early American History* (New York and London: W. W. Norton & Company, 1984), pp. 177–78; Oaks, " 'Things Fearful to Name,' " p. 275; and Chapin, *Criminal Justice in Colonial America*, pp. 38–39, 128–29.

29. Hoadly, *Records . . . of New Haven, from 1638 to 1649*, pp. 295–96; Oaks, " 'Things Fearful to Name,' " p. 276; Murrin, "Magistrates," p. 178; and Gail Sussman Marcus, " 'Due Execution of the Generall Rules of Righteousnesse': Criminal Procedure in New Haven Town and Colony, 1648–1658," in Hall et al., *Saints & Revolutionaries*, pp. 115–16.

30. Cotton Mather, *Magnalia Christi Americana* 2:405–7. On the belief that humans could engender offspring through sexual intercourse with animals, see Thomas, *Man and the Natural World*, pp. 134–35; Oaks, " 'Things Fearful to Name,' " p. 277; and Chapin, *Criminal Justice in Colonial America*, pp. 127–28.

31. Samuel Sewall, *The Diary of Samuel Sewall, 1674–1729*, 2 vols., ed. M. Halsey Thomas (New York: Farrar, Straus & Giroux, 1973), 1:4; Edward Rawson to John Winthrop, Jr., March 14, 1674, in "Winthrop Papers," Massachusetts Historical Society, *Collections*, 3d ser., 10 (1849): 98. Oaks states that this was "The last execution for buggery by the Massachusetts Court of Assistants": " 'Things Fearful to Name,' " p. 277.

32. "Winthrop Papers," Massachusetts Historical Society, *Collections*, 3d ser., 10 (1849): 98.

33. S[amuel] D[anforth], *The Cry of Sodom Enquired Into; Upon Occasion of The Arraignment and Condemnation of Benjamin Goad, For his Prodigious Villany* (Cambridge, Mass., 1674), pp. 3–6.

34. D[anforth], *Cry of Sodom*, pp. 8–9. And see Sewall, *Diary* 1:4. On Sodom's importance for Puritan preachers as a symbol of sexual transgression, see Verduin, " 'Our Cursed Natures,'" pp. 228–29. Verduin also notes the Puritan interpretation of idleness as the prime instigator of uncleanness, following Ezekiel 16:49 (pp. 232–33).

35. D[anforth], *Cry of Sodom*, pp. 9, 11.

36. Ibid., p. 9. On the social value of "deviance," see Erikson, *Wayward Puritans*, passim.

37. The Puritan sense of wilderness as a potential source of cultural and moral contamination was strongly influenced by biblical traditions. For a suggestive discussion of the Hebraic background, see Johannes Pedersen, *Israel: Its Life and Culture, I–II*, trans. Aslaug Møller and Johannes Pedersen (London: Oxford University Press, 1926), pp. 453–96.

38. William Bradford, *History of Plymouth Plantation, 1620–1647*, 2 vols., ed. Worthington Chauncey Ford (Boston: Massachusetts Historical Society, 1912; reprint ed., New York: Russell & Russell, 1968), 2:308–9.

39. Bradford, *Plymouth Plantation* 2:328, 328 n. 1.

40. Ibid., pp. 328–29; Shurtleff and Pulsifer, *Records of the Colony of New Plymouth* 2:44; Oaks, " 'Things Fearful to Name,' " p. 275. According to Bradford, Granger "left a wife and children" (*Plymouth Plantation* 2:329 n. 1).

41. Bradford, *Plymouth Plantation* 2:329–30; and see Oaks, " 'Things Fearful to Name,' " p. 275.

42. Bradford, *Plymouth Plantation* 2:309.

43. John Owen King III makes interesting observations on the psychological implications for Puritans of living in a satanic wilderness environment: *The Iron of Melancholy: Structures of Spiritual Conversion in America from the Puritan Conscience to Victorian Neurosis* (Middletown, Conn.: Wesleyan University Press, 1983), pp. 19–22. See also my chap. 3.

44. Bradford, *Plymouth Plantation* 2:309–10.

45. See my chap. 1, nn. 23–24 (above); and Pedersen, *Israel*, pp. 453–96.

46. Shurtleff and Pulsifer, *Records of the Colony of New Plymouth* 6:74; and see Oaks, " 'Things Fearful to Name,' " p. 278.

47. See Slotkin, *Regeneration Through Violence*, p. 88; and the rhetoric favored by William Hubbard in *The Present State of New-England. Being a Narrative of the Troubles with the Indians in New-England* (London, 1677; reprint ed., with introduction by Cecelia Tichi, Bainbridge, N.Y.: York Mail-Print, 1972), passim. Although the court's reference to the devil's "instigation" is formulaic, the formula here seems especially apt.

48. Shurtleff and Pulsifer, *Records of the Colony of New Plymouth* 6:74–75; Oaks, " 'Things Fearful to Name,' " p. 278.

49. Other cases (and suspected cases) of bestiality— not all resulting in conviction— are cited in: Murrin, "Magistrates"; Marcus, " 'Due Execution' "; Oaks, " 'Things Fearful to Name' "; and Chapin, *Criminal Justice in Colonial America*, p. 128. See also Sewall's *Diary* 1:64; Cotton Mather, *Selected Letters of Cotton Mather*, ed. Kenneth Silverman (Baton Rouge: Louisiana State University Press, 1971), p. 210; and Thompson, *Sex in Middlesex*, p. 73.

50. On the occurrence of bestiality in England, see Thomas, *Man and the Natural World*, pp. 39, 119; and F. G. Emmison, *Elizabethan Life: Disorder* (Chelmsford: Essex County Council, 1970), pp. 197, 318.

51. Thompson, *Sex in Middlesex*, p. 75.

52. J. W., "Letter from New-England Concerning their Customs, Manners, and Religion," in George Parker Winship, ed., *Boston in 1682 and 1699: "A Trip to New-England" by Edward Ward and "A Letter from New-England" by J. W.* (New York: Burt Franklin, 1970), p. 8 (original pagination).

53. Gabriel Towerson, *An Explication of the Decalogue* (1676), quoted in Thomas, *Man and the Natural World*, p. 119.

54. Christopher Hill speculates that buggery and bestiality may have been familiar practices in the English countryside: "Jolly Rogers," review of *Sodomy and the Perception of Evil: English Sea Rovers in the Seventeenth-Century Caribbean*, by B. R. Burg, in *New York Review of Books*, 12 May 1983, p. 42. See also Oaks, " 'Things Fearful to Name,' " p. 277, and Chapin, *Criminal Justice in Colonial America*, p. 128.

55. Farrand, *The Laws and Liberties of Massachusetts*, p. 1 (italics reversed). And for similar phrases, see Trumbull and Hoadly, *The Public Records of the Colony of Connecticut* 1:509; and Shurtleff and Pulsifer, *Records of the Colony of New Plymouth* 11:91.

56. William Hubbard, *A General History of New England, From The Discovery to MDCLXXX* (Boston, 1848; reprint ed., New York: Arno Press, 1972), pp.

146–47. And note Ebenezer Pemberton's remark that without good government, "Men would be like fishes in the sea and as beasts in the wilderness, the greater devour the less": quoted in A. W. Plumstead, ed., *The Wall and the Garden: Selected Massachusetts Election Sermons, 1670–1775* (Minneapolis: University of Minnesota Press, 1968), p. 20. On the Puritan concept of order, see Stephen Foster, *Their Solitary Way: The Puritan Social Ethic in the First Century of Settlement in New England* (New Haven and London: Yale University Press, 1971), chap. 1; and Perry Miller, *The New England Mind: The Seventeenth Century*, chap. 14.

57. John Cotton, *A Brief Exposition With Practical Observations Upon the whole Book of Canticles* (London, 1655), p. 104. Though consonant with American circumstances, this material was probably written in England between 1612 and 1632: see Larzer Ziff's note on the 1642 edition in *The Career of John Cotton: Puritanism and the American Experience* (Princeton, N.J.: Princeton University Press, 1962), p. 263. On the church as Garden of Christ, see also: Peter N. Carroll, *Puritanism and the Wilderness: The Intellectual Significance of the New England Frontier, 1629–1700* (New York and London: Columbia University Press, 1969), chap. 6; George H. Williams, *Wilderness and Paradise in Christian Thought: The Biblical Experience of the Desert in the History of Christianity & The Paradise Theme in the Theological Idea of the University* (New York: Harper & Brothers, 1962), pp. 72, 99–113; and Ann Stanford, "Anne Bradstreet's Emblematic Garden," in Pattie Cowell and Ann Stanford, eds., *Critical Essays on Anne Bradstreet* (Boston: G. K. Hall & Co., 1983), pp. 238–53.

58. Peter Bulkeley, *The Gospel-Covenant; or The Covenant of Grace Opened* (London, 1651), p. 163. And on the role of education in New England society, see James Axtell, *The School upon a Hill: Education and Society in Colonial New England* (New Haven and London: Yale University Press, 1974); and Bernard Bailyn, *Education in the Forming of American Society: Needs and Opportunities for Study* (New York: W. W. Norton & Company for the Institute of Early American History and Culture, 1972), especially pp. 79–83.

59. See Charles Chauncy, *Gods Mercy, Shewed to His People in Giving Them a Faithful Ministry and Schooles of Learning for the Continual Supplyes Therof* (Cambridge, Mass., 1655), pp. 15–16.

60. Edward Johnson, *Johnson's Wonder-Working Providence, 1628–1651*, ed. J. Franklin Jameson (New York: Charles Scribner's Sons, 1910; reprint ed., New York: Barnes & Noble, 1937), p. 253.

61. Francis Bacon, "Of Frendship," in *Essays* (London: Oxford University Press, 1937; reprint ed., 1966), p. 107.

62. Thomas Walkington, *The Optick Glasse of Humors (1631)* (Oxford, [1631]; reprint ed., Delmar, N.Y.: Scholars' Facsimiles & Reprints, 1981), p. 132.

63. Robert Burton, *The Anatomy of Melancholy*, ed. Holbrook Jackson (New York: Vintage Books, 1977), pt. 1, pp. 246, 248–49. On Puritanism and melancholy (including the American environment's significance in this relationship), see King, *Iron of Melancholy*, chap. 1.

64. John Cotton, *A Briefe Exposition with Practicall Observations upon The Whole Book of Ecclesiastes* (London, 1654), pp. 85, 87.

65. Browne, *Religio Medici*, pp. 69, 152.

66. Thomas Tillam, "Uppon the first sight of New-England June 29 1638," in Kenneth Silverman, ed., *Colonial American Poetry* (New York: Hafner, 1968), p. 31 (italics reversed).

67. On the Puritans' solitary devotional exercises, see Charles E. Hambrick-Stowe,

The Practice of Piety: Puritan Devotional Disciplines in Seventeenth-Century New England (Chapel Hill: University of North Carolina Press for the Institute of Early American History and Culture, 1982), pp. 156–93. On Edward Hopkins, see Cotton Mather, *Magnalia Christi Americana* 1:145.

68. Thomas Shepard, "Autobiography," in Michael McGiffert, ed., *God's Plot: The Paradoxes of Puritan Piety, Being the Autobiography and Journal of Thomas Shepard* (n.p.: University of Massachusetts Press, 1972), p. 41.

69. Cotton Mather, *Magnalia Christi Americana* 2:86.

70. Cotton Mather, *Diary* 1:69.

71. Roger Clap quoted in Hambrick-Stowe, *Practice of Piety*, p. 175.

72. Jonathan Edwards's "Account of His Conversion, Experiences, and Religious Exercises, Given by Himself," in Samuel Hopkins, *The Life and Character of Reverend Mr. Jonathan Edwards*, reprinted in David Levin, ed., *Jonathan Edwards: A Profile* (New York: Hill and Wang, 1969), pp. 24, 28.

73. Peter N. Carroll remarks that "the basic problem of Puritan society in the wilderness" was "the need to reconcile expansion and collectivity": *Puritanism and the Wilderness*, p. 220. For a different perspective on the problem, see Alan Heimert, "Puritanism, the Wilderness, and the Frontier," *New England Quarterly* 26 (1953): 361–82.

74. On the half-mile law, see: Shurtleff, *Records of the Governor and Company of the Massachusetts Bay* 1:157, 181, 257, 291; Foster, *Their Solitary Way*, p. 50 n. 24; James T. Lemon, "Spatial Order: Households in Local Communities and Regions," in Jack P. Greene and J. R. Pole, eds., *Colonial British America: Essays in the New History of the Early Modern Era* (Baltimore and London: Johns Hopkins University Press, 1984), p. 93; and David Grayson Allen, "*Vacuum Domicilium*: The Social and Cultural Landscape of Seventeenth-Century New England," in Jonathan L. Fairbanks and Robert F. Trent, eds., *New England Begins: The Seventeenth Century*, 3 vols. (Boston: Museum of Fine Arts, Department of American Decorative Arts and Sculpture, 1982), 1:4-5.

75. Trumbull and Hoadly, *Public Records of the Colony of Connecticut* 1:210.

76. Shurtleff and Pulsifer, *Records of the Colony of New Plymouth* 3:6–7, 102. The court seemed more concerned with the welfare of Ramsden's wife than with what might happen to the man himself. See also James Axtell, *The European and the Indian: Essays in the Ethnohistory of Colonial North America* (New York and Oxford: Oxford University Press, 1981), p. 159.

77. Shurtleff and Pulsifer, *Records of the Colony of New Plymouth* 5:169. And see Axtell, *European and the Indian*, p. 159.

78. Daniel Defoe, *Robinson Crusoe: An Authoritative Text, Backgrounds and Sources, Criticism*, ed. Michael Shinagel (New York: W. W. Norton & Company, 1975), pp. 89, 54. *Robinson Crusoe* was originally published in 1719. My view of the novel, as elaborated in this section, owes much to Maximillian E. Novak, *Defoe and the Nature of Man* (London: Oxford University Press, 1963), especially pp. 22–64. See also Novak's "The Wild Man Comes to Tea," in Edward Dudley and Maximillian E. Novak, eds., *The Wild Man Within: An Image in Western Thought from the Renaissance to Romanticism* (Pittsburgh: University of Pittsburgh Press, 1972), pp. 183–221. Christopher Hill notes Defoe's "emphasis on the individual in isolation" in "Daniel Defoe (1660–1731) and *Robinson Crusoe*," in *The Collected Essays of Christopher Hill*, Vol. 1, *Writing and Revolution in 17th Century England* (Amherst: University of Massachusetts Press, 1985), pp. 122–23. John Seelye suggests an interesting American perspective on *Crusoe* in "Some Green Thoughts on a Green Theme," in George Abbott White and

Charles Newman, eds., *Literature in Revolution* (New York, Chicago, San Francisco: Holt, Rinehart and Winston, 1972), pp. 590–95; and James Holstun applies the Crusoe analogy to John Eliot's Praying Indian towns in *A Rational Millennium: Puritan Utopias of Seventeenth-Century England and America* (New York and Oxford: Oxford University Press, 1987), pp. 108–9, 326 n. 10.

79. Woodes Rogers, "[Account of Alexander Selkirk's Solitary Life on Juan Fernandez Island for Four Years and Four Months]," in Defoe, *Robinson Crusoe*, p. 252.

80. Defoe, *Robinson Crusoe*, pp. 141, 117–18.

81. See ibid., pp. 141, 121–22.

82. Ibid., pp. 166, 161, 162. For another view of the master-servant relationship between Crusoe and Friday and its "American" context, see Leslie A. Fiedler, *The Return of the Vanishing American* (New York: Stein and Day, 1968), p. 53: "Even *Robinson Crusoe*, otherwise so oddly like an American book, with its striking parallel to the myth of the Good Companions in the Wilderness, parts company with our own similar books at the point where Friday is taught 'Master' as his first word."

Chapter 3. Indian Origins and Colonial Destinies

1. On the problem of "Diffusion, Degeneration, and Environmentalism," I follow Margaret T. Hodgen, *Early Anthropology in the Sixteenth and Seventeenth Centuries* (Philadelphia: University of Pennsylvania Press, 1964), chap. 7, especially pp. 257–63. See also Michael T. Ryan, "Assimilating New Worlds in the Sixteenth and Seventeenth Centuries," *Comparative Studies in Society and History* 23 (1981): 519–38; Nicholas Canny, *Kingdom and Colony: Ireland in the Atlantic World, 1560–1800* (Baltimore and London: Johns Hopkins University Press, 1988), pp. 36–37 (where he cites Ryan); and Robert F. Berkhofer, Jr., *The White Man's Indian: Images of the American Indian from Columbus to the Present* (New York: Vintage Books, 1979), pp. 36–38.

2. On the presumed danger of "botanical" degeneration or mutation through colonization, see the sources quoted by Hodgen, *Early Anthropology*, p. 260.

3. The reference to "wild shamrock manners" is from John Derricke (1581), quoted in David Beers Quinn, *The Elizabethans and the Irish* (Ithaca, N.Y.: Cornell University Press for The Folger Shakespeare Library, 1966), p. 62. On the question of Ireland as a precedent for English colonization in America, see: ibid.; Howard Mumford Jones, *O Strange New World; American Culture: The Formative Years* (New York: Viking Press, 1964), pp. 167–79; Canny, *Kingdom and Colony*; Nicholas P. Canny, *The Elizabethan Conquest of Ireland: A Pattern Established, 1565–76* (New York: Barnes & Noble, 1976); Nicholas P. Canny, "The Ideology of English Colonization: From Ireland to America," *William and Mary Quarterly*, 3d ser., 30 (1973): 575–98; Nicholas Canny, "The Permissive Frontier: The Problem of Social Control in English Settlements in Ireland and Virginia, 1550–1650," in K. R. Andrews, N. P. Canny, and P. E. H. Hair, eds., *The Westward Enterprise: English Activities in Ireland, the Atlantic, and America, 1480–1650* (Liverpool: Liverpool University Press, 1978), pp. 17–44; Bernard W. Sheehan, *Savagism and Civility: Indians and Englishmen in Colonial Virginia* (Cambridge: Cambridge University Press, 1980), pp. 54–56; James Muldoon, "The Indian as Irishman," *Essex Institute Historical Collections* 111 (1975): 267–89; W. R. Jones, "England Against the Celtic Fringe: A Study in Cultural Stereotypes," *Cahiers D'Histoire Mondiale* 13 (1971): 155–71; J. F. Lydon, *The Lordship of Ireland in the Middle Ages*

(Toronto and Buffalo: University of Toronto Press, 1972). Nicholas Canny discusses the Anglo-Irish problem (and Edmund Spenser's views of the subject) in "Identity Formation in Ireland: The Emergence of the Anglo-Irish," in Nicholas Canny and Anthony Pagden, eds., *Colonial Identity in the Atlantic World, 1500–1800* (Princeton, N.J.: Princeton University Press, 1987), pp. 159–212.

4. On the book's composition and printing, see C. S. Lewis, *English Literature in the Sixteenth Century Excluding Drama* (Oxford: Oxford University Press, 1954), p. 378.

5. Edmund Spenser, *A View of the Present State of Ireland*, ed. W. L. Renwick (Oxford: Clarendon Press of Oxford University Press, 1970), pp. 48, 64, 66. On "patchocks," see the *OED*, s.v. "patchcock." Note also that the term may derive from an Irish word meaning "worm, reptile"; see the commentary in Rudolf Gottfried, ed., *Spenser's Prose Works*, in *The Works of Edmund Spenser: A Variorum Edition* (Baltimore: Johns Hopkins Press, 1949), 9:346.

6. Quinn, *Elizabethans and the Irish*, pp. 106–22 (the quote is from p. 122).

7. See, in addition to Quinn: Muldoon, "The Indian as Irishman"; Canny, "The Ideology of English Colonization"; Sheehan, *Savagism and Civility*, pp. 55–56; Canny, *Elizabethan Conquest*; and Jones, *O Strange New World*, pp. 170–79. Canny further refines his thoughts on the Indian-Irish analogy in *Kingdom and Colony*, chap. 2.

8. William Bradford, *History of Plymouth Plantation, 1620–1647*, 2 vols., ed. Worthington Chauncey Ford (Boston: Massachusetts Historical Society, 1912; reprint ed., New York: Russell & Russell, 1968), 1:55.

9. See also Richard Slotkin and James K. Folsom, eds., *So Dreadfull a Judgment: Puritan Responses to King Philip's War, 1676–1677* (Middletown, Conn.: Wesleyan University Press, 1978), p. 36; and Edmund S. Morgan, *Roger Williams: The Church and the State* (New York: Harcourt, Brace & World, 1967), p. 81.

10. Edward Winslow, *Hypocrisie Unmasked* (London, 1646; reprint ed., New York: Burt Franklin, 1968), p. 89.

11. Nathaniel Morton, *New Englands Memoriall* (Cambridge, Mass., 1669; reprint ed., New York: Scholars' Facsimiles & Reprints, 1937), p. 3

12. Samuel Maverick, "A Briefe Discription of New England and the Severall Townes therein, together with the Present Government thereof," Massachusetts Historical Society, *Proceedings*, 2d ser., 1 (1884–85): 246.

13. John Brinsley, *A Consolation for Our Grammar Schooles* (London, 1622; reprint ed., New York: Scholars' Facsimiles & Reprints, 1943), sig. A3^r (italics reversed). See also Sheehan, *Savagism and Civility*, p. 48.

14. Richard Eburne, *A Plain Pathway to Plantations (1624)*, ed. Louis B. Wright (Ithaca, N.Y.: Cornell University Press for The Folger Shakespeare Library, 1962), p. 137.

15. Bradford, *Plymouth Plantation* 1:56.

16. Ibid.

17. John Rastell, "A new interlude and a mery of the nature of the .iiii. elementes, &c." (ca. 1519), in Edward Arber, ed., *The First Three English Books on America. [?1511]–1555 A.D.* (Birmingham, England, 1885; reprint ed., New York: Kraus Reprint Co., 1971), p. xxi.

18. Philip Vincent, *A True Relation of the Late Battell fought in New England, between the English, and the Salvages* (London, 1637; reprint ed., Norwood, N.J., and Amsterdam: Walter J. Johnson and Theatrum Orbis Terrarum, 1974), sigs. B^r–B^v.

19. Vincent, *True Relation*, sigs. B^v–B2^r.

20. On humoral physiology, see C. S. Lewis, *The Discarded Image: An Introduction to Medieval and Renaissance Literature* (Cambridge: Cambridge University Press, 1964), pp. 169–74; and E. M. W. Tillyard, *The Elizabethan World Picture* (New York: Vintage Books, n.d.), pp. 68–71.

21. Roger Williams, *A Key into the Language of America*, ed. John J. Teunissen and Evelyn J. Hinz (Detroit: Wayne State University Press, 1973), p. 85.

22. This phrase is from Cotton Mather, *Magnalia Christi Americana; or, The Ecclesiastical History of New-England*, 2 vols. (Hartford, Conn., 1852; reprint ed., New York: Russell & Russell, 1967), 1:25.

23. William Wood, *New Englands Prospect* (London, 1634; reprint ed., Boston: Prince Society, 1865), p. 18 (italics reversed).

24. See Joseph Caryl's preface to John Eliot, *A Late and Further Manifestation of the Progress of the Gospel amongst the Indians in New-England* (1655), Massachusetts Historical Society, *Collections*, 3d ser., 4 (1834): 267. Caryl also saw the colonists as having "Planted themselves in the *Indian Wildernesses*."

25. Wood, *New Englands Prospect*, p. 20.

26. Ibid.

27. Williams, *Key*, p. 85 (and see p. 133).

28. [Thomas Shepard?], *The Day-Breaking, If not the Sun-Rising of the Gospell With the Indians in New-England* (1647), Massachusetts Historical Society, *Collections*, 3d ser., 4 (1834): 14, 17.

29. Nathanael Carpenter, *Geography Delineated Forth in Two Bookes* (Oxford, 1625; reprint ed., Norwood, N.J., and Amsterdam: Walter J. Johnson and Theatrum Orbis Terrarum, 1976), 2:283.

30. William Hubbard, *A General History of New England, From The Discovery to MDCLXXX* (Boston, 1848; reprint ed., New York: Arno Press, 1972), p. 134.

31. Genesis 9:25 (King James Version).

32. William Strachey, *The Historie of Travell into Virginia Britania (1612)*, ed. Louis B. Wright and Virginia Freund (London: Hakluyt Society, 1953), pp. 54–55; and see Hodgen, *Early Anthropology*, pp. 261–63.

33. Strachey, *Virginia Britania*, pp. 53–55.

34. John White, *The Planters Plea* (London, 1630; reprint ed., New York and Amsterdam: Da Capo Press and Theatrum Orbis Terrarum, 1968), pp. 54–55.

35. Ibid., pp. 15–16.

36. Ibid., pp. 13–14.

37. On the millenarianism of this period as it impinged on the Indian-origins problem, see: Richard W. Cogley, "John Eliot and the Origins of the American Indians," *Early American Literature* 21 (1986–87): 210–25; Slotkin and Folsom, *So Dreadfull a Judgment*, pp. 61–62; Christopher Hill, " 'Till the conversion of the Jews,' " in *The Collected Essays of Christopher Hill*, Vol. 2, *Religion and Politics in 17th Century England* (Amherst: University of Massachusetts Press, 1986), pp. 269–300; and Richard H. Popkin, "Jewish Messianism and Christian Millenarianism," in Perez Zagorin, ed., *Culture and Politics: From Puritanism to the Enlightenment* (Berkeley, Los Angeles, London: University of California Press, 1980), pp. 67–90. The most useful surveys of the primary literature on the Indian-origins dispute are: Lee Eldridge Huddleston, *Origins of the American Indians: European Concepts, 1492–1729* (Austin, Tex., and London, England: University of Texas Press for The Institute of Latin American Studies, 1967); and Don Cameron Allen, *The Legend of Noah: Renaissance Rationalism in Art, Science, and Letters* (Urbana: University of Illinois Press, 1963), chap. 6. See also the discussion of "Christian Cosmogony and the Problem of Indian Origins"

in Berkhofer, *White Man's Indian*, pp. 34–38; and Ryan, "Assimilating New Worlds," pp. 532–34.

38. Thorowgood's argument first appeared in *Jewes in America, or, Probabilities That the Americans are of that Race* (London, 1650) and was updated in *Jews in America* (London, 1660). In the 1650 edition he suggested that "the *Jewes* did *Indianize*, or the *Indians* doe *Judaize*, for surely they are alike in many, very many remarkable particulars" (sig. [a3]ʳ).

39. Eliot's ideas (written to Thorowgood ca. 1653–54, according to Cogley) were published as "The learned Conjectures of Reverend Mr. *John Eliot* touching the *Americans*, of new and notable consideration," in the 1660 *Jews in America*, separate pagination (quotes are from pp. 16, 19). See the discussion of this letter in Cogley, "John Eliot."

In the 1650 *Jewes* Thorowgood quoted in favor of his theory a letter Roger Williams had sent from Salem "more than ten yeers since." And in the 1660 edition he again turned to Williams—now represented by *A Key into the Language of America*—for support. By this time, however, Williams had distanced himself from Thorowgood's enterprise. As early as the *Key* itself (1643), Williams had begun to express skepticism about establishing too precise a genealogy for the Indians. He admitted that he had noticed certain similarities between the Indians' customs and ancient Hebrew practices, but random evidence of this sort apparently could not add up to a definite identification: "I dare not conjecture in these *Uncertainties*." And in February 1654 Williams wrote to John Winthrop, Jr., in approval of Sir Hamon L'Estrange's book declaring, contra Thorowgood, *Americans no Jewes* (London, 1652). See Thorowgood, *Jewes in America* (1650), pp. 5–6; *Jews in America* (1660), pp. 31–32; Williams, *Key*, pp. 85–87; and Roger Williams, *Letters of Roger Williams, 1632–1682*, in *The Complete Writings of Roger Williams*, 7 vols., ed. Reuben Aldridge Guild et al. (New York: Russell & Russell, 1963), 6:286 (and see p. 286 n. 2).

40. Eliot, "Conjectures," pp. 2, 12.

41. James Holstun has suggested that, for Eliot, "These archetypal pilgrims [Shem, Eber, etc.] . . . are both the actual ancestors of the Indians and the Old Testament types of the emigrating and planting Congregationalists." He also notes that in the meeting of Puritans and Indians "The New World becomes the appointed site for the millennial encounter of clockwise and counter-clockwise Israelites: the Indian descendants of Shem and Eber bearing themselves eastward, . . . and the Puritan Israelites bearing westward the Hebrew Scriptures . . .": *A Rational Millennium: Puritan Utopias of Seventeenth-Century England and America* (New York and Oxford: Oxford University Press, 1987), pp. 113, 115.

42. Jonathan Mitchell, "A Modell For the Maintaining of Students & Fellows of Choise Abilities at the Colledge in Cambridge" (ca. 1663), in Samuel Eliot Morison, George Lyman Kittredge, and C. K. Shipton, eds., *Harvard College Records*, pt. 3, Colonial Society of Massachusetts, *Publications*, vol. 31, *Collections* (1935): 311.

43. On the reasons for declining belief in the Jews-in-America theory, see Cogley, "John Eliot," pp. 220–21; and Sacvan Bercovitch, *The American Jeremiad* (Madison: University of Wisconsin Press, 1978), p. 75n. See also Hill, " 'Till the conversion of the Jews,' " pp. 290–91.

44. Gookin, *Historical Collections of the Indians in New England*, Massachusetts Historical Society, *Collections*, [1st ser.], 1 (1792): 144 (Gookin devoted his first chapter to "Several Conjectures of their Original": pp. 144–47).

45. See ibid., pp. 144–45.

46. Ibid., p. 145. He also summarized the theory that they were descendants of "the tawny Moors of Africa"—an idea of apparently little importance to Gookin or his contemporaries in New England (p. 146).

47. Ibid., pp. 145–46.

48. Ibid., p. 146. On Puritan "tribalism," see Edmund S. Morgan, *The Puritan Family: Religion & Domestic Relations in Seventeenth-Century New England*, rev. and enlarged ed. (New York: Harper & Row, 1966), chap. 7.

49. Bradford, *Plymouth Plantation* 1:55.

50. Gookin, *Historical Collections*, pp. 146–47.

51. See Cotton Mather, *Magnalia Christi Americana* 1:560–61.

52. Ibid., p. 249 (and see pp. 44–45).

53. On Mather's contradictory attitudes toward Indians and the missionary work, see Kenneth Silverman, *The Life and Times of Cotton Mather* (New York: Harper & Row, 1984), pp. 237–43; and John Seelye, *Prophetic Waters: The River in Early American Life and Literature* (New York: Oxford University Press, 1977), p. 269.

54. Hubbard, *General History*, p. 26 (and for Hubbard's verdict on the Jews-in-America theory, see pp. 27–28). The Mede-Twisse correspondence dated from the 1630s, but was printed in *The Works of The Pious and Profoundly-Learned Joseph Mede, B.D. Sometime Fellow of Christ's Colledge in Cambridge*, 3d ed. (London, 1672), pp. 798–802, 809–10.

55. On the assumption that the Indians' religion was a form of Satanism, see Roy Harvey Pearce, *Savagism and Civilization: A Study of the Indian and the American Mind*, rev. ed. (Baltimore and London: Johns Hopkins Press, 1967), p. 22; Silverman, *Life and Times of Cotton Mather*, p. 239; and William S. Simmons, "Cultural Bias in the New England Puritans' Perception of Indians," *William and Mary Quarterly*, 3d ser., 38 (1981): 56–72.

56. Mede, *Works*, p. 799 (italics reversed). On Gog and Magog, who were regarded as Japhetic in origin, see Revelation 20:7–8 and Genesis 10:2. On Mede's eschatology, see James West Davidson, *The Logic of Millennial Thought: Eighteenth-Century New England* (New Haven and London: Yale University Press, 1977), pp. 43–48, 51–55.

57. Mede, *Works*, pp. 799–800; and see Davidson, *Logic of Millennial Thought*, p. 54.

58. Mede, *Works*, pp. 800, 809 (italics reversed).

59. See the militant rhetoric in Edward Johnson's *Wonder-Working Providence, 1628–1651*, ed. J. Franklin Jameson (New York: Charles Scribner's Sons, 1910; reprint ed., New York: Barnes & Noble, 1937).

60. Increase Mather, "A Discourse Concerning the Danger of Apostacy" (preached May 23, 1677), in *A Call from Heaven*, 2d ed. (Boston, 1685), pp. 77, 87.

61. Increase Mather, *A Discourse Concerning the Uncertainty of the Times of Men, and The Necessity of being Prepared for Sudden Changes & Death* (Boston, 1697), p. 35.

62. Increase Mather, *A Dissertation Concerning the Future Conversion of the Jewish Nation* (London, 1709), pp. 32–33. And see Davidson, *Logic of Millennial Thought*, pp. 61, 65. On Mather's interest in the conversion of the Jews, see also Michael G. Hall, *The Last American Puritan: The Life of Increase Mather, 1639–1723* (Middletown, Conn.: Wesleyan University Press, 1988), pp. 76–77, 273–75.

63. Samuel Sewall, *Phaenomena quaedam Apocalyptica*, 2d ed. (Boston, 1727; originally published, 1697), p. 42, sigs. [B2ʳ] (italics reversed), A2ᵛ, A2ʳ. See also *Letter-Book of Samuel Sewall*, Massachusetts Historical Society, *Collections*, 6th ser., 1 (1886): 22–23; and Davidson, *Logic of Millennial Thought*, pp. 65–67.

64. Cotton Mather, *Magnalia Christi Americana* 1:556.
65. Ibid., p. 556. On Mather's early interest in Mede's theory, see Samuel Sewall, *The Diary of Samuel Sewall, 1674–1729*, 2 vols., ed. M. Halsey Thomas (New York: Farrar, Straus & Giroux, 1973), 1:90; and Cotton Mather, *The Way to Prosperity* (preached 1689), in A. W. Plumstead, ed., *The Wall and the Garden: Selected Massachusetts Election Sermons, 1670–1775* (Minneapolis: University of Minnesota Press, 1968), p. 137.
66. Cotton Mather, *Magnalia Christi Americana* 1:46.
67. Ibid.
68. Mather's "Problema Theologicum," quoted in Robert Middlekauff, *The Mathers: Three Generations of Puritan Intellectuals, 1596–1728* (Oxford, London, and New York: Oxford University Press, 1971), p. 342 (and see pp. 322, 333, 335–37).
69. Cotton Mather, *The Present State of New-England* (Boston, 1690), title page (italics reversed), p. 35.
70. Cotton Mather, *Present State*, p. 35.
71. On Increase Mather's Anglophilia, see my chap. 6.
72. Cotton Mather, *Present State*, p. 38.
73. Cotton Mather, *Decennium Luctuosum* (1699), in Wilcomb E. Washburn, ed., *The Garland Library of Narratives of North American Indian Captivities*, 111 vols. (New York and London: Garland Publishing, 1978), 3:103.
74. Perry Miller, *The New England Mind: From Colony to Province* (Cambridge, Mass., and London, England: Belknap Press of Harvard University Press, 1953), p. 33.
75. Cotton Mather, *Magnalia Christi Americana* 2:508 (this is the final sentence before the appendix, a reprinting of *Decennium Luctuosum*).
76. Urian Oakes, *New-England Pleaded with* (Cambridge, Mass., 1673), p. 17.
77. See also Bercovitch, *American Jeremiad*, p. 75n.
78. See Johannes Pedersen, *Israel: Its Life and Culture, I–II*, trans. Aslaug Møller and Johannes Pedersen (London: Oxford University Press, 1926), pp. 477–79; and Dan Jacobson, *The Story of the Stories: The Chosen People and Its God* (New York: Harper & Row, 1982), pp. 28–41.
79. Genesis 15:18–21.
80. Exodus 23:23.
81. Leviticus 20:23.
82. Joshua 23:12–13.
83. In 1660 the phrase "Uncircumcised Heathens" was applied to the Narragansetts: see J. Hammond Trumbull and Charles Jeremy Hoadly, eds., *The Public Records of the Colony of Connecticut*, 15 vols. (Hartford, Conn., 1850–90), 1:576.
84. See *Public Records of the Colony of Connecticut* 1:149–50 (the quote is from p. 149).
85. Paul J. Lindholdt, ed., *John Josselyn, Colonial Traveler: A Critical Edition of "Two Voyages to New-England"* (Hanover, N.H., and London: University Press of New England, 1988), p. 124. On the threat of intermarriage with Indians, see Slotkin and Folsom, *So Dreadfull a Judgment*, pp. 266, 299 n. 62; James Axtell, *The European and the Indian: Essays in the Ethnohistory of Colonial North America* (New York and Oxford: Oxford University Press, 1981), pp. 153–57; and, for a more southern perspective, David D. Smits, " 'Abominable Mixture': Toward the Repudiation of Anglo-Indian Intermarriage in Seventeenth-Century Virginia," *Virginia Magazine of History and Biography* 95 (1987): 157–92. Yasuhide Kawashima discusses colonial legal attitudes toward English-Indian intermar-

riage—as well as sexual crimes involving Indians—in *Puritan Justice and the Indian: White Man's Law in Massachusetts, 1630–1763* (Middletown, Conn.: Wesleyan University Press, 1986), pp.98–99, 163–67.

86. *Winthrop Papers*, 5 vols. (Boston: Massachusetts Historical Society, 1929–47), 3:149 (and see pp. 171–72).

87. Hubbard, *General History*, p. 60. Even Thomas Morton referred to the disease that had swept through "New Canaan" as the "Minister" of God, sent to destroy the Indians "by heapes": *New English Canaan*, ed. Charles Francis Adams, Jr. (Boston: Prince Society, 1883; reprint ed., New York: Burt Franklin, 1967), p. 120.

88. William Hubbard, *The Present State of New-England. Being a Narrative of the Troubles with the Indians in New-England* (London, 1677; reprint ed., with introduction by Cecelia Tichi, Bainbridge, N.Y.: York Mail-Print, 1972), title page (italics reversed); and see pt. 1, p. 109; pt. 2, pp. 79–81. For similar rhetoric, see: *New Englands First Fruits* (1643), in Samuel Eliot Morison, *The Founding of Harvard College* (Cambridge, Mass.: Harvard University Press, 1935), p. 441; Charles Chauncy, *Gods Mercy* (Cambridge, Mass., 1655), p. 18; Cotton Mather, *Magnalia Christi Americana* 1:344; Cotton Mather, *Decennium Luctuosum*, pp. 246, 249; Cotton Mather, *Present State*, p. 41; Increase Mather, "Diary of Increase Mather," ed. Samuel A. Green, Massachusetts Historical Society, *Proceedings*, 2d ser., 13 (1899–1900): 400; Increase Mather, *A Brief History of the Warr With the Indians in New-England* (1676), in Slotkin and Folsom, *So Dreadfull a Judgment*, p. 139; and Mary Rowlandson, *The Soveraignty & Goodness of God* (1682), in Slotkin and Folsom, *So Dreadfull a Judgment*, p. 360. See also Neal Salisbury, *Manitou and Providence: Indians, Europeans, and the Making of New England, 1500–1643* (New York and Oxford: Oxford University Press, 1982), p. 225; Richard Slotkin, *Regeneration Through Violence: The Mythology of the American Frontier, 1600–1860* (Middletown, Conn.: Wesleyan University Press, 1973), pp. 55, 83–84; and Slotkin and Folsom, *So Dreadfull a Judgment*, especially pp. 61–63.

89. [Samuel Gorton], *Simplicities Defence against Seven-Headed Policy* (1646), in Peter Force, ed., *Tracts and Other Papers*, 4 vols. (Gloucester, Mass.: Peter Smith, 1963), vol. 4, no. 6, p. 45.

90. Roger Williams, *The Bloudy Tenent, of Persecution, for cause of Conscience* (1644), in *The Complete Writings of Roger Williams*, 7 vols., ed. Reuben Aldridge Guild et al. (New York: Russell & Russell, 1963), 3:318 (and see pp. 360–63).

91. Roger Williams, *Christenings make not Christians* (1645), in *Complete Writings* 7:31.

92. See Williams, *Christenings*, pp. 31–33 (quote is from p. 32). In *The Bloudy Tenent* Williams also argued that "Although the tearme *Heathen* is most commonly appropriated to the wilde naked *Americans*, &c.," it seemed equally applicable "even to the civilized *Romanes* &c. and consequently must it be applied to the most *civilized Antichristians*, who are not the *Church* and people of *God* in *Christ*" (p. 400). On the rhetoric of national election in New England, see especially Bercovitch, *American Jeremiad*.

93. Williams, *Christenings*, p. 38.

94. Williams, *Bloudy Tenent*, p. 323.

95. *Winthrop Papers* 3:54–55.

96. Numbers 33:55–56.

97. John Cotton, *Gods Promise to His Plantations* (1630), *Old South Leaflets*, no. 53 (n.d.): 14.

98. Michael Wigglesworth, "God's Controversy with New-England" (1662), in Kenneth Silverman, ed., *Colonial American Poetry* (New York and London: Hafner, 1968), pp. 77, 71, 79–81.

99. See Increase Mather's "Discourse Concerning the Danger of Apostacy," p. 78: "When Predecessors have been eminent for God, their Successours have been most degenerate, . . . Yea, it is a sad Truth that Religion has seldome been upheld in the power of it, for above one or two Generations together."

100. Cotton Mather, *Things for a Distress'd People to think upon* (1696), in Ronald A. Bosco, ed., *The Puritan Sermon in America, 1630–1750*, 4 vols. (Delmar, N.Y.: Scholars' Facsimiles & Reprints, 1978), 3:11–12 (original pagination). On Mather and the problem of Indianization, see also my chap. 6.

Chapter 4. *"Wild Men of Mine Own Nation"*

1. David Beers Quinn, ed., *The Roanoke Voyages, 1584–1590: Documents to Illustrate the English Voyages to North America Under the Patent Granted to Walter Raleigh in 1584*, 2 vols. (London: Hakluyt Society, 1955), 1:204–5. For the sake of clarity, I have modernized Lane's spelling and punctuation.

2. On Lane's rather equivocal recommendation of Roanoke, see David Beers Quinn, *Set Fair for Roanoke: Voyages and Colonies, 1584–1606* (Chapel Hill and London: University of North Carolina Press, 1985), p. 147.

3. On this matter I must again mention my indebtedness to Richard Slotkin's *Regeneration Through Violence: The Mythology of the American Frontier, 1600–1860* (Middletown, Conn.: Wesleyan University Press, 1973); and Richard Slotkin and James K. Folsom, eds., *So Dreadfull a Judgment: Puritan Responses to King Philip's War, 1676–1677* (Middletown, Conn.: Wesleyan University Press, 1978).

4. William Strachey, *A True Reportory of the Wreck and Redemption of Sir Thomas Gates, Knight, upon and from the Islands of the Bermudas*, in Louis B. Wright, ed., *A Voyage to Virginia in 1609: Two Narratives: Strachey's "True Reportory" and Jourdain's "Discovery of the Bermudas"* (Charlottesville: University Press of Virginia, 1964), p. 16; and Silvester Jourdain, *A Discovery of the Bermudas, Otherwise Called the Isle of Devils*, in Wright, *A Voyage to Virginia in 1609*, p. 108. Wright gives a useful summary of the basic facts of the *Sea Venture*'s wreck in his introduction to *A Voyage to Virginia*, which I follow here. See also Leo Marx, *The Machine in the Garden: Technology and the Pastoral Ideal in America* (London, Oxford, and New York: Oxford University Press, 1964), pp. 34–72; and Bernard W. Sheehan, *Savagism and Civility: Indians and Englishmen in Colonial Virginia* (Cambridge, London, and New York: Cambridge University Press, 1980), p. 111.

5. Jourdain, *Discovery*, p. 109.

6. Strachey, *True Reportory*, pp. 32–33; and Jourdain, *Discovery*, p. 110.

7. Strachey, *True Reportory*, pp. 44, 40–41.

8. Ibid., p. 49.

9. Ibid., pp. 43, 52–53; Jourdain, *Discovery*, pp. 113–14; and Sheehan, *Savagism and Civility*, p. 111.

10. Strachey, *True Reportory*, p. 42. And see B. F. De Costa, "Stephen Hopkins of the Mayflower," *New England Historical and Genealogical Register* 33 (1879): 302; and Sheehan, *Savagism and Civility*, p. 111. It has been suggested that there was a more direct link between the *Sea Venture* and the *Mayflower* in the person of Stephen Hopkins—a name shared by one of the leading mutineers on Bermuda and a *Mayflower* passenger. See De Costa, "Stephen Hopkins"; George F. Wil-

lison, *Saints and Strangers: Being the Lives of the Pilgrim Fathers & Their Families, with Their Friends & Foes; & an Account of Their Posthumous Wanderings in Limbo, Their Final Resurrection & Rise to Glory, & the Strange Pilgrimages of Plymouth Rock* (New York: Reynal & Hitchcock, 1945), pp. 140–41; and William Bradford, *Of Plymouth Plantation, 1620–1647*, ed. Samuel Eliot Morison (New York: Alfred A. Knopf, 1982), p. 87 n. 3. In the absence of conclusive evidence, however, it seems more likely that the name is a mere coincidence. On the Bermuda Stephen Hopkins, see also Sheehan, *Savagism and Civility*, p. 111.

11. William Bradford, *History of Plymouth Plantation, 1620–1647*, 2 vols., ed. Worthington Chauncey Ford (Boston: Massachusetts Historical Society, 1912; reprint ed., New York: Russell & Russell, 1968), 1:189, 191; Willison, *Saints and Strangers*, pp. 138–46.

12. For Bradford's encounter with the deer snare, see [William Bradford, Edward Winslow, and Robert Cushman], *A Relation or Journall of the beginning and proceedings of the English Plantation setled at Plimoth in New England* (London, 1622; reprint ed., n.p.: Readex Microprint, 1966), pp. 7–8. Stephen Hopkins explained the device's use to the other Pilgrims, and Willison and De Costa offer this as evidence that Hopkins had been in America before—presumably with the *Sea Venture* company that eventually landed in Virginia: see *Saints and Strangers*, p. 140; and "Stephen Hopkins," pp. 304–5.

13. [Bradford et al.], *Relation*, pp. 4–5.

14. Ibid., pp. 6–10 (and see pp. 13, 51).

15. Ibid., pp. 6–7.

16. Ibid., pp. 6, 11.

17. Ibid., pp. 11–12.

18. John Seelye, *Prophetic Waters: The River in Early American Life and Literature* (New York: Oxford University Press, 1977), pp. 114–15. Seelye's interpretation of this incident has greatly influenced my own.

19. [Bradford et al.], *Relation*, p. 32. And see Bradford, *Plymouth Plantation* 1:198–99.

20. [Bradford et al.], *Relation*, pp. 32, 35; and see Bradford, *Plymouth Plantation* 1:199, 202–4.

21. Bradford, *Plymouth Plantation* 1:202. The Indians themselves understood the importance of Squanto's services to the English. One Indian remarked that "if he [Squanto] were dead, the English had lost their tongue": *Relation*, p. 53. Squanto apparently tried to make the best of his situation by exploiting his role as mediator between the Indians and the English: see Bradford, *Plymouth Plantation* 1:254–55; Edward Winslow, *Good Newes from New England* (1624), in Alexander Young, ed., *Chronicles of the Pilgrim Fathers of the Colony of Plymouth, from 1602 to 1625* (Boston: Charles C. Little and James Brown, 1841), p. 289; and John M. Humins, "Squanto and Massasoit: A Struggle for Power," *New England Quarterly* 60 (1987): 54–70. On Squanto's travels, see Neal Salisbury, *Manitou and Providence: Indians, Europeans, and the Making of New England, 1500–1643* (New York and Oxford: Oxford University Press, 1982), p. 107.

22. Bradford, *Plymouth Plantation* 1:283. George Steiner's thoughts on the implications of multilingualism have influenced my view of Squanto. See especially the title essay in Steiner's *Extraterritorial: Papers on Literature and the Language Revolution* (New York: Atheneum, 1971), pp. 3–11.

23. [Bradford et al.], *Relation*, p. 10.

24. John Smith, *Advertisements for the Unexperienced Planters of New England, or Any Where* (1631), in *The Complete Works of Captain John Smith (1580–1631)*, 3 vols.,

ed. Philip L. Barbour (Chapel Hill and London: University of North Carolina Press for the Institute of Early American History and Culture, 1986), 3:272.

25. See Sheehan, *Savagism and Civility*, pp. 110–15.

26. In *A Map of Virginia* (1612), Smith suggested that some of the Virginia colonists who had complained about conditions in the colony did so out of disappointment at not finding "dissolute liberty" there: in *Complete Works* 1:176.

27. John Smith, *The True Travels, Adventures, and Observations of Captain John Smith* (1630), in *Complete Works* 3:221.

28. Smith, *Advertisements*, pp. 285–86 (see also p. 283).

29. Bradford, *Plymouth Plantation* 1:272. I have borrowed the terms "Westonians" and "Plymotheans" from Cotton Mather, *Magnalia Christi Americana; or, The Ecclesiastical History of New-England*, 2 vols. (Hartford, Conn., 1852; reprint ed., New York: Russell & Russell, 1967), 1:58. Useful modern accounts of the events at Wessagusset include: Willison, *Saints and Strangers*, pp. 214–30; Francis Jennings, *The Invasion of America: Indians, Colonialism, and the Cant of Conquest* (New York: W. W. Norton & Company for the Institute of Early American History and Culture, 1976), pp. 186–87; Salisbury, *Manitou and Providence*, pp. 125–40; and (contra Jennings) see Alden T. Vaughan, *New England Frontier: Puritans and Indians, 1620–1675*, rev. ed. (New York and London: W. W. Norton & Company, 1979), pp. xxii–xxiii.

30. Bradford, *Plymouth Plantation* 1:288, 291.

31. For New England reactions to the hanging at Wessagusset (and Butler's version of it), see ibid., p. 291; William Hubbard, *A General History of New England, From The Discovery to MDCLXXX* (Boston, 1848; reprint ed., New York: Arno Press, 1972), p. 77; and Cotton Mather, *Magnalia Christi Americana* 1:58.

32. Bradford, *Plymouth Plantation* 1:290.

33. Winslow, *Good Newes*, p. 333.

34. Hubbard, *General History*, p. 111 (and see Willison, *Saints and Strangers*, pp. 131–32).

35. For Standish's actions at Wessagusset, see Winslow, *Good Newes* pp. 336–42 (the Indian is quoted from p. 338); Bradford, *Plymouth Plantation* 1:294–96; Jennings, *Invasion of America*, pp. 186–87; Willison, *Saints and Strangers*, pp. 214–30; and Salisbury, *Manitou and Providence*, pp. 125–40.

36. Bradford, *Plymouth Plantation* 1:297.

37. Ibid.

38. Ibid., pp. 367–69, 368 n. 1.

39. Ibid., pp. 295n, 296.

40. Winslow, *Good Newes*, p. 331.

41. See Samuel Maverick's "Briefe Discription of New England and the Severall Townes therein, together with the Present Government thereof," Massachusetts Historical Society, *Proceedings*, 2d ser., 1 (1884–85): 240.

42. Winslow, *Good Newes*, p. 276. Winslow qualified his remarks on the Westonians by adding: "I would not be understood to think there were no well deserving persons amongst them; for of mine knowledge it was a grief to some that they were so yoked; whose deserts, as they were then suitable to their honest protestations, so I desire still may be in respect of their just and true Relations."

43. Ibid., p. 327.

44. Bradford, *Plymouth Plantation* 2:80–83.

45. Ibid., p. 83.

46. Ibid., pp. 83–84, 84 n. 1 (Bradford's note).

47. Ibid., p. 85.

48. Ibid., p. 97.

49. Ibid., p. 107. For the proclamation Ashley allegedly violated, see the plate between pp. 106 and 107. For the testimony against Ashley, see pp. 107–9 n. 5.

50. Ibid., pp. 107–8 (and see pp. 107–9 n. 5).

51. For biographical information on Morton I have relied upon: Charles Francis Adams, Jr., "Morton of Merry-Mount," in his edition of Morton's *New English Canaan* (Boston: Prince Society, 1883; reprint ed., New York: Burt Franklin, 1967), pp. 1–98; Charles Edward Banks, "Thomas Morton of Merry Mount," Massachusetts Historical Society, *Proceedings* 58 (1924–25): 147–93; and Donald F. Connors, *Thomas Morton* (New York: Twayne Publishers, 1969), pp. 17–29 (and see the "Chronology," pp. 13–15).

52. For Morton's seal, see Banks, "Thomas Morton of Merry Mount," p. 160 and the plate facing p. 169.

53. My interpretation of Morton and his book is especially indebted to: Salisbury, *Manitou and Providence*, pp. 152–65; Seelye, *Prophetic Waters*, pp. 166–77; Slotkin, *Regeneration Through Violence*, pp. 58–65; Michael Zuckerman, "Pilgrims in the Wilderness: Community, Modernity, and the May Pole at Merry Mount," *New England Quarterly* 50 (1977): 255–77; and Daniel B. Shea, " 'Our Professed Old Adversary': Thomas Morton and the Naming of New England," *Early American Literature* 23 (1988): 52–69. James Muldoon offers Morton as an example that the same contamination of culture that had plagued the English in Ireland might happen in America: see "The Indian as Irishman," *Essex Institute Historical Collections* 111 (1975): 285. Of course, Nathaniel Hawthorne's "The May-Pole of Merry Mount" may still be the single most influential interpretation.

54. Bradford, *Plymouth Plantation* 2:45, 47–48.

55. Ibid., p. 48.

56. Ibid., p. 49.

57. On the May Games and Pole, see: Frederick J. Furnivall, ed., *Phillip Stubbes's Anatomy of the Abuses in England in Shakspere's Youth, A.D. 1583* (London: New Shakspere Society and N. Trübner & Co., 1877–79), pt. 1, pp. 146–50; Slotkin, *Regeneration Through Violence*, pp. 62–64; E. K. Chambers, *The Mediaeval Stage*, 2 vols. (London: Oxford University Press, 1903), 1:160–81; and Joseph Strutt, *The Sports and Pastimes of the People of England* (London: William Tegg and Co., 1855), pp. 339–42, 351–54. William Hubbard provides an interesting comparison of pagan festivals and the American Indians' practices: "It is not worth the while either to write or read what it [the Indians' religion] was, all of it depending on the uncertain reports of some occasional spectators; but nothing unclean or filthy, like the heathen's feasts of Bacchus and Venus, was ever heard of amongst any of them": *General History*, p. 35.

58. On Robin Hood, see: J. C. Holt, *Robin Hood* (London: Thames and Hudson, 1982); Maurice Keen, *The Outlaws of Medieval Legend*, rev. ed. (London and Henley: Routledge & Kegan Paul, 1977), especially pp. xix, 2; John Seelye, "Some Green Thoughts on a Green Theme," in George Abbott White and Charles Newman, eds., *Literature in Revolution* (New York, Chicago, and San Francisco: Holt, Rinehart and Winston, 1972), pp. 588–89; and W. Gordon Zeeveld, *The Temper of Shakespeare's Thought* (New Haven and London: Yale University Press, 1974), pp. 202–5.

59. *As You Like It*, act 1, scene 1, lines 114–19.

60. Bradford, *Plymouth Plantation* 2:54.

61. Minor White Latham, *The Elizabethan Fairies: The Fairies of Folklore and the Fairies of Shakespeare* (New York: Columbia University Press, 1930), pp. 52, 223, and passim. On notions of fairies in the sixteenth and seventeenth centuries, see also: K. M. Briggs, *The Anatomy of Puck: An Examination of Fairy Beliefs among Shakespeare's Contemporaries and Successors* (London: Routledge and Kegan Paul, 1959); and Keith Thomas, *Religion and the Decline of Magic* (New York: Charles Scribner's Sons, 1971), pp. 606–14.

62. On the fairies' dancing, see Latham, *Elizabethan Fairies*, pp. 91–92.

63. John Milton, *Comus*, in *John Milton: Complete Poems and Major Prose*, ed. Merritt Y. Hughes (Indianapolis: Odyssey Press of Bobbs-Merrill Company, 1957), lines 172, 532–36.

64. Ibid., line 550.

65. On Morton as a relatively conservative challenge to the Puritans' more radical social tendencies, see Zuckerman, "Pilgrims in the Wilderness," pp. 276–77.

66. Bradford, *Plymouth Plantation* 2:51.

67. On the gun-running charge, see: Minor Wallace Major, "William Bradford versus Thomas Morton," *Early American Literature* 5 (1970): 1–13; Robert Daly, "William Bradford's Vision of History," *American Literature* 44 (1973): 564–65; Salisbury, *Manitou and Providence*, pp. 157–58, 162.

68. William Bradford, "Governour Bradford's Letter Book," Massachusetts Historical Society, *Collections*, [1st ser.], 3 (1794): 62.

69. See Bradford, *Plymouth Plantation* 2:56–57.

70. See ibid., p. 76, 76 n. 1; and Adams, "Morton of Merry-Mount," pp. 46–47.

71. Bradford, *Plymouth Plantation* 2:76 (and for a general account of these events, see pp. 73–77).

72. Ibid., p. 76.

73. Morton, *New English Canaan*, p. 276 (and see Zuckerman, "Pilgrims in the Wilderness"). For Morton's reference to himself as "mine Hoste of Ma-re Mount," see, for example, p. 277.

74. See Salisbury, *Manitou and Providence*, pp. 159–60.

75. Morton, *New English Canaan*, p. 280 (italics reversed).

76. Ibid., p. 289 (and see Adams, "Morton of Merry-Mount," p. 29).

77. Morton, *New English Canaan*, p. 276.

78. Ibid., pp. 256–57. For Morton's "Golden Age" view of the Indians, see pp. 175–78.

79. Ibid., p. 178.

80. Ibid., p. 256.

81. Ibid., p. 310 (and see p. 318 for Morton's reference to "greate Josua Temperwell").

82. Ibid., p. 113 (italics reversed).

83. Ibid., p. 248 (and for the entire Indian-grave story, see pp. 247–48).

84. *The Tempest*, act 1, scene 2, line 358. On "vild," see also Roger Williams, *A Key into the Language of America*, ed. John J. Teunissen and Evelyn J. Hinz (Detroit: Wayne State University Press, 1973), p. 290 n. 116.20.

85. Morton, *New English Canaan*, p. 254.

86. Ibid., pp. 282–83. Morton could have found inadvertent support for his charge that the Pilgrims were "masterles people" in a letter John Robinson wrote to his flock reminding them that they were "not furnished with any persons of speitall eminencie above the rest, to be chosen by you into office of goverment": quoted in Bradford, *Plymouth Plantation* 1:134. For Bradford on Morton's "inordinariness," see "Governour Bradford's Letter Book," p. 62. It is impor-

tant to note that Morton, in the *New English Canaan*, was not reacting to the rhetoric of Bradford's *Plymouth Plantation* (in which Bradford is more likely reacting, in part, to Morton's rhetoric), but to Bradford's letters to England (see the "Letter Book," pp. 61–64) and to oral rumors that were surely circulating about him. The *New English Canaan*, through its own strategy against the Puritans, implies the argument (oral or written) that it seeks to refute.

87. Morton, *New English Canaan*, pp. 313–15.
88. Ibid., pp. 313, 316.
89. Ibid., p. 315 (italics reversed).
90. Ibid., pp. 282–83.
91. Ibid., p. 288.
92. Ibid., pp. 278, 332.
93. Ibid., pp. 260–61.
94. Ibid., pp. 322–23, 327.
95. Ibid., pp. 327–30.
96. Ibid., pp. 297–99.
97. Ibid., p. 213.
98. Ibid., p. 277.
99. Ibid., pp. 280–82.
100. Ibid., p. 123.
101. Ibid., pp. 123–24.
102. Ibid., pp. 128–29 (and see p. 126).
103. Charles Francis Adams, Jr., suggests that "Morton's attempt to trace the origin of the North American Indians from Brutus, . . . reads like a humorous satire on the historical methods in vogue with the writers of his time": ibid., p. 129 n. 1. Morton's satirical motives, however, seem directed against more than "historical methods."
104. Morton, *New English Canaan*, pp. 126–27. On the Trojan-origins question, see: Arthur B. Ferguson, *Clio Unbound: Perception of the Social and Cultural Past in Renaissance England* (Durham, N.C.: Duke University Press, 1979), pp. 105–7; and Hugh A. MacDougall, *Racial Myth in English History: Trojans, Teutons, and Anglo-Saxons* (Hanover, N.H.: University Press of New England, 1982), pp. 7–27.
105. Morton, *New English Canaan*, p. 123.
106. On this point, see also Slotkin, *Regeneration Through Violence*, pp. 59–60.
107. See Ferguson, *Clio Unbound*, pp. 106–7; and MacDougall, *Racial Myth*, pp. 21–22, 24.
108. Michael Drayton, "To the Virginian Voyage," in Alexander M. Witherspoon and Frank J. Warnke, eds., *Seventeenth-Century Prose and Poetry*, 2d ed. (New York, Chicago, San Francisco, and Atlanta: Harcourt, Brace & World, 1963), p. 721. On Drayton's Stuart connections, see MacDougall, *Racial Myth*, p. 22.
109. For the chronology of Morton's last years, see Connors, *Thomas Morton*, p. 15.
110. *Winthrop Papers*, 5 vols. (Boston: Massachusetts Historical Society, 1929–47), 4:428.
111. Ibid., p. 464.
112. Ibid., p. 465.
113. Connors, *Thomas Morton*, p. 15.
114. Maverick, "Briefe Discription," p. 238. For Puritan historians' treatment of Morton, see, of course, Bradford's *Plymouth Plantation* and Hubbard's *General History*, pp. 102–4, 137.
115. Roger Williams, *Letters of Roger Williams, 1632–1682*, in *The Complete Writings*

of Roger Williams, 7 vols., ed. Reuben Aldridge Guild et al. (New York: Russell & Russell, 1963), 6:101. See also Sydney V. James, "The Worlds of Roger Williams," *Rhode Island History* 37 (1978): 103.

116. For Williams's letters to Winthrop on Baker, see *Winthrop Papers* 3:500 and 4:7, 15, 31.

117. On the "Holy Wild Man," see Penelope B. R. Doob, *Nebuchadnezzar's Children: Conventions of Madness in Middle English Literature* (New Haven and London: Yale University Press, 1974), pp. 134–207; and Richard Bernheimer, *Wild Men in the Middle Ages: A Study in Art, Sentiment, and Demonology* (Cambridge, Mass.: Harvard University Press, 1952), p. 13. On Williams's view of himself as "witness" (with its scriptural parallels), see W. Clark Gilpin, *The Millenarian Piety of Roger Williams* (Chicago and London: University of Chicago Press, 1979), pp. 78–95; and Jesper Rosenmeier, "The Teacher and the Witness: John Cotton and Roger Williams," *William and Mary Quarterly*, 3d ser., 25 (1968): 408–31.

118. Williams, *Key into the Language of America*, p. 105 (italics reversed).

119. On Nebuchadnezzar as a model for both the holy and unholy wild man, see Doob, *Nebuchadnezzar's Children*, p. 138.

120. Williams, *Letters*, p. 165 (and see James, "Worlds of Roger Williams," p. 106).

121. Bradford, *Plymouth Plantation* 2:161.

122. Hubbard, *General History*, pp. 205–6.

123. Cotton Mather, *Magnalia Christi Americana* 2:497, 495 (and see pp. 495–99, passim).

124. Bruce C. Daniels suggests that Rhode Island's reputation as a pariah existed more in the rhetoric of the period than in actual practice: see his *Dissent and Conformity on Narragansett Bay: The Colonial Rhode Island Town* (Middletown, Conn.: Wesleyan University Press, 1983), especially pp. 22, 111–12.

125. Williams, *Letters*,, pp. 4, 5.

126. *Winthrop Papers* 3:509. And see James, "Worlds of Roger Williams," p. 102.

127. Williams, *Letters*, p. 303.

128. Roger Williams, *The Bloody Tenent Yet More Bloody* (1652), in *Complete Writings* 4:222. See also Rosenmeier, "Teacher and the Witness," p. 419; Theodore Dwight Bozeman, "Religious Liberty and the Problem of Order in Early Rhode Island," *New England Quarterly* 45 (1972): 44–64; and Edmund S. Morgan, *Roger Williams: The Church and the State* (New York: Harcourt, Brace & World, 1967), chaps. 4–5.

129. Roger Williams, *The Hireling Ministry None of Christs* (1652), in *Complete Writings* 7:167, 153, 169. See also Gilpin, *Millenarian Piety*, pp. 142–46.

130. John Norton, *The Heart of N-England rent at the Blasphemies of the Present Generation* (1659), in *Photostat Americana*, 2d ser., 73 (1936): 39. On the Quakers' challenge to New England, see Larzer Ziff, *Puritanism in America: New Culture in a New World* (New York: Viking Press, 1973), pp. 138–43. The General Court of Massachusetts Bay commissioned Norton to write against the Quaker menace—the result being *The Heart of N-England rent*, for which he was duly thanked and rewarded with a grant of land: see Nathaniel B. Shurtleff, ed., *Records of the Governor and Company of the Massachusetts Bay in New England*, 5 vols. (Boston, 1853–54), vol. 4, pt. 1, pp. 348, 397. For views of Williams himself as an infection, see John Winthrop, *The History of New England from 1630 to 1649*, 2 vols., ed. James Savage (Boston: Little, Brown and Company, 1853), 1:209; and John Cotton, *A Reply to Mr. Williams his Examination; And Answer of the Letters sent to him by John Cotton* (1647), in Williams's *Complete Writings* 2:27,

93. Cotton Mather said Williams "infected with his *extravagancies*" members of his Salem congregation: *Magnalia Christi Americana* 2:497.

131. Hubbard, *General History*, pp. 208–9. Hubbard also notes "the fruits of good works that appeared in his life and conversation, especially in his faithfulness to the English of the Massachusetts, by whom he might have accounted he had been so severely handled" (p. 209). See also Cotton Mather, *Magnalia Christi Americana* 2:499; and [Joshua Scottow], *A Narrative of the Planting of the Massachusetts Colony* (Boston, 1694), pp. 21–22. A useful survey of Williams's relations with the Quakers is in Gilpin, *Millenarian Piety*, pp. 167–73; and see Morgan, *Roger Williams*, pp. 56–61. For an account of the circumstances of the debate, see Ola Elizabeth Winslow, *Master Roger Williams: A Biography* (New York: Macmillan, 1957), pp. 272–80.

132. Roger Williams, *George Fox Digg'd out of his Burrowes* (1676), in *Complete Writings* 5:5 (italics reversed).

133. Ibid., p. 308.

134. Ibid., p. 309.

135. Ibid., p. 211.

136. Ibid., pp. 309, 13 (italics reversed).

137. Ibid., p. 28.

138. Ibid., p. 311.

139. Ibid., p. 211. According to Lawrence Stone, "foreign visitors [to England] from the late fifteenth to the late eighteenth centuries noted with astonishment and shock the freedom with which it was the custom in England for persons of different sexes to greet each other by a kiss upon the lips": *The Family, Sex and Marriage in England, 1500–1800* (New York: Harper & Row, 1977), p. 520. The Quakers were apparently trying to pioneer the use of the handshake as a substitute.

140. Williams, *George Fox*, pp. 499, 284.

141. Ibid., p. 53.

142. Ibid., p. 84.

143. Ibid., p. 75.

144. See Gilpin, *Millenarian Piety*, p. 170.

145. Williams, *George Fox*, p. 147.

146. Ibid., p. 283.

147. Ibid., pp. 278–79.

148. For an account of the debates that emphasizes the bitterness of Williams's attack, see Winslow, *Master Roger Williams*, pp. 274–79. But see also Perry Miller, *Roger Williams: His Contribution to the American Tradition* (Indianapolis and New York: Bobbs-Merrill Company, 1953), pp. 241–45. According to Miller, "a good part of the interchange became mere name-calling—Williams giving as good as he got. Unless one is interested in these local spats, most of the book is today unreadable. And yet there are wonderful passages in it, and no understanding of Williams will be complete unless it is taken fully into account" (p. 245).

149. Williams later claimed that John Winthrop had advised him to escape to the Narragansett area, though Winthrop's motives for such advice remain unclear. See Williams's *Letters*, pp. 269, 335; and Cyclone Covey's discussion of this point in *The Gentle Radical: A Biography of Roger Williams* (New York: Macmillan, 1966), pp. 122–23. For the details of Williams's banishment, see, in addition to Covey's treatment, Winslow's *Master Roger Williams*, pp. 107–24.

150. Roger Williams, *Experiments of Spiritual Life & Health, And their Preservatives* (1652), in *Complete Writings* 7:47 (italics reversed). In this paragraph I have also drawn upon Covey, *Gentle Radical*, pp. 122, 2; and Winslow, *Master Roger Williams*, pp. 126–27.

151. Miller, *Roger Williams*, p. 52.

152. Roger Williams, *Mr. Cottons Letter Lately Printed, Examined and Answered* (1644), in *Complete Writings* 1:315 (italics reversed), (and see his *Letters*, pp. 335–37). On Williams's considerable talent for self-dramatization, see (in addition to Miller): Gilpin, *Millenarian Piety*, p. 88; Covey, *Gentle Radical*, p. 122; John Garrett, *Roger Williams: Witness Beyond Christendom, 1603–1683* (New York: Macmillan, 1970), p. 18; and James, "Worlds of Roger Williams," p. 103.

153. Williams, *Mr. Cottons Letter*, p. 319. Regarding his illness, he wrote that he was already "neare unto death" as a result of overwork and traveling back and forth from the court. Then, "(notwithstanding the mediating testimony of two skillfull in Physick) I was unmercifully driven from my chamber to a Winters flight" (p. 340).

154. Ibid., p. 315 (italics reversed).

155. Ibid., pp. 337–38.

156. John Cotton, *Reply to Mr. Williams*, p. 17.

157. Ibid., pp. 92–93.

158. See John Cotton, *A Letter of Mr. John Cottons Teacher of the Church in Boston, in New-England, to Mr. Williams a Preacher there* (1643), in Williams's *Complete Writings* 1:297–98. Covey notes that there is evidence that Cotton's advice in favor of banishment was the determining influence for at least some of the court members: see *Gentle Radical*, p. 116.

159. Cotton, *Reply to Mr. Williams*, p. 19.

160. Ibid., p. 87.

161. For Cotton's belief that "Society in all sorts of humane affaires is better then Solitariness," see his *Briefe Exposition with Practicall Observations upon The Whole Book of Ecclesiastes* (London, 1654), pp. 85, 87.

162. Cotton's poem quoted in John Norton, *Abel being Dead yet speaketh; Or, the Life & Death Of that deservedly Famous Man of GOD, Mr John Cotton* (London, 1658; reprint ed., Delmar, N.Y.: Scholars' Facsimiles & Reprints, 1978), pp. 29–30 (italics reversed).

163. Cotton, *Reply to Mr. Williams*, p. 210.

164. Ibid., p. 22. Cotton used these words in reference to Williams's polemic against him: "I confesse we have . . . cause to admire, and adore the wisdome, and dreadfull Justice of God herein, That seeing Mr. *Williams* hath been now as a branch cut off from the Church of *Salem* these many yeares, he should bring forth no spirituall good fruits in due season: and that which he bringeth forth now at the last is bitter, and wild fruit." On the orthodox Puritan view of the wilderness as the ideal place for the likes of Roger Williams, see Loren Baritz, *City on a Hill: A History of Ideas and Myths in America* (New York, London, Sydney: John Wiley & Sons, 1964), p. 20.

165. Williams, *Key*, pp. 83, 84. My reading of Williams's *Key* has been greatly influenced by John J. Teunissen and Evelyn J. Hinz's introduction to their edition of the work, and I have also benefited from Gilpin's *Millenarian Piety*, pp. 121–25. On the *Key's* publication history, see Teunissen and Hinz, "Introduction," pp. 24–27 (and on the book's extralinguistic ambitions, see pp. 28–29).

166. Williams, *Key*, p. 175.

167. See, for example, *The Bloudy Tenent, of Persecution, for cause of Conscience* (1644),

in *Complete Writings* 3:104: "The *World* lyes in *wickednesse*, is like a *Wildernesse* or a *Sea* of *wilde Beasts* innumerable, *fornicators, covetous, Idolaters*, &c." He also played on wilderness-garden imagery by equating the wilderness with the world, the church with the garden: see ibid., pp. 95, 175, 198. On Williams's use of the wilderness motif, see also Gilpin, *Millenarian Piety*, pp. 58–59, 113–15, 131–34.

168. Williams, *Key*, pp. 225, 226.

169. Teunissen and Hinz, "Introduction," p. 61.

170. Williams, *Key*, p. 225; and Teunissen and Hinz, "Introduction," p. 61.

171. Williams, *Key*, p. 226.

172. Ibid., p. 175 (italics reversed).

173. Williams, *Bloudy Tenent*, p. 11.

174. Ibid., p. 419.

175. Ibid., p. 245.

176. Williams, *Bloody Tenent Yet More Bloody*, p. 143.

177. Ibid., p. 99.

178. Ibid., p. 97.

179. Williams, *Bloudy Tenent*, p. 186.

180. John Cotton, *The Bloudy Tenent, Washed, And Made White in the Bloud of the Lambe* (London, 1647), pp. 61, 171. Thomas Shepard, Jr., in his *Eye-Salve* (Cambridge, Mass., 1673), noted that God had delivered his people in New England "from such *that as ravening Wolves, but in Sheeps cloathing, would have wurried or scattered the Lords flock, if himself had not wrought for us*," and he cited the followers of Samuel Gorton as "Hornets" from whom God had saved them—"and that Ministerially by our Rulers spirited by himself thereunto" (p. 13).

181. See Williams's *Bloody Tenent Yet More Bloody*, pp. 425–29.

182. Williams, *Key*, p. 87.

183. Teunissen and Hinz deal admirably with Williams's use of the Indians to upbraid the English. They are careful, however, to distinguish Williams's approach from Morton's: see their "Introduction," p. 37.

184. Williams, *George Fox*, p. 399.

185. Williams, *Letters*, pp. 14, 321; "Winthrop Papers," Massachusetts Historical Society, *Collections*, 3d ser., 10 (1849): 27. And see James, "Worlds of Roger Williams," pp. 103–4.

186. *Winthrop Papers* 3:445.

187. "Winthrop Papers," Massachusetts Historical Society, *Collections*, 4th ser., 6 (1863): 305–6.

188. Williams, *Key*, p. 192. He came to the same conclusion about "Their publique *Games*" (p. 229).

189. Ibid., p. 90 (italics reversed).

190. Ibid., p. 98. In the original printing of 1643, the sense of linguistic opposition was heightened by heavy vertical lines separating the English and Indian columns—a device dropped in Teunissen and Hinz's edition.

191. Ibid.

192. Ibid., p. 133 (italics reversed). Commenting on this verse, Gilpin suggests that for Williams "The real distinction emerged between those inside and outside the covenant of grace, not between those of different cultural backgrounds": *Millenarian Piety*, p. 124. And Miller has noted that in Williams's view, "Civilization is not essentially superior to barbarism": *Roger Williams*, p. 54.

193. Williams, *Key*, p. 203.

194. Ibid., p. 193.

195. Ibid., p. 104.
196. Ibid., p. 148.
197. Ibid., p. 130.
198. Ibid., p. 241.
199. Ibid., p. 188 (italics reversed).
200. Ibid., p. 249 (italics reversed).
201. Ibid., p. 99 (italics reversed in poem).
202. Ibid., p. 204 (italics reversed).
203. For Morton's appropriation of Jonah's role, see *New English Canaan*, pp. 344–45 (quote is from p. 345).
204. Williams, *Christenings make not Christians* (1645), in *Complete Writings* 7:35.

Chapter 5. The Triumph of Indianism

1. For Williams's rather ambivalent thoughts on Indian conversion, see W. Clark Gilpin, *The Millenarian Piety of Roger Williams* (Chicago and London: University of Chicago Press, 1979), pp. 116, 121, 126–31; Edmund S. Morgan, *Roger Williams: The Church and the State* (New York: Harcourt, Brace & World, 1967), pp. 43–44, 51–52; and Perry Miller, *Roger Williams: His Contribution to the American Tradition* (Indianapolis and New York: Bobbs-Merrill Company, 1953), pp. 49–50. Miller makes the useful observation that, in practice, "Williams was not a great converter of Indians; in fact he hardly tried." In Williams's view, "God's method was to turn the soul from its idols before making it capable of worship, and until God had wrought, Williams would no longer . . . presume to work in God's place."
2. John Eliot, letter of November 13, 1649, in Edward Winslow, *The Glorious Progress of the Gospel, Amongst the Indians in New England* (1649), Massachusetts Historical Society, *Collections*, 3d ser., 4 (1834): 88. For Eliot, "co-habitation, Government, Arts, and trades" seem to have been the essential components of civility. For the term "Indianisme," see Henry Whitfield, *Strength out of Weaknesse* (1652), Massachusetts Historical Society, *Collections*, 3d ser., 4 (1834): 192–93.
3. Eliot, in Thomas Shepard, *The Clear Sun-shine of the Gospel Breaking Forth Upon the Indians in New-England* (1648), Massachusetts Historical Society, *Collections*, 3d ser., 4 (1834): 49–50.
4. For the Briton-Indian analogy, see, for example: [Robert Johnson], *Nova Britannia: Offering Most Excellent fruites by Planting in Virginia* (1609), in Peter Force, ed., *Tracts and Other Papers*, 4 vols. (Gloucester, Mass.: Peter Smith, 1963), vol. 1, no. 6, p. 14; John White, *The Planters Plea* (London, 1630; reprint ed., New York and Amsterdam: Da Capo Press and Theatrum Orbis Terrarum, 1968), p. 11; and Bernard W. Sheehan, *Savagism and Civility: Indians and Englishmen in Colonial Virginia* (Cambridge: Cambridge University Press, 1980), pp. 120–21.
5. Roger Williams, *A Key into the Language of America*, ed. John J. Teunissen and Evelyn J. Hinz (Detroit: Wayne State University Press, 1973), p. 85.
6. Shepard, *Clear Sun-shine*, pp. 60–61.
7. Williams, *Key*, p. 197.
8. Robert Cushman, *Cushman's Discourse [On the Sin and Danger of Self-Love]* (1622), in Alexander Young, ed., *Chronicles of the Pilgrim Fathers of the Colony of Plymouth, from 1602 to 1625* (Boston: Charles C. Little and James Brown, 1841), p. 268.
9. John Cotton, *Gods Promise to His Plantations* (1630), *Old South Leaflets* 53 (n.d.): 14.
10. White, *Planters Plea*, pp. 36, 27. James Axtell has also noted the early English

belief that the Indians' emulation of English material culture would lead easily to spiritual emulation: *The Invasion Within: The Contest of Cultures in Colonial North America* (New York and Oxford: Oxford University Press, 1985), pp. 131–33.

11. Nathaniel B. Shurtleff, ed., *Records of the Governor and Company of the Massachusetts Bay in New England*, 5 vols. (Boston, 1853–54), 1:17.

12. Cradock's letter, in Alexander Young, ed., *Chronicles of the First Planters of the Colony of Massachusetts Bay, from 1623 to 1636* (Boston: Charles C. Little and James Brown, 1846), pp. 133–34.

13. On English ministers' use of the Indian example, see Richard Slotkin and James K. Folsom, eds., *So Dreadfull a Judgment: Puritan Responses to King Philip's War, 1676–1677* (Middletown, Conn.: Wesleyan University Press, 1978), p. 37.

14. Shepard, *Clear Sun-shine*, p. 32 (italics reversed).

15. Henry Whitfield, *The Light appearing more and more towards the perfect Day* (1651), Massachusetts Historical Society, *Collections*, 3d ser., 4 (1834): 146–47 (italics reversed).

16. The phrase is from Shepard, *Clear Sun-shine*, p. 34, and see p. 48: "These things [i.e., evidence of the Indians' growing piety] me thinkes should move bowels, and awaken *English* hearts to be thankfull . . . : I wish the like hearts and wayes were seen in many *English* who professe themselves Christians, and that here in and many the like excellencies they were become *Indians*, excepting that name, as he did in another case, except his bonds."

17. For use of the Indian example to shame congregations in New England as well as Old, see Richard Mather, in [John] Eliot and [Thomas] Mayhew, *Tears of Repentance* (1653), Massachusetts Historical Society, *Collections*, 3d ser., 4 (1834): 224–25; and Daniel Gookin, *Historical Collections of the Indians in New England* (1674), Massachusetts Historical Society, *Collections*, [1st ser.], 1 (1792): 169.

18. Williams, *Key*, p. 197.

19. *New Englands First Fruits* (1643), a missionary promotional tract in Samuel Eliot Morison, *The Founding of Harvard College* (Cambridge, Mass.: Harvard University Press, 1935), p. 424.

20. For the reference to the drunken Indian, see William Hubbard, *The Present State of New-England. Being a Narrative of the Troubles with the Indians in New-England* (London, 1677; reprint ed., with introduction by Cecelia Tichi, Bainbridge, N.Y.: York Mail-Print, 1972), pt. 2, p. 59. See also William Wood, *New Englands Prospect* (London, 1634; reprint ed., Boston: Prince Society, 1865), p. 68; Paul J. Lindholdt, ed., *John Josselyn, Colonial Traveler: A Critical Edition of "Two Voyages to New-England"* (Hanover, N.H., and London: University Press of New England, 1988), p. 99; John Eliot, *Eliot's Brief Narrative [of the Progress of the Gospel amongst the Indians in New England]* (1671), *Old South Leaflets* 21 (n.d.): 6; Gookin, *Historical Collections*, p. 151; Roy Harvey Pearce, *Savagism and Civilization: A Study of the Indian and the American Mind*, rev. ed. (Baltimore and London: Johns Hopkins Press, 1967), p. 30; and James Axtell, *The European and the Indian: Essays in the Ethnohistory of Colonial North America* (New York and Oxford: Oxford University Press, 1981), pp. 257–59.

21. "Winthrop Papers," Massachusetts Historical Society, *Collections*, 3d ser., 10 (1849): 3.

22. Roger Williams, *Letters of Roger Williams, 1632–1682*, in *The Complete Writings of Roger Williams*, 7 vols., ed. Reuben Aldridge Guild et al. (New York: Russell & Russell, 1963), 6:333.

23. Increase Mather, *Wo to Drunkards* (Cambridge, Mass., 1673), p. 21. On Increase

Mather's interest in reforming drunkards, see Michael G. Hall, *The Last American Puritan: The Life of Increase Mather, 1639–1723* (Middletown, Conn.: Wesleyan University Press, 1988), pp. 108, 113, 122–23, 130, 199.

24. [Cotton Mather], *A Monitory, and Hortatory Letter, To those English, who debauch the Indians, By Selling Strong Drink unto them* (Boston, 1700), p. 8.

25. [Cotton Mather], *Monitory, and Hortatory Letter*, p. 7.

26. William Strachey, *The Historie of Travell into Virginia Britania (1612)*, ed. Louis B. Wright and Virginia Freund (London: Hakluyt Society, 1953), p. 19.

27. [William Bradford, Edward Winslow, and Robert Cushman], *A Relation or Journall of the beginning and proceedings of the English Plantation setled at Plimoth in New England* (London, 1622; reprint ed., n.p.: Readex Microprint, 1966), p. 61.

28. *Cushman's Discourse*, pp. 259–60.

29. Cradock's letter, in Young, *Chronicles of the First Planters*, pp. 136, 159.

30. *First Fruits*, p. 428.

31. White, *Planters Plea*, p. 52.

32. Francis Higginson, *New-Englands Plantation* (London, 1630; reprint ed., New York and Amsterdam: Da Capo Press and Theatrum Orbis Terrarum, 1970), sig. [C4ᵛ].

33. Edward Winslow, *Good Newes from New England* (1624), in Young, *Chronicles of the Pilgrim Fathers*, p. 366.

34. Wood, *New Englands Prospect*, p. 103.

35. *First Fruits*, p. 421.

36. Roger Williams, *Christenings make not Christians* (1645), in *Complete Writings* 7:39–40; and see Williams, *Key*, p. 84.

37. Roger Williams, *The Bloody Tenent Yet More Bloody* (1652), in *Complete Writings* 4:371–73. Williams based his skepticism about Eliot's linguistic competence on one of Massachusetts Bay's own conversion tracts, Shepard's *Clear Sun-shine*: "there Mr *Eliot* (the ablest amongst them in the *Indian Speech*) promising an old *Indian* a suit of Cloths, the man (sayth the relation) not well understanding Mr *Eliots* speech, asked another *Indian* what Mr *Eliot* said": ibid., p. 373; and for the original source of the anecdote, see *Clear Sun-shine*, p. 46. In later years Williams felt somewhat more charitable toward Eliot, especially when the immediate Quaker menace made old animosities seem less important than the basic fellowship in the task of conversion: "surely," Williams wrote, "God hath stirred up the Spirit of my ancient dear Friend *Mr. Eliot* to gain their Language, to Translate them the *Bible*, and many other wayes to bring the sound of a Saviour amongst them, which I humbly beg of God to perfect and finish for the Glory of his Great Name, &c.": *George Fox Digg'd out of his Burrowes* (1676), in *Complete Writings* 5:465. For a critical account of Eliot's language studies, see Francis Jennings, *The Invasion of America: Indians, Colonialism, and the Cant of Conquest* (New York: W. W. Norton & Company for the Institute of Early American History and Culture, 1976), pp. 233–34.

38. On the difficulties for the missionary work posed by the fact that "Congregational ministers were tied to their congregations," see Axtell, *Invasion Within*, p. 220.

39. Williams, *George Fox*, pp. 464–65.

40. Williams, *Bloody Tenent Yet More Bloody*, p. 72 n. 2.

41. Roger Williams, *Experiments of Spiritual Life & Health, And their Preservatives* (1652), in *Complete Writings* 7:89. For another example of the "strange *affection*" with which Englishmen endured Indian hospitality, see Edward Winslow's account of "A Journey to Packanokik, The Habitation of the Great King

Massasoyt," in [Bradford et al.], *Relation*, pp. 40–48, especially p. 46: "Very importunate he was to have us stay with them longer: But wee desired to keepe the Sabboth at home: and feared we should either be light-headed for want of sleepe, for what with bad lodging, the Savages barbarous singing, (for they use to sing themselves asleepe) lice and fleas within doores, and Muskeetoes without, wee could hardly sleepe all the time of our being there; we much fearing, that if wee should stay any longer, we should not be able to recover home for want of strength."

42. Alexander Whitaker, *Good Newes from Virginia* (London, 1613; reprint ed., New York: Scholars' Facsimiles & Reprints, n.d.), sig. [A4^r].

43. Endecott quoted in Whitfield, *Strength out of Weaknesse*, p. 191.

44. Chauncy in John W. Ford, ed., *Some Correspondence between the Governors and Treasurers of the New England Company in London and the Commissioners of the United Colonies in America, The Missionaries of the Company, And Others Between the Years 1657 and 1712* (New York: Burt Franklin, 1970), p. 10.

45. Henry W. Bowden and James P. Ronda, eds., *John Eliot's Indian Dialogues: A Study in Cultural Interaction* (Westport, Conn., and London, England: Greenwood Press, 1980), p. 59.

46. Clifford K. Shipton, ed., "The Autobiographical Memoranda of John Brock, 1636–1659," in Sacvan Bercovitch, ed., *A Library of American Puritan Writings: The Seventeenth Century*, 27 vols. (New York: AMS Press, n.d.), 8:101. Axtell notes that "the Harvard graduates who devoted any time to Indian missions were typically in their mid-twenties, with only home study in theology after the B.A. to their credit. Socially and intellectually, they had ranked in the bottom third of their classes": *Invasion Within*, p. 279.

In 1642 Thomas Lechford had perceived the Congregationalists' vulnerability on the missionary question. Pointing out that "there hath not been any sent forth by any Church to learne the Natives language, or to instruct them in the Religion," he cited the Puritans' congregational church polity as well as their millenarian assumptions as the reasons. Moreover, Lechford hinted that Congregationalism might well result in English degeneration rather than in the Indians' conversion. Because of the Puritans' restrictive policy of church membership, "they will (it is to be feared) in stead of propagating the Gospel, spread heathenisme; in stead of gaining to the Church, lose from the Church: for when the major part are unbaptized, as in twenty years undoubtedly they will be, by such a course continued, what is like to become of it, but that either they may goe among their fellow-heathens the Indians, or rise up against the Church, and break forth into many grievous distempers among themselves?" See Thomas Lechford, *Plain Dealing, or News from New England* (1642), ed. J. Hammond Trumbull (Boston, 1867; reprint ed., with introduction by Darrett B. Rutman, New York and London: Johnson Reprint Corporation, 1969), pp. 54–55, 7 (italics reversed).

47. Gookin, *Historical Collections*, p. 183.

48. Ibid., pp. 219–21. Gookin also noted that the Indians would thus "be able to read any English book" and "to understand our English ministers, who are better fitted to instruct them in substantial and orthodox divinity, than teachers of their own nation."

49. Ibid., pp. 221–22. See also Frederick William Gookin, *Daniel Gookin, 1612–1687, Assistant and Major General of the Massachusetts Bay Colony: His Life and Letters and some Account of His Ancestry* (Chicago: Lakeside Press, 1912); and Axtell, *Invasion Within*, pp. 184–85.

50. John Brinsley, *A Consolation for Our Grammar Schooles* (London, 1622; reprint ed., New York and Amsterdam: Da Capo Press and Theatrum Orbis Terrarum, 1969), sig. A3ᵛ (italics reversed) and title page. On Brinsley's proposals, see also Axtell, *Invasion Within*, pp. 181–82.

51. John Cotton, *The Way of Congregational Churches Cleared* (1648), in Larzer Ziff, ed., *John Cotton on the Churches of New England* (Cambridge, Mass.: Harvard University Press, 1968), p. 200. On Indian schools in New England and other colonies, see Axtell, *Invasion Within*, pp. 179–217. For Indians at Harvard, see Samuel Eliot Morison, *Harvard College in the Seventeenth Century*, 2 vols. (Cambridge, Mass.: Harvard University Press, 1936), 1:352–59.

52. Thomas Morton, *New English Canaan*, ed. Charles Francis Adams, Jr. (Boston: Prince Society, 1883; reprint ed., New York: Burt Franklin, 1967), p. 169.

53. For Indian children adopted into English service or bequeathed by their parents to the English, see: John Winthrop, *The History of New England from 1630 to 1649*, 2 vols., ed. James Savage (Boston: Little, Brown and Company, 1853), 1:142–43; Cotton, *Way of Congregational Churches Cleared*, pp. 277–78; John Cotton, *The Bloudy Tenent, Washed, And Made White in the Bloud of the Lambe* (London, 1647), p. 148; *First Fruits*, p. 427; and [Thomas Shepard?], *The Day-Breaking, If not The Sun-Rising of the Gospell With the Indians in New-England* (1647), Massachusetts Historical Society, *Collections*, 3d ser., 4 (1834): 3, 18, 22.

54. See *First Fruits*, pp. 422–25.

55. On this problem, see Neal Salisbury, "Red Puritans: The 'Praying Indians' of Massachusetts Bay and John Eliot," *William and Mary Quarterly*, 3d ser., 31 (1974): 42, 46.

56. [Shepard?], *Day-Breaking*, p. 4.

57. Ibid., p. 15. Shepard, however, did not expect much success until the Indians had been civilized—nor did he believe the English themselves could perform the task of conversion. God would probably use the Indians for this purpose, though the English could take a hand in beginning the process. On Shepard as the probable author of *Day-Breaking*, see J. William T. Youngs, Jr., "The Indian Saints of Early New England," *Early American Literature* 16 (1981–82): 253–54.

58. Eliot and Mayhew, *Tears of Repentance*, p. 208; Shepard, *Clear Sun-shine*, p. 40. On the New England Indians' movement toward civility and Christianity, see the discussion in Axtell, *Invasion Within*, especially chap. 7. James Holstun discusses Eliot and the Praying Towns from the perspective of Puritan Utopianism in *A Rational Millennium: Puritan Utopias of Seventeenth-Century England and America* (New York and Oxford: Oxford University Press, 1987), chap. 3. See also Yasuhide Kawashima's discussion of the Praying Indians' legal status in *Puritan Justice and the Indian: White Man's Law in Massachusetts, 1630–1763* (Middletown, Conn.: Wesleyan University Press, 1986), passim.

59. Shepard, *Clear Sun-shine*, pp. 44–45. On the Indians' adoption (and adaptation) of English clothes, see Axtell, *Invasion Within*, pp. 170–74.

60. Whitfield, *Strength out of Weaknesse*, pp. 178, 190. Increase Mather also described Indian singing in appreciative terms: "some of them are excellent singers": quoted in Cotton Mather, *Magnalia Christi Americana; or, The Ecclesiastical History of New-England*, 2 vols. (Hartford, Conn., 1852; reprint ed., New York: Russell & Russell, 1967), 1:570. See also Axtell, *Invasion Within*, pp. 235–36.

61. Whitfield, *Strength out of Weaknesse*, p. 179.

62. See Salisbury, "Red Puritans," pp. 42, 46.

63. John Underhill, *Newes From America* (1638), Massachusetts Historical Society, *Collections*, 3d ser., 6 (1837): 6.

64. Whitfield, *Light appearing*, pp. 109–10.

65. White, *Planters Plea*, p. 52.

66. Shepard, *Clear Sun-shine*, p. 66.

67. Whitfield, *Light appearing*, p. 107 (italics reversed).

68. *First Fruits*, p. 431. Samuel Eliot Morison aptly described the tract as "a promotion pamphlet; one half-expects to find in it a return postcard, on receipt of which 'our representative will call' ": *Founding of Harvard College*, p. 304.

69. On the returns brought in by *First Fruits*, see Morison, *Founding of Harvard College*, pp. 303–14; and William Kellaway, *The New England Company, 1649–1776: Missionary Society to the American Indians* (London: Longmans, Green and Company, 1961), pp. 8–10.

70. Nathaniel B. Shurtleff and David Pulsifer, eds., *Records of the Colony of New Plymouth in New England*, 12 vols. (Boston: 1855–61), 10:118. See also Samuel Maverick, "A Briefe Discription of New England and the Severall Townes therein, together with the Present Government thereof" (ca. 1660), Massachusetts Historical Society, *Proceedings*, 2d ser., 1 (1884–85): 243: Maverick praised the efforts of the Mayhews on Martha's Vineyard, but he also noted that they had accomplished their successes without much assistance from the collected money. "It were good," he wrote, "to enquire how it hath been disposed of[.] I know in some measure or at least suspect the bussines hath not been rightly carryed." Updating Maverick and other critics' charges, Francis Jennings refers to "the missionary racket" in *Invasion of America*, p. 53 (and see pp. 53–56, 242–43, 243 n. 38).

71. On rumors of Indian plots, see Winthrop, *History of New England* 2:159–60; William Hubbard, *A General History of New England, From The Discovery to MDCLXXX* (Boston, 1848; reprint ed., New York: Arno Press, 1972), p. 546; and Shurtleff and Pulsifer, *Records of the Colony of New Plymouth* 10:22.

72. See John Eliot, *A Late and Further Manifestation of the Progress of the Gospel amongst the Indians in New-England* (1655), Massachusetts Historical Society, *Collections*, 3d ser., 4 (1834): 271–72. And see Axtell, *Invasion Within*, p. 239.

73. Shurtleff and Pulsifer, *Records of the Colony of New Plymouth* 10:140.

74. See Salisbury, "Red Puritans," pp. 40–41, 51–52. Also useful in this context are Holstun, *Rational Millennium*, chap. 3; and Kawashima, *Puritan Justice and the Indian*, passim.

75. On English fears of "Indianization," I have benefited from the following works: Richard Slotkin, *Regeneration Through Violence: The Mythology of the American Frontier, 1600–1860* (Middletown, Conn.: Wesleyan University Press, 1973); Slotkin and Folsom, *So Dreadfull a Judgment*; Axtell, *European and the Indian*; Axtell, *Invasion Within*, pp. 302–27; Neal Salisbury, *Manitou and Providence: Indians, Europeans, and the Making of New England, 1500–1643* (New York and Oxford: Oxford University Press, 1982), pp. 139, 189; Sheehan, *Savagism and Civility*; William S. Simmons, "Cultural Bias in the New England Puritans' Perception of Indians," *William and Mary Quarterly*, 3d ser., 38 (1981): 70–71; Karen Ordahl Kupperman, *Settling With the Indians: The Meeting of English and Indian Cultures in America, 1580–1640* (Totowa, N.J.: Rowman and Littlefield, 1980), especially pp. 156–58; Michael Zuckerman, "The Fabrication of Identity in Early America," *William and Mary Quarterly*, 3d ser., 34 (1977): 183–214; Michael Zuckerman, "Identity in British America: Unease in Eden," in Nicholas

Canny and Anthony Pagden, eds., *Colonial Identity in the Atlantic World, 1500–1800* (Princeton, N.J.: Princeton University Press, 1987), pp. 115–57; James Muldoon, "The Indian as Irishman," *Essex Institute Historical Collections* 111 (1975): 284–85; and (for an alternative view of the "white Indian" question) Alden T. Vaughan and Daniel K. Richter, "Crossing the Cultural Divide: Indians and New Englanders, 1605–1763," *Proceedings of the American Antiquarian Society* 90 (1980): 23–99.

76. Winthrop, *History of New England* 2:327; and see Edward Johnson, *Johnson's Wonder-Working Providence, 1628–1651*, ed. J. Franklin Jameson (New York: Charles Scribner's Sons, 1910; reprint ed., New York: Barnes & Noble, 1937), pp. 186–87.

77. J. Hammond Trumbull and Charles Jeremy Hoadly, eds., *The Public Records of the Colony of Connecticut*, 15 vols. (Hartford, Conn., 1850–90), 1:78.

78. Ibid., pp. 200, 216–18.

79. Regarding the typology of Indianization, James Axtell proposes a view comprehending the situation on the frontier, traders who lived much of the time among Indians, and the "white Indians" who more or less voluntarily became "Indians": see "The Indian Impact on English Colonial Culture," in *European and the Indian*, pp. 275–79.

80. Wood, *New Englands Prospect*, p. 109. According to Robert Burton, "England is a paradise for women, and hell for horses: Italy a paradise for horses, hell for women, as the diverb goes": *The Anatomy of Melancholy*, ed. Holbrook Jackson (New York: Vintage Books, 1977), pt. 3, p. 265. Presumably Wood wanted his readers to know that New England was maintaining the Old English tradition.

81. [Edward Ward], *A Trip to New-England. With a Character of the Country and People, both English and Indians* (1699), in George Parker Winship, ed., *Boston in 1682 and 1699: "A Trip to New-England" by Edward Ward and "A Letter from New-England" by J.W.* (New York: Burt Franklin, 1970), p. 51.

82. Slotkin describes Ward's attitude as "a spectator's amused condescension," not a "hagridden intensity," toward the danger of wilderness acculturation: *Regeneration Through Violence*, pp. 192–93.

83. *Winthrop Papers*, 5 vols. (Boston: Massachusetts Historical Society, 1929–47), 3:367.

84. [Shepard?], *Day-Breaking*, p. 6.

85. Whitfield, *Strength out of Weaknesse*, p. 181 (and see p. 180).

86. Cotton Mather, *Magnalia Christi Americana* 1:594.

87. See Slotkin, *Regeneration Through Violence*, pp. 42, 118.

88. Robert Gray, *A Good Speed to Virginia* (London, 1609; reprint ed., New York: Scholars' Facsimiles & Reprints, 1937), sigs. C^v–C3^r.

89. *Winthrop Papers* 3:451–52.

90. Trumbull and Hoadly, *Public Records of the Colony of Connecticut* 1:576–77.

91. See Jennings, *Invasion of America*, pp. 220–25; and Mason's own *Brief History of the Pequot War*, ed. Thomas Prince (Boston, 1736; reprint ed., n.p.: Readex Microprint, 1966).

92. Trumbull and Hoadly, *Public Records of the Colony of Connecticut* 2:339.

93. Gookin, *Historical Collections*, pp. 200–1.

94. The Massachusetts Bay seal, with its Indian pleading "Come over and help us," alluded to Acts 16:9: see p. 59, above. Note also the Macedonian allusions in the names the English bestowed upon Massasoit's successors, Alexander and Philip. Jennings suggests that these names were "derisive" *Invasion of America*, (p. 290 n. 21), but given the probable link between "Alexander" and "Philip"

and Acts 16:9, derision may not be the best word to describe the English intention in this case. On the significance of the Massachusetts seal, see also Increase Mather, *An Earnest Exhortation To the Inhabitants of New-England* (1676), in Slotkin and Folsom, *So Dreadfull a Judgment*, p. 190.

95. *The Tempest*, act 4, scene 1, lines 188–90.

96. William Hubbard, *Present State*, pt. 1, pp. 14–15; and for an alternative to Hubbard's account of Sassamon's death, see Jennings, *Invasion of America*, pp. 294–97.

97. "Winthrop Papers," Massachusetts Historical Society, *Collections*, 5th ser., 1 (1871): 425.

98. Increase Mather, *Earnest Exhortation*, pp. 189, 170, 179, 171. On Mather's use of the war, see Slotkin, *Regeneration Through Violence*, pp. 83–87; Slotkin and Folsom, *So Dreadfull a Judgment*, pp. 55–78; and Hall, *Last American Puritan*, pp. 106–26. Daniel Gookin, a layman, also believed God was using the Indians to chastise wayward Englishmen: see *An Historical Account of the Doings and Sufferings of the Christian Indians in New England, in the Years 1675, 1676, 1677* (*Archaeologia Americana: Transactions and Collections of the American Antiquarian Society* 2 [1836]; reprint ed., New York: Arno Press, 1972), pp. 437–38. Note also the official recognition among the English of the "*Provoking Evils*" that had presumably brought on the war: "Several Laws and Orders" (1675), in John D. Cushing, ed., *The Laws and Liberties of Massachusetts, 1641–1691: A Facsimile Edition, Containing Also Council Orders and Executive Proclamations*, 3 vols. (Wilmington, Del.: Scholarly Resources, 1976), vol. 2, no. 30, pp. 32–37 (original pagination).

99. Increase Mather, *Earnest Exhortation*, pp. 189–91. Cotton Mather also assumed the mantle of Gildas in a letter of 1719: "Our neglect of Christianizing the eastern savages has been punished, as was that of the Britons to Christianize the Saxons in the days of Gildas": *Selected Letters of Cotton Mather*, ed. Kenneth Silverman (Baton Rouge: Louisiana State University Press, 1971), p. 275.

100. Increase Mather, *A Brief History of the Warr With the Indians in New-England* (1676), in Slotkin and Folsom, *So Dreadfull a Judgment*, p. 89. Mather saw "An awfull Providence" in the incident of the "distracted" soldier—a distraction apparently provoked by the death of an English scout, the use of profanity by some of the other soldiers, and the bad weather that kept the English from getting at the enemy.

101. For Mather's attempt to moderate his darker views of the war as a scourge, see his *Earnest Exhortation*, pp. 191–95.

102. Increase Mather, *Brief History*, p. 86.

103. For the corrective mechanism of public humiliation, thanksgiving, and covenant renewal, see *Brief History*, pp. 127–28, 134; and *Earnest Exhortation*, pp. 182–83.

104. For useful comparisons of Mather and Hubbard as historians of the war, see Hall, *Last American Puritan*, pp. 112–26; Anne Kusener Nelsen, "King Philip's War and the Hubbard-Mather Rivalry," *William and Mary Quarterly*, 3d ser., 27 (1970): 615–29; and Jennings, *Invasion of America*, pp. 184–85. Jennings presents his own study of the war "in one respect, as a detailed refutation of Hubbard's book and tradition" (p. 185). See also Mather's own remarks in his preface, "To the Reader," in *A Relation of the Troubles which have hapned in New-England, By reason of the Indians there. From the Year 1614. to the Year 1675* (Boston, 1677; reprint ed., New York: Arno Press, 1972)—a work he wrote in reply to Hubbard's *Present State*.

105. Hubbard, *Present State*, pt. 1, pp. 29, 115 (italics reversed). I have used the London edition of this work, which had appeared earlier in Boston as *A Narrative of the Troubles with the Indians in New-England*: see Cecelia Tichi's introduction to *Present State*, p. iv. This introduction is also an excellent general essay on the book.

106. See John Seelye, *Prophetic Waters: The River in Early American Life and Literature* (New York: Oxford University Press, 1977), pp. 235–46; and Hall, *Last American Puritan*, pp. 118–19.

107. See Hubbard, *Present State*, pt. 2, pp. 73–77 (quoting from p. 76).

108. Ibid., p. 74.

109. Ibid., pp. 84–85.

110. Ibid., p. 87; and pt. 1, p. 106.

111. Ibid., pt. 2, pp. 74–77. According to Hubbard, "*Thomas Marton* [*sic*] was said to be the first that like *Epimetheus* opened this *Pandora's Box* [of selling firearms and ammunition to the Indians], but he was not the *Vulcan*, that *forged* all their *Guns*, with other *weapons of war* they are found so well furnished withall" (p. 76).

112. Ibid., p. 78 (and see Seelye, *Prophetic Waters*, pp. 247–48).

113. Hubbard, *Present State*, pt. 2, p. 80.

114. See ibid., p. 83.

115. See Increase Mather, *Brief History*, p. 99. And see the commentary in Slotkin and Folsom, *So Dreadfull a Judgment*, pp. 35–39, 55–78.

116. "At a General Court held at Boston, February the 21st. 1675 [1676]," in Cushing, *Laws and Liberties of Massachusetts*, vol. 2, no. 32, broadside.

117. Increase Mather, *Earnest Exhortation*, pp. 174–75.

118. Ibid., p. 177.

119. See Slotkin and Folsom, *So Dreadfull a Judgment*, p. 72.

120. Increase Mather, *Earnest Exhortation*, pp. 181, 196.

121. Increase Mather, *Brief History*, p. 108.

122. Trumbull and Hoadly, *Public Records of the Colony of Connecticut* 2:401, 401n. Roger Williams recorded Tift's examination and confession: see "Winthrop Papers," Massachusetts Historical Society, *Collections*, 4th ser., 6 (1863): 307–11. On Tift, see also Axtell, *European and the Indian*, pp. 156, 280.

123. Hubbard, *Present State*, pt. 1, p. 59.

124. Not surprisingly, no one seems to have exceeded William Hubbard in a sustained rhetorical attack on Philip and the Indians as devilish beasts. The enemy leers and snarls from his pages as "hellish Monsters," "children of the Devil," "*Cannibals*," and "Wild creatures [who] ordinarily love the libeety [*sic*] of the Woods, better than the restraint of a Cage." Philip himself appears as a "cunning Fox" who escapes "through the Bushes" and, "like a Salvage and wild Beast," is "driven to his own Den, upon *Mount-hope*." See Hubbard, *Present State*, pt. 1, pp. 42, 63, 113, 101, 103 (and passim); Slotkin, *Regeneration Through Violence*, p. 88; and (on the Indian as scapegoat) Slotkin and Folsom, *So Dreadfull a Judgment*, pp. 76–77.

On the Indians' use of the wilderness terrain itself against the English, see Increase Mather, *Brief History*, p. 143; Gookin, *Historical Account*, p. 441; and Peter N. Carroll, *Puritanism and the Wilderness: The Intellectual Significance of the New England Frontier, 1629–1700* (New York and London: Columbia University Press, 1969), pp. 206–8.

125. Increase Mather, *Earnest Exhortation*, p. 187. Hall discusses Mather's criticism of the English treatment of Indians in *Last American Puritan*, p. 123. For gestures

toward defending the Praying Indians and other Indian allies, see: Hubbard, *Present State*, pt. 1, pp. 64–66, and pt. 2, p. 85; Increase Mather, *Brief History*, pp. 118, 143; and Mather's *Earnest Exhortation*, pp. 168, 186–87.

126. Gookin, *Historical Account*, p. 494.

127. Ibid., p. 462.

128. Ibid., p. 453.

129. [Nathaniel Saltonstall], *The Present State of New-England, With Respect to the Indian War* (1676), in *King Philip's War Narratives* (n.p.: Readex Microprint, 1966), sig. D. When Gookin confessed to his fear to walk the streets, he was told "you may thank your self." See also Slotkin, *Regeneration Through Violence*, pp. 81–82.

130. Gookin, *Historical Account*, title page. For details of the *Account*'s publication, see the "Preliminary Notice," p. 428; and Frederick William Gookin, *Daniel Gookin*, p. 161.

131. Gookin, *Historical Account*, p. 436.

132. Ibid., pp. 471–72, 474–75.

133. Ibid., pp. 482–84. Note that Gookin's work also tends to support Slotkin's suggestion that there was a class conflict among the English on this matter, with "the 'men of note,' who defend order in society . . . ranged with those who defend the Praying Indians against the popular rage for their destruction": *Regeneration Through Violence*, p. 82. Yet even Gookin stated that it could be "very difficult, unless upon long knowledge, to distinguish Indians from one another": *Historical Account*, p. 492.

134. Gookin, *Historical Account*, pp. 512, 517.

135. For example, ibid., p. 503.

136. Ibid., p. 523.

137. Hubbard, *Present State*, pt. 2, pp. 48, 61, 62.

138. Increase Mather, *Earnest Exhortation*, p. 170.

139. Hubbard, *Present State*, pt. 1, p. 109 (and see pt. 2, pp. 80–81). On the Indians as Canaanites, etc., see my chap. 3.

140. Gookin, *Historical Account*, p. 522.

141. Ibid., p. 462.

142. Increase Mather, *Brief History*, p. 145. Mather referred to Philip as "the perfidious and bloudy Author of the War" (p. 138). See also Josiah Winslow's letter in ibid., pp. 146–47.

143. Ibid., p. 152.

144. Increase Mather, *Earnest Exhortation*, p. 194. See also Hubbard, *Present State*, pt. 1, p. 8. Even the martyrologist of the Christian Indians assumed that one of God's purposes for the war was "the punishment and destruction of many of the wicked heathen," especially after "their malignant opposition to the offers of the Gospel": Gookin, *Historical Account*, p. 438 (and see p. 439).

145. Hubbard, *Present State*, pt. 2, pp. 86–88.

146. Trumbull and Hoadly, *Public Records of the Colony of Connecticut* 2:358.

147. On the question of the confusion of English and Indian identities through cultural and military conflict, see again Slotkin, *Regeneration Through Violence;* the commentary in Slotkin and Folsom, *So Dreadfull a Judgment*; and Axtell, *European and the Indian*, pp. 272–315.

148. For Philip's dismemberment, see Increase Mather, *Brief History*, p. 139; and T[homas] C[hurch], *Entertaining Passages Relating to Philip's War* (1716), in Slotkin and Folsom, *So Dreadfull a Judgment*, pp. 451–52, 469 n. 97.

149. Hubbard, *Present State*, pt. 1, "A Postscript," sigs. [T3ʳ]–[T4ʳ].

150. John Easton, "A Relacion of the Indyan Warre, By Mr. Easton, of Roade Isld.,

1675," in Charles H. Lincoln, ed., *Narratives of the Indian Wars, 1675–1699* (New York: Charles Scribner's Sons, 1913), pp. 13–16.

151. See, on this problem, Axtell, *European and the Indian*, pp. 311–14. Thirty years after King Philip's War, a Jesuit priest in Canada justified Indian attacks on New England by referring to what the English had done to the Indians. Speaking to the captive John Williams, he accused the English of having been "very barbarous and cruel, in burning and killing Indians." Williams replied "that the Indians, in a very perfidious manner, had committed murders on many of our inhabitants, after the signing articles of peace: And as to what they spake of cruelties, they were undoubtedly falsehoods, for I well knew the English were not approvers of any inhumanity or barbarity towards enemies." Despite evidence to the contrary in New England's history, it was still an essential article of faith that the Indians, not the English, were perpetrators of "barbarity": see John Williams, *The Redeemed Captive Returning to Zion*, 6th ed. (Boston, 1795; reprint ed., n.p.: Readex Microprint, 1966), pp. 26–27.

152. See Carroll, *Puritanism and the Wilderness*, pp. 199–222, especially pp. 206–22.

153. C[hurch], *Entertaining Passages*, p. 421.

154. Johnson, *Wonder-Working Providence*, p. 234.

155. Trumbull and Hoadly, *Public Records of the Colony of Connecticut* 2:268–69. On the problem of withdrawal from the frontier, see also: "At a Council Held at Boston April the 4th. 1676," in Cushing, *Laws and Liberties of Massachusetts*, vol. 3, no. 34, broadside; Shurtleff and Pulsifer, *Records of the Colony of New Plymouth* 5:185–86, 193; and Carroll, *Puritanism and the Wilderness*, pp. 208–11.

156. Trumbull and Hoadly, *Public Records of the Colony of Connecticut* 2:328. And on resettlement, see Shurtleff and Pulsifer, *Records of the Colony of New Plymouth* 5:177–79; "Several Laws and Orders" (1679), in *Laws and Liberties of Massachusetts*, vol. 3, no. 55, pp. 67–68 (original pagination); and Carroll, *Puritanism and the Wilderness*, pp. 215–20.

157. Cotton Mather, *Magnalia Christi Americana* 1:88. He adds, "but yet with such variety, that while the *trained companies* of some towns are no bigger than they were thirty or forty years ago, others are as big again."

158. Samuel Nowell, *Abraham in Arms* (1678), in Slotkin and Folsom, *So Dreadfull a Judgment*, p. 287 (and see pp. 265–66, 299 nn. 63–65).

159. Increase Mather, "Diary of Increase Mather," ed. Samuel A. Green, Massachusetts Historical Society, *Proceedings*, 2d ser., 13 (1899–1900): 402.

Chapter 6. "Criolian Degeneracy"

1. Kenneth Silverman, *The Life and Times of Cotton Mather* (New York: Harper & Row, 1984), p. 426.

2. Mather's habit of personalizing public crises is amply documented in *Diary of Cotton Mather*, 2 vols. (New York: Frederick Ungar, n.d.), and in *Selected Letters of Cotton Mather*, ed. Kenneth Silverman (Baton Rouge: Louisiana State University Press, 1971).

3. Mather used the phrase "Criolian degeneracy" in *The Way to Prosperity* (preached 1689), reprinted in A. W. Plumstead, ed., *The Wall and the Garden: Selected Massachusetts Election Sermons, 1670–1775* (Minneapolis: University of Minnesota Press, 1968), p. 137.

4. My discussion of provincialism here and throughout the chapter has been greatly influenced by: Albert J. von Frank, *The Sacred Game: Provincialism and Frontier Consciousness in American Literature, 1630–1860* (Cambridge: Cambridge

University Press, 1985), especially pp. 1–10, 154–58; Perry Miller, *The New England Mind: From Colony to Province* (Cambridge, Mass., and London, England: Belknap Press of Harvard University Press, 1953); David D. Hall, *The Faithful Shepherd: A History of the New England Ministry in the Seventeenth Century* (New York: W. W. Norton & Company for the Institute of Early American History and Culture, 1974), especially chaps. 8 and 12; Peter N. Carroll, *Puritanism and the Wilderness: The Intellectual Significance of the New England Frontier, 1629–1700* (New York and London: Columbia University Press, 1969), especially pp. 82–86; Larzer Ziff, *Puritanism in America: New Culture in a New World* (New York: Viking Press, 1973); John Clive and Bernard Bailyn, "England's Cultural Provinces: Scotland and America," *William and Mary Quarterly*, 3d ser., 11 (1954): 200–13; Bernard Bailyn, *The Peopling of British North America: An Introduction* (New York: Alfred A. Knopf, 1986); Jack P. Greene, "Search for Identity: An Interpretation of the Meaning of Selected Patterns of Social Response in Eighteenth-Century America," *Journal of Social History* 3 (1970): 189–224; Edward Bruce Tucker, "The Founders Remembered: The Anglicization of the Puritan Tradition in New England, 1690–1760" (Ph.D. diss., Brown University, 1978); David Hudson Corkran III, "The New England Colonists' English Image, 1550–1714" (Ph.D. diss., University of California, Berkeley, 1970); Michael Zuckerman, "The Fabrication of Identity in Early America," *William and Mary Quarterly*, 3d ser., 34 (1977): 183–214; Michael Zuckerman, "Identity in British America: Unease in Eden," in Nicholas Canny and Anthony Pagden, eds., *Colonial Identity in the Atlantic World, 1500–1800* (Princeton, N.J.: Princeton University Press, 1987), pp. 115–57; Alan Heimert and Andrew Delbanco, eds., *The Puritans in America: A Narrative Anthology* (Cambridge, Mass., and London, England: Harvard University Press, 1985), especially pp. 381–82, 405–13; Richard R. Johnson, *Adjustment to Empire: The New England Colonies, 1675–1715* (n.p.: Rutgers University Press, 1981), pp. 272–74; Philip S. Haffenden, *New England in the English Nation, 1689–1713* (Oxford: Clarendon Press of Oxford University Press, 1974), chap. 4; Ian K. Steele, *The English Atlantic, 1675–1740: An Exploration of Communication and Community* (New York and Oxford: Oxford University Press, 1986); and David Cressy, *Coming Over: Migration and Communication Between England and New England in the Seventeenth Century* (Cambridge: Cambridge University Press, 1987), especially pp. 292–95. Specifically regarding John Winthrop, Jr.'s significance within provincial culture, Bailyn has suggested an interesting perspective in his *Peopling of British North America*, chap. 3, especially pp. 91–92.

5. On Mather's identification with Winthrop, see Mitchell Robert Breitwieser, *Cotton Mather and Benjamin Franklin: The Price of Representative Personality* (Cambridge: Cambridge University Press, 1984), pp. 145–52.

6. See ibid.

7. Cotton Mather, *Diary* 1:62.

8. Cotton Mather, *Magnalia Christi Americana; or, The Ecclesiastical History of New England*, 2 vols. (Hartford, Conn., 1852; reprint ed., New York: Russell & Russell, 1967), 1:82 (and see Cotton Mather, "Hermes Christianus. The Life of John Winthrop, Esq., Governour of Connecticut and New-Haven United," in ibid., pp. 157–62). On Mather's interest in the Winthropian medical tradition, see *Diary* 2:590–91 (February 1719): "I will prevail with Mr. J. *Winthrop* [John Jr.'s grandson], to furnish me, with some of his Father's and Grandfather's noble Remedies, and I will make myself the Dispenser of them unto the miserable."

9. John Winthrop, Sr., recorded his son's arrival in New England in his journal, *The History of New England from 1630 to 1649*, 2 vols., ed., James Savage (Boston: Little, Brown and Company, 1853), 1:76. For biographical details on John Jr. I have relied on Robert C. Black III, *The Younger John Winthrop* (New York and London: Columbia University Press, 1966); Richard S. Dunn, *Puritans and Yankees: The Winthrop Dynasty of New England, 1630–1717* (Princeton, N.J.: Princeton University Press, 1962); and Samuel Eliot Morison, "John Winthrop, Jr., Industrial Pioneer," in *Builders of the Bay Colony*, rev. ed. (Boston: Houghton Mifflin, 1962), pp. 269–88. On Winthrop's education and travels, see Black, *Younger John Winthrop*, pp. 18–39.

10. See *Winthrop Papers*, 5 vols. (Boston: Massachusetts Historical Society, 1929–47), 2:151.

11. Edward Howes and Robert Child were among Winthrop's most faithful correspondents. On Howes, see Black, *Younger John Winthrop*, pp. 27, 60, 70; and *Winthrop Papers* 2:226 n. 1. The bulk of the Howes-Winthrop correspondence is in *Winthrop Papers*, vols. 3–4. On Winthrop's friendship with Child, see Dunn, *Puritans and Yankees*, pp. 85–86, 91–92; and Black, *Young John Winthrop*, pp. 101–2, 130–32. The Child-Winthrop letters are scattered through *Winthrop Papers*; and see "The Winthrop Papers," Massachusetts Historical Society, *Collections*, 5th ser., 1 (1871): 161–64. On the importance of transatlantic communications in maintaining a sense of English community, see Steele, *English Atlantic*; and (with particular relevance to Winthrop) David Cressy, *Coming Over*, chap. 9.

12. For letters relating to Winthrop's shipments of specimens to England, see *Winthrop Papers* 3:58, 79, 93, 127.

13. Dunn and Black provide useful discussions of Winthrop's early years in New England. On his first return trip to England, see especially Black, *Younger John Winthrop*, pp. 77–90. Cressy discusses "homesickness, return visits and back migration" (including Winthrop's) in *Coming Over*, chap. 8.

14. *Winthrop Papers* 3:278.

15. On this trip, see Black, *Younger John Winthrop*, pp. 111–20. According to Cotton Mather, "That brave old man Johannes Amos Commenius, the *fame* of whose worth hath been *trumpetted* as far as more than *three* languages (whereof every one is indebted unto his *Janua*) could carry it, was indeed agreed withal, by our Mr. Winthrop in his travels through the *low countries*, to come over into New-England, and illuminate this Colledge and *country*, in the quality of a President." But since Comenius went to Sweden instead, "that incomparable Moravian became not an American": see *Magnalia Christi Americana* 2:14. Samuel Eliot Morison is skeptical of this account: see *The Founding of Harvard College* (Cambridge, Mass.: Harvard University Press, 1935), pp. 243–45. Significantly, Morison suggests that Comenius "would have been a complete misfit at Cambridge in New England, doomed to disappointment and frustration" (p. 245). See also Robert Fitzgibbon Young, *Comenius in England* (London: Oxford University Press, 1932), pp. 7–8.

16. See Black, *Younger John Winthrop*, pp. 120, 138, 142.

17. Ibid., p. 150; *Winthrop Papers* 5:315–16, 320.

18. J. Hammond Trumbull and Charles Jeremy Hoadly, eds., *The Public Records of the Colony of Connecticut*, 15 vols. (Hartford, 1850–90), 1:310, 313.

19. *Winthrop Papers* 5:289.

20. Ibid., p. 361.

21. "The Winthrop Papers," Massachusetts Historical Society, *Collections*, 3d ser., 10 (1849): 5–6. And see Cressy, *Coming Over*, p. 209.

22. On Winthrop's 1660s visit to England, see Dunn, *Puritans and Yankees*, pp. 117–42; Black, *Younger John Winthrop*, pp. 206–45; and Cressy, *Coming Over*, p. 209. For the intellectual environment in which the Royal Society emerged, see Charles Webster, *The Great Instauration: Science, Medicine and Reform, 1626–1660* (London: Gerald Duckworth & Company, 1975), especially pp. 32–99. For Winthrop's membership, see this chapter, below.

23. G. H. Turnbull, ed., "Some Correspondence of John Winthrop, Jr., and Samuel Hartlib," Massachusetts Historical Society, *Proceedings* 72 (1957–60): 37. On Winthrop's relationship with Hartlib at this time, see Black, *Younger John Winthrop*, pp. 192–93, 213–17.

24. See Turnbull, "Some Correspondence," pp. 39–40.

25. See ibid., passim. For Hartlib's role in the forming of the Royal Society, see Webster, *Great Instauration*, passim; and Charles Webster, ed., *Samuel Hartlib and the Advancement of Learning* (Cambridge: Cambridge University Press, 1970). See also Frances A. Yates, *The Rosicrucian Enlightenment* (London and Boston: Routledge & Kegan Paul, 1972), pp. 175–81.

26. Turnbull, "Some Correspondence," p. 66.

27. Ibid.

28. B[enjamin] Tompson, *A Funeral Tribute To the Honourable Dust of that most Charitable Christian, Unbiassed Politician, And unimitable Pyrotechnist John Winthrope esq: A Member of the Royal Society, & Governour of Conecticut Colony in New-England. Who expired in his Countreys Service, April. 6th. 1676* [Boston, 1676], broadside. On Winthrop's medical interests, see Black, *Younger John Winthrop*, pp. 169–71, 173, 193, 317–18, 338–39.

29. John Arundell (1656), quoted in Harold Jantz, "America's First Cosmopolitan," Massachusetts Historical Society, *Proceedings* 84 (1972): 19.

30. On Hermeticism in this period, see especially the following works by Frances A. Yates: "The Hermetic Tradition in Renaissance Society," in *Collected Essays*, vol. 3, *Ideas and Ideals in the North European Renaissance* (London: Routledge & Kegan Paul, 1984), pp. 227–46; *Giordano Bruno and the Hermetic Tradition* (Chicago and London: University of Chicago Press, 1964); *The Occult Philosophy in the Elizabethan Age* (London, Boston, and Henley: Routledge & Kegan Paul, 1979); *Rosicrucian Enlightenment*; and *The Art of Memory* (Chicago: University of Chicago Press, 1966). Also useful are: Christopher Hill, "Science and Magic," in *The Collected Essays of Christopher Hill*, vol. 3, *People and Ideas in 17th Century England* (Amherst: University of Massachusetts Press, 1986), pp. 274–99; Peter J. French, *John Dee: The World of an Elizabethan Magus* (London: Routledge & Kegan Paul, 1972); and Keith Thomas, *Religion and the Decline of Magic* (New York: Charles Scribner's Sons, 1971), especially pp. 175–279.

    On Hartlib's "Rosicrucian" connections, see Yates, *Rosicrucian Enlightenment*, pp. 175–81. And for Winthrop's correspondence with Hartlib touching on Rosicrucian concerns, see Turnbull, "Some Correspondence," pp. 47–48, 60, 64. For the Rosicrucian and Hermetic interests of his old friend Edward Howes, see *Winthrop Papers* 3:96–98, 158–59, 241–42. It seems that Howes was especially interested in the work of Robert Fludd, regarding whom see Yates's works cited above and Joscelyn Godwin, *Robert Fludd: Hermetic Philosopher and Surveyor of Two Worlds* (London: Thames and Hudson, 1979). Also useful on this subject are: Black, *Younger John Winthrop*, pp. 27, 87; Ronald Sterne

Wilkinson, "The Alchemical Library of John Winthrop, Jr. (1606–1676) and His Descendants in Colonial America," *Ambix* 11 (1963): 36–38; and C. A. Browne, "Scientific Notes from the Books and Letters of John Winthrop, Jr., (1606–1676). First Governor of Connecticut," *Isis* 11 (1928): 337.

31. Cotton Mather, *Magnalia Christi Americana* 1:157–62; Benjamin Tompson, "Upon the setting of that Occidental Star *John Winthrop* Esq; Governour of *Connecticott* Colony, Member of the Royal Society; who deceased in his Countreys Service *6 April 1676*," in Kenneth Silverman, ed., *Colonial American Poetry* (New York and London: Hafner, 1968), p. 146; and Wilkinson, "Alchemical Library," p. 33.

32. On John Dee, see French, *John Dee*; Yates, *Occult Philosophy*, pp. 75–108 and passim; Yates, *Rosicrucian Enlightenment*; Yates, "Hermetic Tradition"; Yates, *Giordano Bruno*, pp. 148–50, 187–88; and Yates, *Art of Memory*, pp. 262–63, 360–63.

Whatever the extent of Winthrop's identification with Dee, it now seems unlikely that he was (as some have suggested) the "Eirenaeus Philalethes" whose many alchemical writings were well known and respected by European adepti. On the question of the identity of Eirenaeus Philalethes, see the articles by Ronald Sterne Wilkinson, who began by proposing Winthrop as the most likely candidate, then inclined toward George Starkey, an acquaintance of Winthrop's: "George Starkey, Physician and Alchemist," *Ambix* 11 (1963): 121–52; "The Problem of the Identity of Eirenaeus Philalethes," *Ambix* 12 (1964): 24–43; "A Further Note on Eirenaeus Philalethes," *Ambix* 13 (1965): 53–54; "The Hartlib Papers and Seventeenth-Century Chemistry," *Ambix* 15 (1968): 54–69, and *Ambix* 17 (1970): 85–110; "Letter to the Editor: Further Thoughts on the Identity of 'Eirenaeus Philalethes,' " *Ambix* 19 (1972): 204–8; "Some Bibliographical Puzzles Concerning George Starkey," *Ambix* 20 (1973): 235–44. For reactions to Wilkinson's work, see J. W. Hamilton-Jones, "The Identity of Eirenaeus Philalethes," *Ambix* 13 (1965): 52–53; and, above all, Harold Jantz's rather Borgesian essay, "America's First Cosmopolitan."

33. On the libraries of Winthrop and Dee, see Wilkinson, "Alchemical Library"; Browne, "Scientific Notes"; French, *John Dee*, pp. 40–61; and Yates, *Occult Philosophy*, p. 80.

34. On the "*monas hieroglyphica*," see French, *John Dee*, pp. 78–80, 94 (whence the quotation); and Yates, *Occult Philosophy*, pp. 83–84. For Winthrop's use of it, see Wilkinson, "Alchemical Library," pp. 39, 49 (noting its use by Winthrop's son, Wait Still). For an example of Winthrop's use of the *monas* as a bookmark, see Browne, "Scientific Notes," plate 4, fig. 4., facing p. 327. See also Winthrop's use of the emblem in his 1631 memoranda for supplies and other articles relating to his New England voyage: "Memoranda of John Winthrop, Jr.," in Marjorie F. Gutheim, ed., *Microfilm Edition of the Winthrop Papers*, 53 reels (Boston: Massachusetts Historical Society, 1976), reel 35, pt. 1, sec. b, no. 6.

35. French, *John Dee*, pp. 4–19, 55–56, 62–125. On the ambiguous status of alchemy (especially among Calvinists), magic, and occult learning, see Thomas, *Religion and the Decline of Magic*, pp. 230, 253–79. Yates notes that "the Rosicrucian is a secretive type, and has to be": "Hermetic Tradition," p. 235 (and see p. 236). John Aubrey was told by "Old Goodwife Faldo (a Natif of Mortlak in Surrey) [who] did know Dr Dee" that "the Children dreaded him because he was accounted a Conjurer": *Aubrey's Brief Lives*, ed. Oliver Lawson Dick (Harmondsworth, England: Penguin Books, 1972), p. 181.

36. Nathaniel Ward, *The Simple Cobler of Aggawam in America*, ed. P. M. Zall (Lincoln: University of Nebraska Press, 1969), p. 19.

37. Increase Mather, *An Essay for the Recording of Illustrious Providences (1684)*, intro. James A. Levernier (Delmar, N.Y.: Scholars' Facsimiles & Reprints, 1977), pp. 182, 209.

38. For Winthrop's medical interests, see Black, *Younger John Winthrop*, pp. 169–71, 173, 193, 317–18, 338–39.

39. The Mathers (especially Cotton) and Michael Wigglesworth were interested in medicine: see Kenneth Ballard Murdock, *Increase Mather: The Foremost American Puritan* (Cambridge, Mass.: Harvard University Press, 1925), pp. 75–76; Michael G. Hall, *The Last American Puritan: The Life of Increase Mather, 1639–1723* (Middletown, Conn.: Wesleyan University Press, 1988), pp. 290–91, 360; Silverman, *Cotton Mather*, pp. 22, 247, 253, 270–71, 336–63, 406–10; and Richard Crowder, *No Featherbed to Heaven: A Biography of Michael Wigglesworth, 1631–1705* (n.p.: Michigan State University Press, 1962), pp. 125, 131, 218–19, 222–23, 260.

40. On "The Physician as Atheist," see Paul H. Kocher, *Science and Religion in Elizabethan England* (San Marino, Cal.: Huntington Library, 1953), pp. 239–57; and Thomas, *Religion and the Decline of Magic*, p. 85. John Putnam Demos notes the relationship between folk medicine and witchcraft in *Entertaining Satan: Witchcraft and the Culture of Early New England* (Oxford and New York: Oxford University Press, 1982), especially pp. 80–84, 93, 358.

41. Sir Thomas Browne, *Religio Medici*, in *The Major Works*, ed. C. A. Patrides (Harmondsworth, England: Penguin Books, 1977), p. 61. Like Browne (and John Dee), Thomas Hariot also suffered from the nature of his scientific interests: Karen Ordahl Kupperman, *Roanoke: The Abandoned Colony* (Totowa, N.J.: Rowman & Allanheld, 1984), pp. 158–61.

42. John Winthrop, Sr., quoted in Cotton Mather, *Magnalia Christi Americana* 1:161.

43. On Cotton Mather's efforts to portray John Jr. as a full successor to the Winthropian tradition of piety, see Breitwieser, *Cotton Mather and Benjamin Franklin*, pp. 145–52.

44. For Winthrop's election to the Royal Society and related activities, see Thomas Birch, *The History of the Royal Society of London* (London, 1756; reprint ed., Brussels: Culture et Civilisation, 1968), 1:67–68, 76, 80, 82, 87–88, 99–102, 111, 112–13, 162, 166, 167–68, 171, 178, 198, 205, 206, 207, 212, 280, 322, 406–7; Black, *Younger John Winthrop*, pp. 217–18, 232–34, 307–19; Dunn, *Puritans and Yankees*, pp. 129–31, 142, 169–72; and Raymond Phineas Stearns, *Science in the British Colonies of North America* (Urbana, Chicago, London: University of Illinois Press, 1970), pp. 118–38, 691–94.

45. Birch, *History of the Royal Society*, 1:162.

46. The cornbread beer can be traced in ibid., pp. 171, 178, 198, 205, 206 (for the quotation).

47. See ibid., pp. 207, 212, 280; Stearns, *Science in the British Colonies*, p. 129; and [John Winthrop, Jr., et al.], "Correspondence of the Founders of the Royal Society with Governor Winthrop of Connecticut," Massachusetts Historical Society, *Proceedings* 16 (1878): 220.

48. See [Winthrop et al.], "Correspondence," pp. 220–22, 244 (whence the reference to "American Curiosities"), 245, 250; "Winthrop Papers," Massachusetts Historical Society, *Collections*, 5th ser., 8 (1882): 138–40. For Winthrop's Royal Society contributions and publications, see: "The Description, Culture, and Use of Maiz," Royal Society of London, *Philosophical Transactions* 12 (1678–79):

1065–69; "An Extract of a Letter, Written by *John Winthrop Esq*; Governour of *Connecticut* in *New England*," ibid. 5 (1670): 1151–52; and "A further Accompt of the *Stellar Fish*," ibid. 6 (1671): 2221–24. For the Society's ongoing communications with Winthrop, see the "Correspondence." On the transatlantic intellectual community, see also Steele, *English Atlantic*; and Cressy, *Coming Over*, chap. 9.

49. [Winthrop et al.], "Correspondence," pp. 240, 242; and see Black, *Younger John Winthrop*, p. 316.

50. [Winthrop et al.], "Correspondence," pp. 224–25, 225n. See also ibid., pp. 229, 232, 234–35; Dunn, *Puritans and Yankees*, p. 170; Black, *Younger John Winthrop*, p. 317; Stearns, *Science in the British Colonies*, pp. 131, 138; and Cressy, *Coming Over*, pp. 222–28.

51. [Winthrop et al.], "Correspondence," p. 235. See also Dunn, *Puritans and Yankees*, p. 169.

52. Winthrop, "Extract of a Letter," p. 1151.

53. [Winthrop et al.], "Correspondence," p. 223.

54. Winthrop quoted in Black, *Younger John Winthrop*, pp. 312–13.

55. "Winthrop Papers," Massachusetts Historical Society, *Collections*, 3d ser., 10 (1849): 71. Joseph Eliot, Roger Williams, George Starkey, and Jonathan Brewster also borrowed books from Winthrop: see ibid., 5th ser., 1 (1871): 430–31; Wilkinson, "Alchemical Library," p. 46; Wilkinson, "George Starkey"; Roger Williams, *Letters of Roger Williams, 1632–1682*, in *The Complete Writings of Roger Williams*, 7 vols., ed. Reuben Aldridge Guild et al. (New York: Russell & Russell, 1963), 6:167–68, 173. Thomas Goddard Wright notes the importance of book borrowing as a means of overcoming isolation in New England: *Literary Culture in Early New England, 1620–1730* (New York: Russell & Russell, 1966), pp. 61–63; and see Cressy, *Coming Over*, pp. 232–34, 254, 257–58. Winthrop was also able to donate books and a telescope to Harvard: see Black, *Younger John Winthrop*, pp. 172, 310–11; and Ronald Sterne Wilkinson, "John Winthrop, Jr., and America's First Telescopes," *New England Quarterly* 35 (1962): 520–23. Winthrop's friend Sir Kenelm Digby also gave books to Harvard, including a work ascribed to Hermes Trismegistus: Morison, *Founding of Harvard College*, p. 268.

56. Williams, *Letters*, p. 370 (relating the message of Mrs. Richard Smith).

57. On Winthrop's last days, his death, and burial, see Dunn, *Puritans and Yankees*, pp. 164–87; and Black, *Younger John Winthrop*, pp. 320–56.

58. Tompson, "Upon the setting of that Occidental Star," pp. 146, 147 (italics reversed)—and see Tompson's *Funeral Tribute*.

59. On Mather's generation's sense of isolation in New England, see Hall, *Faithful Shepherd*, pp. 180–81. Like Winthrop, Increase Mather was concerned with the advancement of scientific knowledge, and he organized a small "*Philosophical Society*" in Boston. This provincial reflection of the Royal Society was short-lived, however. See [Cotton Mather], *Parentator. Memoirs of Remarkables in the Life and the Death of the Ever-Memorable Dr. Increase Mather. Who Expired, August 23. 1723* (Boston, 1724), p. 86; Stearns, *Science in the British Colonies*, pp. 155–58; Silverman, *Cotton Mather*, p. 41; Murdock, *Increase Mather*, pp. 147–48; and Hall, *Last American Puritan*, pp. 166–67.

60. For Increase Mather's references to Indians as Americans, see Cotton Mather, *Magnalia Christi Americana* 1:563, 566–67, 569.

61. Regarding his problems in England after the Restoration, he wrote that he was "persecuted out of two places, Glocester and Guernsey, before I was 22 years

of age": "The Autobiography of Increase Mather," ed. M. G. Hall, *Proceedings of the American Antiquarian Society* 71 (1961): 285. And see Murdock, *Increase Mather*, pp. 58–70; and Robert Middlekauff, *The Mathers: Three Generations of Puritan Intellectuals, 1596–1728* (Oxford, London, New York: Oxford University Press, 1971), pp. 84–85. In the most thorough biography of Mather to date, Michael G. Hall discusses Mather's return to England and his reluctant retreat to America—while suggesting that by the early 1670s Mather had become more resigned to life in Boston: *Last American Puritan*, chaps. 1–2.

62. Increase Mather, "Autobiography," p. 287. See also Murdock, *Increase Mather*, p. 86; [Cotton Mather], *Parentator*, p. 25; Silverman, *Cotton Mather*, pp. 9–10; and Hall, *Last American Puritan*, chap. 2. And on his "ambivalent relationship with old England," see Cressy, *Coming Over*, pp. 210–12.

63. Samuel Maverick, "A Briefe Discription of New England and the Severall Townes therein, together with the Present Government thereof," Massachusetts Historical Society, *Proceedings*, 2d ser., 1 (1884–85): 237–38.

64. Increase Mather, "Autobiography," p. 300.

65. Silverman, *Cotton Mather*, p. 25; Murdock, *Increase Mather*, pp. 180–286, 339–58; Increase Mather, "Autobiography," pp. 344–45; and Hall, *Last American Puritan*, chaps. 7–8. And, on Mather's mission to England, see also Francis J. Bremer, "Increase Mather's Friends: The Trans-Atlantic Congregational Network of the Seventeenth Century," *Proceedings of the American Antiquarian Society* 94 (1984): 88–91; and Cressy, *Coming Over*, pp. 211–12. Samuel Eliot Morison discusses Mather's troubled relationship with Harvard and his involvement in the maneuvers for a charter mission to England in *Harvard College in the Seventeenth Century*, 2 vols. (Cambridge, Mass.: Harvard University Press, 1936), 2:472–536. For the political context of this period, see Haffenden, *New England in the English Nation*; and Johnson, *Adjustment to Empire*.

66. Increase Mather, "Autobiography," pp. 345, 348, 350 (and see, in general, pp. 345–52). Mather's attempt to rest satisfied with the honors New England had bestowed upon him was obviously not completely successful, since in the following paragraphs he brooded on the slights he had suffered at his countrymen's hands (pp. 351–52). See also Hall, *Last American Puritan*, pp. 281–82.

67. Increase Mather, "Autobiography," pp. 348, 352. And on Mather's interest in angels, see Hall, *Last American Puritan*, p. 273; and Middlekauff, *The Mathers*, pp. 175–77.

68. See Silverman, *Cotton Mather*, p. 179; and Hall, *Last American Puritan*, pp. 309, 313.

69. Increase Mather, "Autobiography," p. 352. On Samuel's departure for England with his father's manuscripts, see also Hall, *Last American Puritan*, p. 291.

70. Increase Mather, "Autobiography," pp. 353–54.

71. Ibid., p. 356.

72. See Murdock, *Increase Mather*, pp. 385–87; and [Cotton Mather], *Parentator*, p. 194.

73. Increase Mather, "Autobiography," pp. 359–60. But see Hall, *Last American Puritan*, p. 313—where, contrary to my interpretation, Mather's professed lack of interest (as of 1705) in a final voyage to England is taken at face value.

74. For Increase's reluctance to leave Cotton in New England, see his "Autobiography," p. 347. On his death in Cotton's arms, see Murdock, *Increase Mather*, p. 388; Silverman, *Cotton Mather*, p. 369; and Hall, *Last American Puritan*, p. 361.

75. Cotton Mather, *A Pillar of Gratitude* (Boston, 1700), p. 11.

76. On Mather's rather limited experience of travel, see also Middlekauff, *The Mathers*, p. 192. As Silverman notes, "Unlike his father, . . . [Cotton] did not hanker to live and die in England" (*Cotton Mather*, p. 426), but a voyage to England was not out of the question for him: see his *Selected Letters*, p.179, 306; and David Levin, *Cotton Mather: The Young Life of the Lord's Remembrancer, 1663–1703* (Cambridge, Mass., and London, England: Harvard University Press, 1978), p. 192.

77. For the *"Particular Faith,"* see, for example, *Diary* 1:305–6, 353–56.

78. Cotton Mather, *Selected Letters*, pp. 25–26. Cotton was also concerned that his father might desert Boston for Cambridge, in accord with his duties as president of Harvard: see *Diary* 1:358–60.

79. See Cotton Mather, *Diary* 1:148.

80. Ibid., p. 354.

81. [Cotton Mather], *Parentator*, p. 193.

82. For Mather on the heathen scourge, see *Observable Things*, published with *Decennium Luctuosum* (Boston, 1699), pp. 214–15; and *Selected Letters*, p. 275.

83. See Silverman, *Cotton Mather*, pp. 237–43; John Seelye, *Prophetic Waters: The River in Early American Life and Literature* (New York: Oxford University Press, 1977), p. 269; and Mather's life of John Eliot in *Magnalia Christi Americana* 1:526–83.

84. For Mather's reference to the Indians as *"devils in flesh,"* see *Magnalia Christi Americana* 2:566. In *Decennium Luctuosum* he demonstrated his inventiveness in slurring the enemy—for example, *"Myrmidons"* (p. 49), "hideous *Loup garou*" (p. 52), *"Indian Rooks"* (p. 58), "Blood-Hounds" (p. 84), "Fierce Things in the Shape of *Men*" (p. 89), and *"Wasps"* (p. 137). He suggested that if the English sufficiently humbled themselves before God it might lead to the Indian enemy's "Extirpation" in *Humiliations follow'd with Deliverances* (1697), in *Photostat Americana*, 2d ser., no. 149 (1936): 47. Regarding this attitude, see also Silverman, *Cotton Mather*, pp. 238–39.

85. Cotton Mather, *Observable Things*, pp. 210–12.

86. Cotton Mather, *Diary* 1:217; Cotton Mather, *The Diary of Cotton Mather, D.D., F.R.S., for the Year 1712*, ed. William R. Manierre II (Charlottesville: University Press of Virginia, 1964), p. 38.

87. Cotton Mather, "Pietas in Patriam. The Life of His Excellency Sir William Phips, Knt.," in *Magnalia Christi Americana* 1:164–230 (see especially pp. 167, 213–14).

88. Cotton Mather, *Observable Things*, pp. 212, 210.

89. Cotton Mather, *The Bostonian Ebenezer* (1698), in *Magnalia Christi Americana* 1:99.

90. [Cotton Mather], *Frontiers Well-Defended* (Boston, 1707), p. 8.

91. Cotton Mather, *Things for a Distress'd People to think upon* (1696), in Ronald A. Bosco, ed., *The Puritan Sermon in America, 1630–1750*, 4 vols. (Delmar, N.Y.: Scholars' Facsimiles & Reprints, 1978), 3:14 (original pagination). And see James Axtell, *The European and the Indian: Essays in the Ethnohistory of Colonial North America* (New York and Oxford: Oxford University Press, 1981), pp. 281–82. For Mather's use of the vine metaphor, see also *Magnalia Christi Americana* 1:249.

92. For use of the term *Americans* in reference to the Indians, see, for example, Roger Williams, *A Key into the Language of America*, ed. John J. Teunissen and Evelyn J. Hinz (Detroit: Wayne State University Press, 1973), p. 133.

93. Paul J. Lindholdt, ed., *John Josselyn, Colonial Traveler: A Critical Edition of "Two*

Voyages to New-England" (Hanover, N.H., and London: University Press of New England, 1988), p. 126.

94. Cotton Mather, *Selected Letters*, p. 178.

95. Cotton Mather, *Pillar of Gratitude*, p. 10. For Mather's spiritual applications of "a very extreme Winter," see *Diary* 2:152–53.

96. Cotton Mather, *Selected Letters*, pp. 397–98.

97. Ibid., p. 398. On Mather's problems with his son Increase, or "Creasy," see Silverman, *Cotton Mather*, pp. 174–75, 292–94, 307–8, 315, 319–20, 346, 366, 387–90, 392.

98. Cotton Mather, *Selected Letters*, p. 399.

99. Ibid.

100. Silverman, *Cotton Mather*, p. 255.

101. Cotton Mather, *Way to Prosperity*, p. 137; and see Plumstead, *Wall and the Garden*, p. 135 n. 24.

102. On creolism in colonial Latin America and the attendant problems of cultural identity, see Lyle N. McAlister, *Spain and Portugal in the New World, 1492–1700* (Minneapolis: University of Minnesota Press, 1984), pp. 401–3; Antonello Gerbi, *The Dispute of the New World: The History of a Polemic, 1750–1900*, rev. and enlarged ed., trans. Jeremy Moyle (Pittsburgh: University of Pittsburgh Press, 1973), pp. 182–91; and Anthony Pagden, "Identity Formation in Spanish America," in Canny and Pagden, *Colonial Identity in the Atlantic World*, pp. 51–93.

103. Thomas Thorowgood, *Jewes in America* (London, 1650), sig. (c3)ᵛ (italics reversed). It is unlikely that Mather borrowed the word "Criolian" directly from Spanish sources, since he first announced his desire to learn Spanish in October 1696 (*Diary* 1:206). In their use of the word, both Mather and Thorowgood predate the earliest example (1702) cited by the *OED* (s.v. "creolian"). Bernard Bailyn has suggested that the notion of creolian degeneracy may have been given its first modern expression in Charles Francis Adams's "glacial age" interpretation: see *Education in the Forming of American Society: Needs and Opportunities for Study* (New York: W. W. Norton & Company for the Institute of Early American History and Culture, 1972), p. 79.

104. Cotton Mather, *Magnalia Christi Americana* 1:25. And see Gerbi, *Dispute of the New World*, pp. 182–91.

105. Cotton Mather, *Way to Prosperity*, p. 137 (and see pp. 131, 133–34, 136). In March 1711 Mather noted that "A lively Discourse about the Benefit and Importance of *Education*, should be given to the Countrey. The Countrey is perishing for want of it; they are sinking apace into Barbarism and all Wickedness. It should be considered of": *Diary* 2:51. And on the linkage of "Criolian degeneracy," Indianization, and environmentalism, see also Axtell, *European and the Indian*, pp. 160, 281–84.

106. Cotton Mather, *Way to Prosperity*, p. 137.

107. Cotton Mather, *Diary* 2:242.

108. Ibid., p. 528.

109. Cotton Mather, *Selected Letters*, p. 388; and Silverman, *Cotton Mather*, p. 305.

110. For Mather's many projects for public improvement, see his *Diary*, passim. In 1712, for example, Mather reminded himself to "Renew my Proposal, for Some honest and prudent men, to Walk the Streets at the Times and Places, where the children most carry on their Play, and observe their Language and if they find any to use Wicked Language, immediately to threaten them, or use

the most proper Methods to Reform them": *Diary . . . 1712*, p. 109 (and see pp. 31–32).

111. Cotton Mather, *Selected Letters*, p. 376. And on the singing controversy and Puritan psalmody, see Mather's *Diary* 2:373, 606; John Atlee Kouwenhoven, "Some Unfamiliar Aspects of Singing in New England, 1620–1810," *New England Quarterly* 6 (1933): 567–88; Kenneth Silverman, "Cotton Mather and the Reform of Puritan Psalmody," *Seventeenth-Century News* 34 (1976): 53–57; Silverman, *Cotton Mather*, pp. 303–6; Ola Elizabeth Winslow, *Meetinghouse Hill, 1630–1783* (New York: W. W. Norton & Company, 1972), pp. 150–70; Gilbert Chase, *America's Music: From the Pilgrims to the Present*, rev. 2d ed. (New York: McGraw-Hill, 1966), pp. 22–40; Laura L. Becker, "Ministers vs. Laymen: The Singing Controversy in Puritan New England, 1720–1740," *New England Quarterly* 55 (1982): 79–95; Joyce Irwin, "The Theology of 'Regular Singing,' " *New England Quarterly* 51 (1978): 176–92; and Eldon R. Turner, "Earwitnesses to Resonance in Space: An Interpretation of Puritan Psalmody in Early 18th-Century New England," *American Studies* 25 (1984): 25–47.

112. For a similar point, regarding the traditional "lining-out" of psalms, see Chase, *America's Music*, p. 39.

113. Cotton Mather, *Diary* 2:216–17.

114. Bernard Bailyn has observed that "American culture in this early period becomes most fully comprehensible when seen as the exotic far western periphery, a marchland, of the metropolitan European culture system": *Peopling of British North America*, see pp. 112–31. See also the discussion of "the dilemma of provincialism" faced by Mather and his generation in Hall, *Faithful Shepherd*, chap. 12.

115. John M. Murrin pioneered the "Anglicization" thesis—which can be conveniently sampled in "The Legal Transformation: The Bench and Bar of Eighteenth-Century Massachusetts," in Stanley N. Katz, ed., *Colonial America: Essays in Politics and Social Development* (Boston: Little, Brown and Company, 1971), pp. 415–49. Variations on Murrin's theme from the perspective of religious history are offered by Edward Bruce Tucker, "Founders Remembered"; and Harry S. Stout, *The New England Soul: Preaching and Religious Culture in Colonial New England* (New York and Oxford: Oxford University Press, 1986), chap. 7. On the colonists' changing image of England in this period, see also Corkran, "New England Colonists' English Image." For a cultural perspective, see Richard L. Bushman, "American High-Style and Vernacular Cultures," in Jack P. Greene and J. R. Pole, eds., *Colonial British America: Essays in the New History of the Early Modern Era* (Baltimore and London: Johns Hopkins University Press, 1984), pp. 345–83.

116. Larzer Ziff argues that "At no points in their colonial history did New Englanders more acutely develop their knowledge of English law and their sense of being Englishmen than at those when they wanted most to assert their differences from England": *Puritanism in America*, p. 223. Ziff also presents a useful general discussion of New England's provincial era (chaps. 8–12). For the Mathers' reaction to the changing political climate, see Levin, *Cotton Mather*, pp. 101–5; Silverman, *Cotton Mather*, pp. 139–40, 144–45, 160–61; and Hall, *Last American Puritan*, chaps. 6–8.

117. Cotton Mather, *Pillar of Gratitude*, pp. 32–33 (and see p. 10).

118. Cotton Mather, *Magnalia Christi Americana* 1:26 (and see pp. 69, 362, 504); and Silverman, *Cotton Mather*, pp. 160–61.

119. Cotton Mather, *Magnalia Christi Americana* 1:43–44.

120. Cotton Mather, *Selected Letters*, p. 135; Cotton Mather, *Magnalia Christi Americana* 1:41; [Cotton Mather], *Parentator*, p. IX.

121. Cotton Mather, *Magnalia Christi Americana* 1:527; Cotton Mather, *Selected Letters*, p. 205; *Magnalia Christi Americana* 1:580.

122. Mather's relations with the Royal Society can be followed in Silverman, *Cotton Mather*. And on Mather's scientific interests, see also Stearns, *Science in the British Colonies*, pp. 403–26.

123. Cotton Mather, *Selected Letters*, p. 138.

124. [Cotton Mather], *Parentator*, p. IX. On Mather's sense of himself as "American," see especially Silverman, *Cotton Mather*, pp. 425–26.

125. Cotton Mather, *Diary* 2:162 (and see p. 212).

126. Cotton Mather, *Diary . . . 1712*, p. 108 (and see Silverman, *Cotton Mather*, p. 199).

127. Cotton Mather, *Diary* 1:533 (and see pp. 534, 2:542–43; and *Diary . . . 1712*, pp. 106–7).

128. Cotton Mather, *Magnalia Christi Americana* 1:100.

129. Cotton Mather, *Diary* 2:634, 641 (and see pp. 632–58, 705–8).

130. Cotton Mather, *Magnalia Christi Americana* 1:91.

131. Cotton Mather, *Diary* 1:53; and Silverman, *Cotton Mather*, pp. 27–28.

132. Cotton Mather, *Diary* 1:311 (and see pp. 68, 227).

133. Ibid., pp. 343, 77. An English visitor in 1686 pronounced Mather's library "the Glory of New-England, if not of all America": quoted in Silverman, *Cotton Mather*, p. 263 (and see p. 262).

134. Cotton Mather, *Diary* 1:343.

135. Ibid., p. 311; Silverman, *Cotton Mather*, p. 197. In 1697 Mather had also thanked God "For his favouring mee, with the *Liberty of the Press*, and publishing more of my Composures than any Man's, that ever was in *America*, while I am yett a young Man" (*Diary* 1:228; and see 2:162, 505–6).

136. Cotton Mather, *Diary* 1:340. Silverman estimates Mather's total output at "some 388 separate titles": see *Cotton Mather*, pp. 197–99.

137. Cotton Mather, *Selected Letters*, p. 103.

138. Cotton Mather, *Diary* 1:548.

139. Ibid., pp. 86–87, 87 n. 2. On the dating of this interview, see Silverman, *Cotton Mather*, pp. 127–29; and Levin, *Cotton Mather*, pp. 106–8, 176.

140. Cotton Mather, *Diary* 1:228.

141. Ibid., p. 343. And on Mather's wide-ranging correspondence, see Silverman, *Cotton Mather*, pp. 199, 424.

142. Mather's worries about manuscripts shipped to England are documented throughout his *Diary*. For his ecstatic reaction to his first sight of the printed *Magnalia*, see *Diary* 1:445.

143. On Mather's Glasgow degree, see *Diary* 2:40, 49, 63–64; and Silverman, *Cotton Mather*, pp. 222–25. On his relations with the Royal Society, see *Diary* 2:245–46; *Diary . . . 1712*, pp. 93–94; and Silverman, *Cotton Mather*, p. 254—where Mather is described as "Giddy with delight in the distinction" of his election to the Society.

144. Cotton Mather, *Diary* 1:570.

145. Ibid. 2:40–41, 162, 178, 283, 376, 436; and Silverman, *Cotton Mather*, especially pp. 257–60.

146. Cotton Mather, *Selected Letters*, p. 190 (and see pp. 155, 170).

147. Cotton Mather, *Diary* 1:498.

148. See Silverman, *Cotton Mather*, p. 165.

149. Cotton Mather, *Magnalia Christi Americana* 1:31.
150. Ibid.
151. On the comparison to Robert Burton's *Anatomy of Melancholy*, see: Samuel Eliot Morison, *The Intellectual Life of Colonial New England* (Ithaca, N.Y.: Cornell University Press, 1960), pp. 196–97; Ziff, *Puritanism in America*, p. 216; Seelye, *Prophetic Waters*, p. 261; and Breitwieser, *Cotton Mather and Benjamin Franklin*, pp. 93–94.
152. Thomas Hooker, *A Survey of the Summe of Church-Discipline* (London, 1648), preface, sig. [a4ʳ]. Perry Miller read this passage as "a perfect summation of the ideal of the plain style as it was brought to New England and there made the presiding rule of American prose." To the imported ideal, Hooker added a new justification (in Miller's words): "We are plain speakers not so much because we learned simplicity in European universities, but because we have to do with the wilderness": "An American Language," in *Nature's Nation* (Cambridge, Mass.: Belknap Press of Harvard University Press, 1967), pp. 213, 215.
153. Increase Mather, in Cotton Mather, *Magnalia Christi Americana* 1:246.
154. On the provincial character of the *Magnalia*, see Silverman, *Cotton Mather*, p. 165; Levin, *Cotton Mather*, pp. 254, 257; Ziff, *Puritanism in America*, pp. 216–17; and Hall, *Faithful Shepherd*, pp. 276–78.
155. Cotton Mather, *Magnalia Christi Americana* 1:34 (translation from p. 34n).
156. [John Oldmixon], *The British Empire in America*, 2d ed., 2 vols. (London, 1741), 1:197 (and see p. 226).
157. [John Oldmixon], *The British Empire in America*, 2 vols. (London, 1708), 1:ix (italics reversed), 109. On Oldmixon, see also Silverman, *Cotton Mather*, p. 222.
158. Cotton Mather, *Selected Letters*, p. 312.
159. See Mather's *Parentator*, pp. v–xiv.
160. Cotton Mather, *Selected Letters*, p. 351.
161. Mather, quoted in Silverman, *Cotton Mather*, p. 403 (and see p. 402).
162. Cotton Mather, *Selected Letters*, pp. 311–12.
163. Mather's *Some American Sentiments on the Great Controversy of the Time* (1720), quoted in Silverman, *Cotton Mather*, p. 331.
164. See Silverman, *Cotton Mather*, p. 426. Silverman has also noted "Mather's evident discomfort in addressing sophisticated, cosmopolitan men, members of the Commonwealth of Learning to which he aspired but felt inadequate." Before such men, "he was at once proud and embarrassed" of his Americanness (p. 245).

Epilogue

1. On Benjamin Colman and Mather, see Kenneth Silverman, *The Life and Times of Cotton Mather* (New York: Harper & Row, 1984), pp. 146–56; and Larzer Ziff, *Puritanism in America: New Culture in a New World* (New York: Viking Press, 1973), pp. 272–79, 295. On Barnard, see ibid., pp. 286–88.
2. Mather's reference (from the 1690s) to the "learned *witlings*," quoted in David Levin, *Cotton Mather: The Young Life of the Lord's Remembrancer, 1663–1703* (Cambridge, Mass., and London, England: Harvard University Press, 1978), p. 246. The war of wits in provincial Boston is masterfully described in Perry Miller, *The New England Mind: From Colony to Province* (Cambridge, Mass., and London, England: Belknap Press of Harvard University Press, 1953), especially bk. 3. And on New England's "Augustan voice," see Alan Heimert and Andrew

Delbanco, eds., *The Puritans in America: A Narrative Anthology* (Cambridge, Mass., and London, England: Harvard University Press, 1985), pp. 405–9.

3. On Mather, Silence Dogood, and Mrs. Dogood's literary venue (James Franklin's *New-England Courant*), see Silverman, *Cotton Mather*, pp. 344–60.

4. In her first letter to the *New-England Courant* (April 2, 1722) Mrs. Dogood remarked that "At the time of my Birth, my Parents were on Ship-board in their Way from *London* to *N. England*": Benjamin Franklin, *Writings*, ed. J. A. Leo Lemay (New York: Literary Classics of the United States, 1987), p. 5.

5. On Franklin's literary apprenticeship, see: Heimert and Delbanco, *Puritans in America*, pp. 395–96, 406 ("he seemed to view America from a position halfway between, as it were, Philadelphia and London"); Arthur Bernon Tourtellot, *Benjamin Franklin: The Shaping of Genius, The Boston Years* (Garden City, N.Y.: Doubleday & Company, 1977); Esmond Wright, *Franklin of Philadelphia* (Cambridge, Mass., and London, England: Belknap Press of Harvard University Press, 1986), chap. 2; Bruce Ingham Granger, *Benjamin Franklin: An American Man of Letters* (Ithaca, N.Y.: Cornell University Press, 1964), chaps. 1–2; James A. Sappenfield, *A Sweet Instruction: Franklin's Journalism as a Literary Apprenticeship* (Carbondale and Edwardsville: Southern Illinois University Press, 1973), chaps. 1–2; Albert Furtwangler, "Franklin's Apprenticeship and the *Spectator*," *New England Quarterly* 52 (1979): 377–96; and Kenneth Silverman, "From Cotton Mather to Benjamin Franklin," in Emory Elliott et al., eds., *Columbia Literary History of the United States* (New York: Columbia University Press, 1988), pp. 106–12. Franklin's provincial attitudes in literary and intellectual matters were oddly consonant with his culture's changing sense of religious identity. David D. Hall has suggested that third-generation New England ministers, "indifferent to the Puritan identity handed on to them, turned increasingly for direction to the world that lay beyond New England. In place of their native tradition they proposed to substitute an identity based on English modes of religious life": *The Faithful Shepherd: A History of the New England Ministry in the Seventeenth Century* (New York: W. W. Norton & Company for the Institute of Early American History and Culture, 1974), p. 272.

6. Franklin acknowledged his debt to Mather in his autobiography and in a letter of 1784 to Mather's son Samuel: see Franklin, *Writings*, pp. 1092, 1317.

7. Benjamin Franklin, *Observations Concerning the Increase of Mankind, Peopling of Countries, &c.* (1751), in *Writings*, pp. 373–74; and Wright, *Franklin of Philadelphia*, pp. 81–84.

8. On Franklin's later ambivalence toward England, see Esmond Wright, " 'The fine and noble china vase, the British Empire': Benjamin Franklin's 'Love-Hate' View of England," *Pennsylvania Magazine of History and Biography* 111 (1987): 435–64.

9. For example, Franklin, *Writings*, pp. 93, 518–30.

10. Henry Hulton, quoted in Esmond Wright, *Fabric of Freedom, 1763–1800*, rev. ed. (New York: Hill and Wang, 1978), p. 72 (and see p. 71).

11. Ralph Waldo Emerson, *English Traits* (1856), in *Essays & Lectures*, ed. Joel Porte (New York: Literary Classics of the United States, 1983), pp. 784–85.

12. Ibid., p. 923 (and see p. 784).

Index

ABOUT THE AUTHOR

John Canup has been interested in nature and environmental problems since childhood. "New England," he writes, "is a more recent obsession." He is a Southerner, born in Atlanta, Georgia, and received his A.B. at the University of Georgia. He returned to the South, after a period of study in Hawaii (M.A. 1975) and of teaching in Japan, to study at the University of North Carolina at Chapel Hill (Ph.D. 1986). He is now assistant professor of history at Texas A&M University. His home is in Bryan, Texas.

ABOUT THE BOOK

This book was composed on the Mergenthaler 202 in Baskerville, a contemporary rendering of a fine transitional typeface named for the eighteenth-century English printer John Baskerville. It was adapted for the 202 from the Linotype version by the Mergenthaler Corporation. The book was composed by WorldComp of Sterling, Virginia, and designed and produced by Kachergis Book Design, Pittsboro, North Carolina.

WITHDRAWN